T0215542

jQuery Recipes

Find Ready-Made Solutions to All Your jQuery Problems

Second Edition

Bintu Harwani

Apress®

jQuery Recipes: Find Ready-Made Solutions to All Your jQuery Problems

Bintu Harwani
Ajmer, Rajasthan, India

ISBN-13 (pbk): 978-1-4842-7303-6   ISBN-13 (electronic): 978-1-4842-7304-3
https://doi.org/10.1007/978-1-4842-7304-3

Managing Director, Apress Media LLC: Welmoed Spahr
Acquisitions Editor: Louise Corrigan
Development Editor: James Markham
Coordinating Editor: Nancy Chen

Cover designed by eStudioCalamar

Cover image by Shyam on Unsplash (www.unsplash.com)

Distributed to the book trade worldwide by Apress Media, LLC, 1 New York Plaza, New York, NY 10004, U.S.A. Phone 1-800-SPRINGER, fax (201) 348-4505, e-mail orders-ny@springer-sbm.com, or visit www.springeronline.com. Apress Media, LLC is a California LLC and the sole member (owner) is Springer Science + Business Media Finance Inc (SSBM Finance Inc). SSBM Finance Inc is a **Delaware** corporation.

For information on translations, please e-mail booktranslations@springernature.com; for reprint, paperback, or audio rights, please e-mail bookpermissions@springernature.com.

Apress titles may be purchased in bulk for academic, corporate, or promotional use. eBook versions and licenses are also available for most titles. For more information, reference our Print and eBook Bulk Sales web page at www.apress.com/bulk-sales.

Any source code or other supplementary material referenced by the author in this book is available to readers on GitHub via the book's product page, located at www.apress.com/9781484273036. For more detailed information, please visit www.apress.com/source-code.

Printed on acid-free paper

I dedicate this book to my lovely mom, dad, wife, and two dearest children. My mom, Mrs. Neeta, and my dad, Mr. Mohan, have been and will always be my inspiration. My sweet wife, Anushka, always stands beside me as my strength and my two sons, Chirag and Naman, are not only part of my small world but also my life line.

Table of Contents

About the Author xxvii

About the Technical Reviewer xxix

Acknowledgments xxxi

Introduction xxxiii

Chapter 1: JQuery Basics 1

What Is jQuery? 2

Understanding the DOM 3

Selectors 4

    Types of Selectors 4

1-1. Including the jQuery Library in a Web Page 5

    Problem 5

    Solution 5

    How It Works 6

1-2. Getting the Document Ready Before Processing 7

    Problem 7

    Solution 7

    How It Works 7

1-3. Applying a Style to a Wrapper Set 8

    Problem 8

    Solution 8

    How It Works 9

1-4. Applying a Style to Specific Paragraphs 10

    Problem 10

    Solution 10

    How It Works 12

1-5. Counting Paragraphs of a Specific Class and Applying Styles to Them 13

    Problem 13

    Solution 13

    How It Works 15

1-6. Returning to a Prior Selection 16

    Problem 16

    Solution 16

    How It Works 18

1-7. Removing a DOM and Prepending and Appending Elements 20

    Problem 20

    Solution 20

    How It Works 22

1-8. Applying Chaining to Apply Styles on Selected List Elements 23

    Problem 23

    Solution 23

    How It Works 25

1-9. Using a for Loop to Display Elements of an Unordered List... 26

    Problem 26

    Solution 26

    How It Works 27

1-10. Replacing a DOM Element 29

    Problem 29

    Solution 29

    How It Works 30

1-11. Replacing Text and HTML 31

    Problem 31

    Solution 31

    How It Works 32

1-12. Cloning a DOM 32

    Problem 32

    Solution 32

    How It Works 33

1-13. Displaying Siblings 35

    Problem 35

    Solution 35

    How It Works 37

1-14. Setting and Getting Attributes 38

    Problem 38

    Solution 38

    How It Works 40

1-15. Counting the Number of Nodes in the DOM and Displaying Their Text 42

    Problem 42

    Solution 42

    How It Works 43

1-16. Obtaining the HTML of an Element 46

    Problem 46

    Solution 46

1-17. Assigning the Same Class Name to Different HTML Elements and
Applying Styles to Them 48

    Problem 48

    Solution 48

1-18. Summary 50

Chapter 2: Arrays and Iteration **51**

2-1. Sorting an Array 51

    Problem 51

    Solution 52

    How It Works 54

2-2. Splitting an Array into Two 56

    Problem 56

    Solution 56

    join( ) 58

    How It Works 58

2-3. Searching and Displaying Desired Values from a Numerical Array 59

Problem 59

Solution 59

How It Works 62

2-4. Concatenating Two Arrays 63

Problem 63

Solution 63

How It Works 65

2-5. Searching for Desired Information in a String Array 67

Problem 67

Solution 67

How It Works 69

2-6. Manipulating Array Elements 71

Problem 71

Solution 71

How It Works 74

2-7. Converting a Numerical Array into a String and Finding Its Substring 75

Problem 75

Solution 76

How It Works 77

2-8. Creating an Array of Objects and Displaying the Content 78

Problem 78

Solution 78

How It Works 80

2-9. Using Associative Arrays 81

Problem 81

Solution 81

How It Works 82

2-10. Sorting an Array of Objects...83

    Problem 83

    Solution 83

    How It Works 85

2-11. Summary..86

Chapter 3: Understanding the Event Model **87**

3-1. Displaying a Message on Getting Focus and When Blurred 88

    Problem 88

    Solution 88

    How It Works 91

3-2. Finding Which Mouse Button Is Pressed 93

    Problem 93

    Solution 93

    How It Works 95

3-3. Changing the Style on a Mouse Entering and Leaving an HTML Element 96

    Problem 96

    Solution 96

    How It Works 101

3-4. Using a Mouse Hover Event to Change the Style on a Button 102

    Problem 102

    Solution 102

    How It Works 104

3-5. Using Mouse Up and Down Events to Show and Hide an Image 105

    Problem 105

    Solution 106

    How It Works 109

3-6. Making Two Buttons, One for Hiding and One for Displaying an Image............................110

    Problem 110

    Solution 110

    How It Works 114

3-7. Zoom In and Out of an Image Using toggleClass 116

Problem 116

Solution 116

How It Works 118

3-8. Avoiding Event Bubbling 119

Problem 119

Solution 120

How It Works 121

3-9. Knowing Which Key Is Down, Pressed, or Released 124

Problem 124

Solution 124

How It Works 126

3-10. Applying a Fading Effect to an Image 128

Problem 128

Solution 128

How It Works 130

3-11. Applying Animation on an Image 131

Problem 131

Solution 132

How It Works 133

3-12. Triggering Events Automatically 136

Problem 136

Solution 136

How It Works 138

3-13. Disabling a Button After It Is Clicked Once 139

Problem 139

Solution 139

How It Works 140

3-14. Finding the Screen Coordinates of a Mouse-Button Press 142

Problem 142

Solution 142

How It Works 143

3-15. Highlighting Text Dynamically 144

    Problem 144

    Solution 144

    How It Works 145

3-16. Making an Image Bright or Blurred with Mouse Movements 147

    Problem 147

    Solution 147

    How It Works 148

3-17. Creating Image-Based Rollovers 150

    Problem 150

    Solution 150

    How It Works 152

3-18. Adding and Removing Text in Response to Events 155

    Problem 155

    Solution 155

    How It Works 156

3-19. Displaying Word Balloons 157

    Problem 157

    Solution 157

    How It Works 159

3-20. Creating "Return to Top" Links 161

    Problem 161

    Solution 161

    How It Works 162

3-21. Displaying Text with an Animation Effect 163

    Problem 163

    Solution 164

    How It Works 166

3-22. Replacing Text with a Sliding Effect 168

    Problem 168

    Solution 168

    How It Works 169

3-23. Summary 171

Chapter 4: Form Validation 173

4-1. Confirming a Required Field Is Not Left Blank 174

    Problem 174

    Solution 174

    How It Works 176

4-2. Validating a Numerical Field 177

    Problem 177

    Solution 177

    How It Works 181

4-3. Validating Phone Numbers 184

    Problem 184

    Solution 184

    How It Works 186

4-4. Validating a User Id 187

    Problem 187

    Solution 187

    How It Works 189

4-5. Validating a Date 190

    Problem 190

    Solution 190

    How It Works 192

4-6. Validating an Email Address 193

    Problem 193

    Solution 194

    How It Works 195

4-7. Checking Whether a Checkbox Is Checked or Not 197

    Problem 197

    Solution 197

    How It Works 201

4-8. Checking If a Radio Button Is Selected 203

    Problem 203

    Solution 204

    How It Works 205

4-9. Checking That an Option in a Select Element is Selected 207

    Problem 207

    Solution 207

    How It Works 209

4-10. Applying Styles to Options and a Form Button 213

    Problem 213

    Solution 213

    How It Works 215

4-11. Checking and Unchecking All Checkboxes Together 219

    Problem 219

    Solution 219

    How It Works 221

4-12. Validating Two Fields 223

    Problem 223

    Solution 223

    How It Works 225

4-13. Matching the Password and Confirming Password Fields 229

    Problem 229

    Solution 229

    How It Works 231

4-14. Disabling Certain Fields 233

    Problem 233

    Solution 233

    How It Works 236

4-15. Validating a Complete Form 238

    Problem 238

    Solution 238

    How It Works 243

4-16. Summary 254

Chapter 5: Page Navigation **255**

5-1. Writing a Breadcrumb Menu 255

    Problem 255

    Solution 256

    How It Works 257

5-2. Adding a Hover Effect to Menu Items 258

    Problem 258

    Solution 258

    How It Works 261

5-3. Creating a Contextual Menu 262

    Problem 262

    Solution 263

    How It Works 266

5-4. Creating a Navigation Menu with Access Keys 268

    Problem 268

    Solution 268

    How It Works 272

5-5. Creating a Context Menu on Right Click 274

    Problem 274

    Solution 274

    How It Works 277

5-6. Creating Two Menus with Separate Menu Items 279

    Problem 279

    Solution 279

    How It Works 281

5-7. Creating Two Menus with Submenu Items 283

    Problem 283

    Solution 284

    How It Works 286

5-8. Making an Accordion Menu 290

    Problem 290

    Solution 291

    How It Works 293

5-9. Making a Dynamic Visual Menu 296

    Problem 296

    Solution 296

    How It Works 300

5-10. Summary 304

Chapter 6: Implementing Animation **305**

6-1. Animating an Image to the Right and Then the Left 305

    Problem 305

    Solution 305

    How It Works 307

6-2. Managing and Manipulating the jQuery Queue 311

    Problem 311

    Solution 311

    How It Works 313

    Popping the Last Function from the Queue 314

6-3. Showing Images One by One by Clicking the Next and Previous buttons 315

    Problem 315

    Solution 316

    How It Works 321

    Displaying All Hidden Images One by One When Any Arrow Key Is Pressed 323

    Making the Images Slide Continuously 325

6-4. Zooming In on an Image When the Mouse Hovers Over It 326

    Problem 326

    Solution 326

    How It Works 328

6-5. Displaying Detailed Information on Clicking the "Read More" Link 329

    Problem 329

    Solution 330

    How It Works 332

6-6. Expanding and Collapsing a List Using Animation 333

    Problem 333

    Solution 333

    How It Works 335

6-7. Summary 337

Chapter 7: Sliding and Visual Effects **339**

7-1. Displaying Images, One at a Time Infinitely 340

    Problem 340

    Solution 340

7-2. Making a Ball Bounce 346

    Problem 346

    Solution 346

7-3. Making Images Scroll Vertically Upward Within a Box 348

    Problem 348

    Solution 349

7-4. Displaying Images Vertically, Each Replaced by the Next in Sequence 352

    Problem 352

    Solution 352

7-5. Making a News Scroller 357

    Problem 357

    Solution 357

7-6. Showing Images One After the Other on Hover 362

    Problem 362

    Solution 362

    How It Works 364

7-7. Showing Images Pagewise 367

    Problem 367

    Solution 367

    How It Works 369

7-8. Shuffling Images in Either Direction 371

    Problem 371

    Solution 371

    How It Works 374

7-9. Writing a Pendulum Scroller 377

    Problem 377

    Solution 377

    How It Works 379

7-10. Scrolling Images Using Arrays 380

    Problem 380

    Solution 381

7-11. Summary 386

Chapter 8: Dealing with Tables **387**

8-1. Hovering Over Table Rows 387

    Problem 387

    Solution 388

    How It Works 389

8-2. Highlighting Alternate Columns 390

    Problem 390

    Solution 390

    How It Works 391

8-3. Filtering Rows..396

    Problem...396

    Solution..396

    How It Works..397

8-4. Hiding the Selected Column...399

    Problem...399

    Solution..399

    How It Works..400

    How It Works..402

8-5. Paginating the Table..403

    Problem...403

    Solution..403

    How It Works..405

8-6. Expanding and Collapsing List Items..408

    Problem...408

    Solution..408

    How It Works..411

8-7. Expanding and Collapsing Rows of the Table..413

    Problem...413

    Solution..414

    How It Works..416

8-8. Sorting List Items...422

    Problem...422

    Solution..422

    How It Works..423

8-9. Sorting a Table...424

    Problem...424

    Solution..424

    How It Works..427

    How It Works..432

8-10. Filtering Rows from a Table 434

    Problem 434

    Solution 434

    How It Works 437

8-11. Summary 438

Chapter 9: jQuery UI 439

9-1. Using Datepicker 439

    Problem 439

    Solution 440

    Configuring Properties of the Datepicker Widget 441

    Changing the Date Format 444

    Applying Styles to the Datepicker 446

9-2. Using the Autocomplete Widget 448

    Problem 448

    Solution 448

    Configuring the Autocomplete Widget 450

9-3. Using an Accordion 453

    Problem 454

    Solution 454

    Configuring an Accordion 457

9-4. Using Dialogs 460

    Problem 461

    Solution 461

    Options to Configure a Dialog Box 462

9-5. Using the Tabs Widget 466

    Problem 466

    Solution 467

    Options to Configure Tabs 470

9-6. Summary 471

Chapter 10: AJAX **473**

10-1. Returning a Single Line of Text from the Server 474

Problem 474

Solution 474

10-2. Returning Multiple Lines of Text from Server 476

Problem 476

Solution 476

10-3. Returning a Name/Value Pair Using JSON 479

Problem 479

Solution 479

10-4. Returning a JSON Object 482

Problem 482

Solution 482

10-5. Returning the JSON Object That Displays Images 484

Problem 484

Solution 484

10-6. Converting a String to Uppercase Using AJAX 489

Problem 489

Solution 489

10-7. Displaying the Price of the Selected Product Through an AJAX Request 492

Problem 492

Solution 492

10-8. Authenticating a User Using AJAX 495

Problem 495

Solution 495

10-9. Validating a User Name 506

Problem 506

Solution 507

How It Works 509

10-10. Using Autocomplete 510

    Problem 510

    Solution 510

    How It Works 514

10-11. Importing HTML 518

    Problem 518

    Solution 518

    How It Works 520

10-12. Getting XML Data 521

    Problem 521

    Solution 522

    How It Works 525

10-13. Paginating Tables 527

    Problem 527

    Solution 527

    How It Works 530

10-14. Summary 531

Chapter 11: Creating and Using jQuery Plugins 533

Creating a Plugin 533

11-1. Creating a Plugin That Changes the Font Size, Font Style, and Foreground and
Background Color of an Element 535

    Problem 535

    Solution 535

11-2. Making a Plugin Chainable 537

11-3. Enabling Passing Customization Options to a Plugin 539

    Problem 539

    Solution 539

    Modifying Content Using a Plugin 542

    Using Plugins 544

11-4. Displaying Images Slider Using a Magnific Popup Plugin 544

Problem 544

Solution 545

11-5. Displaying Dynamic Checkboxes and Radio Buttons Using an iCheck Plugin 554

Problem 554

Solution 554

11-6. Creating an Image Gallery and Carousel Using a blueimp Gallery Plugin 562

Problem 563

Solution 563

11-7. Validating a Form Using a jQuery Validation Plugin 571

Problem 571

Solution 572

11-8. Summary 576

Chapter 12: Using CSS 577

12-1. Distinguishing HTML Elements 578

Problem 578

Solution 578

How It Works 580

12-2. Applying Styles to an Element Nested Inside Another Element 580

Problem 580

Solution 580

How It Works 582

12-3. Indenting Paragraphs 583

Problem 583

Solution 583

How It Works 584

12-4. Applying an Initial Cap to a Paragraph 585

Problem 585

Solution 585

How It Works 586

12-5. Removing the Gap Between Heading and Paragraph 587

    Problem 587

    Solution 587

    How It Works 588

12-6. Applying Styles to Heading Text 589

    Problem 589

    Solution 589

    How It Works 590

12-7. Indenting the First Line Of Multiple Paragraphs 590

    Problem 590

    Solution 591

    How It Works 592

12-8. Creating Paragraphs with Hanging Indents 592

    Problem 592

    Solution 593

    How It Works 593

12-9. Creating a Bordered Pull Quote 594

    Problem 594

    Solution 594

    How It Works 596

12-10. Creating a Pull Quote with Images 596

    Problem 596

    Solution 596

    How It Works 599

12-11. Applying List Properties to List Items 600

    Problem 600

    Solution 600

    How It Works 602

12-12. Applying Styles to Only Selected List Items 602

    Problem 602

    Solution 602

    How It Works 606

12-13. Placing Dividers Between List Items 607

    Problem 607

    Solution 607

    How It Works 608

12-14. Applying Image Markers to the List 608

    Problem 608

    Solution 609

    How It Works 610

12-15. Creating Inline Lists 611

    Problem 611

    Solution 611

    How It Works 613

12-16. Applying Styles to Hyperlinks and mailto 613

    Problem 613

    Solution 613

    How It Works 616

12-17. Assigning Different Dimensions to HTML Elements 617

    Problem 617

    Solution 617

    How It Works 618

12-18. Placing HTML Elements 619

    Problem 619

    Solution 619

    How It Works 621

12-19. Creating a Multicolumn Layout 622

    Problem 622

    Solution 622

    How It Works 625

12-20. Wrapping Text Around Images 626

    Problem 626

    Solution 626

    How It Works 627

12-21. Placing a Drop Shadow Behind an Image 628

    Problem 628

    Solution 628

    How It Works 630

12-22. Changing the Cursor When the Mouse Moves Over a Link 632

    Problem 632

    Solution 632

    How It Works 633

12-23. Displaying a Long Piece of Text Within a Specific Area 634

    Problem 634

    Solution 634

    How It Works 635

12-24. Making a Rounded Corner Column 637

    Problem 637

    Solution 637

    How It Works 639

12-25. Applying Text Decorations 639

    Problem 639

    Solution 640

    How It Works 641

12-26. Scaling Images 642

    Problem 642

    Solution 642

    How It Works 643

12-27. Setting a Background Image 645

    Problem 645

    Solution 645

    How It Works 647

12-28. Centering a Background Image in the Browser 647

    Problem 647

    Solution 647

    How It Works 648

12-29. Making the Background Image Stationary 649

    Problem 649

    Solution 649

    How It Works 650

12-30. Summary 651

Appendix A: Installing WampServer **653**

A-1. Downloading WampServer 653

A-2. Installing WampServer 654

Index **667**

About the Author

Bintu Harwani is the founder of Microchip Computer Education, which is based in Ajmer, India and provides computer literacy in programming and web development to learners of all ages. He further helps the community by sharing his knowledge and expertise gained through 20 years of teaching through writing books. His recent publications include *jQuery Recipes*, published by Apress; *Introduction to Python Programming and Developing GUI Applications with PyQT*, published by Cengage Learning; *The Android Tablet Developer's Cookbook*, published by Addison-Wesley Professional; *Make an E-commerce Site in a Weekend: Using PHP*, by Apress; *UNIX & Shell Programming*, published by Oxford University Press; *Qt5 Python GUI Programming Cookbook*, published by Packt; and *Practical C Programming: Solutions for modern C Developers to Create Efficient and Well-structured Programs*, by Packt.

About the Technical Reviewer

Kenneth Fukizi is a software engineer, architect, and consultant with experience in coding on different platforms internationally. Prior to dedicated software development, he worked as a lecturer for a year and was then head of IT at different organizations. He has domain experience working with technology for companies in a wide variety of sectors. When he's not working, he likes reading up on emerging technologies and strives to be an active member of the software community.

Acknowledgments

I am very grateful to Louise Corrigan, the Acquisitions Editor at Apress, for believing in me and giving me an opportunity to write the second edition of *jQuery Recipes*. I am also thankful to the whole team at Apress for their constant cooperation and contributions.

I offer my gratitude to Kenneth Fukizi who, as the Technical Reviewer, offered a significant amount of feedback that helped to improve the chapters. She did a first-class job at structural and language editing, and played a vital role in improving the structure and quality of information. I appreciate her efforts in enhancing the contents of the book and giving it a polished look.

I also thank Nirmal Selvaraj, the project manager of the book, for his constant support.

A great big thank you to Mark Powers, the Editorial Operations Manager, and the editorial and production staff and the entire team at Apress who worked tirelessly to produce this book. Really, I enjoyed working with each of you.

Introduction

jQuery is a rich bundle of JavaScript libraries that helps users apply dynamic functionality to web pages with great ease. jQuery provides several powerful features, including the ability to access a part of a web page, modify content on fly, add animation, apply AJAX, and more.

This book uses a problem-solution approach to understanding the wide features provided by this open source project. You'll begin by using selectors to apply effects to paragraphs and lists. You'll learn how to set the layouts of a web page. After that, you will explore techniques involving event handling and performing validations to different form elements. Applying visual effects, navigations, AJAX, and many more facets of jQuery will also explained in the form of recipes. The coding used in the recipes is completely explained with screen shots at each step. If you know a bit of HTML, CSS, and jQuery, then this is the book is for you, because it covers most of the problems a person faces when working with jQuery.

Who the Book Is For

This book is suitable for web developers, professionals, trainers, students, and professionals who are looking for quick solutions to problems that are usually encountered while applying features to web pages.

What You Will Learn From this Book

You will learn the following from this book:

- Applying effects to paragraphs and lists
- Setting layouts
- Event handling
- Form validation

- Page navigations

- Visual effects

- Dealing with tables

- AJAX

- Using plugins

Source Code

You can access all of the source code used in this book by clicking the **Download Source Code** button located at www.apress.com/9781484273036.

CHAPTER 1

JQuery Basics

In this chapter, we will be dealing with the basics of jQuery, such as selecting elements, applying styles, and so on. We will be covering the following recipes in this chapter:

- Including the jQuery library on a web page
- Getting the document ready before being processed
- Applying a style to a wrapper set
- Applying a style to specific paragraphs
- Counting paragraphs of a specific class and applying styles to them
- Returning to a prior selection
- Removing the DOM (Document Object Model) and prepending and appending elements
- Applying chaining in order to apply styles on selected list elements
- Using a `for` loop to display elements of an unordered list
- Replacing the DOM element
- Replacing text and HTML
- Cloning the DOM
- Displaying siblings
- Setting and getting attributes
- Counting the number of nodes in the DOM and displaying their text
- Obtaining the HTML of an element
- Assigning the same class name to different HTML

Before we begin, let's quickly review some JQuery fundamentals.

© Bintu Harwani 2022
B. Harwani, *jQuery Recipes*, https://doi.org/10.1007/978-1-4842-7304-3_1

What Is jQuery?

jQuery is a lightweight, cross-platform JavaScript library. Because of its easy-to-use syntax, jQuery makes it quite easy to include JavaScript on any website. It not only simplifies complex coding, but also reduces the size of code.

The following are some features of jQuery:

- jQuery is an open source project that is licensed under the MIT License to permit free use of it on any site, and if required, it can be relicensed under the GNU Public License for inclusion in other GNU-licensed open source projects.

- It has a large community of users and contributors making it better every day. A huge number of posts are published by its community on bug fixes and enhancements.

- It has a huge number of plugins, enabling you to add features to your web page and develop apps that are compatible with different platforms.

- Its API is fully documented, making it easy to use and easy to access its full features.

- It supports most of the CSS3 selectors. Also, jQuery has powerful DOM interaction and manipulation methods. That is, jQuery provides several methods that make it quite easy to select the desired DOM and iterate and traverse the DOM easily.

- Its learning curve is very shallow. Because it uses CSS and HTML, it is very easy to learn its concepts.

- It is optimized for most modern browsers including Chrome, Internet Explorer, Opera, Firefox, and Safari.

- Coding is highly reduced in jQuery because it supports chained method calls. A chained method call means calling one method after another and the result of one method is supplied as input to another method, hence reducing lots of statements.

To use jQuery, no installation is required. Just download jQuery from the official website, `http://jquery.com/`, which has several versions of jQuery. You can download the most stable version.

After downloading jQuery onto your local file system, you simply refer to the file's location using the HTML `<script>` element. Also, jQuery is freely available through content delivery networks (CDNs). Many companies like Google and Microsoft offer the jQuery file on powerful, low-latency servers distributed around the world for fast access. A CDN-hosted copy of jQuery is quite fast to access because of server distribution and caching, but if you don't have access to the Internet, you can always download a copy of jQuery and access it from your local disk.

In this book, we will be using two terms very frequently, *DOM* and *selectors*. So, let's understand them before we start with the first recipe.

Understanding the DOM

The DOM provides a representation of the HTML elements as a network of objects, like a tree of elements on the page. The following example will help you understand how a tree of elements exists on a web page:

```html
<html>
    <head>
        <title>web page title</title>
    </head>
    <body>
        <ul>
            <li>First list item</li>
            <li>Second list item</li>
            <li>Third list item</li>
        </ul>
    </body>
</html>
```

Here, <html> is the ancestor or parent of all of the elements on the web page. That is, all elements are descendants or children of <html>. The <head> and <body> elements are descendants or children of <html>. The <li> elements are children or descendants of <ul>. The <ul> element is the parent of all <li> elements and all <li> elements are siblings of each other.

Selectors

As the name suggests, the jQuery selectors help in finding a DOM element in an HTML document based on id, name, types, attributes, class, etc. The jQuery selectors return either an element or a list of elements.

Types of Selectors

Elements on a web page can be selected using different element properties like type, class, id, attribute, or index location, as shown below:

- **Type:** The following jQuery selector will select all <p> elements:
  $("p")
  $("*") will select all elements.

- **Class:** The following jQuery selector will select all elements of the class named info.
  $(".info")
  $(".info,.features") will select all elements with the class info or features.

- **ID:** The following jQuery selector will select the element with the ID of ElectronicsProducts:
  $("#ElectronicsProducts")

- **Attribute:** The following jQuery selector will select all elements with a defined href attribute:
  $("[href]")

- **Indexed location:** The following jQuery selector will select the second <p> element. Like all programming languages, the indexing is 0-based, so the first element is considered at index 0, the second element at index 1 position, and so on.
  $("p:eq(1)")

1-1. Including the jQuery Library in a Web Page

Problem

You want to use the jQuery JavaScript library in a web page.

Solution

Consider the following HTML file, where you want to use a jQuery library:
    selectprg.html

```
<!DOCTYPE html PUBLIC "-//W3C//DTD XHTML 1.0 Transitional//EN"
        "http://www.w3.org/TR/xhtml1/DTD/xhtml1-transitional.dtd">

<html xmlns="http://www.w3.org/1999/xhtml" xml:lang="en" lang="en">
   <head>
     <meta http-equiv="Content-Type" content="text/html; charset=utf-8"/>
     <title>First jQuery Example</title>
<link rel="stylesheet" href="selectprgstyle.css" type="text/css"
media="screen" />
<script src="https://ajax.googleapis.com/ajax/libs/jquery/3.5.1/jquery.min.js">
</script>
     <script src="selectprgjq.js" type="text/javascript"></script>
   </head>
   <body>
.....
   </body>
</html>
```

To include the jQuery JavaScript library, you need to use the HTML `<script>` element and provide either the URL or directory path in the `src` attribute of the jQuery file.

There are two ways of embedding the jQuery library in a web page:

- Use any hosted content delivery network to include jQuery in the web page.

- Download jQuery from `jQuery.com` and use it in your web page from your file system.

In order to use a Google-hosted CDN, use the following statement in your HTML page:

```
<script src="https://ajax.googleapis.com/ajax/libs/jquery/3.5.1/jquery.min.js"></script>
```

In the above HTML file, `selectprgstyle.css` is assumed to be a cascade style sheet file and `selectprgjq.js` is assumed to be the file that contains the jQuery code to be applied on the web page.

How It Works

The HTML `<script>` element will link the jQuery library that is provided at the specified URL via its `src=""` attribute in the current web page. The benefit of using a Google-hosted version of jQuery is that you get a stable, reliable, bug-free, globally available copy of jQuery.

If you don't have access to the Internet and don't want to use a Google-hosted copy of the jQuery code, you can always download jQuery from `jQuery.com` and host it in your local file system and replace the `src` attribute value with the directory path to the location of the jQuery file. The following script tag includes the jQuery library from the local file system:

```
<script src="jquery-3.5.1.js" type="text/javascript"></script>
```

1-2. Getting the Document Ready Before Processing

Problem

Before traversing or manipulating the DOM, it is essential to ensure that the DOM is loaded before it can be operated on. Not just the DOM; you want to ensure that images and other files are loaded before jQuery code is applied.

Solution

JavaScript code runs immediately when it appears in the browser and at the time the header is being processed. So you need to delay the execution of the code until after the DOM is available to apply the processing. In other words, you need to delay the execution of the jQuery function until the DOM is "ready" to be processed. With the `$(document).ready()` method, jQuery defers the function calls until the DOM is loaded

Once the DOM is ready, jQuery executes the callback function that does the following tasks:

- Accesses the element using the required selector. The selector returns the matching element(s).

- Manipulates the selected element(s) or applies the desired task on it.

The following is the jQuery code that demonstrates how to wait for the document to get ready before executing any jQuery code on it:

```
$(document).ready(function() {
.................
.................
})
```

How It Works

To be more precise, the `ready()` method specifies a function to execute when the DOM is fully loaded. The `function` keyword is used without the function name and the body of the function contains the code to be applied on the DOM. The body of the function is also passed as an argument to the `ready` method because you want the function to be executed immediately but only once.

1-3. Applying a Style to a Wrapper Set

Problem

You need to get the jQuery wrapper set and apply styles. When you select certain DOM elements from the HTML page, they are wrapped with jQuery functionality. To this wrapper set, you want to apply different jQuery functions and properties. Let's see how it is done.

Solution

Here is a HTML file that contains few paragraph elements and a heading 1 element. The text **Welcome to our site** is displayed using heading level 1. Three <p> elements are used to display certain text.

Wrapperpage.html

```
<!DOCTYPE html PUBLIC "-//W3C//DTD XHTML 1.0 Transitional//EN"
        "http://www.w3.org/TR/xhtml1/DTD/xhtml1-transitional.dtd">

<html xmlns="http://www.w3.org/1999/xhtml" xml:lang="en" lang="en">
  <head>
    <meta http-equiv="Content-Type" content="text/html; charset=utf-8"/>
    <title>jQuery Wrapper Set</title>
<link rel="stylesheet" href="wrapperstyle.css" type="text/css"
media="screen" />
    <script src="jquery-3.5.1.js" type="text/javascript"></script>
    <script src="wrapperjq.js" type="text/javascript"></script>
  </head>
  <body>
    <H1>Welcome to our site </H1>
<p> We deal with electronic products like mobile phones, laptops, washing
machine at very reasonable prices </p>
<p> We do provide home delivery also </p>
<p> Best products and very reasonable prices </p>
  </body>
</html>
```

You want to apply a certain style to all paragraph elements of the HTML file. The wrapperstyle.css file is created and a style is created in it, as shown.

Wrapperstyle.css

```
.highlight{
        font-style: italic;
        background-color: #0f0;
}
```

In the above CSS stylesheet file, a CSS style class called highlight is created to change the font style to italic and the background color to green.

In order to apply the style named highlight defined in the CSS file to the paragraph elements of the HTML page, the following jQuery code is written in the wrapperjq.js file:

Wrapperjq.js

```
$(document).ready(function() {
        $('p').addClass('highlight');
})
```

How It Works

In order to select a desired DOM, you need to use the Selectors API in jQuery. To use the Selectors API, you simply write an object called $ (dollar sign). The dollar sign can also be replaced by the string "jQuery". In fact, the $ variable contains the entire jQuery framework and is required to begin jQuery coding. The $ variable has several member properties and methods that can be called to select the desired DOM. Shortly, the $ variable is an alias for the jQuery function and namespace. The $() function usually takes a string as a parameter, which can be a CSS selector, and it returns a new jQuery object instance which might include zero or more DOM elements upon which the desired processing can be applied.

jQuery will scan the complete HTML page and will place all <p> elements in the wrapper set so that the jQuery methods can be applied to them. Implicit iteration is applied automatically, so each DOM element in the wrapper set is observed and the specified highlight class is applied to each paragraph element in the wrapper set. The addClass method is applied to each <p> element on the page without any loop being used, which means an implicit iteration is applied on all of the elements in the wrapper set.

Upon running the HTML file, you see that the H1 heading level displays the text in the highest heading level. Also, upon application of the CSS class named `highlight`, the text of the three paragraphs will appear in italics mode and with a green background color, as shown in Figure 1-1.

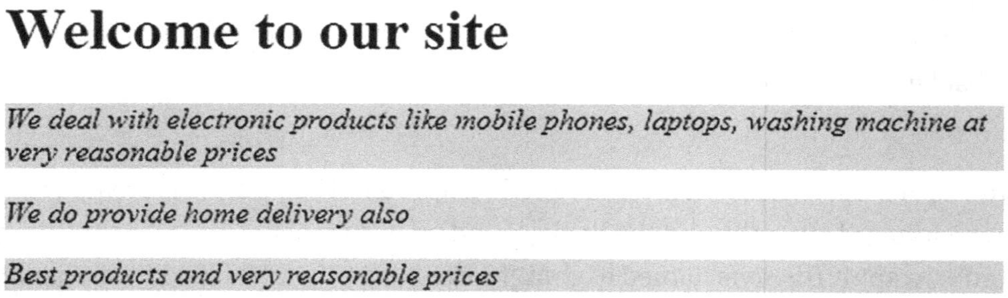

Welcome to our site

We deal with electronic products like mobile phones, laptops, washing machine at very reasonable prices

We do provide home delivery also

Best products and very reasonable prices

Figure 1-1. *Applying styles to the <p> elements*

1-4. Applying a Style to Specific Paragraphs

Problem

You have an HTML file and you want to select paragraphs on the basis of their location to apply styles to them.

Solution

Consider the following HTML file that contains a heading level 1 element and three paragraphs:

selectprg.html

```
<!DOCTYPE html PUBLIC "-//W3C//DTD XHTML 1.0 Transitional//EN"
        "http://www.w3.org/TR/xhtml1/DTD/xhtml1-transitional.dtd">

<html xmlns="http://www.w3.org/1999/xhtml" xml:lang="en" lang="en">
  <head>
    <meta http-equiv="Content-Type" content="text/html; charset=utf-8"/>
    <title>JQuery Examples</title>
    <link rel="stylesheet" href="selectprgstyle.css" type="text/css"
    media="screen" />
```

```
<script src="jquery-3.5.1.js" type="text/javascript"></script>
<script src="selectprgjq.js" type="text/javascript"></script>
</head>
<body>
        <H1>Welcome to our site </H1>
            <p> We deal with electronic products like mobile phones,
            laptops, washing machine at very reasonable prices </p>
            <p> We do provide home delivery also </p>
            <p> Best products and very reasonable prices </p>
</body>
</html>
```

In this HTML file, the text **Welcome to our site** is displayed in heading level 1 and three paragraph elements are used to display certain text.

selectprgstyle.css

```
.highlight1{
        font-style: italic;
        background-color: #0f0;
}
.highlight2{
        font-style: bold;
        background-color: #f00;  .
}
```

Two CSS styles appear in this style sheet file, highlight1 and highlight2. The highlight1 style contains the code to make the text appear in italics and changes the background to green. The highlight2 style contains the code to make the text appear in bold and changes the background color to red.

selectprgjq.js

```
$(document).ready(function() {
    $('p:even').addClass('highlight1');
        $('p:eq(1)').addClass('highlight2');
})
```

In the above jQuery code, the addClass() method is used, so let's have a look at this method.

11

addClass( ) Method

The .addClass() method applies a CSS class to the DOM element that is selected.

Syntax

$(selector).addClass(class_name)

where the class_name parameter represents the class to be added.

You can use the .removeClass() method to remove the specified CSS class from the selected DOM.

How It Works

The p:even selector selects the paragraph elements that are at even index locations (i.e. at 0th, at 2nd, at 4th index locations, and so on). Remember, 0-based indexing is used in almost all programming languages, so the paragraph element at the 0th index location means the first paragraph and the paragraph element at the 2nd index location means the third paragraph, and the style highlight1 will be applied to them.

The eq(1) selector selects the <p> element at the first index location, so the style highlight2 will be applied to the second paragraph element.

In this code, you find all of the <p> elements in the document that are at even index locations (i.e. the <p> element at 0th index location, 2nd index location, 4th index location, and so on). And the class highlight1 is applied to all of those <p> elements.

Note   No iteration is required to add the class to all of the even indexed <p> elements because jQuery uses implicit iteration within it.

Upon running the HTML file, you will see that the CSS style highlight1 is applied on the paragraph elements with index locations 0 and 2, making the text appear in italics mode and in green background color. Also, the CSS style highlight2 is applied to the paragraph element with an index location of 1, making its text appear in bold and with a red background color, as shown in Figure 1-2.

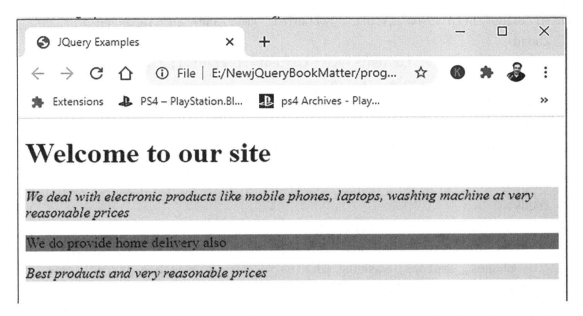

Figure 1-2. *Different styles applied to <p> elements at even index locations and to a <p> element at the first index location*

1-5. Counting Paragraphs of a Specific Class and Applying Styles to Them

Problem

You have some paragraphs in a web page, and you want to count the paragraphs that are assigned a specific class, and you want to apply a CSS style class to them.

Solution

Consider the following HTML file that has a heading level 1 element and a few paragraphs that are assigned a certain class to distinguish them:

countprg.html

```
<!DOCTYPE html PUBLIC "-//W3C//DTD XHTML 1.0 Transitional//EN"
        "http://www.w3.org/TR/xhtml1/DTD/xhtml1-transitional.dtd">
```

```
<html xmlns="http://www.w3.org/1999/xhtml" xml:lang="en" lang="en">
   <head>
    <meta http-equiv="Content-Type" content="text/html; charset=utf-8"/>
    <title>JQuery Examples</title>
    <link rel="stylesheet" href="countprgstyle.css" type="text/css"
    media="screen" />
    <script src="jquery-3.5.1.js" type="text/javascript"></script>
    <script src="countprgjq.js" type="text/javascript"></script>
   </head>
   <body>
        <H1>Welcome to our site </H1>
        <p class="info"> We deal with electronic products like mobile
        phones, laptops, washing machine at very reasonable prices </p>
        <p> We do provide home delivery also </p>
        <p class="info"> Best products and very reasonable prices </p>
   </body>
</html>
```

You can see in the above code that a text message, **Welcome to our site**, is displayed in heading level 1. Three paragraph elements are used to display certain text. The first and third paragraph elements are assigned the class of info.

The following is the CSS file that contains the style rules that you want to apply on the selected paragraphs:

countprgstyle.css

```
.highlight1{
        font-style: italic;
        background-color: #0f0;
}
```

The CSS file contains the style called highlight1 that contains the code to make text appear in italics mode and set its background color to green.

countprgjq.js

```
$(document).ready(function() {
        alert($('p').filter('.info').length+" paragraphs match the given
        class");
        $('p').filter('.info').addClass('highlight1');
})
```

How It Works

The alert() method displays a dialog box with a specified message. The dialog box has an OK button, and until the user clicks the OK button, the dialog box showing the message remains there. In other words, the alert dialog box takes the focus away from the current window and compels the viewer to read the message. The alert method displays a dialog box that shows the count of the paragraph elements that have the class info.

The .filter() method iterates through the matched set of elements (i.e., through all the <p> elements) and will filter out the elements that have the class of info. That is, all the <p> elements that have the class info are selected and returned so that the style highlight1 can be applied to them. All the <p> elements that do not have class info are filtered out (i.e., removed from the matched set).

The alert dialog box will appear, revealing the number of paragraphs that match the info class (see Figure 1-3 (a)). The count of 2 will be displayed via the alert dialog box and the CSS style of highlight1 will be applied to the paragraphs that have the info class (i.e., the text of the first and third paragraphs will change to italics mode and their background color will change to green). See Figure 1-3(b).

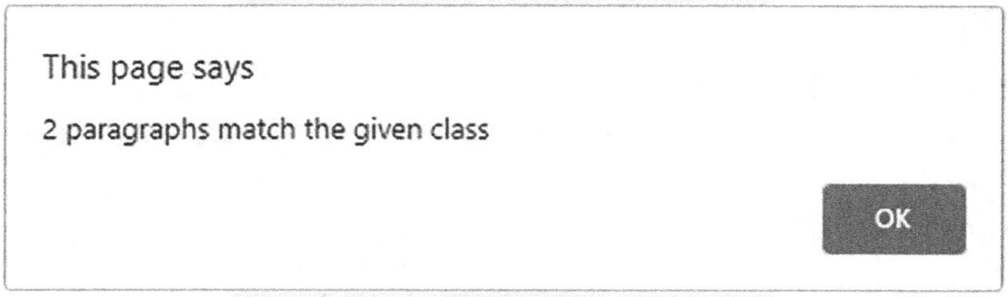

This page says

2 paragraphs match the given class

OK

(a)

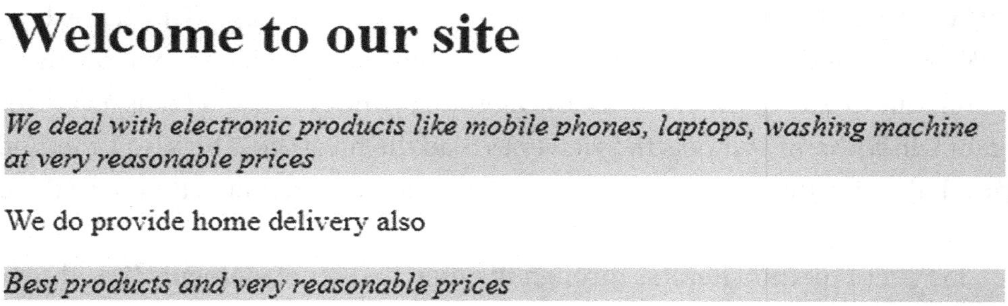

Welcome to our site

We deal with electronic products like mobile phones, laptops, washing machine at very reasonable prices

We do provide home delivery also

Best products and very reasonable prices

(b)

Figure 1-3. *(a) Alert dialog showing the count of <p> element with a specific style (b) Styles applied to the <p> elements that are of the info class*

1-6. Returning to a Prior Selection

Problem

You have selected a certain DOM using selectors and now you want to return to the previous DOM to perform some task.

Solution

The following is an HTML file that contains a heading level 1 element and few paragraphs:

Returnpriorpage.html

```
<!DOCTYPE html PUBLIC "-//W3C//DTD XHTML 1.0 Transitional//EN"
        "http://www.w3.org/TR/xhtml1/DTD/xhtml1-transitional.dtd">
```

```
<html xmlns="http://www.w3.org/1999/xhtml" xml:lang="en" lang="en">
  <head>
    <meta http-equiv="Content-Type" content="text/html; charset=utf-8"/>
    <title>JQuery Examples</title>
    <link rel="stylesheet" href="returnpriorstyle.css" type="text/css"
    media="screen" />
    <script src="jquery-3.5.1.js" type="text/javascript"></script>
    <script src="returnpriorjq.js" type="text/javascript"></script>
  </head>
  <body>
        <H1>Welcome to our site </H1>
        <p class="info"> We deal with electronic products like mobile
        phones, laptops, washing machine at very reasonable prices </p>
        <p> We do provide home delivery also </p>
        <p class="info"> Best products and very reasonable prices. <a
        href="bmharwani.com">Click for details </a> </p>
  </body>
</html>
```

You can see in the above code that the heading level 1 element is used for displaying the text **Welcome to our site**. Certain text is displayed via three paragraph elements. To specifically access them in jQuery code, the first and third paragraphs are assigned the class info.

The following is the CSS file that contains the styles that you want to apply on the selected paragraphs:

Returnpriorstyle.css

```
.highlight1{
    font-style: italic;
    background-color: #0f0;
}
```

The highlight1 style contains the code to make the text appear in italics mode and set its background color to green.

The following is the jQuery code to distinguish the required paragraphs to apply CSS styles on:

```
Returnpriorjq.js

$(document).ready(function() {
        $('p').filter('.info').addClass('highlight1');
})
```

How It Works

The paragraph elements with the class info are filtered out (i.e., selected and the CSS style of highlight1 is applied to them, making their text appear in italics and in green background color as shown in Figure 1-4).

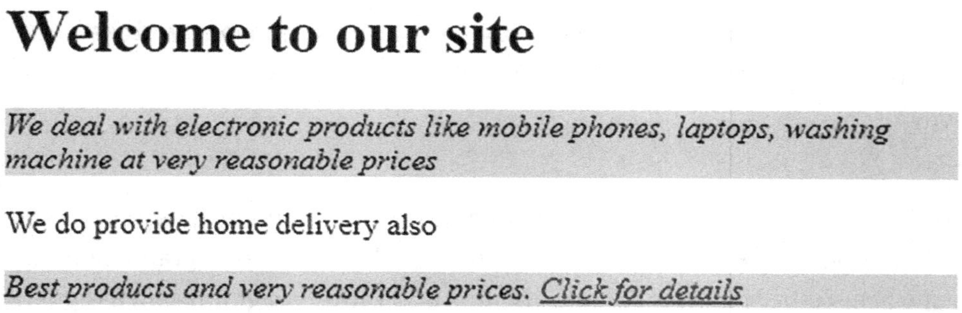

Welcome to our site

We deal with electronic products like mobile phones, laptops, washing machine at very reasonable prices

We do provide home delivery also

Best products and very reasonable prices. Click for details

Figure 1-4. *The CSS style of highlight1 is applied to the <p> element with the class info*

If you add the end() method, the control will return to the previous DOM (i.e., to all three paragraph elements):

```
$(document).ready(function() {
        $('p').filter('.info').end().addClass('highlight1');
})
```

Consequently, the CSS style of highlight1 will be applied to all three paragraph elements, as shown in Figure 1-5.

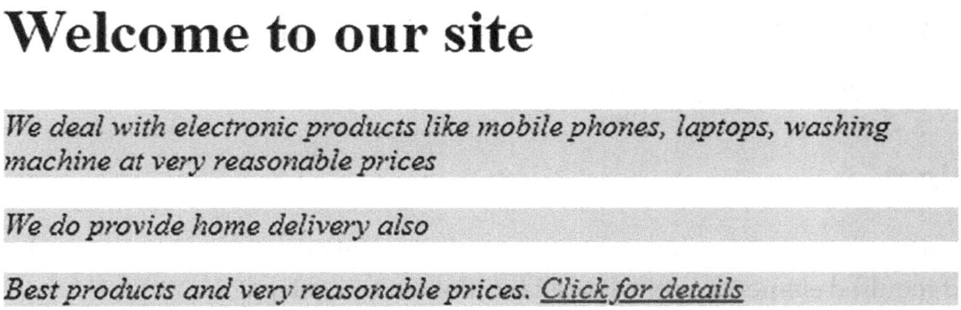

Welcome to our site

We deal with electronic products like mobile phones, laptops, washing machine at very reasonable prices

We do provide home delivery also

Best products and very reasonable prices. Click for details

Figure 1-5. *The CSS style of highlight1 applied to all the three <p> elements*

You can apply the `filter()` and `find()` methods on the jQuery code to select the paragraph more precisely:

```
$(document).ready(function() {
    $('p').filter('.info').find('a').addClass('highlight1');
})
```

The paragraph elements with class `info` are filtered out (selected), and out of them, the `<a>` element (the hyperlink) is searched and the CSS style `highlight1` is applied to that hyperlink if it is found. Eventually, only the hyperlink text appears in italics mode and in the green background color (see Figure 1-6).

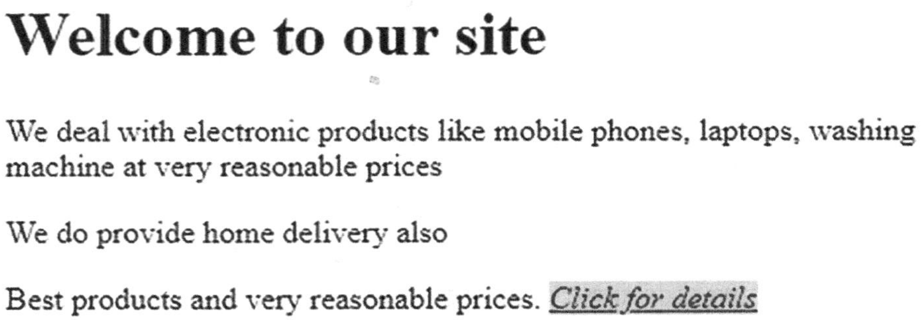

Welcome to our site

We deal with electronic products like mobile phones, laptops, washing machine at very reasonable prices

We do provide home delivery also

Best products and very reasonable prices. *Click for details*

Figure 1-6. *The CSS style of highlight1 applied to the hyperlink*

Note   You can apply more than one `end()` method to go to more previously selected DOMs.

19

1-7. Removing a DOM and Prepending and Appending Elements

Problem

In this recipe, you will learn how to remove undesired DOMs and how to prepend and append required elements at the desired location on the web page.

Solution

The following is the HTML file that contains heading level 1 element and three paragraphs:

removingdom.html

```
<!DOCTYPE html PUBLIC "-//W3C//DTD XHTML 1.0 Transitional//EN"
        "http://www.w3.org/TR/xhtml1/DTD/xhtml1-transitional.dtd">

<html xmlns="http://www.w3.org/1999/xhtml" xml:lang="en" lang="en">
   <head>
     <meta http-equiv="Content-Type" content="text/html; charset=utf-8"/>
     <title>JQuery Examples</title>
     <script src="jquery-3.5.1.js" type="text/javascript"></script>
     <script src="removingdomjq.js" type="text/javascript"></script>
   </head>
   <body>
        <H1>Welcome to our site </H1>
        <p> We deal with electronic products like mobile phones, laptops,
        washing machine at very reasonable prices </p>
        <p> We do provide home delivery also </p>
        <p> Best products and very reasonable prices </p>
   </body>
</html>
```

You can see that in the above code, the text **Welcome to our site** appears at heading level 1. Three paragraph elements are used to display certain text.

removingdomjq.js

```
$(document).ready(function() {
        $('H1').remove();
        $('p:eq(0)').prepend('<img src="a1.jpg" /></a><br/>');
        $('p:eq(2)').remove();
        $('p:eq(1)').append('<p>Festivals Offers starts</p>');
})
```

In the above jQuery code, a few methods are used: remove(), prepend(), and append. Let's have a look at these three methods.

remove( )

The remove() method removes the matching element from the DOM. It not only deletes the specified element but also all of the elements inside it. In other words, all of the children elements of the matching element are also deleted.

Syntax

$(selector).remove(selector)

where the parameter selector represents one or more elements to be removed. If multiple elements are to be removed, the elements need to be separated with a comma (,).

prepend( )

The prepend() method is used to insert the specified content at the beginning of the selected element.

Syntax:

$(selector).prepend(content_to_be_inserted)

where selector is used for selecting the element to which the content has to be inserted and the content_to_be_inserted parameter is the content that will be added before the DOM selected via the selector.

append( )

The append() method inserts the specified content at the end of the selected elements.

Syntax:

`$(selector).append(content_to_append)`

where `selector` helps in selecting the DOM at the end of which you want to add the content and `content_to_append` is the content that must be added at the end of the selected DOM.

How It Works

The heading 1 element is removed from the web page. Before the paragraph element at index location 0 (i.e., before the first paragraph) an image named `a1.jpg` is added. Thereafter a line break is inserted and the paragraph element at index location 2 (i.e., the third paragraph) is removed from the web page. Also, after the paragraph element at index location 1 (i.e., after the second paragraph), a paragraph element is added with the text **Festivals Offers starts**. After running the program, you get the output shown in Figure 1-7.

We deal with electronic products like mobile phones, laptops, washing machine at very reasonable prices

We do provide home delivery also

Festivals Offers starts

Figure 1-7. *Output after removing H1, prepending an image, removing a <p> element at index location 2, and appending a text*

1-8. Applying Chaining to Apply Styles on Selected List Elements

Problem

You have an unordered list containing a few list items and you want to apply a certain style on the desired list items using chaining.

Solution

Chaining in jQuery enables you to run several jQuery methods on the same element with a single statement. The multiple jQuery methods used in chaining will execute one after the other on the selected element. For chaining, you just add another jQuery action to the previous action.

The following is an HTML file displaying an unordered list:

chaining.html

```
<!DOCTYPE html PUBLIC "-//W3C//DTD XHTML 1.0 Transitional//EN"
        "http://www.w3.org/TR/xhtml1/DTD/xhtml1-transitional.dtd">

<html xmlns="http://www.w3.org/1999/xhtml" xml:lang="en" lang="en">
  <head>
    <meta http-equiv="Content-Type" content="text/html; charset=utf-8"/>
    <title>JQuery Examples</title>
    <link rel="stylesheet" href="chainingstyle.css" type="text/css"
    media="screen" />
    <script src="jquery-3.5.1.js" type="text/javascript"></script>
    <script src="chainingjq.js" type="text/javascript"></script>
  </head>
  <body>
<ul id="ElectronicsProducts">
                <li>Cameras</li>
                <li>Cell Phones</li>
                <li>Laptops</li>
            </ul>
  </body>
</html>
```

You can see in the above code that an unordered list is created with the id of ElectronicsProducts and consists of three list items: Cameras, Cell Phones, and Laptops.

To apply styles to the selected list items, the following style rules are written into the CSS file:

chainingstyle.css

```css
.highlight1{
      font-style: italic;
      background-color: #0f0;
}
.highlight2{
      font-style: bold;
      background-color: #f00;
}
```

The style sheet contains two styles named highlight1 and highlight2. The highlight1 style contains the code to convert text into italics mode and to change its background color to green. Similarly, the highlight2 class contains the code to convert text into bold and to change its background color to red.

To apply different styles to different list items of the unordered list by making use of the chaining method, the following jQuery code is written:

chainingjq.js

```javascript
$(document).ready(function() {
      $('li:contains(Cell Phones)').parent().find('li:eq(0)')
      .addClass('highlight1').end().find('li:eq(2)')
      .addClass('highlight2');
});
```

In the above jQuery code, the find() method is used, so let's look at this method.

find( )

The find() method is used to find all descendant elements of the selected element. The method scans all of the elements until the last leaf of the selected element in the DOM. The following are the two ways of using the find() method:

Syntax:

```
$(selector).find()
```

where `selector` is the element of which all the descendant elements have to be found. The function returns all of the found descendent elements.

Syntax:

```
selector.find( selector )
```

where the `selector` to the left of the `find` method helps in selecting the element whose descendants have to be scanned and the `selector` sent as a parameter to the find method is used for selecting the elements from the found descendants.

How It Works

All list items are searched to see if any of them contain the string **Cell Phones**. If that list item is found, its parent is selected. The `Cell Phones` text is found in second list item and the parent of the `<li>` elements is a `<ul>` element, so an unordered list element is selected and from its descendants, the list item at the 0th index location (i.e., the first list item) element is selected (i.e., the list item with text `Cameras` is selected and the style `highlight1` is applied to it). When the `end()` method calls, the control goes back to the parent element (i.e., to the unordered list element). Again, from the descendants of the unordered list, the list item element at second index location is selected (i.e., the third list item) (with a text of `Laptops`) is selected and to that list item the style `highlight2` is applied (as shown in Figure 1-8).

- *Cameras*
- Cell Phones
- Laptops

Figure 1-8. *The highlight1 style is applied to the list item at index location 0 and the highlight2 style is applied to the list item at the second index location*

1-9. Using a for Loop to Display Elements of an Unordered List

Problem

You have an unordered list of certain list items. You want to display all list items of the unordered list using a for loop.

Solution

The following HTML program contains an unordered list containing few list items.

fordisplay.html

```
<!DOCTYPE html PUBLIC "-//W3C//DTD XHTML 1.0 Transitional//EN"
        "http://www.w3.org/TR/xhtml1/DTD/xhtml1-transitional.dtd">
<html xmlns="http://www.w3.org/1999/xhtml" xml:lang="en" lang="en">
  <head>
    <meta http-equiv="Content-Type" content="text/html; charset=utf-8"/>
    <title> </title>
    <script src="jquery-3.5.1.js" type="text/javascript"></script>
    <script src="fordisplayjq.js" type="text/javascript"></script>
  </head>
  <body>
<ul id="ElectronicsProducts">
                <li>Cameras</li>
                <li>Cell Phones</li>
                <li>Laptops</li>
        </ul>
  </body>
</html>
```

You can see in the above code that an unordered list is created with the id of ElectronicsProducts and consists of three list items: Cameras, Cell Phones, and Laptops. The id is assigned to the unordered list so that it can be accessed in jQuery code precisely.

The following is the jQuery code to access the list items of the unordered list and display them:

fordisplayjq.js

```
$(document).ready(function() {
        var $nodes = $('#ElectronicsProducts').children();
        alert('Number of nodes is '+$nodes.length);
        var txt="";
        for (var i = 0; i < $nodes.length; i++){
                        txt+=$('#ElectronicsProducts').find('li:eq('+i+')').
                        text()+" ";
        }
        alert("Items in the unordered lists are "+txt);
});
```

In the above jQuery code, the `children()` method is used, so let's have a look at it first.

children( )

The `children()` method finds all of the children of the selected element and returns them. This method traverses all children elements down to the leaf element of the selected element and returns all of them.

Syntax:

$(selector).children()

where `selector` is the element whose children have to be returned.

How It Works

All children nodes of the element whose id is `ElectronicsProducts` will be accessed and returned to the `nodes` variable. The unordered list has the id of `ElectronicsProducts` so its three list items will be assigned to the `nodes` variable. Because there is more than one list item, the nodes will become an array containing the three list items.

An alert dialog box will be displayed showing the count of the number of children (i.e., the count of the list items), so 3 will be displayed in the dialog box (see Figure 1-9(a)).

A string variable is initialized and a for loop is set to execute from index value 0 until one less than the nodes arrays' length. That is, the for loop will run with its variable i's value ranging from 0 to 2. Using the for loop ranging from the 0th value to 2nd value, the list items at index location 0 until 2 are accessed and their text is concatenated to the string variable txt. The text of the first three list items (i.e., Cameras, Cell Phones, and Laptops) is assigned to the txt variable. Finally, the text of the three list items is displayed via an alert dialog box (see Figure 1-9(b)).

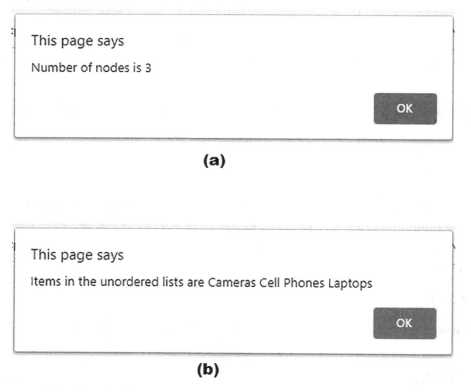

(a)

(b)

Figure 1-9. *(a) Alert dialog showing the count of nodes (b) Alert dialog showing the text of all of the list items*

1-10. Replacing a DOM Element

Problem

You have a paragraph element in an HTML file that you want to replace with an unordered list.

Solution

The following HTML program contains three paragraph elements with certain text. To distinguish the paragraphs, unique classes are assigned to them.

replacedom.html

```
<!DOCTYPE html PUBLIC "-//W3C//DTD XHTML 1.0 Transitional//EN"
        "http://www.w3.org/TR/xhtml1/DTD/xhtml1-transitional.dtd">

<html xmlns="http://www.w3.org/1999/xhtml" xml:lang="en" lang="en">
   <head>
    <meta http-equiv="Content-Type" content="text/html; charset=utf-8"/>
    <title>JQuery Examples</title>
    <script src="jquery-3.5.1.js" type="text/javascript"></script>
    <script src="replacedomjq.js" type="text/javascript"></script>
   </head>
   <body>
        <p class="features"> We deal with electronic products like mobile
        phones, laptops, washing machine at very reasonable prices </p>
        <p class="info"> We do provide home delivery also </p>
        <p class="features"> Best products and very reasonable prices </p>
   </body>
</html>
```

In the above HTML code you can see that certain text is displayed via three paragraph elements. The first and third paragraph elements are assigned the class features and the second paragraph element is assigned the class info.

The following is the jQuery code to replace a paragraph element with an unordered list:

replacedomjq.js

```
$(document).ready(function() {
        $( "p.info" ).replaceWith( "<ul>We provide: <li>Free Home Delivery
        </li><li>Fast Delivery with Charges </li></ul>" );
});
```

In the above jQuery code, a method called replaceWith() is used, so let's have a look at this method.

replaceWith(new_content)

This method replaces each element in the set of selected elements with the desired new content. The parameter new_content can be an HTML string, DOM element, array, or jQuery object. Remember, the content of the selected element will be removed and the new_content will be pasted at its place.

How It Works

The second paragraph (i.e., the paragraph with the class of info) is replaced by an unordered list that consists of the text We provide and two list items, Free Home Delivery and Fast Delivery with Charges. Hence, an unordered list will appear between the first and third paragraphs as shown in Figure 1-10.

We deal with electronic products like mobile phones, laptops, washing machine at very reasonable prices

We provide:
- Free Home Delivery
- Fast Delivery with Charges

Best products and very reasonable prices

Figure 1-10. *The <p> element replaced by an unordered list*

1-11. Replacing Text and HTML

Problem

You have a heading element and a paragraph element and you want to replace the text of the heading element and assign HTML code to the paragraph element.

Solution

The following HTML file has a heading element and a paragraph element:

Replacehtmltextpage.html

```
<!DOCTYPE html PUBLIC "-//W3C//DTD XHTML 1.0 Transitional//EN"
        "http://www.w3.org/TR/xhtml1/DTD/xhtml1-transitional.dtd">

<html xmlns="http://www.w3.org/1999/xhtml" xml:lang="en" lang="en">
   <head>
     <meta http-equiv="Content-Type" content="text/html; charset=utf-8"/>
     <title>JQuery Examples</title>
     <script src="jquery-3.5.1.js" type="text/javascript"></script>
     <script src="replacehtmltextjq.js" type="text/javascript"></script>
   </head>
   <body>
       <H1>Welcome to our site </H1>
       <p> We deal with electronic products like mobile phones, laptops,
       washing machine at very reasonable prices </p>
   </body>
</html>
```

In the above code, you can see that a text message, **Welcome to our site**, is displayed through heading level 1. Below the heading is a paragraph element displaying some text.

The jQuery code to replace the text of the heading level 1 element and to set the HTML for the paragraph element is as follows:

Replacehtmltextjq.js

```
$(document).ready(function() {
$("h1").text("Welcome to latest Innovations");
```

31

```
$("p").html("<b>Latest Laptops, Cameras, Mobile Phones at attractive prices
available</b>");
})
```

How It Works

The text of heading level 1 is replaced by the text **Welcome to latest Innovations**. The text of the paragraph element is replaced by the HTML **<b> Latest Laptops, Cameras, Mobile Phones at attractive prices available </b>**. This text will appear in bold and will replace the original paragraph text as shown in Figure 1-11.

Welcome to latest Innovations

Latest Laptops, Cameras, Mobile Phones at attractive prices available

Figure 1-11. *The text of H1 and the <p> element are replaced*

1-12. Cloning a DOM

Problem

You have HTML element and you want to make a copy of it. More precisely, you want to make a copy of a paragraph element and paste it at the required location.

Solution

The following is an HTML program that contains certain paragraph elements showing certain text:

`cloningdom.html`

```
<!DOCTYPE html PUBLIC "-//W3C//DTD XHTML 1.0 Transitional//EN"
        "http://www.w3.org/TR/xhtml1/DTD/xhtml1-transitional.dtd">

<html xmlns="http://www.w3.org/1999/xhtml" xml:lang="en" lang="en">
  <head>
    <meta http-equiv="Content-Type" content="text/html; charset=utf-8"/>
```

```
<title> </title>
<script src="jquery-3.5.1.js" type="text/javascript"></script>
<script src="cloningdomjq.js" type="text/javascript"></script>
</head>
<body>
    <p> We deal with electronic products like mobile phones, laptops,
    washing machine at very reasonable prices </p>
    <p class="info"> We do provide home delivery also </p>
    <p class="features"> Best products and very reasonable prices </p>
</body>
</html>
```

You can see in the above code that certain text is displayed through three paragraph elements. In order to access them through jQuery code, the second and third paragraphs are assigned the classes info and features, respectively.

The jQuery code to make a copy of a paragraph element and paste it after another paragraph is the following:

cloningdomjq.js

```
$(document).ready(function() {
$( "p.info" ).clone().appendTo("p.features");
});
```

How It Works

The clone() method makes a copy of selected element(s) including its children. As is clear from its name, this method makes an exact duplicate of the element including text and attributes.

The paragraph element with the class info is selected, its clone (i.e., its copy) is made, and that clone is added at the end of the paragraph element with the class features, as shown in Figure 1-12.

We deal with electronic products like mobile phones, laptops, washing machine at very reasonable prices

We do provide home delivery also

Best products and very reasonable prices

We do provide home delivery also

Figure 1-12. *A clone of the <p> element of class info is made and appended to the <p> element of class features*

Note   When using the `.clone()` method, you can modify the cloned element or its appearance before inserting it.

Let's apply the style to the paragraph element being cloned. To do so, replace the script line with the following jQuery script file:

```
<script src="cloningdombjq.js" type="text/javascript"></script>
```

where `cloningdombjq.js` contains the following jQuery code:

```
$(document).ready(function() {
        $( "p.info" ).clone().appendTo("p.features").addClass('highlight1');
});
```

You can see that the paragraph element with the class info is selected and its clone is made. The clone is then added at the end of the paragraph element with the class features. To the cloned paragraph element, the CSS class of highlight1 is applied.

To apply the style to the cloned paragraph, add the following statement to access the CSS file in the <head> element of the HTML file:

```
<link rel="stylesheet" href="cloningdomstyle.css" type="text/css"
media="screen" />
```

where `cloningdomstyle.css` contains the following CSS styles:

```
.highlight1{
    font-style: italic;
    background-color: #0f0;
```

```
}
.highlight2{
    font-style: bold;
    background-color: #f00;
}
```

The CSS file contains two CSS classes, highlight1 and highlight2. You will be using the highlight1 style in the jQuery code. The CSS style highlight1 contains the code that converts the text to appear in italics mode and changes its background color to green. On running the program, you can see that to the cloned paragraph (i.e., the second graph before it is added at the end) has the CSS style highlight1 applied to it first, as shown in Figure 1-13.

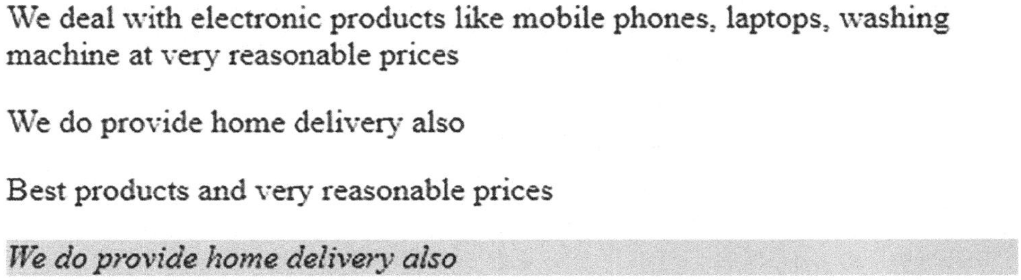

We deal with electronic products like mobile phones, laptops, washing machine at very reasonable prices

We do provide home delivery also

Best products and very reasonable prices

We do provide home delivery also

Figure 1-13. *A clone of the <p> element is made and appended after applying the highlight1 style to it*

1-13. Displaying Siblings

Problem

You have certain HTML elements nested within each other and you want to display or find out the siblings of a specific HTML element.

Solution

The following HTML program contains a <div> element and several other HTML elements nested within it:

Siblingpage.html

```
<!DOCTYPE html PUBLIC "-//W3C//DTD XHTML 1.0 Transitional//EN"
        "http://www.w3.org/TR/xhtml1/DTD/xhtml1-transitional.dtd">

<html xmlns="http://www.w3.org/1999/xhtml" xml:lang="en" lang="en">
  <head>
    <meta http-equiv="Content-Type" content="text/html; charset=utf-8"/>
    <title>JQuery Examples</title>
    <link rel="stylesheet" href="siblingstyle.css" type="text/css"
    media="screen" />
    <script src="jquery-3.5.1.js" type="text/javascript"></script>
    <script src="siblingjq.js" type="text/javascript"></script>
  </head>
  <body>
        <div>
                <p> Electronic Products </p>
                <ul>
                        <li>Cameras</li>
                        <li>Cell Phones</li>
                        <li>Laptops</li>
                </ul>
                <H1> Snacks </H1>
                <ul>
                        <li>Pizza</li>
                        <li>Burger</li>
                </ul>
        </div>
  </body>
</html>
```

You can see in the above HTML program that a `<div>` element is made. Within the `<div>` element is a `<p>` element, a `<ul>` element, an `<H1>` element, and one more `<ul>` element. The two `<ul>` elements have their respective `<li>` elements.

To apply a style to the desired siblings of the desired HTML element, define certain style rules in a CSS file as shown below:

Siblingstyle.css

```
.highlight{
```

```
        font-style: italic;
        background-color: #0f0;
}
```

You can see that the CSS file contains a style called `highlight` which converts a text into italics mode and changes its background color to green.

The following is the jQuery code to display siblings of the `<div>` element:

Siblingjq.js

```
$(document).ready(function() {
        $('div').siblings();
})
```

How It Works

The siblings of the `<div>` element are to be displayed (i.e., the paragraph element, the unordered list consisting of its three list items, the heading level 1 element, and again the unordered list with its two list items) as shown in Figure 1-14.

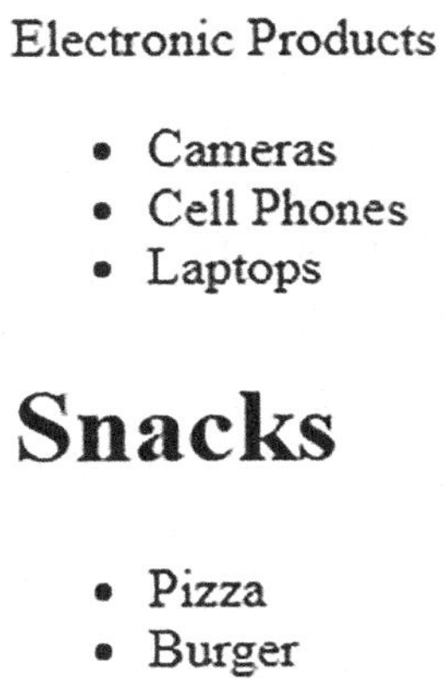

Electronic Products

- Cameras
- Cell Phones
- Laptops

Snacks

- Pizza
- Burger

Figure 1-14. *The two siblings of <div> element are displayed*

To apply the `highlight` style to only specific siblings of the `<div>` element (i.e., only to the unordered lists), modify the jQuery code to appear as follows:

```
$(document).ready(function() {
 $('p').siblings('ul').addClass('highlight');
})
```

37

Out of all of the siblings of the <div> elements (i.e., out of the <p>, <ul>, <h1>, and <ul> elements), the <ul> elements are selected and the highlight style is applied to both unordered list items, converting the text of the list items to italics mode and changing their background color to green (see Figure 1-15).

Electronic Products

- *Cameras*
- *Cell Phones*
- *Laptops*

Snacks

- *Pizza*
- *Burger*

Figure 1-15. *The highlight style is applied to the siblings' unordered list elements*

1-14. Setting and Getting Attributes

Problem

You want to set and get attributes of HTML elements dynamically. In this recipe, you will learn how to access the attribute value of a hyperlink and how to set or change its attribute value.

Solution

The following HTML file has two paragraph elements defined with certain text. The second paragraph is assigned the class info and thereafter a hyperlink is defined as shown:

Getsetattribpage.html

```
<!DOCTYPE html PUBLIC "-//W3C//DTD XHTML 1.0 Transitional//EN"
        "http://www.w3.org/TR/xhtml1/DTD/xhtml1-transitional.dtd">

<html xmlns="http://www.w3.org/1999/xhtml" xml:lang="en" lang="en">
```

```
<head>
 <meta http-equiv="Content-Type" content="text/html; charset=utf-8"/>
 <title>jQuery Examples</title>
 <script src="jquery-3.5.1.js" type="text/javascript"></script>
 <script src="getsetattribjq.js" type="text/javascript"></script>
</head>
<body>
    <p> We do provide home delivery also </p>
    <p class="info"> Best products and very reasonable prices. </p>
    <a href="http://bmharwani.com">Click for details </a>
</body>
</html>
```

The method that you will be using for getting and setting the attribute value of the HTML element is attr(), so let's look at the attr() method now.

attr( )

The attr() method is used for getting and setting the attribute value of the HTML element. When a single parameter is passed to the .attr() function, it returns the value of the passed attribute on the selected element.

Syntax:

$([selector]).attr([attribute name]);

In order to assign a value to some element, you need to supply the attribute value after the attribute name.

Syntax:

attr(attributeName, attributeValue)

Example:

```
$('a').attr('title', 'Click for  details');
```

The title attribute helps in assigning the text to the HTML element that appears when the mouse is hovered over that element.

In order to set and get the hyperlink attribute values, you need to write the following jQuery code:

Getsetattribjq.js

```
$(document).ready(function() {
      alert($('a').attr('href'));
      $('a').attr('title', 'Click for bmharwani.com');
      $('a').attr('href','http://jquery.com');
      alert($('a').attr('href'));
})
```

How It Works

The attribute value of the hyperlink will be displayed via an alert dialog box. Because the hyperlink is pointing at `http://bmharwani.com` initially, this URL will be displayed in the alert dialog box (see Figure 1-16(a)). The title of the hyperlink is set to "Click for bmharwani.com" so, upon pointing at the hyperlink, the title will be displayed (see Figure 1-16(c)). The hyperlink is set to point at `http://query.com`. The `href` attribute of the hyperlink is displayed via an alert dialog box (i.e., the URL where the hyperlink is pointing is displayed using the alert dialog box). See Figure 1-16(b).

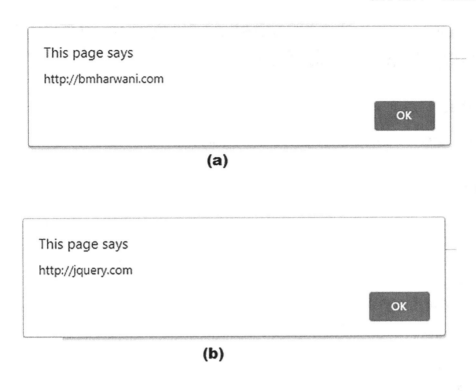

(a)

(b)

(c)

Figure 1-16. *(a) Alert dialog showing the URL pointed to by the hyperlink (b) Alert dialog displaying the href attribute of the hyperlink (c) The title of the hyperlink displayed upon pointing at the hyperlink*

1-15. Counting the Number of Nodes in the DOM and Displaying Their Text

Problem

You want to access the DOM and its nodes via jQuery.

Solution

In the DOM, a web page is represented in the form of a tree structure with a root node (parent) and several branches (children) where each HTML element is represented in the form of a node. These nodes can be accessed and manipulated as desired with the help of jQuery.

Let's look at the following HTML page:

countnodes.html

```
<!DOCTYPE html PUBLIC "-//W3C//DTD XHTML 1.0 Transitional//EN"
"http://www.w3.org/TR/xhtml1/DTD/xhtml1-transitional.dtd">
<html xmlns="http://www.w3.org/1999/xhtml" xml:lang="en" lang="en">
   <head>
    <meta http-equiv="Content-Type" content="text/html; charset=utf-8"/>
    <title>JQuery Examples</title>
    <script src="jquery-3.5.1.js" type="text/javascript"></script>
    <script src="countnodesjq.js" type="text/javascript"></script>
   </head>
   <body>
      <div id="root">
      <div>Darjeeling</div>
      <div>Assam</div>
      <div>Kerala</div>
      </div>
   </body>
</html>
```

You can see that the preceding HTML file includes the <script> tags for loading the jQuery library as well as for including the JavaScript file that contains the jQuery code (countnodesjq.js). You can also see that the HTML file contains a div element with id="root". All of the elements inside this div element are child elements (i.e., the div with id="root" is the parent of all the div elements described inside it). To count the DOM nodes and display their text, write the following jQuery code:

countnodesjq.js

```
$(document).ready(function() {
        var $nodes = $('#root').children();
        alert('Number of nodes is '+$nodes.length);
        var txt="";
        $('#root').children().each( function() {
        txt+=$(this).text();
    });
        alert(txt);
});
```

How It Works

All the child elements of the div of id="root" are accessed and assigned to variable $nodes. You display the length of the collection of child nodes using the first alert statement (see Figure 1-17(a). Thereafter, with the help of the each() method, you access all of the elements stored in $nodes one at a time. You use the text() method and access and concatenate the text of the elements in the string variable $txt. At the end, the text of all the children is displayed via another alert() method, as shown in Figure 1-17(b).

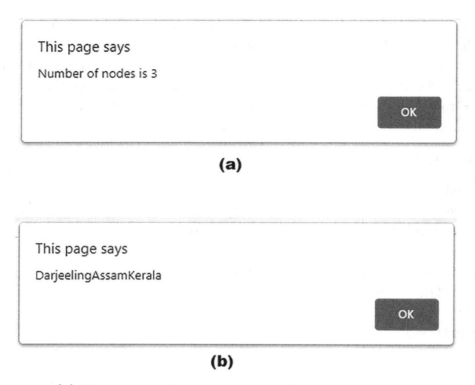

Figure 1-17. (a) The count of the nodes displayed through an alert dialog (b) The text content of the HTML elements displayed

Let's look at the methods used in the preceding jQuery code one by one.

each( )

each() is a method that is used to iterate over each element in the wrapped collection (selected elements). It contains an iterator function in which you write the code to be applied to each individual element of the collection.

text( )

text() is a method of the jQuery object that accesses the text contents of the selected element(s). The text contents of the selected element(s) are combined and returned in the form of a string. To see the text contents of a paragraph element, you may write following jQuery code:

```
alert($('p').text());
```

Let's assume that the paragraph element appears as shown in the following example:

```
<p>Styles make the formatting job much easier and more efficient. To
give an attractive look to web sites, styles are heavily used.
<span>jQuery is a powerful JavaScript library that allows us to add
dynamic elements to our web sites. </span>Not only is it easy to learn,
but it's easy to implement too.<br>
<a href="a1.htm"> jQuery Selectors</a> are used for selecting the area
of the document where we want to apply styles </p>
```

The preceding jQuery code will display the output shown in Figure 1-18.

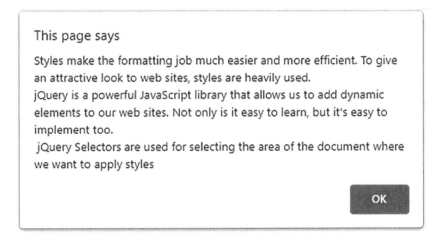

Figure 1-18. *The text content of the paragraph element of an HTML file*

You can see the text contents of the children of a paragraph element by using the following statement:

```
$(document).ready(function() {
     alert($('p').children().text());
});
```

parent( )

The parent() method is a tree-traversal method that searches for the immediate parent of each of the selected elements and returns a new jQuery object. This method travels only a single level up in the DOM tree. To get the text content of the parent of the span element, you may use the following jQuery code:

```
alert($('span').parent().text());
```

1-16. Obtaining the HTML of an Element

Problem

You want to see the HTML code of the selected element(s).

Solution

First, assume that the HTML file contains the following paragraph element:

obtainhtml.html

```
<!DOCTYPE html PUBLIC "-//W3C//DTD XHTML 1.0 Transitional//EN"
"http://www.w3.org/TR/xhtml1/DTD/xhtml1-transitional.dtd">
<html xmlns="http://www.w3.org/1999/xhtml" xml:lang="en" lang="en">
  <head>
    <meta http-equiv="Content-Type" content="text/html; charset=utf-8"/>
    <title>JQuery Examples</title>
    <script src="jquery-3.5.1.js" type="text/javascript"></script>
    <script src="obtainhtmljq.js" type="text/javascript"></script>
  </head>
  <body>

    <p>Styles make the formatting job much easier and more efficient. To
    give an attractive look to web sites, styles are heavily used.
    <span>jQuery is a powerful JavaScript library that allows us to add
    dynamic elements to our web sites. </span>Not only is it easy to learn,
    but it's easy to implement too.<br>
```

```
<a href="a1.htm"> jQuery Selectors</a> are used for selecting the area
of the document where we want to apply styles </p>

  </body>
</html>
```

The jQuery code to display the HTML code of the paragraph element appears as follows:

obtainhtmljq.js

```
$(document).ready(function() {
        alert($('p').html());
});
```

How It Works

The contents of the paragraph element are accessed and with the help of the html() method and its HTML code are displayed. The html() method gets the HTML content of the first element of the selected elements. It returns the HTML contents in the form of a string. The difference between html() and text() is that the text() method can be used in XML as well as in HTML documents, whereas html() can be used only in an HTML document. Another difference is that the html() method displays the tags along with the text.

The output you will get is shown in Figure 1-19. You can see that the output includes the tags together with the text.

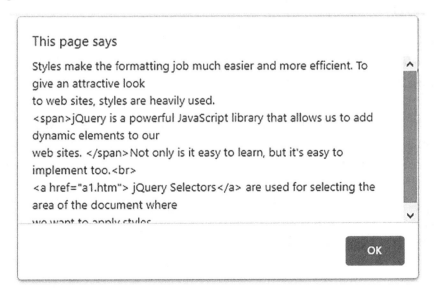

Figure 1-19. *The HTML content of the paragraph element of an HTML file*

To get the HTML content of the span element, you use following statement:

```
alert($('span').html());
```

To get the HTML content of the parent of the span element, you use the following jQuery code:

```
alert($('span').parent().html());
```

1-17. Assigning the Same Class Name to Different HTML Elements and Applying Styles to Them

Problem

You want to assign the same class name to two HTML elements and apply styles to them. The two elements can be a paragraph and an h1 element.

Solution

Let's examine the following HTML file, where the class named features is assigned to a paragraph and the h1 element:

assignsameclass.html

```
<!DOCTYPE html PUBLIC "-//W3C//DTD XHTML 1.0 Transitional//EN"
"http://www.w3.org/TR/xhtml1/DTD/xhtml1-transitional.dtd">
<html xmlns="http://www.w3.org/1999/xhtml" xml:lang="en" lang="en">
   <head>
    <meta http-equiv="Content-Type" content="text/html; charset=utf-8"/>
    <title>JQuery Examples</title>
    <link rel="stylesheet" href="style.css" type="text/css" media="screen" />
    <script src="jquery-3.5.1.js" type="text/javascript"></script>
    <script src="sameclassjq.js" type="text/javascript"></script>
   </head>
```

```
<body>
    <p class="features">Styles make the formatting job much easier and
    more efficient.</p>
    To give an attractive look to web sites, styles are heavily used.
        <h1 class="features">Using jQuery</h1>
</body>
</html>
```

To apply a style to the elements of class features in the preceding HTML file, the external style sheet (style.css) may be created with the following content:

```
.features{color:green;font-style:italic}
```

If you want the style rule to be applied to the HTML element via jQuery code (and not automatically), you need to assign some other name to the style rule in the style sheet.

```
.highlight{color:green;font-style:italic}
```

Then you need to write the following jQuery code:

sameclassjq.js

```
$(document).ready(function() {
    $('.features').addClass('highlight');
});
```

How It Works

In the HTML file, the paragraph and h1 elements both belong to class features. In the final style sheet, the style rule has the selector .highlight, which means the properties defined in this rule will be applied to all HTML elements that belong to class highlight. The style rule has two properties defined in it, color and font-style, and these properties apply the green color and italic style.

The preceding jQuery code will set the CSS class highlight on all HTML elements with class name features. The output appears as shown in Figure 1-20.

49

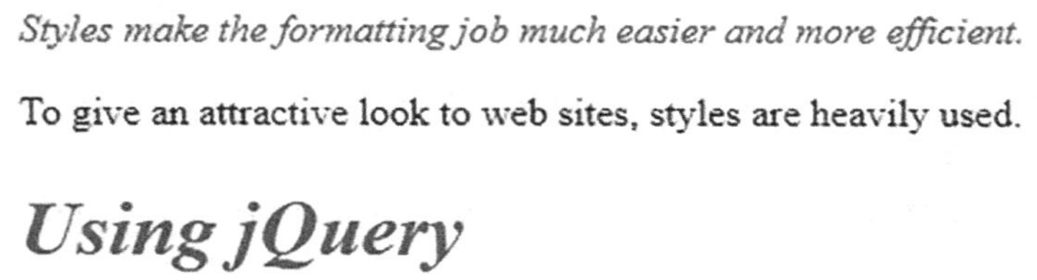

Styles make the formatting job much easier and more efficient.

To give an attractive look to web sites, styles are heavily used.

Using jQuery

Figure 1-20. *The same class applied to <p> and <h1> tags*

1-18. Summary

This chapter not only focused on explaining the basic features of jQuery but explained the concept of the DOM and different selector types. You learned how to include jQuery in a web page; applying styles to a wrapper set; specifying paragraphs; counting content with specific class; and applying styles. You also learned how to return to the previous DOM, how to remove a specific DOM, and how to prepend and append elements. You also learned the process of applying chaining, using for loops to display unordered list elements, replacing a DOM element, replacing text and HTML, cloning a DOM, displaying siblings, and setting and getting attributes of HTML elements.

The next chapter will explain how to use arrays and different iteration techniques. You will learn to sort arrays, split an array, search and display a desired value in numerical and in a string array, and the process of concatenating two arrays. You will also learn how to create an array of objects and how to use associative arrays.

CHAPTER 2

Arrays and Iteration

In this chapter, you will be learning how to use arrays and the different iteration techniques used to search for desired information in the arrays. We will be covering the following recipes in this chapter:

- Sorting an array
- Splitting an array into two
- Searching and displaying desired values from a numeric array
- Concatenating two arrays
- Searching desired information in a string array
- Manipulating array elements
- Converting a numerical array into a string and finding its substring
- Creating an array of objects and displaying the content
- Using associative arrays
- Sorting an array of objects

2-1. Sorting an Array

Problem

You have an array of elements and you want to sort them in a desired order.

© Bintu Harwani 2022
B. Harwani, *jQuery Recipes*, https://doi.org/10.1007/978-1-4842-7304-3_2

Solution

The following is an HTML file containing a `<div>` element and an unordered list:

Sortarray.html

```
<!DOCTYPE html PUBLIC "-//W3C//DTD XHTML 1.0 Transitional//EN"
        "http://www.w3.org/TR/xhtml1/DTD/xhtml1-transitional.dtd">
<html xmlns="http://www.w3.org/1999/xhtml" xml:lang="en" lang="en">
  <head>
    <meta http-equiv="Content-Type" content="text/html; charset=utf-8"/>
    <title></title>
    <script src="jquery-3.5.1.js" type="text/javascript"></script>
    <script src="sortarrayjq.js" type="text/javascript"></script>
  </head>
  <body>
<div></div>
<ul class="sorted"></ul>
  </body>
</html>
```

You can see in the above code that a `<div>` element is defined and an unordered list is defined and is assigned the class `sorted`. A text will be displayed via `<div>` element and the sorted electronics items will be displayed through an unordered list.

The jQuery code to sort the array elements in ascending order and display them on the screen is as follows:

Sortarrayjq.js

```
$(document).ready(function() {
    var items=["Television", "Referigerator", "Cameras", "Cell Phones",
    "Laptops" ]
    items.sort();
    $('div').text("Following are the " +  items.length + " electronic
    items for sale");
    for (var i = 0; i < items.length; i++){
        $('ul.sorted').append($("<li>" + items[i] + "</li>"));
    }
});
```

In the above jQuery code, a few methods are used, such as sort(), append(), and the length property, so let's look at them first.

sort( )

As the name suggest, the sort() method sorts the elements of an array in place. By default the elements will be sorted in ascending order. The original array itself is sorted by this method:

Syntax:

array.sort(compare_function)

where compare_function is optional and defines the sort order.
Example:

```
array.sort(function(a,b){
return a-b;
});
```

The comparison function might return value <0, =0, or >0.

- When <0, it means the second value is larger than the first value and is hence pushed down in the array.

- When >0, the first value is larger and is hence pushed down in the array.

- When =0, no change will happen as both values are equal.

append( )

The append() method inserts specified info at the end of each of the selected elements.
Syntax:

$(selector).append(info,function(index,html))

- The info parameter represents the data that has to be inserted. This data can be simple HTML element(s) or a jQuery object.

- function(index,html) where the function parameter returns the data to insert where the index parameter points to the location of the element and html returns the HTML content of the selected element.

length Property

The length property counts the number of the elements in the mentioned jQuery object and returns it.

Syntax:

```
$(selector).length
```

where selector is the jQuery object whose count has to be determined.

How It Works

A string array is defined by the name items and is assigned certain electronic items. The sort method is invoked and the array items is arranged alphabetically. Using the text() method, a text message is displayed via a <div> element indicating the count of electronic items for sale. A for loop is used to access each element of the array one by one and is displayed in the form of list items of the unordered list as shown in Figure 2-1.

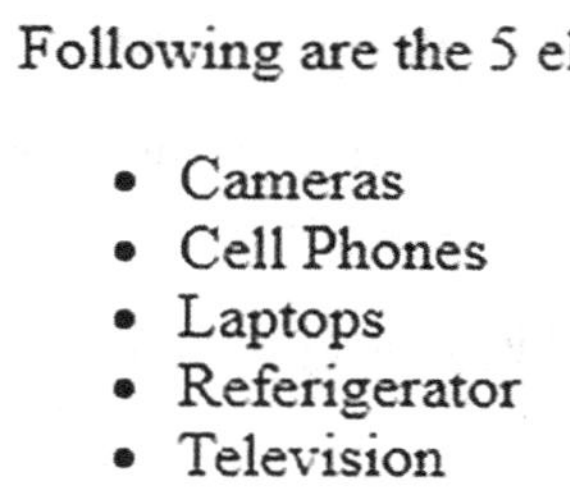

Following are the 5 electronic items for sale

- Cameras
- Cell Phones
- Laptops
- Referigerator
- Television

Figure 2-1. Count of items and its sorted order

In order to reverse the sort (i.e., to get the items arranged in reverse alphabetical order), after the items.sort() method, add the following statement:

items.reverse();

A small introduction to the reverse() method is given next.

reverse( )

The reverse() method reverses the order of the elements in an array. The array itself is modified.

Syntax:

`array.reverse()`

On adding the reverse() method, you will get the output shown in Figure 2-2.

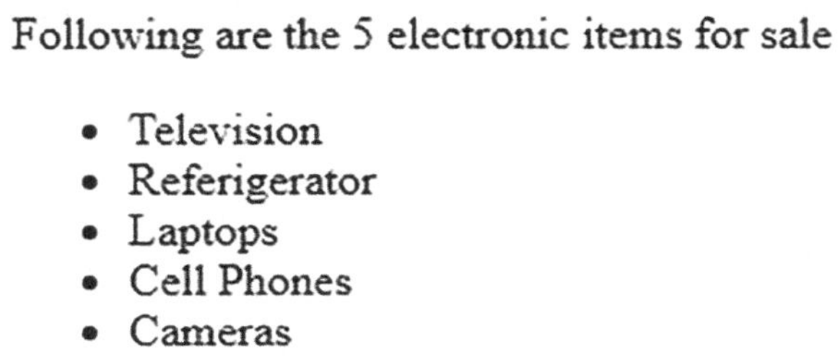

Following are the 5 electronic items for sale

- Television
- Referigerator
- Laptops
- Cell Phones
- Cameras

Figure 2-2. *The count of the items is displayed and the items are displayed in reverse order*

Note   The items.sort() will not give a correct result with a numeric array because 125 will be considered smaller than 45 because the number starting with 1 is considered smaller than the number beginning with 4. To sort the numeric array, you need to replace the items.sort statement with the following statement:

```
items.sort(function(a,b){
     return a-b;
});
```

Here is the complete jQuery code:

```
$(document).ready(function() {
    var items=[67,51,125,39,84, 44]
    items.sort(function(a,b){
       return a-b;
    });
    $('div').text("Following are the " +  items.length + " numericals in
    ascending order");
    for (var i = 0; i < items.length; i++){
        $('ul.sorted').append($("<li>" + items[i] + "</li>"));
    }
});
```

On running the program, you get the numeric array sorted in ascending order, as shown in Figure 2-3.

Following are the 6 numericals in ascending order

- 39
- 44
- 51
- 67
- 84
- 125

Figure 2-3. *The length of the array is displayed and its elements are displayed in ascending order*

2-2. Splitting an Array into Two

Problem

You have an array of items and you want to divide it into two.

Solution

The following is the HTML file containing two pairs of `<div>` and `<p>` elements:

Splitarray.html

```
<!DOCTYPE html PUBLIC "-//W3C//DTD XHTML 1.0 Transitional//EN"
        "http://www.w3.org/TR/xhtml1/DTD/xhtml1-transitional.dtd">
<html xmlns="http://www.w3.org/1999/xhtml" xml:lang="en" lang="en">
  <head>
    <meta http-equiv="Content-Type" content="text/html; charset=utf-8"/>
    <title></title>
    <script src="jquery-3.5.1.js" type="text/javascript"></script>
    <script src="splitarrayjq.js" type="text/javascript"></script>
  </head>
  <body>
<div id="electronics"></div>
```

```
<p class="electronics"></ul>
<div id="garments"></div>
<p class="garments"></ul>
  </body>
</html>
```

You can see in the above code that there are two pairs of `<div>` and `<p>` elements since you want to display electronics items and garments separately. Each `<div>` element will display the respective heading (i.e., whether the items shown below it are electronics items or are garments). Similarly, each `<p>` element will be used to display the respective items. To distinguish the two `<div>` elements, they are assigned the IDs `electronics` and `garments`, respectively. Similarly, the two `<p>` elements are assigned the classes `electronics` and `garments`, respectively.

The jQuery code to initialize an array, to split the array, and to display their contents separately is as follows:

Splitarrayjq.js

```
$(document).ready(function() {
    var items=["Television", "Refrigerator", "Cameras", "Cell Phones",
    "Laptops", "Jeans", "Shirts", "Blazers" ]
    electronics=items.splice(0,5);
    $('div#electronics').text("Following are the " + electronics.length +
    " electronic items for sale");
    $('p.electronics').html(electronics.join());
    $('div#garments').text("Following are the " + items.length + "
    garments for sale");
    $('p.garments').html(items.join());
});
```

In the above jQuery code, the `splice()` and `join()` methods are used, so let's have a quick look at these two methods first.

splice( )

The `splice()` method does the task of adding new elements to an array and removing the existing elements from the array. The method returns the modified array.

Syntax:

`array.splice(location, number, items_to_insert )`

- The `location` parameter represents the subscript or index position from where to add or remove elements. If this value is negative, it means the location is from the end of the array.

- The `number` parameter specifies the number of elements to be removed from the mentioned location.

- The `items_to_insert` parameter is a list of items separated by commas that you want to be inserted at the specified location. This parameter is optional.

The method modifies the array and returns the list of elements that are removed. If no element is removed, an empty array is returned.

join( )

The `join()` method joins the elements of an array and returns them in the form of a string.

Syntax:

`array.join(separator)`

where the `separator` parameter is a delimiter to separate each elements of the array. The default separator is a comma.

The method returns a string consisting of all the joined elements separated by the supplied separator.

How It Works

The `items` array is initialized and a few electronics and garment items are assigned to it. Because the first five elements in the array `items` are electronics items, the `splice()` method is used to extract the first five elements from the `items` array and assign them to another array called `electronics`. After the application of the `splice()` method, the sixth element and onwards (until the end) will remain in the `items` array only (i.e., the garments will remain in the `items` array). The count of electronics items is displayed via the `<div>` element with the id `electronics`. Next, all the electronics items in the electronic array are displayed through the <p> element with class electronics. Similarly, the count of the garment items is displayed via the <div> element with the id garments. The garment names in the items array are displayed through the <p> element that is assigned the garments class (see Figure 2-4).

   If you want the elements to appear one below the other, you can pass <br/> as a parameter in the join() method.

Following are the 5 electronic items for sale

Television,Referigerator,Cameras,Cell Phones,Laptops

Following are the 3 garments for sale

Jeans,Shirts,Blazers

Figure 2-4. *Dividing an array, one displaying the electronics items and other displaying the garments*

Note   In this recipe, you are learning to split an array on the basis of its indices. Splitting an array on the basis of content is covered later in this chapter.

2-3. Searching and Displaying Desired Values from a Numerical Array

Problem

You have some values in a numerical array and you want to display the first five values in that array and also the values that are less than 5.

Solution

In order to display all of the elements of array, the first five elements, and the elements with a value of less than 5, three pairs of <div> and <p> elements are defined in an HTML file, as shown:

Searchnumarr.html

```
<!DOCTYPE html PUBLIC "-//W3C//DTD XHTML 1.0 Transitional//EN"
        "http://www.w3.org/TR/xhtml1/DTD/xhtml1-transitional.dtd">
<html xmlns="http://www.w3.org/1999/xhtml" xml:lang="en" lang="en">
  <head>
    <meta http-equiv="Content-Type" content="text/html; charset=utf-8"/>
    <title></title>
    <script src="jquery-3.5.1.js" type="text/javascript"></script>
    <script src="searchnumarrjq.js" type="text/javascript"></script>
  </head>
  <body>
<div id="allnums"></div>
<p class="allnums"></ul>
<div id="first5"></div>
<p class="first5"></ul>
<div id="lessthan5"></div>
<p class="lessthan5"></ul>
  </body>
</html>
```

Because you want to display three categories of values (all values, first five values, and the values that are less than 5), three <div> and <p> element pairs are made. The three <div> elements are assigned the IDs allnums, first5, and lessthan5. Similarly, to distinguish the three <p> elements, they are assigned the classes allnums, first5, and lessthan5, respectively.

In order to display all items from the array, to display first five elements, and the elements that are less than 5, the jQuery code is as shown:

Searchnumarrjq.js

```
$(document).ready(function() {
    var nums=[5,0,4,2,7,1,9,3,6,8]
    $('div#allnums').text("Complete list");
    $('p.allnums').html(nums.join(", "));
    first5 =$.grep(nums, function( n, i ) {
        return ( i<=4 );
    });
```

```
$('div#first5').text("First 5 values");
$( "p.first5" ).text(first5.join( ", " ) );
lessthan5 =$.grep(nums, function( n, i ) {
      return ( n<5 );
});
$('div#lessthan5').text("Values less than 5");
$( "p.lessthan5" ).text(lessthan5.join( ", " ) );
});
```

In the above jQuery code, the grep() method is used, so let's understand how it works.

grep( )

The grep() method is used to search the elements of an array that satisfy a filter function.

Syntax:

jQuery.grep(array, function(value, location) [, invert])

- The array parameter represents the array in which the searching has to be done.

- The function(value, location) parameter represents the filter function that takes two arguments:

  - value points at the current element of the array.

  - location points at the subscript of the current element.

- The invert parameter, if ignored, returns an array having all elements for which the function has returned true. But if this parameter is passed as true, then the inverse will happen. You get an array having all elements for which the function returns false.

The grep() method returns the elements that satisfy the filter function without affecting the original array.

How It Works

An integer array is defined by the name nums and is initialized with a few integer values. The div element with the ID allnums is assigned the text **Complete list** to display.

All of the integer values in the nums array are displayed through the <p> element that is assigned the class allnums. The elements being displayed are separated by comma and will be displayed on the same line. To display the array elements on a separate line, replace the comma in the join() method with the <br/> element.

The grep() method is used along with the filter function() where the filter() function is set to the condition i<=4 so it will extract the elements with the index value less than or equal to 4 from the nums array and will be assigned to the array first5. The elements in the array first5 will be displayed through the paragraph that is assigned the class first5 (see Figure 2-5).

Again, the grep() method is used along with the filter function() where the filter() function is set to the condition n< 5 so the filter function will extract the elements from the nums array whose value is less than 5 and are assigned to the array lessthan5. The elements in the lessthan5 array will be displayed via the paragraph that is assigned the class lessthan5, as shown in Figure 2-5.

Complete list

5, 0, 4, 2, 7, 1, 9, 3, 6, 8

First 5 values

5, 0, 4, 2, 7

Values less than 5

0, 4, 2, 1, 3

Figure 2-5. *Showing the complete array, the first five values, and the values that are less than 5*

2-4. Concatenating Two Arrays

Problem

You have a numerical array containing a few values. You want to create two arrays out of it, one array having all the numbers that are divisible by 3 and another array having the values that are divisible by 5. Then you want to concatenate the two arrays into one that contains the numbers that are divisible by 3 or 5.

Solution

In order to display the original array, the array containing elements divisible by 3, the array containing elements divisible by 5, and the concatenation of two arrays, four pairs of <div> and <p> elements are defined in an HTML file:

Arrconcatenate.html

```
<!DOCTYPE html PUBLIC "-//W3C//DTD XHTML 1.0 Transitional//EN"
        "http://www.w3.org/TR/xhtml1/DTD/xhtml1-transitional.dtd">
<html xmlns="http://www.w3.org/1999/xhtml" xml:lang="en" lang="en">
  <head>
    <meta http-equiv="Content-Type" content="text/html; charset=utf-8"/>
    <title></title>
    <script src="jquery-3.5.1.js" type="text/javascript"></script>
    <script src="arrconcatenatejq.js" type="text/javascript"></script>
  </head>
  <body>
  <div id="allnums"></div>
      <p class="allnums"></ul>
      <div id="divisibleby5"></div>
      <p class="divisibleby5"></ul>
      <div id="divisibleby3"></div>
      <p class="divisibleby3"></ul>
      <div id="divisibleby3or5"></div>
      <p class="divisibleby3or5"></ul>
  </body>
</html>
```

63

You can see in the above code that four pairs of <div> and <p> elements are defined where the <p> element will be used to display content and the <div> element will be used to display headings (i.e., informing what is being shown through the <p> elements). To distinguish among themselves, the elements are assigned the IDs allnums, divisibleby5, divisibleby3, and divisibleby3or5.

The jQuery first creates two arrays from the main array, one containing the elements divisible by 3 and the other containing the elements divisible by 5, and finally the two arrays are concatenated to make an array that contains the elements divisible by 3 or 5. The complete jQuery code for doing above said tasks is as follows:

Arrconcatenatejq.js

```
$(document).ready(function() {
    var nums=[5,0,4,2,7,1,9,3,6,8]
    $('div#allnums').text("Complete list");
    $('p.allnums').html(nums.join(", "));
    divby5 =$.grep(nums, function( n, i ) {
        return ( (n!=0) && (n%5==0 ));
    });
    $('div#divisibleby5').text("Values divisible by 5");
    $( "p.divisibleby5" ).text(divby5.join( ", " ) );
    divby3 =$.grep(nums, function( n, i ) {
        return ( (n!=0) && (n%3==0) );
    });
    $('div#divisibleby3').text("Values divisible by 3");
    $( "p.divisibleby3" ).text(divby3.join( ", " ) );
    $.merge( divby3,divby5 )
    //divby3or5=divby3.concat(divby5);
    $('div#divisibleby3or5').text("Values divisible by 3 or 5");
    $( "p.divisibleby3or5" ).text(divby3.join( ", " ) );
    //$( "p.divisibleby3or5" ).text(divby3or5.join( ", " ) );
});
```

In the above jQuery code, two methods are used, merge() and concat(), so let's first have a quick view of them.

merge( )

The merge() method merges the content of two arrays into the first array.

Syntax:

$.merge(first_array, second_array)

where first_array is the array to which the elements of second_array will be merged. The contents of second_array remain unaffected.

concat( )

The concat() method can be used to join two strings and arrays. The two arrays being concatenated will remain unaffected and the concatenated version is returned.

Syntax:

concatenated_array = array1.concat(array2, ...)

where array1, array2, etc. are the arrays to be concatenated and the concatenated array (i.e., the merged elements) are returned and can be assigned to the new array.

How It Works

An integer array called nums array is defined and contains a few values. To display the numerical ones first, the heading **Complete list** is displayed through the <div> element of the id allnums. Below the <div> element, using the <p> element of class allnums, all of the numerical values in the nums array are displayed.

To get the numbers from the nums arrays that are divisible by 5, a grep() method is used along with the filter function and the %5 expression is used in the filter function to find the numbers that are divisible by 5. Hence all the numbers that are divisible by 5 are extracted from the nums arrays and are assigned to the array called divby5. The elements in the divby5 array are displayed via the <p> element of class divisibleby5. The heading for these elements is the text Values divisible by 5 through the <div> element of ID divisibleby5. Using the same procedure, elements that are divisible by 3 are extracted from the nums array and are assigned to the array called divby3.

Thereafter, the merge() method is invoked and both arrays, divby3 and divby5, are passed to the method and the contents of the divby5 array are added to the divby3 array.

The merged elements (i.e., the elements divisible by 3 or 5 in the divby3 array) are then displayed via the <p> element of class divisibleby3or5. Figure 2-6 shows the output of the program.

Note   There is one more way to display the array elements that are divisible by 3 or 5. You can also replace the merge() method with the concat method. That is, the contents of the divby3 and divby5 arrays are concatenated and the combined elements are assigned to the divby3or5 array. The first commented out statement in the above code does the same:

```
//divby3or5=divby3.concat(divby5);
```

Thereafter, the concatenated elements in the divby3or5 array can be displayed on the screen using the <p> element of class divisibleby3or5. The second commented out statement does this task:

```
//$( "p.divisibleby3or5" ).text(divby3or5.join( ", " ) );
```

Complete list

5, 0, 4, 2, 7, 1, 9, 3, 6, 8

Values divisble by 5

5

Values divisible by 3

9, 3, 6

Values divisible by 3 or 5

9, 3, 6, 5

Figure 2-6. *Displaying all array elements and the elements that are divisible by 5, the elements that are divisible by 3, and the elements that are divisible by 3 or 5*

2-5. Searching for Desired Information in a String Array

Problem

You have a string array and out of that array, you want to display strings that are of a specific length, strings that end with a specific character, and strings that have a specific substring.

Solution

In order to display the results of different queries performed on the string array, four pairs of <div> and <p> elements are defined in the following HTML program:

Desiredstr.html

```
<!DOCTYPE html PUBLIC "-//W3C//DTD XHTML 1.0 Transitional//EN"
        "http://www.w3.org/TR/xhtml1/DTD/xhtml1-transitional.dtd">
<html xmlns="http://www.w3.org/1999/xhtml" xml:lang="en" lang="en">
   <head>
    <meta http-equiv="Content-Type" content="text/html; charset=utf-8"/>
    <title></title>
    <script src="jquery-3.5.1.js" type="text/javascript"></script>
    <script src="desiredstrjq.js" type="text/javascript"></script>
   </head>
   <body>
     <div id="allitems"></div>
     <p class="allitems"></ul>
     <div id="length8"></div>
     <p class="length8"></ul>
     <div id="endingwiths"></div>
     <p class="endingwiths"></ul>
     <div id="juices"></div>
     <p class="juices"></ul>
   </body>
</html>
```

You can see in the above code that there are four pairs of `<div>` and `<p>` elements that will be used to display all of the items, items exactly 8 characters in length, the items that end with the character s, and all of the juices on the list. The `<div>` elements will be used to display a heading for the category of items being displayed and that is why they are assigned the IDs allitems, length8, endingwiths, and juices, respectively. The `<p>` elements are meant for displaying the items falling into the categories and hence are assigned the classes allitems, length8, endingwiths, and juices, respectively.

The jQuery code to display the desired strings from the string array (i.e., the strings that meet the specific criteria are searched) is as follows:

Desiredstrjq.js

```
$(document).ready(function() {
    var items=["Aloe vera juice", "Apple juice", "Biscuits", "Juice of
    oranges", "Cakes", "Brownies", "Doughnut", "Juice of pomegranate" ]
    $('div#allitems').text("Complete list");
    $('p.allitems').html(items.join(", "));

    $('div#length8').text("Items of length 8 characters");
    length8items =$.grep(items, function( n, i ) {
        return ( n.length ==8 );
    });
    $( "p.length8" ).text(length8items.join( ", " ) );

    $('div#endingwiths').text("Items ending with 's'");
    endingwithsitems =$.grep(items, function( n, i ) {
        return n.match(/[s]$/)
    });
    $( "p.endingwiths" ).text(endingwithsitems.join( ", " ) );
    $('div#juices').text("List of juices");
     juiceitems =$.grep(items, function( n, i ) {
        return ( n.toLowerCase().indexOf("juice") >= 0 );
    });
    $( "p.juices" ).text(juiceitems.join( ", " ) );
});
```

In the above jQuery code, the indexOf() method is used, so let's have a look at this method first.

indexOf( )

The indexOf() method searches for the specified string in the main string and returns the location of the first occurrence of the specified string. The location returned is 0-based and the method returns -1 if the string being searched is not found in the main string.

Syntax:

string.indexOf(string_to_search, location_to_start)

- The string_to_search parameter represents the string to search. It is case sensitive.

- The location_to_start parameter specifies the location to start the search. This parameter is optional and its default value is 0.

In order to search a substring in the specific selector, the index() method is used. Let's have a look at this method too.

index( )

The index() method searches the specified element in the selector and returns an integer representing the index location of the element.

Syntax:

$(selector).index(element_to_search)

Where the element_to_search parameter represents the element to be searched. If no parameter is used, the method returns the index location of the first element of the selector in relations to its siblings.

How It Works

The <div> element with the ID of allitems is accessed and its text is set to **Complete list**. All elements in the items array are displayed on the screen by assigning them to the <p> element of class allitems.

Similarly, the `<div>` element with the ID of `length8` is assigned the text **Items of length 8 characters**. A grep method is used along with a filter function that extracts all items with length equal to 8 characters from the `items` array and assigns them to the array `length8items`. Thereafter, all the elements in the array `length8items` are displayed via the `<p>` element of class `length8`.

Similarly, the `<div>` element with the ID of `endingwiths` is assigned the text **Items ending with s**. A grep method is used along with a filter function that uses a regular expression to extract the elements from the `items` array that have the last character as s and such elements are then assigned to the array called `endingwithsitems`. Finally, the elements in the array `endingwithsitems` are displayed through the `<p>` element of class `endingwiths`.

The last `<div>` element with the ID of `juices` is set to display the text **List of juices**. The `grep()` method is used along with the filter function that searches for the word **juices** in the elements of the `items` array and those elements are assigned to the array `juiceitems`. Thereafter, all elements in the array `juiceitems` are displayed via the `<p>` element of class `juices` as shown in Figure 2-7.

Complete list

Aloe vera juice, Apple juice, Biscuits, Juice of oranges, Cakes, Brownies, Doughnut, Juice of pomegranate

Items of length 8 characters

Biscuits, Brownies, Doughnut

Items ending with 's'

Biscuits, Juice of oranges, Cakes, Brownies

List of juices

Aloe vera juice, Apple juice, Juice of oranges, Juice of pomegranate

Figure 2-7. *Displaying the entire string array and the elements that are 8 characters in length, elements ending with s, and all elements with a substring of juice*

2-6. Manipulating Array Elements

Problem

You want to manipulate array elements for tasks like applying serial numbers to them, converting them to uppercase, and other tasks.

Solution

Let's assume an HTML file that has a heading element to display the message Members of my Group along with an empty paragraph element, as shown here:

manipulatearray.html

```
<!DOCTYPE html PUBLIC "-//W3C//DTD XHTML 1.0 Transitional//EN"
        "http://www.w3.org/TR/xhtml1/DTD/xhtml1-transitional.dtd">
<html xmlns="http://www.w3.org/1999/xhtml" xml:lang="en" lang="en">
  <head>
    <meta http-equiv="Content-Type" content="text/html; charset=utf-8"/>
    <title></title>
    <script src="jquery-3.5.1.js" type="text/javascript"></script>
    <script src="manipulatearrayjq.js" type="text/javascript"></script>
  </head>
  <body>
        <h3> Members of my Group are </h3>
        <p></p>
  </body>
</html>
```

This blank paragraph element will display names taken from an array, with serial numbers applied.

The jQuery code to display the array elements along with the serial number is shown here:

manipulatearrayjq.js

```
$(document).ready(function() {
    var members = [ "John", "Steve", "Ben", "Damon", "Ian" ];
```

```
        members = $.map(members, function(n,i){ return(i+1+"."+n); });
        $('p').html(members.join("<br />"));
});
```

Converting Names to Uppercase

Let's see how to use other useful methods in the callback method to manipulate members of the array. The first solution shows how to convert all names to uppercase with the toUpperCase() method.

convnamestoupperjq.js

```
$(document).ready(function() {
    var members = [ "John", "Steve", "Ben", "Damon", "Ian" ];
    members=$.map(members, function(n,i){ return(i+1+"."+n.
    toUpperCase());});
        $('p').html(members.join("<br/>"));
});
```

Using an Ordered List

Another method of displaying the array elements in capital letters along with serial numbers is to make use of the ordered-list element. Here is an HTML file that displays a heading element and an empty ordered-list element.

orderedlist.html

```
<!DOCTYPE html PUBLIC "-//W3C//DTD XHTML 1.0 Transitional//EN"
        "http://www.w3.org/TR/xhtml1/DTD/xhtml1-transitional.dtd">
<html xmlns="http://www.w3.org/1999/xhtml" xml:lang="en" lang="en">
  <head>
    <meta http-equiv="Content-Type" content="text/html; charset=utf-8"/>
    <title></title>
    <script src="jquery-3.5.1.js" type="text/javascript"></script>
    <script src="orderedlistupperjq.js" type="text/javascript"></script>
  </head>
  <body>
      <h3> Members of my Group are </h3>
```

```
    <ol id="list">
     </ol>
</body>
</html>
```

The jQuery code to display the array elements in uppercase is as follows:

orderedlistupperjq.js

```
$(document).ready(function() {
    var memlist = $( "#list" );
    var members = [ "John", "Steve", "Ben", "Damon", "Ian" ];
    members=$.map(members, function(n){ return(n.toUpperCase());});
    $.each(members,function( index, value ){
        memlist.append($( "<li>" + value + "</li>" ));
    });
});
```

In the above jQuery code, the each() method is used, so let's have a quick look at this method.

each( )

The each() method is used to define a function that executes on each of the selected elements. That is, the loop iterates over all of the selected DOM and executes the code defined in the function.

Syntax

```
$(selector).each(function(index,element))
```

- The function(index,element) parameter contains the statements that need to execute on each selected element.

- The index represents the position of the selector.

- The element represent the current element.

How It Works

To understand this recipe, you need to know about the map() method. This method iterates through each element of the array and invokes a callback function on each of the array elements. The returned elements can be assigned to another array or the same array if you prefer. The map() method can also iterate through array-like objects that have a length property. Here is the syntax for map():

map(array, callback);

The callback function here contains the statements for performing the processing task on the array elements. In the first solution, you want to display the names stored in the array along with serial numbers. You can see that the array members is defined and contains the names you want to display. You next pass this array to the map() method. The callback function in the map() method contains two arguments, n and i, where n refers to the elements of the array (names) being passed to the map() method and i is the index of the individual array element (the index begins with 0). To make the serial numbers begin with 1 instead of 0, you can add 1 to i in each iteration. The values returned by the callback function thus appear as follows:

```
return(i+1+"."+n)
```

This statement returns all the elements of the array one by one with the index beginning from 1. The output is shown in Figure 2-8.

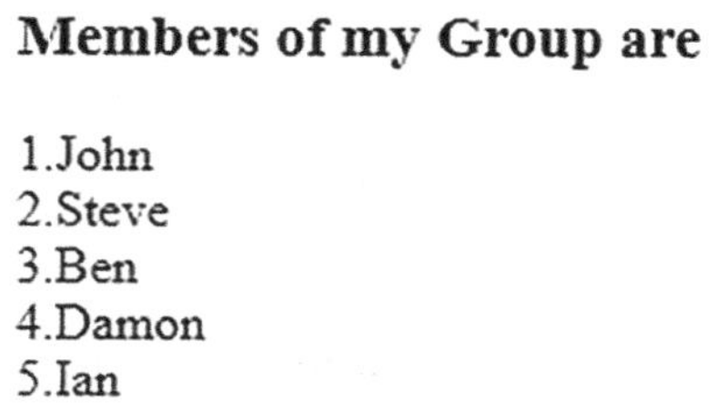

Members of my Group are

1.John
2.Steve
3.Ben
4.Damon
5.Ian

Figure 2-8. *Using array mapping to assign serial numbers to elements of the array*

Next, you use the toUpperCase() method in the callback function to convert into uppercase all names stored in the array:

```
members=$.map(members, function(n,i){ return(i+1+"."+n.toUpperCase()); });
```

Recall that the arguments n and i in the callback function refer to the array element and index number, respectively. You can see that the application of `toUpperCase()` to n (that is, the names stored in the array in the form of array elements) converts the names into uppercase and returns them for display in the paragraph element. The output will be the names converted to uppercase, along with serial numbers, as shown in Figure 2-9.

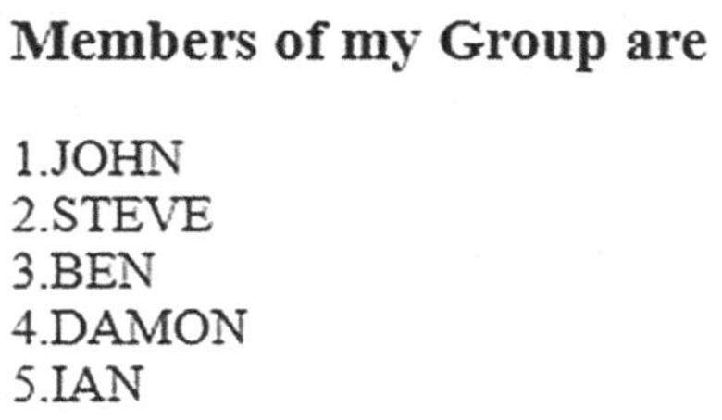

Members of my Group are

1.JOHN
2.STEVE
3.BEN
4.DAMON
5.IAN

Figure 2-9. *Using array mappings to convert array elements to uppercase*

The ordered-list solution applies autonumbering to its list elements. To the members array, you assign the result of the `map()` method, which will convert each array element into uppercase. You then append each member of the `members` array one by one to the ordered list (which has an id of `list` to identify it through jQuery code). You will get the output shown in Figure 2-10.

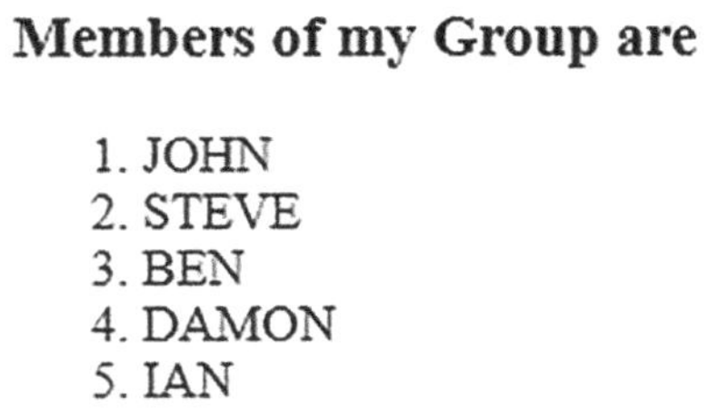

Members of my Group are

1. JOHN
2. STEVE
3. BEN
4. DAMON
5. IAN

Figure 2-10. *Displaying array elements in uppercase via list items*

2-7. Converting a Numerical Array into a String and Finding Its Substring

Problem

You have a numerical array and you want it to be converted into a string so that you can apply the `substr()` method to take out a part of the string.

Solution

Here is an HTML file that contains three headings elements to display the titles for the original numerical array you're working with, the array converted into string form, and finally the substring of the string. Also, below each heading element is a paragraph element. The three paragraph elements are assigned class names origarr, arrstring, and partstring. The paragraph of the class origarr will be used to display elements of the numerical array. The paragraph of the class arrstring will be used for displaying the string (the array after converted into string form) and the paragraph of the class partstring will be used for displaying the part of the string that you want to take out. The HTML file is as follows:

convnumarrayintostring.html

```
<!DOCTYPE html PUBLIC "-//W3C//DTD XHTML 1.0 Transitional//EN"
        "http://www.w3.org/TR/xhtml1/DTD/xhtml1-transitional.dtd">
<html xmlns="http://www.w3.org/1999/xhtml" xml:lang="en" lang="en">
  <head>
    <meta http-equiv="Content-Type" content="text/html; charset=utf-8"/>
    <title></title>
    <script src="jquery-3.5.1.js" type="text/javascript"></script>
    <script src="convnumtostringjq.js" type="text/javascript"></script>
  </head>
  <body>
      <h3>Original array is </h3>
      <p class="origarr"></p>
      <h3> Array in form of string </h3>
       <p class="arrstring"></p>
      <h3> Substring is </h3>
      <p class="partstring"></p>
  </body>
</html>
```

The jQuery code to convert the numerical array into a string and then to take out a part of it is as follows:

convnumtostringjq.js

```
$(document).ready(function() {
    var members = [67,51,125,39,84];
    $('p.origarr').html(members.join("<br/>"));
    var str = members.join("");
    $('p.arrstring').text(str);
    var substr = str.substr(0,3);
    $('p.partstring').text(substr);
});
```

How It Works

You define a numerical array named members of five elements and display the contents in the paragraph element of the class origarray, delimiting each array element with a line break (<br/>) so that the array elements are displayed one below the other.

Next, you convert the numerical array members into a string by joining each of its elements into the string variable str without any white space in between. That is, the string str will contain all the numerical values of the numerical array joined one after the other, without any space in between. The str variable is displayed in the paragraph element of the class arrstring.

Finally, you take out a part of the string from the str variable, beginning from index location 0. From there, three characters are extracted and stored in the string variable substr. The contents of the variable substr will be displayed in the paragraph element of the class partstring. The output is shown in Figure 2-11.

Original array is

67
51
125
39
84

Array in form of string

67511253984

Substring is

675

Figure 2-11. *A numerical array converted to a string*

2-8. Creating an Array of Objects and Displaying the Content

Problem

You want to create an array of objects where each object contains a pair comprising a country's name and its capital.

Solution

To display the content in array of objects (i.e., to display country name and the corresponding capital), a `<div>` element and a `<p>` element are created as shown below:

Countrycap.html

```
<!DOCTYPE html PUBLIC "-//W3C//DTD XHTML 1.0 Transitional//EN"
        "http://www.w3.org/TR/xhtml1/DTD/xhtml1-transitional.dtd">
<html xmlns="http://www.w3.org/1999/xhtml" xml:lang="en" lang="en">
  <head>
    <meta http-equiv="Content-Type" content="text/html; charset=utf-8"/>
```

```
    <title></title>
    <script src="jquery-3.5.1.js" type="text/javascript"></script>
    <script src="countrycapjq.js" type="text/javascript"></script>
  </head>
  <body>
<div id="allcountries"></div>
<p class="allcountries">
  </body>
</html>
```

You can see in the above code that to give a unique identity, the <div> element is assigned an ID of allcountries and the <p> element is assigned the class allcountries.

The following is the jQuery code to create an array of objects and to display information about different countries and their capitals stored in i:

Countrycapjq.js

```
$(document).ready(function() {
    var countries=[
    {
        "country": "India",
        "capital": "New Delhi"
    },
    {
        "country": "United States",
        "capital": "Washington D.C."
    },
    {
        "country": "England",
        "capital": "London"
    },
    {
        "country": "Australia",
        "capital": "Canberra"
    }
    ];
```

```
    $('div#allcountries').text("List of countries and their capitals");
    for(var i=0;i<countries.length;i++){
        $('p.allcountries').append("<tr><td>"+countries[i].country+ "
        </td><td>"+countries[i].capital+"</td><tr/>");
    }
});
```

How It Works

An array of objects called countries is created where each object comprises two attributes, country and capital. A few objects are created with some country names and their respective capitals.

The <div> element with ID allcountries is assigned the text List of countries and their capitals. A for loop is used to access each object from the array and display the value in the country and capital attributes, and display them through the <p> element with an ID of allcountries, as shown in Figure 2-12.

List of countries and their capitals

India   New Delhi
United States Washington D.C.
England   London
Australia   Canberra

Figure 2-12. *Displaying all the elements of the array of objects where each object is comprised of a country and capital pair*

In order to sort this array of objects on the basis of an ascending order of country names, add the following whole code before displaying the array through a <div> element:

```
countries=countries.sort(function(a,b){
    if(a.country < b.country){return -1};
    if(a.country > b.country){return 1};
     return 0;
});
```

Add the above code in jQuery above the following statement:

```
$('div#allcountries').text("List of countries and their capitals");
```

The sort() method was explained in the first recipe. The array will be objects in the ascending order of country names, as shown in Figure 2-13.

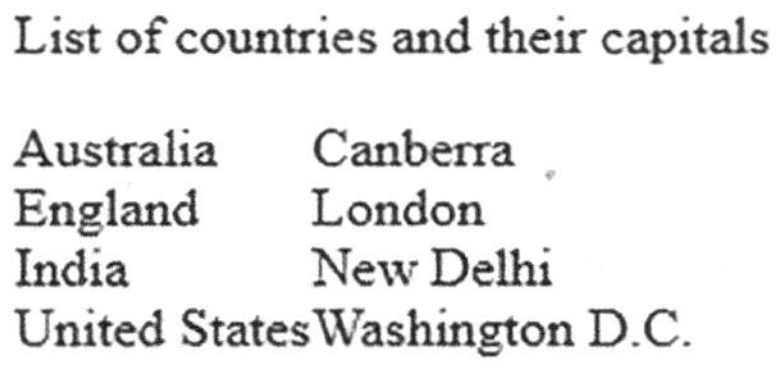

List of countries and their capitals

Australia   Canberra
England   London
India   New Delhi
United States Washington D.C.

Figure 2-13. Displaying the array of objects after sorting on country names

2-9. Using Associative Arrays

Associative arrays are the arrays where the indexes are not essentially numerical but strings as well. These string indexes are also known as keys (i.e., associative arrays are nothing but a sequence of key/value pairs).

Problem

You want to display certain countries and their capitals in the form of an associative array.

Solution

To display a heading and the countries and their respective capitals, create the following HTML file with <div> and <p> elements:

Associativearr.html

```
<!DOCTYPE html PUBLIC "-//W3C//DTD XHTML 1.0 Transitional//EN"
        "http://www.w3.org/TR/xhtml1/DTD/xhtml1-transitional.dtd">
<html xmlns="http://www.w3.org/1999/xhtml" xml:lang="en" lang="en">
  <head>
    <meta http-equiv="Content-Type" content="text/html; charset=utf-8"/>
    <title></title>
    <script src="jquery-3.5.1.js" type="text/javascript"></script>
    <script src="associativearrjq.js" type="text/javascript"></script>
  </head>
  <body>
```

```
<div id="allcountries"></div>
<p class="allcountries">
  </body>
</html>
```

You can see in the above code that a `<div>` element of ID `allcountries` and a `<p>` element of class `allcountries` are defined where the `<div>` element will be used for displaying the heading and the `<p>` element will be used for displaying content

You need to write the jQuery code to define an associative array, assigning the country and capital in the form of a key and value, and then to display them.

Associativearrjq.js

```
$(document).ready(function() {
    var countries={
        "India" : "New Delhi",
        "United States" : "Washington D.C.",
        "England" : "London",
        "Australia" : "Canberra"
    };
    $('div#allcountries').text("List of countries and their capitals");
    $.each(countries, function(key, value) {
        $('p.allcountries').append("<tr><td>"+key+ " </td><td>"+value+"
        </td><tr/>");
    });
});
```

How It Works

An associative array is created by name the of `countries` comprising a key/value pair were the key is the country name and the value is its capital. Four countries and their respective capitals are used to initialize the associative array.

The text `List of countries and their capitals` is displayed using the `<div>` element of ID `allcountries`. Using an `each()` loop, the specified function is executed on all elements of the associative array. The function accesses the key and its associated value and displays it through the `<p>` element of the class `allcountries`, as shown in Figure 2-14.

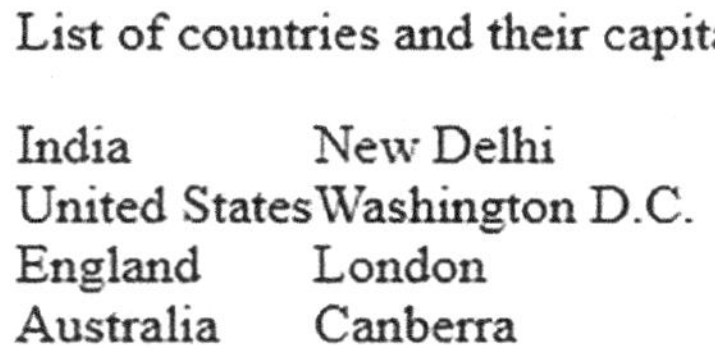

List of countries and their capitals

India   New Delhi
United States Washington D.C.
England   London
Australia   Canberra

Figure 2-14. *Displaying the contents of the associative array*

2-10. Sorting an Array of Objects

Problem

You have student information stored in the form of an array of objects. Each student object is assumed to consist of three attributes: roll, name, and emailId. You want to sort the array on the basis of the attribute roll.

Solution

Let's create an HTML file that displays a heading and an empty table element of the class listofstud. The table element will be used to display a sorted array of objects. The HTML file may appear as shown here:

sortarrobject.html

```
<!DOCTYPE html PUBLIC "-//W3C//DTD XHTML 1.0 Transitional//EN"
        "http://www.w3.org/TR/xhtml1/DTD/xhtml1-transitional.dtd">
<html xmlns="http://www.w3.org/1999/xhtml" xml:lang="en" lang="en">
  <head>
    <meta http-equiv="Content-Type" content="text/html; charset=utf-8"/>
    <title></title>
    <script src="jquery-3.5.1.js" type="text/javascript"></script>
    <script src="sortarrobjectjq.js" type="text/javascript"></script>
  </head>
  <body>
      <h3>List of students is </h3>
      <table class="listofstud"></table>
  </body>
</html>
```

Now write the jQuery code to create an array of objects to store information of three students with attributes of roll, name, and emailId. Also, you need to include the code to perform sorting on the roll attribute of the student object. The jQuery code is shown here, and in the next section you'll look at how it all works.

sortarrobjectjq.js

```
$(document).ready(function() {
    var students=[
    {
        "roll": 101,
        "name": "Ben",
        "emailId":"ben@gmail.com"
    },
    {
         "roll": 102,
        "name": "Ian",
        "emailId":"ian@gmail.com"
    },
    {
        "roll": 103,
        "name": "Caroline",
        "emailId":"carol@gmail.com"
    }
    ];
    students = students.sort(function(a,b){
        return b.roll-a.roll;
    });
    $.each(students,function( index, value ){
        $('table.listofstud').append("<tr><td>"+value.roll+"
        </td><td>"+value.name+"</td><td>"+
value.emailId+"</td></tr>");
    });
});
```

If you want to sort the array on the alphabetical order of its name attribute, you need to replace the preceding sort() function with one like this:

```
students = students.sort(function(a,b){
    if(a.name<b.name){ return -1 };
    if(a.name>b.name){ return 1 };
    return 0;
});
```

How It Works

In the `sort()` method you needed to add the comparison function that repeatedly takes a pair of values from the array and returns the values <0, =0, and >0 on the basis of comparison. You can see that in the comparison function you are comparing the `roll` attributes of the `students` object. That function returns the following:

```
return b.roll-a.roll;
```

This means the function will sort the array in descending order of the attribute `roll`. Thereafter, you use `each()` to parse each of the array elements and process them via their callback function. In the callback function, each of the array element's attributes, that is, `roll`, `name`, and `emailId`, are displayed by enclosing them in the `<td>` and `</td>` tags. This means that each array element is stored in a table data element in a separate row and each of the attributes of the array element are displayed in the form of columns. The result is that now the array of objects appears in tabular format, as shown in Figure 2-15.

List of students is

103 Caroline carol@gmail.com
102 Ian   ian@gmail.com
101 Ben   ben@gmail.com

Figure 2-15. *An array of student objects, sorted in descending order of the roll attribute*

When you sort on the `name` attribute, you can see that this time you are comparing the `name` attributes of the `students` object. The function returns -1 if the `name` attribute of the first element is smaller (in ASCII value) than the `name` attribute of the second element and returns 1 in the opposite scenario. The result will be the array of `student` objects sorted on the basis of the `name` attribute. You'll see output like Figure 2-16.

List of students is

101 Ben   ben@gmail.com
103 Caroline carol@gmail.com
102 Ian   ian@gmail.com

Figure 2-16. *An array of student objects, sorted in alphabetical order of the name attribute*

2-11. Summary

In this chapter, you learned about working with numerical arrays, string arrays, associative arrays, and an array of objects. You also learned to sort an array, split the array into parts, search for desired elements in the arrays, and how to concatenating arrays. Also, you learned how an array of objects is defined and how an associative array works.

The next chapter focuses on understanding the event handling methods. You will learn how to take actions when a mouse button is clicked or when an input box gets focus or when a mouse is hovered over any button. You will also learn to perform tasks on mouse up and down events and when a key is pressed or released. Also, you will learn to zoom in and out of an image and apply a fading effect and animation to an image when some event occurs.

CHAPTER 3

Understanding the Event Model

In this chapter, you will be learning different event handling methods. We will be covering the following recipes in this chapter:

- Displaying a message upon getting focus and when blurred
- Finding out which mouse button is pressed
- Changing the style on mouse entering and leaving an HTML element
- Using a mouse hover event to change the style of a button
- Using mouse up and down events to show and hide an image
- Making two buttons, one for hiding and one for displaying an image
- Zooming in and out of an image using `toggleClass`
- Avoiding event bubbling
- Knowing which key is down, pressed, or released
- Applying a fading effect on an image
- Applying animation on an image
- Triggering events automatically
- Disabling a button after it is clicked once
- Finding the screen coordinates of a mouse button press
- Highlighting text dynamically
- Making an image bright or blurred with mouse movements
- Creating image-based rollovers

© Bintu Harwani 2022
B. Harwani, *jQuery Recipes*, https://doi.org/10.1007/978-1-4842-7304-3_3

- Adding and removing text in response to events

- Displaying word balloons

- Creating "Return to Top" links

- Displaying text with an animation

- Replacing text with a sliding effect

The event model, as the name suggests, deals with events like click events, key presses, mouse up, mouseover, etc. You will learn how an action is performed when some event occurs.

3-1. Displaying a Message on Getting Focus and When Blurred

Problem

You want to display a message when an input box gets the user's focus and also when the user leaves that input box.

Solution

The following is an HTML file that contains a paragraph element, a form, and within the form, an input box and a button:

Inputfocus.html

```
<!DOCTYPE html PUBLIC "-//W3C//DTD XHTML 1.0 Transitional//EN"
        "http://www.w3.org/TR/xhtml1/DTD/xhtml1-transitional.dtd">

<html xmlns="http://www.w3.org/1999/xhtml" xml:lang="en" lang="en">
  <head>
    <meta http-equiv="Content-Type" content="text/html; charset=utf-8"/>
    <title></title>
    <script src="jquery-3.5.1.js" type="text/javascript"></script>
    <script src="inputfocusjq.js" type="text/javascript"></script>
  </head>
```

```
<body>
<p>We deal with Electronics Products</p>
<form action="destinationfile" method="get">
 <label>Product to search: </label>
 <input type="text" name="product" >
 <input type="submit" id="submit" value="Submit">
</form>
  </body>
</html>
```

You can see in the above code that a paragraph element is used to display the text **We deal with Electronics Products**. A form is made with a label, an input box, and a button. When the button is pressed in the form, the user will be navigated to the web page called destinationfile. The label is set to display the text **Product to search** and the name of the input box is set to **product**.

To display the message when the input box gets focus and when the user clicks anywhere outside the input box, use the following jQuery code:

Inputfocusjq.js

```
$(document).ready(function() {
    $("input").on("focus", function() {
        alert("Enter product to search");
    }).on("blur", function() {
        alert("We will mail you the related products");
        //$("#submit").trigger( "click" );
    });
});
```

In the above jQuery code, you use the methods on(), focus(), blur() , and trigger(). Let's look at these methods first.

on( )

The on() method is for associating or connecting one or more event handlers to the selected elements and their children.

Syntax:

$(selector).on(event, child_selector,passed_data,function,map)

- The event parameter represents one or more event(s) to be linked with the selected elements. If more events are there, they need to be separated by a space.

- The child_selector parameter is optional, but if used, it means that the event handler has to be attached to the specified child elements only and not the main selector.

- The passed_data parameter represents the data to be passed to the function. It is optional.

- The function parameter represents the function that has to be executed when the event occurs.

- The map parameter specifies the event function pair in the format (event:function, event:function, ...) where the respective function will execute on the occurrence of an event.

To remove an event handler from the selected element, the off() method is used.

focus( )

The focus event occurs when an input element gets focus. The focus on an input element can be achieved either by pressing the Tab key or via a mouse click. On getting the focus (i.e., when the focus event occurs on the input event), the code in the attached function is executed.

Syntax:

$(selector).focus(function)

where the function parameter includes the code that has to be executed on getting the focus on the input element. It is optional.

The focus method is usually used along with the blur method

The alert() method was discussed in Chapter 1. For your reference, recall that it is used for displaying a dialog box with a message and an OK button. Until and unless the user clicks the OK button and closes the alert box, the user cannot access any other part of the page.

blur( )

The blur event occurs when an element loses focus. The blur() method can be used for doing following two things:

- Triggering the blur event

- Attaching a function that runs the code when a blur event occurs

Syntax:
The following syntax fires the blur event on the specified selector(s):

$(selector).blur()

The following syntax attaches a function to the blur event. The function includes the code to be executed on the occurrence of the blur event.

$(selector).blur(function)
The blur method is usually used with the focus() method.

trigger( )

The trigger() method is used for firing a specified event handler on the selected element. That is, the default behavior of an event can be invoked for the selected elements using the trigger() method.

Syntax:

$(selector).trigger(event,parameter1,parameter2,...)

where the event parameter represents the event you want to fire on the selected element. parameter1 and parameter2 are the parameters to be passed to the event handler. These parameters are optional.

How It Works

An alert dialog box will be displayed whenever there is focus on any input element (i.e., the moment the user clicks the input box, the focus event will be fired and the alert dialog will display the message **Enter product to search**). After entering the product information in the input box, when the user presses the Tab button or clicks anywhere outside the input box, the blur() event will be fired, which in turn will display an alert dialog box with the message **We will mail you the related products**.

If you want the form to be automatically submitted and navigated to the target file, `destinationfile` should take place. Then you can remove the comment from the `trigger()` method. The `trigger()` method will invoke the click event on the Submit button; consequently the form will be submitted and you will navigate to the target file mentioned in the `action` attribute, `destinationfile`. Because no `destinationfile` exists currently, the *page not found* error will appear on the navigation.

Upon running the HTML file, you get the screen shown in Figure 3-1(a). Upon clicking the input box (i.e., the moment the input box gets the focus), an alert dialog box appears showing the message **Enter product to search** (see Figure 3-1(b)). After closing the alert dialog box by clicking OK, when the user clicks anywhere outside the input box or presses the Tab key, the input box loses the focus and an alert dialog box is displayed with the message **We will mail you the related products** (see Figure 3-1(c)).

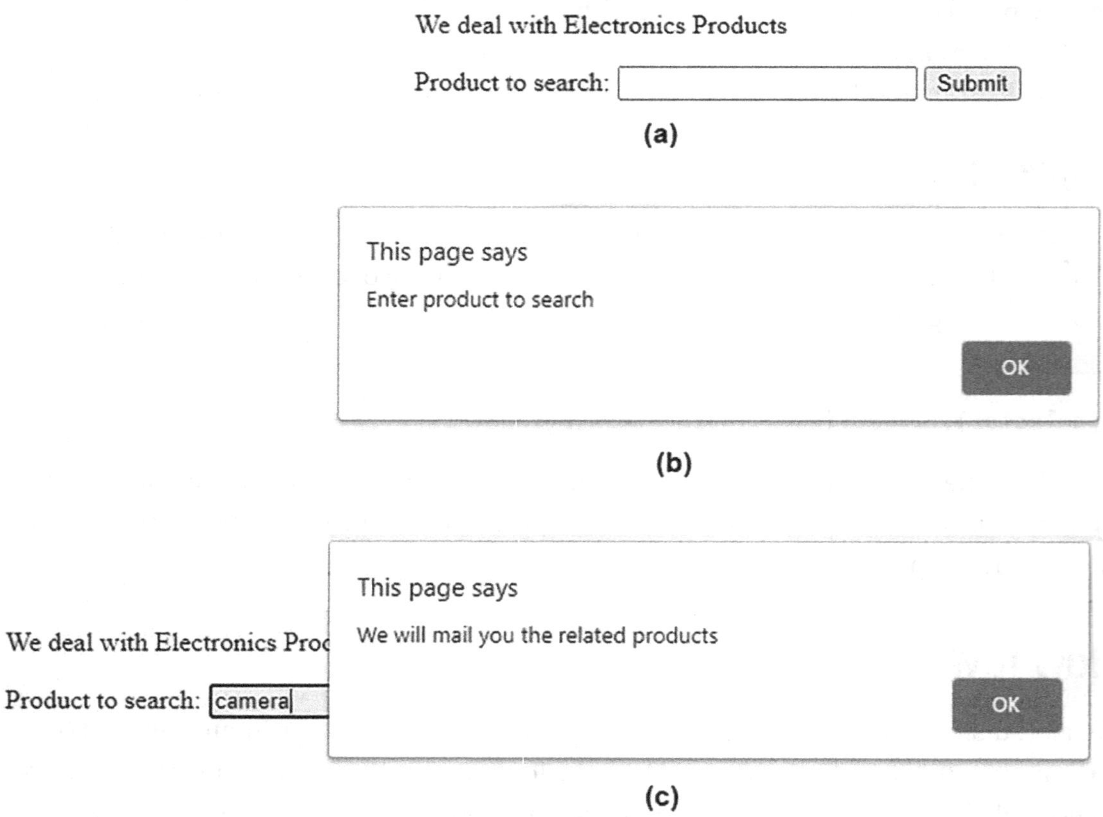

(a)

(b)

(c)

Figure 3-1. *(a) Screen asking for the product to search (b) Alert dialog displays the message "Enter product to search" when the input element gets focus (c) Alert dialog displaying the message "We will mail you the related products" when the focus is removed from the input box*

3-2. Finding Which Mouse Button Is Pressed

Problem

You have certain HTML elements on a web page and you want to know which mouse button, whether left, right, or middle, is pressed on any of the HTML elements.

Solution

Make an HTML file with an unordered list, as follows:

Mousebutton.html

```
<!DOCTYPE html PUBLIC "-//W3C//DTD XHTML 1.0 Transitional//EN"
        "http://www.w3.org/TR/xhtml1/DTD/xhtml1-transitional.dtd">

<html xmlns="http://www.w3.org/1999/xhtml" xml:lang="en" lang="en">
  <head>
    <meta http-equiv="Content-Type" content="text/html; charset=utf-8"/>
    <title></title>
    <script src="jquery-3.5.1.js" type="text/javascript"></script>
    <script src="mousebuttonjq.js" type="text/javascript"></script>
  </head>
  <body>
        <ul id="ElectronicsProducts">
          <li class="product">Cameras</li>
          <li class="product">Cell Phones</li>
          <li class="product">Laptops</li>
        </ul>
  </body>
</html>
```

In this HTML file, you can see that an unordered list is created with the ID of ElectronicsProducts consisting of three list items with the text Cameras, Cell Phones, and Laptops. The three list items are assigned a class name of product.

In order to display which mouse button is pressed on which element, the following jQuery code is written:

93

Mousebuttonjq.js

```
$(document).ready(function() {
$(".product").on("mousedown", function(event) {
    if(event.which==1){
        alert("Left mouse button is pressed on "+$(this).text());
    }
    else
    {
        alert("Right mouse button is pressed on "+$(this).text());
    }
});
});
```

Let's look at the method and the properties that are used in preceding jQuery code: the mousedown() method and the event.which property.

mousedown( )

As the name suggests, the mousedown event occurs when the mouse pointer is over some element and the mouse button is pressed down over that element. The mousedown() method does following two tasks:

- It fires the mousedown event.

- It connects a function with the mousedown event. The function contains the code that is required to run when the mousedown event occurs.

Syntax:

The following syntax fires the mousedown event on the selected element(s):

$(selector).mousedown()

The following syntax associates a function to the mousedown event:

$(selector).mousedown(function)

where the parameter function contains the code to be executed when the mouse event occurs on the selected element(s).

event.which

The event.which property indicates which keyboard key or mouse button is pressed during the event. The property represents value 1 for the left button, 2 for middle, and 3 for the right button.

Syntax:

event.which

where event is the parameter used in the **event-binding** function.

How It Works

When the mouse button is clicked over any element with the class of product, the mousedown() event will be fired. All three list items are assigned the product class, so if the left mouse button is clicked on any of the list items, the event.which property is checked to know which mouse button is pressed. Accordingly, an alert dialog box is displayed indicating whether the left, middle, or right mouse button is pressed along with the list item on which the mouse button is pressed.

On pressing the left mouse button on the Cameras list item, the alert dialog box will appear, informing that the left mouse button is pressed on Cameras, as shown in Figure 3-1(a). When the right mouse button is clicked on the Laptops list item, the alert dialog box will show the message shown in Figure 3-2(b).

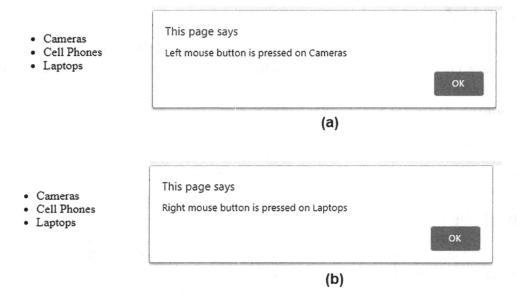

Figure 3-2. *(a) Alert dialog informing that the left mouse button is pressed on Cameras (b) Alert dialog informing that right mouse button is clicked on Laptops*

3-3. Changing the Style on a Mouse Entering and Leaving an HTML Element

Problem

You have a button with some CSS style already applied to it. You want to change the style when the mouse pointer enters the button and reapply the original CSS style when the mouse pointer leaves the button.

Solution

Make an HTML file with an unordered list, as shown:

Mousehover.html

```
<!DOCTYPE html PUBLIC "-//W3C//DTD XHTML 1.0 Transitional//EN"
        "http://www.w3.org/TR/xhtml1/DTD/xhtml1-transitional.dtd">

<html xmlns="http://www.w3.org/1999/xhtml" xml:lang="en" lang="en">
  <head>
```

```
    <meta http-equiv="Content-Type" content="text/html; charset=utf-8"/>
    <title></title>
<link rel="stylesheet" href="mousehoverstyle.css" type="text/css"
media="screen" />
    <script src="jquery-3.5.1.js" type="text/javascript"></script>
    <script src="mousehoverjq.js" type="text/javascript"></script>
  </head>
  <body>
<p>We deal with Electronics Products</p>
<img src="a1.jpg" width="200" height="100"><br/>
<button class="btn" id="hide">Hide Image</button>
<button class="btn" id="show">Show Image</button>
  </body>
</html>
```

A paragraph element is used to display the text **We deal with Electronics Products.** An image is displayed, 200px wide and 100px high. Two buttons are displayed below the image with text **Hide Image** and **Show Image**. The class btn is assigned to the two buttons. In order to access the jQuery code, the two buttons are assigned the IDs hide and show, respectively.

To apply the CSS class to the button and to define the CSS class that needs to be applied when the mouse pointer is hovered over it, write different CSS classes in the stylesheet, as follows:

Mousehoverstyle.css

```
.btn{
    font-style: italic;
    background-color: #0f0;
}
.highlight{
    font-style: bold;
    background-color: #f00;
}
```

In order to apply a CSS class on the mouse button when the mouse pointer hovers over it and to remove the CSS class when the mouse pointer is moved away from the button, write the following jQuery code:

Mousehoverjq.js

```
$(document).ready(function() {
    $("button#hide").on("mouseenter", function() {
        // alert("hovered over");
        $("button#hide").addClass("highlight");
    }).on("mouseleave", function() {
        $("button#hide").removeClass("highlight");
        // alert("hovered out");
    });
});
```

In this jQuery code, methods mouseenter(), mouseleave(), mouseover() and mouseout() are used. Let's have a quick look at these methods first.

mouseenter( )

The mouseenter event occurs when the mouse pointer is over the selected element. The mouseenter() method does the following two tasks:

- It triggers the mouseenter event.

- It associates a function that contains the code that is required to run when the mouseenter event occurs.

Syntax:
The following syntax fires the mouseenter event on the selected element(s):

$(selector).mouseenter()

The following syntax associates a function to the mouseenter event:

$(selector).mouseenter(function)

where the function parameter contains the code that has to be run when the mouseenter event is fired.

The difference between the mouseover and mouseenter events is that the mouseenter event fires only when the mouse pointer enters the selected element whereas the mouseover event fires even if the mouse pointer enters any of its child elements too.

The mouseenter method is usually used along with the mouseleave event.

mouseleave( )

The mouseleave event occurs when the mouse pointer leaves the selected element. The mouseleave() method does the following two tasks:

- It fires the mouseleave event.

- It attaches a function to run when a mouseleave event occurs.

Syntax:
The following syntax fires the mouseleave event for the selected element(s):

$(selector).mouseleave()

The following syntax associates a function to the mouseleave event:

$(selector).mouseleave(function)

where the parameter function contains the code to be executed when the mouseleave event occurs.

The difference between the mouseout and mouseleave events is that the mouseleave event fires only when the mouse pointer leaves the selected elements whereas the mouseout event is fired even if the mouse pointer leaves any of its child elements too.

The mouseleave() method is usually used with the mouseenter() event.

mouseover( )

The mouseover event occurs when the mouse pointer is over the selected element. The mouseover() method does the following tasks:

- It triggers the mouseover event.

- It associates a function with the mouseover event that contains the code to run when the mouseover event occurs.

Syntax:
The following syntax fires the mouseover event on the selected element(s):

$(selector).mouseover()

The following syntax associates a function to the mouseover event:

$(selector).mouseover(function)

99

where the `function` parameter contains the code that is required to run when the mouseover event occurs.

The difference between the mouseenter and mouseover events is that the mouseover event fires if the mouse pointer enters the selected element or any of its child elements whereas the mouseenter event fires only when the mouse pointer enters the selected element.

The `mouseover` method is usually used with the mouseout event.

mouseout( )

The mouseout event occurs when the mouse pointer leaves the selected element. The `mouseout()` method does the following two tasks:

- It fires the mouseout event.

- It associates a function with the mouseout event that contains the code to execute when the mouseout event occurs.

Syntax

The following syntax fires the mouseout event for the selected element(s):

$(selector).mouseout()

The following syntax associates a function to the mouseout event:

$(selector).mouseout(function)

where the parameter `function` contains the code to be executed when the mouseout event occurs.

The difference between the mouseleave and mouseout events is that the mouseout event fires if the mouse pointer leaves the selected element or any of its child elements whereas the mouseleave event fires only when the mouse pointer leaves the selected element.

The `mouseout()` method is usually used with the mouseover event.

How It Works

The CSS style btn is automatically applied to the two buttons, **Hide Image** and **Show Image**, as both the buttons are assigned the class btn. The button caption appears in italics mode and in a green color. The CSS style highlight is applied to the **Hide Image** button when mouse hovers over it.

When the mouse is over the button with the caption **Hide Image**, the style class highlight is applied to the button, making its caption bold and the color red. When the mouse leaves the **Hide Image** button, the highlight style class is removed from the button, making it the same as it was previously.

Note   If the comments are removed from the two statements, an alert dialog box with the message **hovered over** will be displayed when the mouse is over the **Hide Image** button and the alert dialog box will display the message **hovered out** when the mouse leaves the **Hide Image** button.

Initially, an image will appear with two buttons, **Hide Image** and **Show Image**. Both buttons will appear in a green color with their captions in italics mode (see Figure 3-3(a)).

On hovering the mouse over the **Hide Image** button, the caption will turn into bold and the color of the button will turn into red (see Figure 3-3(b)).

We deal with Electronics Products

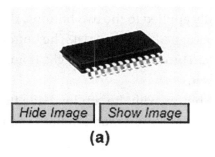

(a)

We deal with Electronics Products

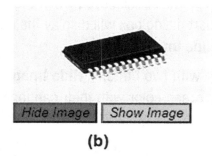

(b)

Figure 3-3. *(a) Two buttons, Hide Image and Show Image, appear in a green color (b) The color of the Hide Image button turns into red*

3-4. Using a Mouse Hover Event to Change the Style on a Button

Problem

You have a button on a web page and you want the CSS style of that button to change when the user hovers over the button.

Solution

Make an HTML file with a paragraph element, an image, and two buttons, as follows:

Mousehover2.html

```
<!DOCTYPE html PUBLIC "-//W3C//DTD XHTML 1.0 Transitional//EN"
        "http://www.w3.org/TR/xhtml1/DTD/xhtml1-transitional.dtd">
<html xmlns="http://www.w3.org/1999/xhtml" xml:lang="en" lang="en">
  <head>
    <meta http-equiv="Content-Type" content="text/html; charset=utf-8"/>
    <title></title>
    <link rel="stylesheet" href="mousehoverstyle.css" type="text/css"
    media="screen" />
    <script src="jquery-3.5.1.js" type="text/javascript"></script>
    <script src="mousehover2jq.js" type="text/javascript"></script>
  </head>
  <body>
    <p>We deal with Electronics Products</p>
    <img src="a1.jpg" width="200" height="100"><br/>
    <button class="btn" id="hide">Hide Image</button>
    <button class="btn" id="show">Show Image</button>
  </body>
</html>
```

A paragraph is set to display the text **We deal with Electronics Products**. An image 200px wide and 100px high is displayed below the paragraph. Two buttons with captions **Hide Image** and **Show Image** are displayed below the image. The class btn is assigned and the IDs hide and show are assigned to the two buttons, respectively.

To define the original CSS class for the button and also to define the CSS class that needs to be applied when the mouse pointer is hovered over it, you will use the CSS style file mousehoverstyle.css that you created in the previous recipe.

The jQuery code to apply the CSS style class on the button when the mouse pointer hovers over it is as follows:

Mousehover2jq.js

```
$(document).ready(function() {
    $("button.btn").hover( function() {
        $(this).addClass("highlight");
    }, function() {
```

103

```
        $(this).removeClass("highlight");
    });
});
```

In this jQuery code, the hover() method is used, so let's have a look at this method first.

hover( )

As the name suggests, the hover() method represents the function that contains the code to be executed when the mouse pointer hovers over an element (i.e., the mouse pointer enters and leaves the specified element(s)). It also means that the hover method fires both the mouseenter as well as the mouseleave events. The hover() method specifies two functions to run, as shown:

Syntax:

$(selector).hover(enterFunction,leaveFunction)

- enterFunction is a function that contains the code to execute when the mouseenter event occurs.

- leaveFunction is a function that contains the code to execute when the mouseleave event occurs. This function is optional. If this function is not used, the same function is executed for both the mouseenter and mouseleave events.

How It Works

Because the two buttons are assigned the class btn, the CSS class btn will be applied automatically to both buttons, making their captions appear in italics mode and the background color as green.

When the mouse pointer hovers over any of the buttons, the CSS class highlight will be applied on it, making its caption bold and changing its background color to red.

Initially, on running the web page, you get the output shown in Figure 3-4(a), which is two buttons with the captions **Hide Image** and **Show Image** where both captions are in italics mode and the background color of the two buttons is green. Upon hovering over any button, the caption of the button will change to bold and the background color of the button will change to red (as shown in Figure 3-4(b)).

We deal with Electronics Products

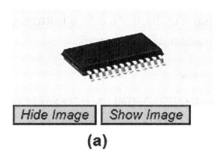

(a)

We deal with Electronics Products

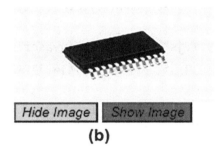

(b)

Figure 3-4. *(a) Two buttons with captions Hide Image and Show Image have green backgrounds. (b) The caption of the button changes to bold and the background color turns into red when hovered over*

3-5. Using Mouse Up and Down Events to Show and Hide an Image

Problem

In this recipe, you will make a button that when pressed by the user will display an image. Upon releasing the mouse button from the image, the image will become invisible again.

Solution

The following is an HTML file that will display a text, a button, and an image. The image will be initially hidden via application of a CSS style.

Mouseupdown.html

```
<!DOCTYPE html PUBLIC "-//W3C//DTD XHTML 1.0 Transitional//EN"
        "http://www.w3.org/TR/xhtml1/DTD/xhtml1-transitional.dtd">

<html xmlns="http://www.w3.org/1999/xhtml" xml:lang="en" lang="en">
  <head>
    <meta http-equiv="Content-Type" content="text/html; charset=utf-8"/>
    <title></title>
<link rel="stylesheet" href="mouseupdownstyle.css" type="text/css"
media="screen" />
    <script src="jquery-3.5.1.js" type="text/javascript"></script>
    <script src="mouseupdownjq.js" type="text/javascript"></script>
  </head>
  <body>
<p>We deal with Electronics Products</p>
<button id="show">Show Image</button>
<img src="a1.jpg" width="200" height="100"><br/>
  </body>
</html>
```

In this code, you can see that the paragraph element is set to display the text **We deal with Electronics Products**. A button is displayed with the caption **Show Image** and the id of the button is set to show. Below the button is an image displayed as 200px wide and 100px high.

To apply the style to the image upon launching the HTML file, the external style sheet may be created as follows:

Mouseupdownstyle.css

```
img{
      display: none;
}
```

The display: none style rule in the img style will make the image invisible when the program launches.

The jQuery code to display the image on pressing the button is as follows:

Mouseupdownjq.js

```
$(document).ready(function() {
    $("button#show").on("mousedown", function() {
        $("img").fadeIn();
    });
     $("button#show").on("mouseup", function() {
        $("img").fadeOut();
    });
});
```

This jQuery code uses the mouseup(), fadeOut(), and fadeIn() methods, so let's have a look at these methods first.

mouseup( )

When the left mouse button is released on the selected element, the mouseup event fires. The mouseup() method does the following two tasks:

- It fires the mouseup event.

- It associates a function that contains the code that needs to run when the mouseup event occurs.

Syntax:
The following syntax fires the mouseup event on the selected element(s):

$(selector).mouseup()

The following syntax associates a function that contains the code that has to be executed on occurrence of the mouseup event:

$(selector).mouseup(function)

where the parameter function is the function that is invoked when the mouseup event occurs.

Note   The `mouseup()` method is usually used with the `mousedown()` method.

---

fadeOut( )

This method fades the selected element, making it transparent (i.e., the opacity of the selected element is gradually changed, making it completely invisible).

Syntax:

`$(selector).fadeOut(speed,easing,function)`

- The parameter `speed` defines the speed of fading out. Valid options are

  - `slow`: The selected element fades out slowly.

  - `fast`: The selected element fades out quite quickly.

  - `milliseconds`: The selected element fades out in the specified milliseconds. If you don't use the `speed` parameter, the default value is 400ms.

- The `easing` parameter represents the speed of fading out at different points. Valid values for this parameter are `swing` or `linear`. The `swing` option makes the process of fading out slower at the beginning or end and faster in the middle. The `linear` option continues the process of fading out at a constant speed. The default easing value is `swing`.

- The `function` parameter represents the function that you want to execute after the fading out is done.

Note   The `fadeOut` method is usually used along with the `fadeIn()` method.

---

fadeIn( )

The `fadeIn()` method makes the hidden element visible (i.e. the opacity of the element is changed to make it visible).

Syntax:

`$(selector).fadeIn(speed,easing,function)`

- The `speed` parameter defines the speed by which the selected element will be made visible. Valid options are

  - `slow`: The hidden element will be made visible slowly.

  - `fast`: The hidden element will be made visible quickly.

  - `milliseconds`: The hidden element will be made visible in the specified milliseconds.

  - The `speed` parameter is optional. If not used, the default value is 400 milliseconds.

- The `easing` parameter defines the speed at different points while the hidden element is being made visible. Valid values are

  - `swing`: Unhides the element slowly at the beginning or end and fast in the middle.

  - `linear`: Unhides the element at a constant speed.

  - The default value of easing parameter is `swing`.

- The `function` parameter is optional and is used to write the code that you want to execute once the `fadeIn()` method is complete.

The `fadeIn()` method is usually used along with the `fadeOut()` method.

How It Works

When the mouse button is pressed over the button, the image will gradually fade in (i.e., it will become visible slowly) and when the mouse button is released, the image will fade out (i.e., the image will become invisible gradually).

The `img` style class will be automatically applied to the image, making it invisible.

Upon running the HTML file, you get the screen shown in Figure 3-5(a), with the text **We deal with Electronic Products** and a button below called **Show Image**. Upon pressing the button, an image appears, as shown in Figure 3-5(b). The moment you release the mouse button, the image disappears again.

We deal with Electronics Products

Show Image

(a)

We deal with Electronics Products

Show Image

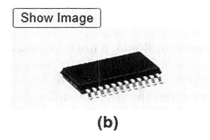

(b)

Figure 3-5. *(a) Text and a button named Show Image are displayed. (b) An image appears upon pressing the Show Image button*

3-6. Making Two Buttons, One for Hiding and One for Displaying an Image

Problem

You want to create two buttons for individual tasks. One button when clicked makes an image invisible and the other button when clicked makes the image reappear.

Solution

The following is the HTML file that contains a paragraph element, an image, and two buttons that will be assigned the task of hiding and displaying the image:

Showhideimage.html

```
<!DOCTYPE html PUBLIC "-//W3C//DTD XHTML 1.0 Transitional//EN"
        "http://www.w3.org/TR/xhtml1/DTD/xhtml1-transitional.dtd">
<html xmlns="http://www.w3.org/1999/xhtml" xml:lang="en" lang="en">
  <head>
```

```
    <meta http-equiv="Content-Type" content="text/html; charset=utf-8"/>
    <title></title>
    <script src="jquery-3.5.1.js" type="text/javascript"></script>
    <script src="showhidejq.js" type="text/javascript"></script>
  </head>
  <body>
<p>We deal with Electronics Products</p>
<img src="a1.jpg" width="200" height="100"><br/>
<button id="hide">Hide Image</button>
<button id="show">Show Image</button>
  </body>
</html>
```

You can see in the code that a paragraph element is used to display the text **We deal with Electronic Products**. Thereafter, an image is shown at 200px wide and 100px high. Below the image are two buttons with captions **Hide Image** and **Show Image**.

The jQuery code to enable the buttons to hide the image and to make it reappear again is as follows:

Showhidejq.js

```
$(document).ready(function() {
    $("button#hide").on("click", function() {
        $("img").fadeOut();
    });
    $("button#show").on("click", function() {
        $("img").fadeIn();
    });
});
```

In this jQuery code, you are using methods fadeOut(), fadeIn(). slideDown(), off(), and hide(). Out of these methods, the fadeOut() and fadeIn() methods were explained in a previous recipe. Let's have a quick look at the rest of the methods.

slideDown( )

The slideDown() method makes the hidden element slide down (i.e., makes it visible gradually).

Syntax:

$(selector).slideDown(speed,easing,function)

- The speed parameter determines the speed by which the element will become visible. The following are the valid options:
  - slow: The hidden element will become visible gradually.
  - fast: The hidden element will become visible quickly.
  - milliseconds: The hidden element will become visible in the specified milliseconds.
  - The speed parameter is optional. If it is not specified, the default value is 400 ms.
- The easing parameter defines the speed at different points while unhiding the element. Valid options are
  - swing: Makes the hidden element visible slowly at the beginning or end and fast in the middle.
  - linear: Unhides the hidden element at a constant speed.
  - The default value of the easing parameter is swing.
- The function parameter is optional and is used for writing the code that you want to execute after the hidden element is completely visible.

Only the element that is hidden using jQuery methods and using the display:hone attribute in CSS is made visible using the slideDown() method.

off( )

The off() method is the reverse of the on() method. Consequently it removes the event handler that is attached to any element using the on() method.

Syntax:

$(selector).off(event,selector,function(event_object),map)

- The event parameter represents the event that is required to be removed from the selected element. If there is more than one event, they need to be separated by a space.

- The selector parameter represents the element from which the event must be removed. These are the elements that were used in the on() method.

- The function(event_object) parameter contains the code to run when the off event occurs. This parameter is optional.

- The map parameter represents the pair of events and associated functions in the format (event:function, event:function, ...), indicating the respective function that executes when an event occurs.

The one() method is usually used to associate an event to an element if the event is required to execute only once. The event is automatically removed after execution.

hide( )

As the name suggests, the hide() method hides the selected elements.

Syntax:

$(selector).hide(speed,easing, function)

- The speed parameter determines the speed of hiding the element. Valid options are

  - slow: It hides the selected element gradually.

  - fast: It hides the selected element quite quickly.

  - milliseconds: It hides the selected element in the specified milliseconds. The default value is 400 ms.

- The easing parameter determines the speed of hiding the element at different points. Valid options are

- swing: Hides the element slowly at the beginning or end and fast in the middle.

- linear: Hides the element at a constant speed.

- The easing parameter is optional. If not used, its default value is swing.

- The function parameter is a function that contains the code to be executed after the element is completely hidden. It is optional.

To show the hidden elements, the show() method is usually used.

How It Works

When the button with the id hide is clicked (i.e., when the button with the caption **Hide Image** is clicked), the fadeOut() method will be invoked on the image element, making the image invisible gradually. Similarly, when the button with the id show is clicked (i.e., when the button with the caption **Show Image** is clicked), the fadeIn() method is invoked on the image element, making the image visible slowly. A similar action will take place if the fadeOut() method is replaced with the hide() method. Also, the fadeIn() method can be replaced by the slideDown() method, which makes the image visible slowly. You can also modify the jQuery code to appear as follows:

Showhidejq.js

```
$(document).ready(function() {
    $("button#hide").on("click", function() {
        $("img").hide();
        $("button#hide").off("click");
    });
    $("button#show").on("click", function() {
        $("img").slideDown();
        $("button#show").off("click");
    });
});
```

The hide() method hides the selected element (i.e., the image will be hidden upon clicking the Hide Image button). The effect of using the off() method is that the click event will be removed from these buttons after the click event takes place once. Thus the **Show Image** and **Hide Image** buttons will work only once.

Upon running the HTML file, you get the screen shown in Figure 3-6(a). The paragraph element displays the text **We deal with Electronics Products**. Below the text is an image followed by two buttons with the captions **Hide Image** and **Show Image**. Upon clicking the **Hide Image** button, the image will gradually disappear as in Figure 3-6(b). Upon clicking the **Show Image** button, the image will reappear, as in Figure 3-6(a).

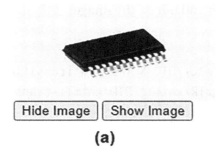

Figure 3-6. *(a) A paragraph element, image, and two buttons, Hide Image and Show Image, are displayed. (b) The image disappears upon clicking the Hide Image button*

3-7. Zoom In and Out of an Image Using toggleClass

Problem

You have an image on a web page and you want to zoom in on that image when a button is pressed and zoom out when the button is clicked again.

Solution

The following is the HTML file that contains the image and the button that will be assigned the task of zooming in and out on the image:

Zoominoutimage.html

```
<!DOCTYPE html PUBLIC "-//W3C//DTD XHTML 1.0 Transitional//EN"
        "http://www.w3.org/TR/xhtml1/DTD/xhtml1-transitional.dtd">

<html xmlns="http://www.w3.org/1999/xhtml" xml:lang="en" lang="en">
  <head>
    <meta http-equiv="Content-Type" content="text/html; charset=utf-8"/>
    <title></title>
<link rel="stylesheet" href="zoominoutstyle.css" type="text/css"
media="screen" />
    <script src="jquery-3.5.1.js" type="text/javascript"></script>
    <script src="zoominoutjq.js" type="text/javascript"></script>
  </head>
  <body>
<p>We deal with Electronics Products</p>
<button id="zoom">Zoom In / Out Image</button><br/>
<img src="a1.jpg" width="200" height="100">
  </body>
</html>
```

In this program, you can see that the text **We deal with Electronics Products** is displayed via a paragraph element. Thereafter, a button is displayed with the caption

Zoom In / Out Image. An id of zoom is assigned to the button to make it accessible in the jQuery code. After the button, an image is displayed at 200px wide and 100px high.

A CSS style called enlarge is created and when applied to an element will make its width 300px and height 300px. The following is the CSS file:

Zoominoutstyle.css

```
.enlarge{
  width: 300px;
  height: 300px;
}
```

The jQuery code to apply the CSS style on the first click of the button and to remove the CSS style on another click is as follows:

Zoominoutjq.js

```
$(document).ready(function() {
    $("button#zoom").on("click", function() {
        $("img").toggleClass('enlarge');
    });
});
```

In the above jQuery code, the method toggleClass() is used, so let's understand it.

toggleClass( )

As the name suggests, the method applies the class on the selected elements if the class is not yet applied. Also, the method removes the class from the selected elements if it is already applied.

Syntax:

$(selector).toggleClass(class,function(location,class),switch)

- class represents the class to be added or removed. If more than one class is used, they need to be separated by a space.

- function(location,class) is a function that returns one or more class names to be added or removed. It is optional.

- location returns the subscript or location of the element.

117

- `class` returns the class name of selected elements.

- The `switch` parameter is a Boolean value which if set to true means the class needs to be added and if set to false means the class need to be removed. It is optional.

How It Works

When the button with the id of `zoom` is clicked (i.e., when the **Zoom In / Out Image** button is clicked) using the `toggleClass()` method, the CSS style `enlarge` is applied to the image, enhancing its size to 300px wide and 300px high. When the user clicks the **Zoom In / Out Image** button again, the `toggleClass()` method will remove the CSS style `enlarge` from the image, reducing it to its original size of 200px wide and 100px high.

Upon running the HTML file, the text message **We deal with Electronics Products** will be displayed. A button with the caption **Zoom In / Out Image** will be displayed below the text followed by an image 200px wide and 100px high (see Figure 3-7(a)). On clicking the **Zoom In / Out Image** button, the image will be zoomed (i.e., enlarged) to 300px wide and 300px high (see Figure 3-7(b)). On clicking the Zoom In / Out Image button again, the image will be reduced to its original size.

We deal with Electronics Products

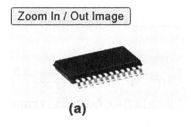

(a)

We deal with Electronics Products

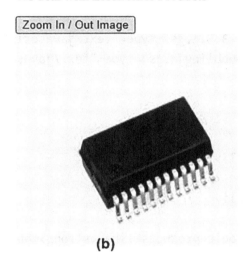

(b)

Figure 3-7. *(a) A text message, a Zoom In / Out Image button, and an image are displayed. (b) The image is enlarged upon clicking the Zoom In / Out Image button*

3-8. Avoiding Event Bubbling

Problem

When an event is triggered on an element that is nested inside other elements, what happens is that the event is fired on that element as well as for all of the elements that contain it (i.e., the event will be fired on all of the elements up the DOM). You want to avoid event bubbling when an event occurs on any nested element.

Solution

Here is an HTML file that contains a few elements, one inside the other:

Eventbublling.html

```
<!DOCTYPE html PUBLIC "-//W3C//DTD XHTML 1.0 Transitional//EN"
        "http://www.w3.org/TR/xhtml1/DTD/xhtml1-transitional.dtd">
<html xmlns="http://www.w3.org/1999/xhtml" xml:lang="en" lang="en">
  <head>
    <meta http-equiv="Content-Type" content="text/html; charset=utf-8"/>
    <title></title>
    <script src="jquery-3.5.1.js" type="text/javascript"></script>
    <script src="eventbubblingjq.js" type="text/javascript"></script>
  </head>
  <body>
    <div>Welcome to our site
        <ul>
          <li>Cameras</li>
          <li>Cell Phones</li>
          <li>Laptops</li>
        </ul>
<p> We deal with electronic products like <strong>mobile phones, laptops,
washing machine </strong at very reasonable prices </p>
    </div>
  </body>
</html>
```

You can see in this code that a `<div>` element is set to display the text **Welcome to our site**. Within the `<div>` element, an unordered list element is defined with three list items: `Cameras`, `Cell Phones`, and `Laptops`. Below the unordered list, within the `<div>` element is a `<p>` element and within the `<p>` element is a `<strong>` element. Each element is set to display certain text.

The following jQuery code will result in event bubbling:

Eventbubblingjq.js

```
$(document).ready(function() {
    $('div').click(function(event){
```

```
                alert('<div> element is clicked');
        });
        $('ul').click(function(event){
                alert('<ul> element is clicked');
        });
         $('p').click(function(event){
                alert('<p> element is clicked');
        });
        $('strong').click(function(event){
                alert('<strong> element is clicked');
        });
});
```

How It Works

When the user clicks on the `<div>` element, an alert dialog box will appear showing the message **`<div>` element is clicked**. Because the `<div>` element is the parent of all the elements, no event propagation will take place.

When the user clicks the `<ul>` element, an alert dialog box will appear displaying the message **`<ul>` element is clicked**. Now because the `<ul>` element is nested within the `<div>` element, the click event will be propagated to the parent (i.e., to the `<div>` element); consequently, one more alert box will appear showing the message **`<div>` element is clicked**.

When the user clicks the `<p>` element, an alert dialog box will appear displaying the message **`<p>` element is clicked**. Again, the `<p>` element is nested within the `<div>` element, so the click event will be propagated to the `<div>` element as well; consequently, one more alert box will appear showing the message **`<div>` element is clicked.**

When the user clicks the `<strong>` element, an alert dialog box will appear displaying the message **`<strong>` element is clicked** (see Figure 3-8(a)). Because the `<strong>` element is nested within the `<p>` element which in turn is nested within the `<div>` element, the click event will be propagated to both the `<p>` and the `<div>` element as well. Hence two more alert boxes will appear showing the messages **`<p>` element is clicked** and **`<div>` element is clicked**, respectively (see Figure 3-8(b)).

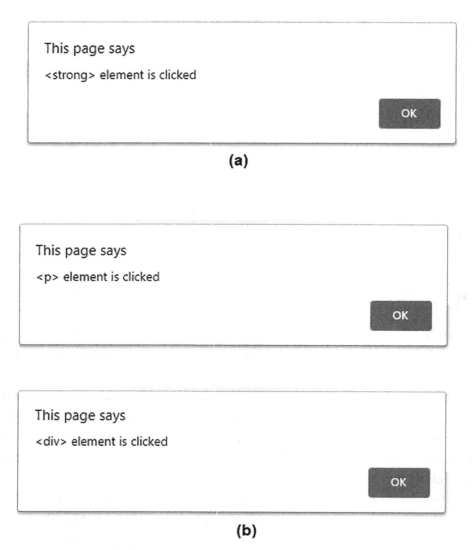

Figure 3-8. *(a) The alert dialog box informing that the <strong> element is clicked. (b) Because of event propagation, two alert dialog boxes appear one by one showing the messages "<p> element is clicked" and "<div> element is clicked"*

To stop event bubbling, you need to invoke the `stopPropagation()` method. So, change the jQuery code to appear as shown below. You can see that the `event.stopPropagation()` statement is added (marked in bold).

```
$(document).ready(function() {
    $('div').click(function(event){
        alert('<div> element is clicked');
    });
    $('ul').click(function(event){
        event.stopPropagation();
        alert('<ul> element is clicked');
    });
    $('p').click(function(event){
        event.stopPropagation();
        alert('<p> element is clicked');
    });
    $('strong').click(function(event){
        event.stopPropagation();
        alert('<strong> element is clicked');
    });
});
```

In this jQuery code, the stopPropagation() method is used, so let's have a quick look at it first.

stopPropagation( )

As the name suggests, the stopPropagation() method stops the bubbling of an event to the parent elements (i.e., the event will take place only on the selected element and will not occur on the elements within which the selected element is nested).

Syntax:

event.stopPropagation()

In this jQuery code, when the user clicks any element, the task assigned to that event is performed, but by using the event.stopPropagation() method within the event handlers, the event will occur on the selected element only and the event will not be navigated to the parent element(s).

3-9. Knowing Which Key Is Down, Pressed, or Released

Problem

You have an input box and you want to know which key is down in it, which key is pressed in that input box, and which key is released.

Solution

The HTML file to display an input box and to define paragraph elements to display which key is down, pressed, or released is as follows:

Keypressdown.html

```
<!DOCTYPE html PUBLIC "-//W3C//DTD XHTML 1.0 Transitional//EN"
        "http://www.w3.org/TR/xhtml1/DTD/xhtml1-transitional.dtd">

<html xmlns="http://www.w3.org/1999/xhtml" xml:lang="en" lang="en">
  <head>
    <meta http-equiv="Content-Type" content="text/html; charset=utf-8"/>
    <title></title>
    <script src="jquery-3.5.1.js" type="text/javascript"></script>
    <script src="keypressdownjq.js" type="text/javascript"></script>
  </head>
  <body>
<p>We deal with Electronics Products</p>
 <label>Product to search: </label>
 <input type="text" name="product" >
 <p id="kdown"></p>
 <p id="kpress"></p>
 <p id="kup"></p>
  </body>
</html>
```

You can see in this code that a paragraph element is used to display the text **We deal with Electronics Products**. The user is asked to enter a product to search via an input box. Three paragraph elements are defined below the input box with IDs kdown, kpress, and kup. It is through these paragraph elements that you will display which key is down, pressed, or released in the input box.

The following is the jQuery code that handles the keydown, keypress, and keyup events and displays the code of the respective event through the respective paragraph elements:

Keypressdownjq.js

```
$(document).ready(function() {
    $("input").on("keydown", function(event) {
        $('p#kdown').text('Key down is '+ event.keyCode);
        //$('p#kdown').text('Key down is '+String.fromCharCode(event.
        keyCode));
    });
    $("input").on("keypress", function(event) {
        $('p#kpress').text('Key pressed is '+event.keyCode);
    });
    $("input").on("keyup", function(event) {
        $('p#kup').text('Key up is '+ event.keyCode);
    });
});
```

Note   The commented out statement in the above code is to do typecasting (i.e., convert the key code in the integer format to the string format).

The above jQuery code uses the methods keydown(), keypress(), and keyup(), so let's have a look at these methods first.

keydown( )

On pressing a key, the keydown() event occurs.

Syntax:

$(selector).keydown()

The keydown event will be fired on the selected element(s).

$(selector).keydown(function)

The function is executed when the keydown event occurs.

keypress( )

The method indicates that the key is pressed down.

Syntax:

$(selector).keypress()

The above syntax fires the keypress event for the selected element(s).

$(selector).keypress(function)

where the function is executed when the keypress event occurs.

Although the keypress event appears similar to the keydown event, the keypress event is not fired for all keys. It is not fired for the keys Alt, Ctrl, Shift, Esc, etc.

keyup( )

The method indicates that the key is released.

Syntax:

$(selector).keyup()

The keyup event will be fired on the selected element by the above syntax.

$(selector).keyup(function)

where the function is executed when the keyup event occurs.

How It Works

When the keydown event occurs on the input box, the Unicode value of the key pressed is assigned to the keyCode or charCode property.

The charCode is a number that represents the ASCII character of the key pressed. The ASCII characters of a and A are different, whereas the keyCode is a keyboard code that is same for uppercase and lowercase.

The Unicode value of the key pressed is displayed via the <p> element with the ID kdown. The ASCII character of the key pressed is displayed through the <p> element with the ID kpress. When the pressed key is released, the Unicode of the released key is displayed through the <p> element that is assigned the ID kup.

On pressing a key, say a in the input box, the keycode of a is displayed through the keydown() event and its ASCII value is displayed through the keypress() event, and when a is released, its keycode is displayed via the keyup() event, as shown in Figure 3-9(a).

On pressing the Shift key, the keypress() event will not fire and the keyCode of the Shift key will be displayed via the keydown() event and through the keyup() event when the Shift key is released (see Figure 3-9(b)).

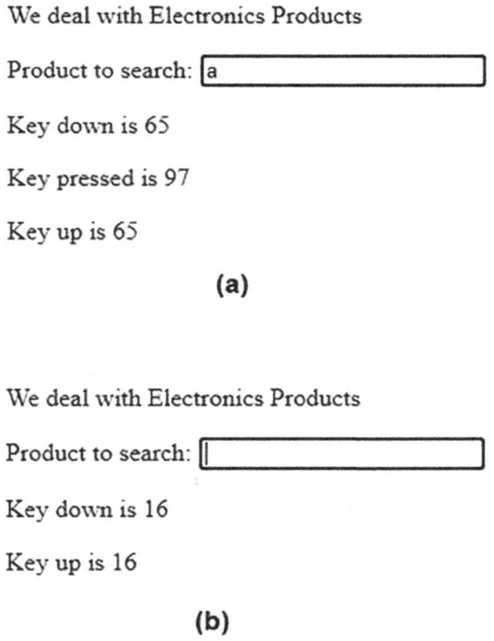

We deal with Electronics Products

Product to search: a

Key down is 65

Key pressed is 97

Key up is 65

(a)

We deal with Electronics Products

Product to search:

Key down is 16

Key up is 16

(b)

Figure 3-9. (a) The keycode and ASCII values of character a are displayed. (b) The keycode of the Shift key is displayed

3-10. Applying a Fading Effect to an Image

Problem

You have an image and you want the following to happen: when the mouse pointer hovers over a button, the image fades away and is replaced by its enlarged size (at its original location), and when mouse pointer moves away from the button, the enlarged size fades away and is replaced by the image in its original size.

Solution

Consider the following HTML file that contains an image and a button:

fadingeffect.html

```
<!DOCTYPE html PUBLIC "-//W3C//DTD XHTML 1.0 Transitional//EN"
        "http://www.w3.org/TR/xhtml1/DTD/xhtml1-transitional.dtd">

<html xmlns="http://www.w3.org/1999/xhtml" xml:lang="en" lang="en">
  <head>
    <meta http-equiv="Content-Type" content="text/html; charset=utf-8"/>
    <title></title>
<link rel="stylesheet" href="fadingeffectstyle.css" type="text/css"
media="screen" />
    <script src="jquery-3.5.1.js" type="text/javascript"></script>
    <script src="fadingeffectjq.js" type="text/javascript"></script>
  </head>
  <body>
<p>We deal with Electronics Products</p>
<button id="fade">Fade In / Out Image</button><br/>
<img id="pic1" src="a1.jpg" width="200" height="100">
  </body>
</html>
```

You can see in this file that a message of **We deal with Electronics Products** is displayed through a paragraph element. A button is displayed with the caption **Fade In / Out Image**. To access it through jQuery code, the button is assigned the ID fade.

Below the button is an image with a width of 200px and a height of 100px. The image is assigned the id pic1.

A CSS style named enlarge sets the width of an element to 300px and the height to 300px. The CSS style sheet file is as shown here:

Fadingeffectstyle.css

```
.enlarge{
  width: 300px;
  height: 300px;
}
```

The jQuery code to apply the fading image on hovering over the button and replacing the image with its enlarged size and again fading away the enlarged size and getting back the original size when the mouse is moved away from the button is as follows:

```
Fadingeffectjq.js
$(document).ready(function() {
    $("button#fade").hover( function() {
        $("img#pic1").fadeTo('slow',0,"linear");
        $("img#pic1").addClass("enlarge").fadeTo('fast',1, "swing");
    }, function() {
        $("img#pic1").removeClass("enlarge").fadeTo('slow',0, "linear");
        $("img#pic1").fadeTo('slow',1);
    });
});
```

In this jQuery code, the fadeTo() method is used, so let's have a quick look at this method first.

fadeTo( )

The fadeTo() method gradually changes the opacity of the selected elements to the specified fading effect.

Syntax:

$(selector).fadeTo(speed,opacity,easing,function)

129

- The speed parameter determines the speed of the fading effect. Its value can be slow or fast.

- The opacity parameter specifies the opacity to fade to. It is a number between 0.00 and 1.00 where 0.00 will make the element completely fade out and 1.00 will make the element fade in (i.e., fully visible).

- The easing parameter specifies the speed of the element in different points of the animation. Its value can be swing or linear. The swing value moves slower at the beginning or end and faster in the middle. The linear value moves at a constant speed. The default value is swing.

- The function parameter contains the code that is executed after the fadeTo() method is completed. It is optional.

How It Works

When the user hovers over the button, the original image will gradually fade out (i.e., it will become invisible). Immediately after making the image invisible, it is made visible and the CSS style enlarge is applied to it, increasing the size of the image to 300px wide and 300px high.

When the mouse goes away from the button, the CSS style class enlarge is removed from the image, returning it to its original size and gradually making it invisible. Immediately after making it invisible, the image is made visible again.

Initially, the image will appear in its original size, as shown in Figure 3-10(a). When the user hovers over the button, the original image will gradually fade out and then it will be enlarged in size and slowly made visible (see Figure 3-10(b)).

We deal with Electronics Products

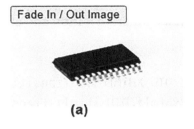

(a)

We deal with Electronics Products

(b)

Figure 3-10. *(a) The image appears in its original size. (b) The enlarged image appears slowly on hovering over the button*

3-11. Applying Animation on an Image

Problem

You have an image that you want to animate upon a clicking of the button. That is, you want the image to move to the right upon clicking the button. Also, while moving, the image should get bigger in size gradually.

Solution

Consider the following HTML file that contains a button and an image:

Animation1.html

```
<!DOCTYPE html PUBLIC "-//W3C//DTD XHTML 1.0 Transitional//EN"
        "http://www.w3.org/TR/xhtml1/DTD/xhtml1-transitional.dtd">

<html xmlns="http://www.w3.org/1999/xhtml" xml:lang="en" lang="en">
  <head>
    <meta http-equiv="Content-Type" content="text/html; charset=utf-8"/>
    <title></title>
    <script src="jquery-3.5.1.js" type="text/javascript"></script>
    <script src="animation1jq.js" type="text/javascript"></script>
  </head>
  <body>
<p>We deal with Electronics Products</p>
<button id="anim">Animate Image</button><br/>
<img id="pic1" src="a1.jpg" width="200" height="100">
  </body>
</html>
```

You can see in this code that a message of **We deal with Electronics Products** is displayed using the paragraph element. Below the text, a button is displayed with the caption of **Animate Image**. In order to access the button in jQuery code, an id of anim is assigned to the button. Below the button, an image 200px wide and 100px high is displayed.

The jQuery code to enlarge the image in size with an animation effect is shown here:

Animation1jq.js

```
$(document).ready(function() {
    $("button#anim").click( function() {
        $("img#pic1").animate({width: '400px',height: '500px'}, 'slow');
});
});
```

In this jQuery code, the animate() method is used, so let's understand this method first.

animate( )

The animate() method is used to create custom animations.

Syntax:

`$(selector).animate({style},speed, easing, function);`

- The style parameter defines the CSS properties to be animated.

- The speed parameter specifies the duration of the animation and its valid values are slow, fast, or a value in milliseconds. It is optional.

- The easing parameter specifies the speed of the element during the animation. Valid values are swing and linear. The swing value makes the element move slower at the beginning and end, and faster in the middle. The linear value makes the element move at a constant speed.

- The function parameter represents the function that is to be executed after the animation completes. It is optional.

How It Works

When the button is clicked, the image will animate to 400px wide and 500px high slowly. Upon running the HTML file, you get the output shown in Figure 3-11(a). A text message, a button, and an image are displayed. Upon clicking the button, the image will increase its size slowly (see Figure 3-11(b)).

We deal with Electronics Products

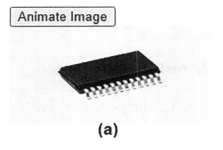

(a)

We deal with Electronics Products

(b)

Figure 3-11. (a) *A text message, a button, and an image are displayed.* (b) *The image size will increase slowly upon clicking the button*

To apply a CSS style to the image automatically when the HTML file loads, create a file called `Animation1style.css` with the following code:

Animation1style.css

```
.pic{
    position: absolute;
    width: 150px;
    height: 100px;
}
```

The `position` property of the image is set to `absolute` so that the image will be positioned in relation to its nearest positioned ancestor. Because there is no ancestor to the image, the image will be positioned in relation to the web page boundary. Also, the width and height of the image are initially set to 150px and 100px, respectively.

To include the above CSS style sheet file in the HTML file, add the following statement in the <head> section:

<link rel="stylesheet" href="animation1style.css" type="text/css" media="screen" />

To make the image animate from its current location to the right, change the jQuery code to appear as follows:

Animation1jq.js

```
$(document).ready(function() {
    $("button#anim").click( function() {
        $("img#pic1").animate({ left: '350px'}, 'slow');
});
});
```

In this jQuery code, the image will animate towards the right slowly when the **Animate Image** button is clicked. The image will animate towards the right from its current position and will stop when the image reaches a distance of 350px from the left edge.

Initially, the HTML page will appear as shown in Figure 3-12(a). Upon clicking the button, the image will animate to the right slowly and will stop when it is at a distance of 350px from the left edge of the web page (see Figure 3-12(b)).

We deal with Electronics Products

Animate Image

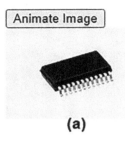

(a)

We deal with Electronics Products

Animate Image

(b)

Figure 3-12. *(a) A text message, an Animate Image button, and an image are displayed. (b) The image is animated towards the right upon clicking the Animate Image button*

3-12. Triggering Events Automatically

Problem

You have a web page with two buttons that say **Bold** and **Italic** and you want the click event to trigger automatically on either button.

Solution

In this recipe, there are two buttons and you want to fire an event automatically. Let's define an HTML file that contains the text **Bold** and **Italic** for the buttons that you want to create:

triggerautomatically.html

```
<!DOCTYPE html PUBLIC "-//W3C//DTD XHTML 1.0 Transitional//EN"
        "http://www.w3.org/TR/xhtml1/DTD/xhtml1-transitional.dtd">
<html xmlns="http://www.w3.org/1999/xhtml" xml:lang="en" lang="en">
  <head>
    <meta http-equiv="Content-Type" content="text/html; charset=utf-8"/>
    <title></title>
    <link rel="stylesheet" href="stylebuttons.css" type="text/css"
    media="screen" />
    <script src="jquery-3.5.1.js" type="text/javascript"></script>
    <script src="triggerautojq.js" type="text/javascript"></script>
  </head>
  <body>
      <span class="bold buttons">Bold</span>
      <span class="italic buttons">Italic</span>
  </body>
</html>
```

In the external style sheet stylebuttons.css, you write the CSS class buttons to give the shape of the button to the text:

stylebuttons.css

```
.buttons{
    width: 100px;
    float: left;
    text-align: center;
    margin: 5px;
    border: 2px solid;
    font-weight: bold;
}
```

Let's write the jQuery code to make an event occur automatically (that is, to be triggered by the script instead of by the user). You may require certain events to occur automatically, like the autoclick of a button or the autosubmission of a form. The method provided by jQuery to trigger an event is trigger().

Make the click event trigger automatically on the **Italic** button. The jQuery code for doing so is as follows:

triggerautojq.js

```
$(document).ready(function() {
    $('.buttons').bind('click', function(){
        alert('You have clicked the ' +$(this).text()+' button');
    });
     $('.italic').trigger('click');
});
```

How It Works

In the HTML file, the statement

<span class="bold buttons">Bold</span>

defines the text **Bold** in a span element of the classes bold and buttons. The class bold is used to apply the jQuery code to the span element, and the class button is used to apply the styles defined in the CSS class buttons specified in the style sheet.

Similarly, the second statement defines the text **Italic** of the span element of the classes italic and buttons. The italic class is for applying the jQuery code and the buttons class is for applying the CSS class. In the jQuery code, use the method trigger() to trigger an event. Let's have a brief introduction to the method.

trigger( )

This method invokes the event handler of the specified event type (passed to this method).

Syntax:

trigger(eventType)

where eventType is a string that specifies the type of the event (that is, whether it is a click, double-click, focus, etc.).

The method returns a jQuery object. When you trigger the event, the code in the respective event handler will be executed. So before using the trigger() method on any element, you need to confirm that it has an event handler defined.

In the jQuery code, you can see that the click event is attached to the elements of the buttons class (that is, to both the **Bold** and **Italic** buttons). In addition, the inline functions in the form of event handlers are also defined for them. After that, the statement

```
$('.italic').trigger('click');
```

fires the click event on the **Italic** button, causing its event handler to be invoked. The event handler displays an alert message that indicates that the button is clicked. This will happen without clicking the **Italic** button and also when it is clicked, as shown in Figure 3-13.

Figure 3-13. *Alert message on the autotriggering of a click event on the Italic button*

3-13. Disabling a Button After It Is Clicked Once

Problem

Sometimes you want an event to fire only once or you want to disable it when certain conditions are met. For example, you might want to disable the Submit button after it is has been clicked once.

Solution

In this recipe, there are two buttons and you want to disable a button after it is clicked once. The following is an HTML file that contains the text **Bold** and **Italic** for the buttons that you want to create:

disablingbutton.html

```
<!DOCTYPE html PUBLIC "-//W3C//DTD XHTML 1.0 Transitional//EN"
        "http://www.w3.org/TR/xhtml1/DTD/xhtml1-transitional.dtd">
```

```
<html xmlns="http://www.w3.org/1999/xhtml" xml:lang="en" lang="en">
  <head>
    <meta http-equiv="Content-Type" content="text/html; charset=utf-8"/>
    <title></title>
    <link rel="stylesheet" href="stylebuttons.css" type="text/css"
    media="screen" />
    <script src="jquery-3.5.1.js" type="text/javascript"></script>
    <script src="disablingbuttonjq.js" type="text/javascript"></script>
  </head>
  <body>
        <span class="bold buttons">Bold</span>
        <span class="italic buttons">Italic</span>
  </body>
</html>
```

In this recipe, you will use the same external style sheet, stylebuttons.css, that you created in Recipe 3-12. The style sheet contains the CSS class buttons to give the shape of the button to the text.

Let's write the jQuery code to disable the event handlers after being clicked once:

disablingbuttonjq.js

```
$(document).ready(function() {
    $('.buttons').bind('click', function(){
        alert('You have clicked the ' +$(this).text()+' button');
        $('.buttons').unbind('click');
    });
});
```

How It Works

jQuery provides the unbind() method to remove the event type from the specified element. jQuery also supports namespaced events, which allow you to trigger or unbind specific groups of bound handlers without having to reference them directly.

The unbind() method removes the previously attached event handler from the specified element:

Syntax:

unbind(eventType, handler)
unbind(eventType)
unbind()

- eventType refers to different events, like click, double-click, etc. All event handlers attached to the specified eventType will be stopped from being executed.

- handler is the event handler to remove; it should be the same as the one passed to bind().

- If you pass no arguments, all events will be removed.

In the jQuery code, you can see that the click event is bound to the buttons. Clicking either button will display an alert message showing the text of the button selected. So, if you select the **Bold** button, you will get the output shown in Figure 3-14.

Figure 3-14. *Alert message upon clicking the Bold button*

But thereafter, the statement

$('.buttons').unbind('click');

unbinds the event handler (inline function) of the click event, so clicking any button will not display any message.

3-14. Finding the Screen Coordinates of a Mouse-Button Press

Problem

You have an image on a web page and you want to display the screen coordinates of the location where the mouse button is pressed on the image.

Solution

Let's make an HTML file that displays an image and an empty paragraph element, as shown here:

mousecoordinate.html

```
<!DOCTYPE html PUBLIC "-//W3C//DTD XHTML 1.0 Transitional//EN"
        "http://www.w3.org/TR/xhtml1/DTD/xhtml1-transitional.dtd">
<html xmlns="http://www.w3.org/1999/xhtml" xml:lang="en" lang="en">
  <head>
    <meta http-equiv="Content-Type" content="text/html; charset=utf-8"/>
    <title></title>
    <script src="jquery-3.5.1.js" type="text/javascript"></script>
    <script src="mousecoordinatejq.js" type="text/javascript"></script>
  </head>
  <body>
        <img src="a1.jpg"/>
        <p></p>
  </body>
</html>
```

The empty paragraph will be used for displaying the screen coordinates. Now write the jQuery code to attach the mousedown event to the image to sense if the mouse button is pressed on any part of it. The code is shown here:

mousecoordinatejq.js

```
$(document).ready(function() {
    $('img').mousedown(function(event){
```

```
        $('p').text('Mouse is clicked at horizontal coordinate: '+event.
        screenX+
' and at vertical coordinate: '+event.screenY);
    });
});
```

How It Works

In this recipe, you use the attributes of the event object. The event object is the one that is automatically sent by JavaScript to the event-handling function when an event occurs. The event object has several properties or attributes. The two properties you are going to use in this solution are as follows:

- screenX specifies the horizontal coordinate of the occurrence of the event relative to the screen origin.

- screenY specifies the vertical coordinate of the occurrence of the event relative to the screen origin.

In the event-handling function of the mousedown event, you write the code to display the values of the screenX and screenY attributes of the event object in the form of text of the paragraph element. Upon the execution of the jQuery code, you get the output shown in Figure 3-15.

Mouse is clicked at horizontal coordinate: 113 and at vertical coordinate: 142

Figure 3-15. *The location of screen coordinates displaying where the mouse button is clicked on the image*

3-15. Highlighting Text Dynamically

Problem

You have certain text on a web page along with a button, and you want to highlight the text (by changing its background and foreground colors) when the mouse moves over the button.

Solution

The following is the HTML file that has the text **Highlight** enclosed in a span element of the class buttons and paragraph text:

highlighttextdyn.html

```
<!DOCTYPE html PUBLIC "-//W3C//DTD XHTML 1.0 Transitional//EN"
        "http://www.w3.org/TR/xhtml1/DTD/xhtml1-transitional.dtd">
<html xmlns="http://www.w3.org/1999/xhtml" xml:lang="en" lang="en">
  <head>
    <meta http-equiv="Content-Type" content="text/html; charset=utf-8"/>
    <title></title>
    <link rel="stylesheet" href="stylebuttons.css" type="text/css"
    media="screen" />
    <script src="jquery-3.5.1.js" type="text/javascript"></script>
    <script src="highlighttextdynjq.js" type="text/javascript"></script>
  </head>
  <body>
        <span class="buttons">Highlight</span><br/><br/>
        <p>Styles make the formatting job much easier and more efficient.
        To give an attractive look to web sites, styles are heavily used.
        A person must have a good knowledge of HTML and CSS
        and a bit of JavaScript. </p>
  </body>
</html>
```

For the text **Highlight**, the style rule buttons defined in the style sheet `stylebuttons.css` will be applied to give it the shape of a button. Use the same style sheet, `stylebuttons.css`, you used in Recipe 3-12.

To apply the styles to the text dynamically (when the mouse is moved over the text), write the following jQuery code:

highlighttextdynjq.js

```
$(document).ready(function() {
    $('.buttons').mouseover(function(){
        $('p').css({
            'background-color':'cyan',
            'font-weight':'bold',
            'color':'blue'
        });
    });
});
```

How It Works

In this recipe, you use a technique by which the style properties defined in the style sheet are overridden and the CSS properties are applied to the specified element(s) directly. jQuery provides a method called `css()` for applying CSS properties to the HTML directly. This method sets CSS properties to the specified elements directly, overriding the styles defined in the style sheet (if any). It allows you to have better control over the application of styles on the individual elements as well as a collection of elements.

.css(property, value)

Here `property` is the CSS property name that you want to set and `value` can be either the property value that you want to assign to the property or it can be a function that returns the property value to set. Here's an example:

$('p').css('color':'blue');

145

It sets the color of the paragraph text to blue. The following code uses a function that returns the height of the img element after incrementing it by 30; that is, it will increase the height of the img element by 30px:

```
$('img').css('height',function(){ return $(this).height()+30;});
```

The output of this solution will display the button and the paragraph text as shown in Figure 3-16.

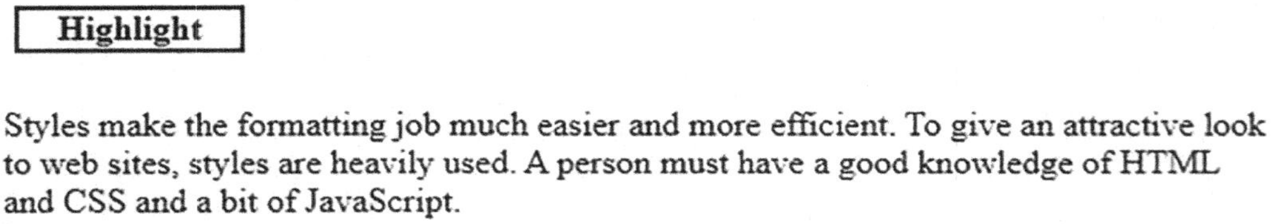

| Highlight |

Styles make the formatting job much easier and more efficient. To give an attractive look to web sites, styles are heavily used. A person must have a good knowledge of HTML and CSS and a bit of JavaScript.

Figure 3-16. *The button and the paragraph text*

You can see in the jQuery code that css() defines several properties, like the background-color property to apply cyan as the background of the paragraph text, font-weight to make the text appear in bold, and color to change the foreground color of the paragraph text to blue. The properties in the css() method will be applied to the paragraph text when the mouse is moved over the button and may appear as shown in Figure 3-17 (despite this being in black and white, you get the general idea).

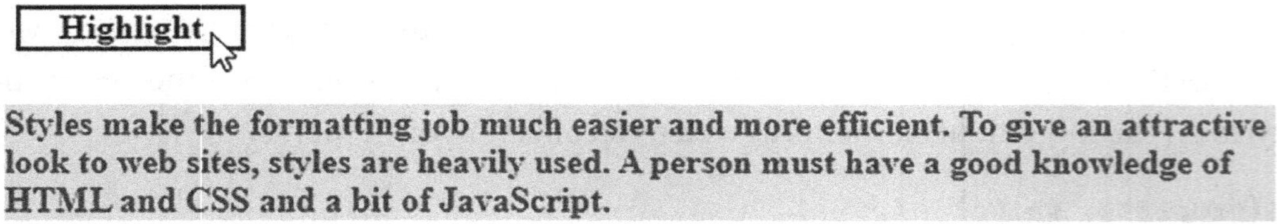

| Highlight |

Styles make the formatting job much easier and more efficient. To give an attractive look to web sites, styles are heavily used. A person must have a good knowledge of HTML and CSS and a bit of JavaScript.

Figure 3-17. *The paragraph text gets highlighted when the mouse is moved over the button*

3-16. Making an Image Bright or Blurred with Mouse Movements

Problem

Imagine you have an image displayed on your web page along with a button. The image is initially blurred. You want to make it so that when the mouse is moved over the button, the image becomes bright, and when the mouse is moved away from the button, the image again becomes blurred. Also, you want to increase the height and width of the image when you click the button.

Solution

Here is an HTML file that displays a button and an image:

brightblurr.html

```
<!DOCTYPE html PUBLIC "-//W3C//DTD XHTML 1.0 Transitional//EN"
        "http://www.w3.org/TR/xhtml1/DTD/xhtml1-transitional.dtd">
<html xmlns="http://www.w3.org/1999/xhtml" xml:lang="en" lang="en">
  <head>
    <meta http-equiv="Content-Type" content="text/html; charset=utf-8"/>
    <title></title>
    <link rel="stylesheet" href="stylebuttons.css" type="text/css"
    media="screen" />
    <script src="jquery-3.5.1.js" type="text/javascript"></script>
    <script src="brightblurrjq.js" type="text/javascript"></script>
  </head>
  <body>
        <span class="buttons" id="bright">Bright Image</span>
        <img src="a1.jpg"/>
  </body>
</html>
```

The text **Bright Image** is enclosed within a span element of the class buttons so that the style rule buttons defined in the external style sheet stylebuttons.css is applied to the text to give it the shape of a button. In this recipe, use the style sheet file from Recipe 3-12.

The jQuery code to apply effects to the image is as follows:

brightblurjq.js

```
$(document).ready(function() {
    $('img').css('opacity',0.4);
    $("span#bright").on("mouseenter", function() {
        $('img').css('opacity',1.0);
    }).on("mouseleave", function() {
        $('img').css('opacity',0.4);
    });
    $("span#bright").on("mousedown", function(event) {
        $('img').css('width',function(){ return $(this).width()+50;});
        $('img').css('height',function(){ return $(this).height()+30;});
    });
});
```

How It Works

In this solution, you will be using the opacity CSS property. The value of the opacity property ranges from 0 (transparent) to 1 (opaque) or from 0% to 100%.

Let's examine the code line by line:

$('img').css('opacity',0.4);

This line makes the image blur at the beginning and when the mouse is moved away from the button.

$('img').css('opacity',1.0);

This line makes the image bright (opaque) when the mouse is over the **Bright Image** button.

$('img').css('width',function(){ return $(this).width()+50;});

This line increases the width of the image by 50px when the mouse presses the **Bright Image** button.

```
$('img').css('height',function(){ return $(this).height()+30;});
```

This line increases the height of the image by 30px when the mouse is pressed on the **Bright Image** button.

The image appears blurred initially when the mouse is away from the **Bright Image** button, as shown in Figure 3-18.

Figure 3-18. *The button and a blurred image appear when mouse is away from the button*

The image becomes bright (that is, opaque) when the mouse pointer is moved over the **Bright Image** button, as shown in Figure 3-19.

Figure 3-19. *The image becomes bright (opaque) when the mouse is moved over the the Bright Image button*

The width and height of the image are increased by 50 and 30 pixels, respectively, when the mouse button is pressed on the **Bright Image** button, as shown in Figure 3-20.

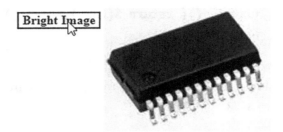

Figure 3-20. *The height and width of the image increase when the Bright Image button is clicked*

3-17. Creating Image-Based Rollovers

Problem

You want to create an image-based rollover. Image rollovers are those that change shape when the mouse is moved over an image and they designate a hyperlink to some web site. The image also changes if it is clicked once, to designate that it has already been visited.

Solution

Make an HTML file that contains a hyperlink element:

rollover.html

```
<!DOCTYPE html PUBLIC "-//W3C//DTD XHTML 1.0 Transitional//EN"
        "http://www.w3.org/TR/xhtml1/DTD/xhtml1-transitional.dtd">
<html xmlns="http://www.w3.org/1999/xhtml" xml:lang="en" lang="en">
  <head>
    <meta http-equiv="Content-Type" content="text/html; charset=utf-8"/>
    <title></title>
    <link rel="stylesheet" href="stylesrollover.css" type="text/css"
    media="screen" />
    <script src="jquery-3.5.1.js" type="text/javascript"></script>
    <script src="rolloverjq.js" type="text/javascript"></script>
  </head>
  <body>
```

```
        <a href="abc.com"><span class="roll"></span></a>
    </body>
</html>
```

In the style sheet, write style rules called link, hover, and active. The style sheet also needs a type selector called img, the properties of which will be automatically applied to the img element without using jQuery code. The style sheet file may appear as shown here:

stylesrollover.css

```
.link{
    display:block;
    width:170px;
    height:55px;
    background-image:url(btn1.png);
    background-repeat:no-repeat;
    background-position: top left;
}
.hover{
    display:block;
    width:220px;
    height:100px;
    background-image:url(btn2.png);
    background-repeat:no-repeat;
    background-position: top left;
}
.active{
    display:block;
    width:170px;
    height:55px;
    background-image:url(btn3.png);
    background-repeat:no-repeat;
    background-position: top left;
}
img{
    border:0;
}
```

The jQuery code to apply the style rules defined in the style sheet to the empty span element of the class roll is shown here:

rolloverjq.js

```
$(document).ready(function() {
    $('.roll').addClass('link');
    $('.roll').hover(
        function(){
            $(this).addClass('hover');
        },
        function(){
            $(this).removeClass('hover');
        }
    );
    $('.roll').click(function(event){
        $(this).addClass('active');
        event.preventDefault();
    });
});
```

How It Works

The preceding HTML file contains a span element of the class roll, which will be filled with images through style rules and jQuery code. You will be using three images in this solution: btn1.png, btn2.png, and btn3.png, shown in Figures 3-21 through 3-23.

In the style sheet, the style rule link contains the properties that will be applied to the image when the web page is loaded. It assigns the width and height of 170px and 55px, respectively, to the image.

Also the image btn1.png is loaded in the background and the value of the background-repeat property is set to no-repeat so as to avoid repetition of the image and make it appear only once.

Since you want the button to become larger when the mouse pointer is moved over it, the hover style rule contains the second image: btn2.png (shown in Figure 3-21). The rest of the properties in this style rule are the same as those in the link style rule.

The third style rule designates the image when the link is visited once, so use the image named `btn3.png`. The only change between the two images, `btn1.png` and `btn3.png`, is in the color of the button text. The color of the text on the button in `btn3.png` is set to maroon to represent that its link has been visited. The style sheet also contains a type selector `img` that has a single property border with its value set to zero to remove the border from the three images that will be displayed.

In the jQuery code, the statement

$('.roll').addClass('link');

will apply the `link` style rule to the span element, making the image in `btn1.bmp` appear on the screen.

The statements

```
$('.roll').hover(
    function(){
        $(this).addClass('hover');
    },
    function(){
        $(this).removeClass('hover');
    }
);
```

add the `hover` event to the span element, with two inline functions attached to it. The first function applies the style rule `hover` to the span element (when the mouse pointer is moved over the image), making `btn2.png` (the enlarged image) appear in place of `btn1.png`. The `btn1.png` image will be hidden by the image in `btn2.png` because the position of the images is set to top left via the `background-position` property. The second inline function (applied when the mouse pointer is moved away from the image) removes the style rule `hover` from the image, making it appear as it was previously (that is, just like `btn1.png`).

The statement

$(this).addClass('active');

applies the property defined in the `active` style rule to the image, setting the background image `btn3.png` to appear. This image has the button text set to maroon to make it appear different from the initial image, to show that it has been visited already.

The statement

`event.preventDefault();`

prevents the browser from navigating to the hyperlinked web site. That is, it makes the hyperlink ignore its default action (which is navigating to the linked web site). As a result, you remain at the same web page even after clicking the image. Initially the image may appear as shown in Figure 3-21.

Figure 3-21. *The button that appears in the default state*

When the mouse pointer is moved over the image, the image becomes enlarged, as shown in Figure 3-22.

Figure 3-22. *The button in the enlarged state when the mouse moves over it*

The image changes if you click the image link, as shown in Figure 3-23.

Figure 3-23. *The color of the button text changes in active state (when it is clicked)*

3-18. Adding and Removing Text in Response to Events

Problem

You have two buttons on the web page with the text **Add** and **Remove**, respectively. You want to have certain text added to the web page when the user selects the **Add** button and have the added text removed when the user selects the **Remove** button.

Solution

Begin by making an HTML file that contains the text **Add** and **Remove** enclosed in the span element of class buttons so that the class selector buttons defined in the style sheet can be applied to them:

addingremovingtext.html

```
<!DOCTYPE html PUBLIC "-//W3C//DTD XHTML 1.0 Transitional//EN"
        "http://www.w3.org/TR/xhtml1/DTD/xhtml1-transitional.dtd">
<html xmlns="http://www.w3.org/1999/xhtml" xml:lang="en" lang="en">
  <head>
    <meta http-equiv="Content-Type" content="text/html; charset=utf-8"/>
    <title></title>
    <link rel="stylesheet" href="stylebuttons.css" type="text/css"
    media="screen" />
    <script src="jquery-3.5.1.js" type="text/javascript"></script>
    <script src="addingremovingjq.js" type="text/javascript"></script>
  </head>
  <body>
    <span class="add buttons">Add</span>
    <span class="remove buttons">Remove</span><br><br>
    <div></div>
  </body>
</html>
```

Use the style sheet stylebuttons.css from Recipe 3-12. The following is the jQuery code to add click events to both buttons along with their inline functions to add and remove text:

addingremovingjq.js

```
$(document).ready(function() {
    $('.add').on("mousedown", function() {
        $('div').prepend('<p>Styles make the formatting job much easier
        and more efficient. To give an attractive look to web sites,
        styles are heavily used. A person must have a good knowledge of
        HTML and CSS and a bit of JavaScript. </p>');
    });
    $('.remove').on("mousedown", function() {
        $('p').remove();
    });
});
```

How It Works

You see that the HTML file has an empty div element. To this div element you add a paragraph element (with some text in it) when the **Add button** is clicked. Also the newly added paragraph element will be removed from the div element when the **Remove** button is clicked. In order to add the paragraph, you use the prepend() method. To remove the paragraph element, you use the remove() method.

The remove() method removes the set of selected elements from the DOM and returns a jQuery object. It also removes all event handlers and internally cached data. You don't need to pass any parameter with this method.

In the jQuery code, the statement

$('div').prepend('<p>Styles...</p>');

adds the paragraph element at the beginning of the div element when the **Add** button is clicked, while the statement

$('p').remove();

accesses the paragraph element(s) in the HTML file and removes them. Since there is only a single paragraph element in the HTML file (added via the **Add** button), it will be removed when the **Remove** button is clicked.

On execution of the jQuery code, you will initially get two buttons displayed with the text **Add** and **Remove** on them, as shown in Figure 3-24.

Figure 3-24. *Two buttons for adding and removing text*

Upon selecting the **Add** button, the paragraph element with some text appears, as shown in Figure 3-25.

Styles make the formatting job much easier and more efficient. To give an attractive look to web sites, styles are heavily used. A person must have a good knowledge of HTML and CSS and a bit of JavaScript.

Figure 3-25. *The text appears upon selecting the Add button*

On selecting the **Remove** button, the text disappears.

3-19. Displaying Word Balloons

Problem

You have two buttons on the web page, one named **Bold** and the other named **Italic**. You want to create a word-balloon effect when either of the buttons is clicked. If the **Bold** button is clicked, you want the text **This is Bold menu** to appear in the word balloon (shown later in Figure 3-28) and if the **Italic** button is clicked, you want the text **This is Italic menu** to appear in the word balloon (shown later in Figure 3-29).

Solution

Use the following HTML file to display two buttons, **Bold** and **Italic**:

wordballoons.html

```
<!DOCTYPE html PUBLIC "-//W3C//DTD XHTML 1.0 Transitional//EN"
        "http://www.w3.org/TR/xhtml1/DTD/xhtml1-transitional.dtd">
<html xmlns="http://www.w3.org/1999/xhtml" xml:lang="en" lang="en">
  <head>
    <meta http-equiv="Content-Type" content="text/html; charset=utf-8"/>
    <title></title>
    <link rel="stylesheet" href="styleswordballoons.css" type="text/css"
    media="screen" />
    <script src="jquery-3.5.1.js" type="text/javascript"></script>
    <script src="wordballoonsjq.js" type="text/javascript"></script>
  </head>
  <body>
    <span class="bold buttons">Bold</span>
    <span class="italic buttons">Italic</span>
  </body>
</html>
```

Create a style sheet that contains the class selector buttons to apply the properties to the span elements so as to give them the shape of the buttons. The style sheet also contains two style rules, hover and showtip, to give the hover effect on the buttons and to display the text in the word balloons. The style sheet file is as follows:

styleswordballoons.css

```
.buttons{
    width: 150px;
    float: left;
    text-align: center;
    color:#000;
    background-color:red;
    margin: 5px;
    font-weight: bold;
}
.hover{
    color:red;
    background:url(balloon.png);
```

```
    background-repeat:no-repeat;
    background-position:bottom;
}
.showtip{
    display:block;
    margin:25px;
}
```

The jQuery code to apply the style rules to the buttons is shown here:

wordballoonsjq.js

```
$(document).ready(function() {
    $('.buttons').hover(
        function(event){
            $(this).addClass('hover');
            var $txt=$(this).text();
            $('<span class="showtip"> This is '+$txt+' menu </span>').
            appendTo($(this));
        },
        function(){
            $(this).removeClass('hover');
            $('.showtip').remove();
        }
    );
});
```

How It Works

The image file balloon.jpg used in the aforementioned style sheet contains the image shown in Figure 3-26.

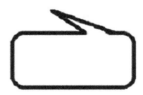

Figure 3-26. *The balloon image in the file balloon.png*

In the style sheet, the `hover` style rule contains the following properties:

- `color` sets the foreground color of the button's text to red.

- `background` displays the word balloon image as the background.

- `background-repeat` is set to `no-repeat` to make the word balloon image appear only once.

- `background-position` makes the word balloon image appear at the bottom.

In the style sheet file, the `showtip` style rule contains the display property with its value set to `block` to treat the text (that will be displayed in the word balloon) as a block element having white space at the beginning and at the end. It also contains the `margin` property that is set to 25px to set the gap between the text and the balloon boundaries.

In the jQuery code, the `hover` event is assigned to the class `buttons` (that is, to both buttons). So, when the mouse pointer enters either of the buttons, first the properties defined in the style rule `hover` will be applied, creating a blank word balloon on the screen. Second, the text of the button in question will be stored in the variable `$txt`. Also a span element will be appended before the button.

The span element is assigned the class `showtip` (so that the properties defined in the class selector showtip can be automatically applied to its text). The text content of the span element is set to **This is $txt menu** where `$txt` contains the text of the button over which the mouse pointer is hovering, hence making the desired text appear inside the word balloon. The second inline function of the `hover` event removes the properties defined in both the style rules `hover` and `showtip`.

Initially, the buttons appear as shown in Figure 3-27.

Figure 3-27. *The Bold and Italic buttons when neither is selected*

When the mouse pointer moves over the **Bold** button, the styles will be applied to change the foreground and background color of the button and to display the word balloon along with the text **This is Bold menu**, as shown in Figure 3-28.

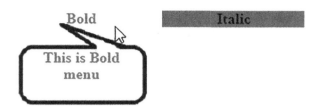

Figure 3-28. *The text This is Bold menu appears in a word balloon when the Bold button is moused over*

Similarly, when the mouse pointer is moved over the **Italic** button, its foreground and background color will be changed and the word balloon with the text **This is Italic menu** will appear, as shown in Figure 3-29.

Figure 3-29. *The text This is Italic menu appears in a word balloon when the Italic button is moused over*

3-20. Creating "Return to Top" Links

Problem

You have a web page with lots of text. After every block of text, you want to display a link that says **Return to Top**, which should navigate the user to the beginning of the web page.

Solution

Let's make an HTML file that contains a few blocks of text in the form of paragraph elements, as shown here:

returntotop.html

```
!DOCTYPE html PUBLIC "-//W3C//DTD XHTML 1.0 Transitional//EN"
```

```
        "http://www.w3.org/TR/xhtml1/DTD/xhtml1-transitional.dtd">
<html xmlns="http://www.w3.org/1999/xhtml" xml:lang="en" lang="en">
  <head>
    <meta http-equiv="Content-Type" content="text/html; charset=utf-8"/>
    <title></title>
    <script src="jquery-3.5.1.js" type="text/javascript"></script>
    <script src="returntotopjq.js" type="text/javascript"></script>
  </head>
  <body>
    <p>Styles make the formatting job much easier and more efficient.
    To give an attractive look to web sites, styles are heavily used.
    jQuery is a powerful JavaScript library that allows us to add dynamic
    elements to our web sites. Not only it is easy to learn, but it's easy
    to implement too.</p>
    <p> A person must have a good knowledge of HTML and CSS and a bit of
    JavaScript. jQuery is an open source project that provides a wide
    range of features with cross-platform
    compatibility</p>
  </body>
</html>
```

The jQuery code to create a hyperlink with the text **Return to top** after every paragraph element and make that text navigate to the beginning of the web page is shown here:

returntotopjq.js

```
$(document).ready(function() {
    $('<a href="#topofpage">Return to top</a>').insertAfter('p');
    $('<a id="topofpage" name="topofpage"></a>').prependTo('body');
});
```

How It Works

The statement

```
$('<a href="#topofpage">Return to top</a>').insertAfter('p');
```

adds a hyperlink with the text **Return to top** after every paragraph element of the HTML file, and when the link is selected by the user, they will be navigated to the element of id topofpage.

The statement

```
$('<a id="topofpage" name="topofpage"></a>').prependTo('body');
```

adds an anchor element with a name and id assigned to it as topofpage before the body of the HTML file. In other words, an anchor element of id topofpage is created at the beginning of the web page. The output of the preceding jQuery code is shown in Figure 3-30.

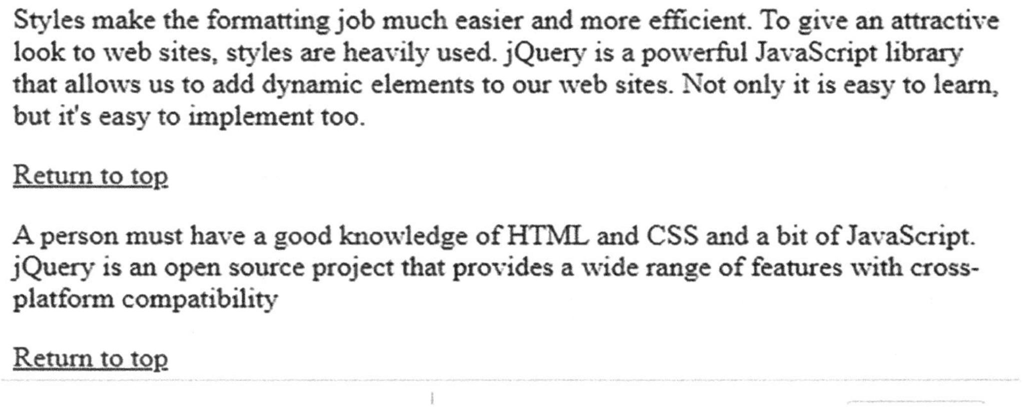

Styles make the formatting job much easier and more efficient. To give an attractive look to web sites, styles are heavily used. jQuery is a powerful JavaScript library that allows us to add dynamic elements to our web sites. Not only it is easy to learn, but it's easy to implement too.

Return to top

A person must have a good knowledge of HTML and CSS and a bit of JavaScript. jQuery is an open source project that provides a wide range of features with cross-platform compatibility

Return to top

Figure 3-30. *The text "Return to top" appears after every paragraph*

If you click any of the **Return to top** links, you will be navigated to the beginning of the web page.

3-21. Displaying Text with an Animation Effect

Problem

You have three buttons on the web page, namely **Books**, **Movies**, and **Music**. You want to display the appropriate text when one of these buttons is clicked. You want the text that is displayed upon clicking the button to have an animation effect.

Solution

Let's make an HTML file that has three buttons, **Books**, **Movies**, and **Music**, and three paragraphs with class names assigned as books, movies, and music, respectively. These paragraphs contain the text to be displayed when each button is clicked. Initially, the text of these paragraphs will be kept invisible. It will be displayed with an animation effect only when its button is clicked. The HTML file appears as shown here:

textanimation.html

```
<!DOCTYPE html PUBLIC "-//W3C//DTD XHTML 1.0 Transitional//EN"
        "http://www.w3.org/TR/xhtml1/DTD/xhtml1-transitional.dtd">
<html xmlns="http://www.w3.org/1999/xhtml" xml:lang="en" lang="en">
  <head>
    <meta http-equiv="Content-Type" content="text/html; charset=utf-8"/>
    <title></title>
    <link rel="stylesheet" href="stylebuttons.css" type="text/css"
    media="screen" />
    <script src="jquery-3.5.1.js" type="text/javascript"></script>
    <script src="textanimationjq.js" type="text/javascript"></script>
  </head>
  <body>
    <span class="buttons" id="booksbutton"> Books </span>
    <span class="buttons" id="moviesbutton"> Movies </span>
    <span class="buttons" id="musicbutton"> Music </span><br><br>
    <p class="books">Books on a range of different subjects available at
    reasonable prices.
Ranging from web development, programming languages, and text books, all
are available at heavy discount. Shipping is free. Also available in stock
are popular magazines, e-books, and tutorial DVDs at affordable prices.</p>
    <p class="movies">Find new movie reviews & the latest Hollywood movie
    news. Includes new movie trailers, latest Hollywood releases, movie
    showtimes, entertainment news, celebrity interviews etc. Also find
    Hollywood actresses, actors, videos, biographies, filmography,
photos, wallpaper, music, jokes, and live TV channels at your doorstep.</p>
```

```
<p class="music">Find music videos, internet radio, music downloads
and all the latest music news and information. We have a large
collection of music and songs classified by type, language, and
region. All downloads are streamed through RealAudio. You can also
watch free music videos, tune in to AOL Radio, and search for your
favorite music artists.</p>
  </body>
</html>
```

In this recipe, you will use the same external style sheet file, **stylebuttons.css,** that you used in Recipe 3-12. The content of the style sheet is repeated here for your reference:

stylebuttons.css

```
.buttons{
    width: 100px;
    float: left;
    text-align: center;
    margin: 5px;
    border: 2px solid;
    font-weight: bold;
}
```

The following is the jQuery code to hide the paragraph text initially and display the contents of the paragraph with an animation effect when its button is clicked:

textanimationjq.js

```
$(document).ready(function() {
    $('.books').hide();
    $('.movies').hide();
    $('.music').hide();
    $('#booksbutton').on("mousedown", function() {
        $('.books').show('slow');
        $('.movies').hide();
        $('.music').hide();
    });
```

```
    $('#moviesbutton').on("mousedown", function() {
        $('.movies').show('slow');
        $('.books').hide();
        $('.music').hide();
    });
    $('#musicbutton').on("mousedown", function() {
        $('.music').show('slow');
        $('.books').hide();
        $('.movies').hide();
    });
});
```

How It Works

In the HTML file, you can see that the text **Books**, **Movies**, and **Music** is enclosed in the span element of the class buttons so that the properties defined in the class selector buttons defined in the style sheet can be automatically applied to it. The class selector buttons contains the properties to give the shape of the button to this text. Also, the buttons are assigned the unique IDs of booksbutton, moviesbutton, and musicbutton so that you can attach click events (i.e., mousedown events) to them individually and write code for hiding the old text (information from an earlier button click) and for displaying the information related to the clicked button.

In the jQuery code, you start by hiding the text of the paragraphs of classes books, movies, and music (that is, only the buttons will be visible initially when the web page is loaded). You then link the mousedown event to the HTML element of id booksbutton (that is, to the **Books** button). When the **Books** button is clicked, the contents of the paragraph of the class books becomes visible slowly, giving it an animation effect (it contains information related to books) and the contents of the paragraph of the classes movies and music are made invisible, hence displaying only the information for the button that is clicked on the screen.

Initially only the three buttons **Books**, **Movies**, and **Music** will be displayed, as shown in Figure 3-31.

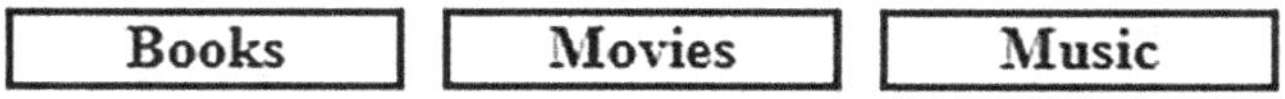

Figure 3-31. *Three buttons: Books, Movies, and Music*

When the **Books** button is clicked, it will display the information related to it; that is, the paragraph of the class books will be displayed as shown in Figure 3-32.

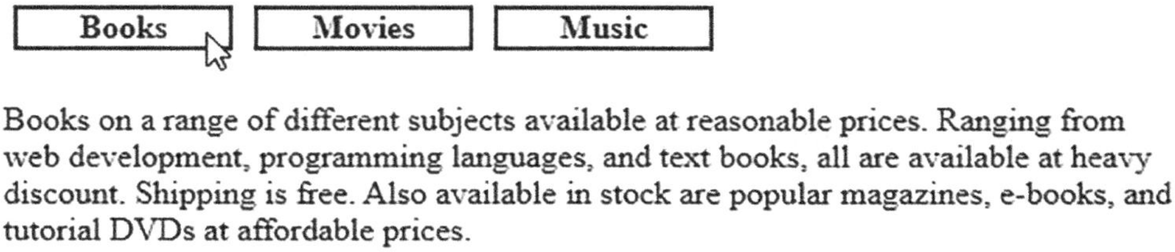

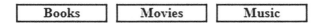

Books on a range of different subjects available at reasonable prices. Ranging from web development, programming languages, and text books, all are available at heavy discount. Shipping is free. Also available in stock are popular magazines, e-books, and tutorial DVDs at affordable prices.

Figure 3-32. *Information related to books is displayed when the Books button is clicked*

Similarly, if the **Movies** button is clicked, it will hide the information related to books or music and will make the information related to movies (that is, the paragraph of class movies) appear slowly on the screen with an animation effect, as shown in Figure 3-33.

Books	Movies	Music

Find new movie reviews & the latest Hollywood movie news. Includes new movie trailers, latest Hollywood releases, movie showtimes, entertainment news, celebrity interviews etc. Also find Hollywood actresses, actors, videos, biographies, filmography, photos, wallpaper, music, jokes, and live TV channels at your doorstep.

Figure 3-33. *Information related to movies is displayed when the Movies button is clicked*

Adding a Mouseover Event

Instead of applying click events to the buttons, you can also attach the mouseover event to them. The mouseover event will make the appropriate information appear when the mouse pointer enters the button (there is no need to click the button). The jQuery code for attaching the mouseover event is as follows:

textanimationhoverjq.js

```
$(document).ready(function() {
    $('.books').hide();
    $('.movies').hide();
    $('.music').hide();
    $('#booksbutton').mouseover(function(){
        $('.books').show('slow');
        $('.movies').hide();
        $('.music').hide();
    });
    $('#moviesbutton').mouseover(function(){
        $('.movies').show('slow');
        $('.books').hide();
        $('.music').hide();
    });
    $('#musicbutton').mouseover(function(){
        $('.music').show('slow');
        $('.books').hide();
        $('.movies').hide();
    });
});
```

3-22. Replacing Text with a Sliding Effect

Problem

You want one piece of text to be replaced by another; the first piece is slowly made invisible while the other appears gradually.

Solution

In this solution, you will be applying CSS styles directly to the elements using css() instead of picking them up from the style sheet. Let's assume you have an HTML file that has two paragraph elements that are distinguished from each other by assigning them the IDs message1 and message2.

replacingtext.html

```
<!DOCTYPE html PUBLIC "-//W3C//DTD XHTML 1.0 Transitional//EN"
        "http://www.w3.org/TR/xhtml1/DTD/xhtml1-transitional.dtd">
<html xmlns="http://www.w3.org/1999/xhtml" xml:lang="en" lang="en">
  <head>
    <meta http-equiv="Content-Type" content="text/html; charset=utf-8"/>
    <title></title>
    <script src="jquery-3.5.1.js" type="text/javascript"></script>
    <script src="replacingtextjq.js" type="text/javascript"></script>
  </head>
  <body>
    <p id="message1">jQuery is an open source project</p>
    <p id="message2">Manipulating DOM using jQuery</p>
  </body>
</html>
```

Here is the jQuery code for applying the sliding effect:

replacingtextjq.js

```
$(document).ready(function() {
    $('p#message1').css({'border': '2px solid', 'text-align':
    'center','fontweight':'bold'}).hide();
    $('p#message2').css({'backgroundColor': '#f00','color':'#fff','text-
    align': 'center','font-weight':'bold'}).on("mousedown", function() {
            $(this).slideUp('slow');
            $('p#message1').slideDown('slow');
        }
    );
});
```

How It Works

To the paragraph of id message1, you assign a solid border of 2px thickness, align its text at the center of the browser window, and set it to appear in bold. The background color of the paragraph of id message2 is set to red and the foreground color of the text is set to white and is aligned at the center of the browser window.

In the jQuery code, some text will gradually disappear using the `slideDown()` method and will be replaced with other text that slowly appears using the `slideUp()` method, so let's take a look at the workings of these two methods.

`slideDown()` displays the selected element with a sliding motion.

.slideDown(speed, callback)

`speed` decides the duration of the animation. It can be specified in terms of strings as `fast`, `normal`, or `slow`, or in milliseconds. The higher the number of milliseconds, the longer the animation will take.

`callback` is the function that is fired on completion of the animation.

Conversely, `slideUp()` makes the selected element invisible with a sliding motion.

.slideUp(speed, callback)

`speed` and `callback` have the same meaning as they do for `slideUp()`.

In the jQuery code, you can see that the paragraph of id `message1` is hidden and only the paragraph of id `message2` is set to be visible. So, the output that you get initially is shown in Figure 3-34. Also, a mousedown event is attached to the visible paragraph. In the inline function of the mousedown event, you have written code to make the visible paragraph (the paragraph of id `message2`) become slowly invisible by sliding up, and the paragraph of id `message1` (which was initially invisible) to become visible slowly by sliding down.

Manipulating DOM using jQuery

Figure 3-34. *Applying slideUp() and slideDown()*

On clicking the visible paragraph it will slowly become invisible and the paragraph that was initially invisible will start becoming slowly visible, as shown in Figure 3-35.

Figure 3-35. *One paragraph in the process of sliding down and another in the process of sliding up*

The paragraph is totally replaced by another paragraph, as shown in Figure 3-36.

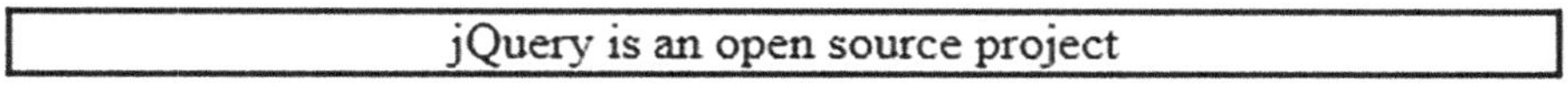

```
jQuery is an open source project
```

Figure 3-36. *One paragraph totally removed and the other now visible*

3-23. Summary

In this chapter, you learned about displaying a message when an element gets focus and when blurred; finding which mouse button is pressed; changing the style of an element when the mouse enters the element or leaves; and using mouseup and mousedown events for displaying and hiding an image. You also learned to hide and display an image upon the click of a button; how to zoom in and out of an image; how to avoid event bubbling; how to know which key is down, pressed, or released; how to applying fading; and how to apply an animation effect on an image.

In the next chapter, you will learn different ways of form validation. You will learn to confirm that the essential field is not left blank; how specific values are allowed; how to validate phone numbers, user ids, dates, and email addresses; finding if the checkbox and radio button are selected or not; matching passwords and confirming password fields; and validating a complete form.

CHAPTER 4

Form Validation

In this chapter, you will explore different ways of form validation. You will be learning the following recipes in this chapter:

- Confirming the essential field is not left blank
- Confirming only numerals are allowed
- Validating phone numbers
- Validating the user id
- Validating a date
- Validating an email address
- Checking whether a checkbox is checked or not
- Finding if a radio button is selected or not
- Finding if any option from a select element is selected or not
- Applying styles to options and form buttons
- Checking and unchecking all checkboxes together
- Validating two fields
- Matching a password and confirming a password
- Disabling certain fields
- Validating a complete form

© Bintu Harwani 2022
B. Harwani, *jQuery Recipes*, https://doi.org/10.1007/978-1-4842-7304-3_4

4-1. Confirming a Required Field Is Not Left Blank

Problem

You have an input text field in a form and you want that it should not be left blank. The user must enter the required data in it or get an error message if it is left blank.

Solution

Make an HTML file that displays a form that contains a label, a text field, an error message, and a Submit button as follows:

Signupform.html

```
<!DOCTYPE html PUBLIC "-//W3C//DTD XHTML 1.0 Transitional//EN"
        "http://www.w3.org/TR/xhtml1/DTD/xhtml1-transitional.dtd">

<html xmlns="http://www.w3.org/1999/xhtml" xml:lang="en" lang="en">
  <head>
    <meta http-equiv="Content-Type" content="text/html; charset=utf-8"/>
    <title></title>
    <link rel="stylesheet" href="style.css" type="text/css" media="screen" />
    <script src="jquery-3.5.1.js" type="text/javascript"></script>
    <script src="signupformjq.js" type="text/javascript"></script>
  </head>
<body>
<form id="signup" method="post" action="">
<div><span class="label">User Id *</span><input
type="text"  class="infobox" name="userid" /><span class="error"> This
field cannot be blank</span></div>
<input class="submit" type="submit" value="Submit">
</form>
</body>
</html>
```

Since the purpose of the HTML form is to validate the input text field and not to send the entered data to some other page for processing, the action attribute of the form is left blank. The form is assigned an id of signup and the method is set to post, although it will have no effect on the validation procedure.

The label message **User Id** is enclosed in a span element of the class label. The input text field is assigned class name infobox and the error message (**This field cannot be blank**) is stored as a span element of class error and the Submit button is assigned the class submit.

The reason for assigning the classes to all four items of the form is to apply the properties defined in the class selectors .label, .infobox, .error, and .submit (defined in the style sheet style.css) automatically to these four items of the form. The style sheet with the respective class selectors is as follows:

style.css

```
.label {float: left; width: 120px; }
.infobox {width: 200px; }
.error { color: red; padding-left: 10px; }
.submit { margin-left: 125px; margin-top: 10px;}
```

The jQuery code to confirm that the input text field is not left blank and to display an error message if it is left blank is as follows:

Signupformjq.js

```
$(document).ready(function() {
  $('.error').hide();
  $('.submit').click(function(event){
    var data=$('.infobox').val();
    var len=data.length;
    if(len<1)
    {
      $('.error').show();
      event.preventDefault();
    }
    else
    {
      $('.error').hide();
    }
  });
});
```

How It Works

The class selector .label has float property set to left so that the next item (the input text field) may appear to its right and its width property is set to 120px to give enough space for the label to display. The class selector .infobox has its width property set to 200px, the size of the input text field. The class selector .error has the color property set to red to highlight it and the padding from the left is set to 10px to keep the distance from the input text field. The class selector .submit has its margin-left and margin-top properties set to 125px and 10px, respectively, to set the distance from the left boundary of the browser window and from the input text field since you want the Submit button to appear below the input text field.

In the above jQuery code, you can see that initially the error message is hidden and a click event is attached to the Submit button. In the event handling function of the click event, you extract the data entered by the user in the input text field (assigned the class name infobox) and store it in a variable called data. You find out the length of the data and if it is less than 1 (which means the user has not entered anything in the text field), you make the error message visible on the screen. The method preventDefault() of the event object is used to keep the Submit button from sending the data entered by the user to the server.

On execution of the jQuery code, you get a form displayed with a label, an input text field, and a Submit button. If you select the Submit button without entering anything in the text field, you get an error message of **This field cannot be blank** displayed in red beside the text field, as shown in Figure 4-1.

Figure 4-1. *An error message is displayed when the input text field is left blank*

If you enter some name in the text field and select the Submit button, you will not get any error message, as shown in Figure 4-2.

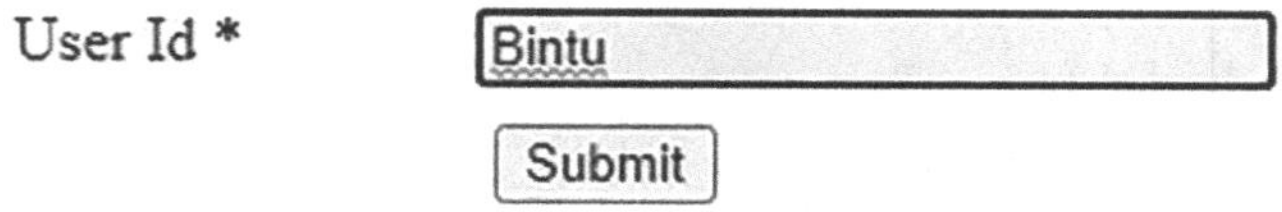

Figure 4-2. *No error message if data is entered in the input text field*

4-2. Validating a Numerical Field

Problem

You have a text field for entering the age of a person and you want to confirm that a numerical value is entered in it and no character or symbol is entered.

Solution

The HTML code to display the form that contains a label, an input text field, an error message, and a Submit button is as follows:

Validatenum.html

```
<!DOCTYPE html PUBLIC "-//W3C//DTD XHTML 1.0 Transitional//EN"
        "http://www.w3.org/TR/xhtml1/DTD/xhtml1-transitional.dtd">

<html xmlns="http://www.w3.org/1999/xhtml" xml:lang="en" lang="en">
  <head>
    <meta http-equiv="Content-Type" content="text/html; charset=utf-8"/>
    <title></title>
    <link rel="stylesheet" href="style.css" type="text/css" media="screen" />
    <script src="jquery-3.5.1.js" type="text/javascript"></script>
    <script src="validatenumjq.js" type="text/javascript"></script>
  </head>
<body>
<form id="signup" method="post" action="">
 <div><span class="label">Enter Age </span><input
type="text"  class="infobox" name="age" /><span class="error"> Only
numericals allowed</span></div>
<input class="submit" type="submit" value="Submit">
</form>
</body>
</html>
```

Since the purpose of this HTML form is to validate the input text field and not to send the entered data to some other page for processing, the action attribute of the form is left blank. The form is assigned an id of `signup` and the method is set to `post`, although it will have no effect on the validation procedure.

The label message `User Id` is enclosed in a span element of class `label`. The input text field is assigned a class name of `infobox` and the error message (**This field cannot be blank**) is stored as a span element of the class `error` and the Submit button is assigned the class `submit`.

The reason for assigning classes to all four items of the form is to apply the properties defined in the class selectors `.label`, `.infobox`, `.error`, and `.submit` (defined in the style sheet `style.css`) automatically to the respective four items of the form. The style sheet with the class selectors is as follows:

style.css

```
.label {float: left; width: 120px; }
.infobox {width: 200px; }
.error { color: red; padding-left: 10px; }
.submit { margin-left: 125px; margin-top: 10px;}
```

Allowing Only Numerical Values

The jQuery code to check that the age entered in the text field contains only numerical values and no text or symbol is as follows:

Validatenumjq.js

```
$(document).ready(function() {
  $('.error').hide();
  $('.submit').click(function(event){
    var data=$('.infobox').val();
    var len=data.length;
    var c;
    for(var i=0;i<len;i++)
    {
      c=data.charAt(i).charCodeAt(0);
      if(c <48 || c >57)
      {
```

```
      $('.error').show();
      event.preventDefault();
      break;
    }
    else
    {
      $('.error').hide();
    }
  }
});
});
```

You can see in this code that the ASCII values of 0 and 9 are used to ensure that the value entered by the user is between 0 and 9. The ASCII value of 0 is 48 and of 9 is 57. If the ASCII value entered is less than 48 or more than 57, an error will be displayed.

Allowing a Negative Value Also

Sometimes it happens that while entering numerical values you come across negative values also. In the above jQuery code, no symbol is allowed (i.e., you cannot use a – (hyphen or minus)), so you cannot enter a negative value in the text field with the above code. Let's modify the jQuery code to accept negative values also:

Allownegativejq.js

```
$(document).ready(function() {
  $('.error').hide();
  $('.submit').click(function(event){
    var data=$('.infobox').val();
    var len=data.length;
    var c;
    for(var i=0;i<len;i++)
    {
      c=data.charAt(i).charCodeAt(0);
      if(c==45 && i==0)
      {
        continue;
      }
```

```
      if(c <48 || c >57)
      {
        $('.error').show();
        event.preventDefault();
        break;
      }
      else
      {
        $('.error').hide();
      }
    }
  });
});
```

Allowing a Range of Values

You want to enter the age of the person and want it to be within the range of 5 to 99 (i.e., if the age entered is below or above the given range, you want an error message to be displayed on the screen).

The jQuery code for entering a numerical value between the range 5 to 99 is as follows:

Allowrangejq.js

```
$(document).ready(function() {
  $('.error').hide();
  $('.submit').click(function(event){
    var data=$('.infobox').val();
    var len=data.length;
    var c=0;
    var age=0;
    var flag=0;
    for(var i=0;i<len;i++)
    {
      c=data.charAt(i).charCodeAt(0);
      if(c <48 || c >57)
```

```
    {
      $('.error').show();
      flag=1;
      event.preventDefault();
      break;
    }
    else
    {
      $('.error').hide();
    }
  }

  if(flag==0)
  {
    age=parseInt(data);
    if(age<5 || age>99)
    {
      $('.error').show();
      $('.error').text('Invalid Age. Please enter the age within the
      range 5 to 99');
      event.preventDefault();
    }
  }
});
});
```

How It Works

You can see in the above HTML file that the label is set to display the text **Enter Age** and the error message is assigned the text **Only numerical allowed**. Also, the four items (label, input text field, error message, and Submit button) are assigned different class names (`label, infobox, error,` and `submit`) so as to apply the properties defined in the class selectors (defined in the style sheet `style.css`) to them. In this recipe, you use the same external style sheet, `style.css`, from Recipe 4-1.

You can see in the jQuery code of the *Allowing Only Numerical Values* section that the error message is initially set to `invisible`. The click event is attached to the Submit button so as to execute its event handling function if the Submit button is clicked. In the event handling function, you see that the data in the input text field (the text field is enclosed in the span element of class `infobox`) is retrieved and is stored in a variable called `data`. Its length is calculated and a `for` loop is executed for the length of the input data to parse each of its individual characters.

In the `for` loop, you take one character at a time (of the input data) and with the help of `charCodeAt()` find its ASCII value. If the ASCII value of the character is below 48 (meaning 0) or more than 57 (meaning 9), meaning it is not a numerical value, you make the error message visible on the screen and exit from the loop. The `preventDefault()` method of the event object is used to prevent the data entered by the user from being sent to the server or the user navigating to the target form.

On execution of the program, if you enter some characters after the age, you get the error message **Only numericals allowed**, as shown in Figure 4-3.

Figure 4-3. *An error message is displayed if a character appears after the age*

Even if the character appears between the digits, the error will be displayed, as shown in Figure 4-4.

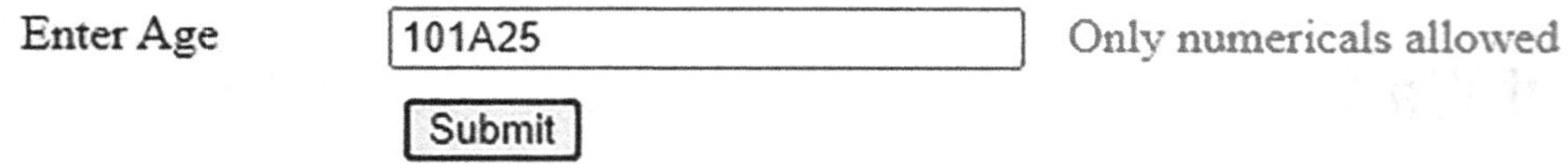

Enter Age   101A25   Only numericals allowed
                   Submit

Figure 4-4. *An error message is displayed if the character appears between the numerals*

Also, if you add any symbol, like a minus or underscore, you get an error message, as shown in Figure 4-5.

Figure 4-5. *An error message is displayed on entering symbols*

You can see in the jQuery code from the *Allowing Negative Values Also* section that the error message is made hidden at the beginning. The event handling function of the click event attached to the Submit button extracts the data from the input text field and stores it in the variable data. Each individual character stored in data is parsed with the help of a for loop. In the loop, you convert each character in the data variable to its ASCII value and check that if the first character has an ASCII value of 45 (which is the ASCII value of the minus sign) and then you continue checking the rest of the characters without displaying any error message. The second condition in the for loop is the one that you saw earlier (i.e., checking if the characters in the data variable are numerical values and displaying the error message if not).

In the jQuery code of the *Allowing a Range of Values* section, you first make the error message invisible. Then you attach the click event to the Submit button. The event handling function of the click event does several jobs, like extracting the numerical value entered in the input text field (assigned the class name infobox) and storing it in the variable data. You then find out the length of the data and execute the loop to parse each of its individual characters. If any of the individual contents in data has an ASCII value lower than 48 (ASCII value of 0) or greater than 57 (ASCII value of 9), it means the data variable contains some value other than a numerical value, so you make the error message visible. Also, you set the value of a variable flag to 1 to indicate that only numbers are allowed and exit from the for loop. If the value of flag is set to 1, it means there is no point in checking the range of the numerical value as it is invalid data.

If the data is a number, you need to check the range of the numerical value (i.e., whether it is between 5 and 99). So, if the value of the flag variable is 0 (after the execution of the for loop, so after inspecting all characters of the data variable), it means the data entered is valid and consist only of numbers; you then apply the conditional statement that if it is less than 5 or greater than 99, make the error message visible and set the text of the error message to **Invalid Age**. The preventDefault() method of the event object is used to prevent the submission of the entered data in case it is invalid. You get the error message displayed in Figure 4-6 if the value is not within the range of 5 and 99.

Enter Age `[140                    ]` Invalid Age. Please enter the age within the range 5 to 99

`[ Submit ]`

Figure 4-6. *The error message displayed if the value is not within the range of 5 to 99*

4-3. Validating Phone Numbers

Problem

You want to use a phone number field and you want the user to be able to enter only numerical digits and + or – (plus or minus) signs and nothing else.

Solution

Make an HTML file that displays a form that consists of a label, an input text field, an error message, and a Submit button:

Validatephone.html

```
<!DOCTYPE html PUBLIC "-//W3C//DTD XHTML 1.0 Transitional//EN"
        "http://www.w3.org/TR/xhtml1/DTD/xhtml1-transitional.dtd">

<html xmlns="http://www.w3.org/1999/xhtml" xml:lang="en" lang="en">
  <head>
    <meta http-equiv="Content-Type" content="text/html; charset=utf-8"/>
    <title></title>
    <link rel="stylesheet" href="style.css" type="text/css" media="screen" />
    <script src="jquery-3.5.1.js" type="text/javascript"></script>
    <script src="validatephonejq.js" type="text/javascript"></script>
  </head>
<body>
    <form id="signup" method="post" action="">
        <div><span class="label">Enter Phone number </span><input
        type="text"  class="infobox" name="phone" /><span class="error">
        Phone number can contain only numbers, + and -</span></div>
```

```
        <input class="submit" type="submit" value="Submit">
    </form>
</body>
</html>
```

All four items in this HTML file are assigned the respective class names of `label`, `infobox`, `error`, and `submit` so that the style properties defined in the class selectors specified in the external style sheet `style.css` can be automatically applied to these items. The class selectors defined in the style sheet file are as follows:

style.css

```
.label {float: left; width: 150px; }
.infobox {width: 200px; }
.error { color: red; padding-left: 10px; }
.submit { margin-left: 150px; margin-top: 10px;}
```

The jQuery code to confirm that the input text field accepts only numerical digits along with – or + signs and nothing else is as follows:

Validatephonejq.js

```
$(document).ready(function() {
  $('.error').hide();
  $('.submit').click(function(event){
    var data=$('.infobox').val();
    if(validate_phoneno(data))
    {
      $('.error').hide();
    }
    else
    {
      $('.error').show();
      event.preventDefault();
    }
  });
});
```

```
function validate_phoneno(ph)
{
  var pattern=new RegExp(/^[0-9-+]+$/);
  return pattern.test(ph);
}
```

How It Works

The class selector .label has the float property set to left so that the next item (the input text field) may appear to its right and its width property is set to 150px to give enough space for the label message **Enter Phone number** to display. The class selector .infobox has its width property set to 200px, which ultimately becomes the width of the input text field. The class selector .error has its color property set to red to highlight it and the padding from the left is set to 10px to keep the distance from the input text field. The class selector .submit has its margin-left and margin-top properties set to 150px and 10px, respectively, to set the distance from the left boundary of the browser window and from the input text field because you want the Submit button to appear just below the input text field.

You can see in the jQuery code that the error message is made invisible at the beginning. The click event is attached to the Submit button. In the event handling function of the click event, the phone number entered by the user in the text field (that is enclosed in the span element of class name infobox) is retrieved and stored in the data variable. The data variable is passed to the validate_phoneno() method for validation.

Here, the contents of the data variable are assigned to the ph parameter of the validate_phoneno() method. In validate_phoneno(), an instance of the RegExp class is created. The regular expression passed to the RegExp constructor is /^[0-9-+]+$/ which means the data in the input text field may begin or end (^ means beginning and $ means end) with any numerical value from 0 to 9 or with a – or + sign. The + sign after the closing bracket (]) means that this pattern can repeat for one or more times (i.e., you can enter the numerals or – or + any number of times in the phone number entered in the input text field).

validate_phoneno() tests the contents of the ph parameter with the regular expression and returns true if the contents of the ph variable match with the regular expression supplied; otherwise it returns false. On the basis of the Boolean value returned by validate_phoneno(), the error message is made visible or invisible. If while entering the phone number you use a symbol other than the + or – sign, you get the error message **Phone number can contain only numbers, + and –**, as shown in Figure 4-7.

Figure 4-7. The error message displayed when data other than numbers, +, or – is entered

If the phone number consists of numbers and a + or – sign, it will be considered a valid phone number and is accepted without displaying any error message, as shown in Figure 4-8.

Figure 4-8. The phone number is considered valid if it consists of numerals and the + or – signs

4-4. Validating a User Id
Problem

You want to validate a user id that may consist of characters, numbers, and underscores and no other symbol.

Solution

Make an HTML file that displays a form that contains a label, an input text field, an error message, and a Submit button. The text of the label is set to **Enter User id** and the message is set to **User id can contain only letters, numbers or underscore**. These four items are also assigned the class names as label, infobox, error, and submit, respectively. For these class names, the respective class selectors are written in the external style sheet. The HTML file is as follows:

Validateuser.html

```
<!DOCTYPE html PUBLIC "-//W3C//DTD XHTML 1.0 Transitional//EN"
        "http://www.w3.org/TR/xhtml1/DTD/xhtml1-transitional.dtd">

<html xmlns="http://www.w3.org/1999/xhtml" xml:lang="en" lang="en">
  <head>
    <meta http-equiv="Content-Type" content="text/html; charset=utf-8"/>
    <title></title>
    <link rel="stylesheet" href="style.css" type="text/css" media="screen" />
    <script src="jquery-3.5.1.js" type="text/javascript"></script>
    <script src="validateuserjq.js" type="text/javascript"></script>
  </head>
  <body>
      <form id="signup" method="post" action="">
          <div><span class="label">Enter User id </span><input type=
          "text"  class="infobox" name="userid" /><span class="error"> User
          id can contain only letters, numbers or underscore</span></div>
          <input class="submit" type="submit" value="Submit">
      </form>
  </body>
</html>
```

The class selectors consist of style properties that are automatically applied to the HTML elements and are defined in the style sheet **style.css**. You use the same style sheet file (style.css) that you used in Recipe 4-3.

The jQuery code to accept the user id that consists of numerals, characters, and underscores only is as follows:

Validateuserjq.js

```
$(document).ready(function() {
  $('.error').hide();
  $('.submit').click(function(event){
    var data=$('.infobox').val();
    if(validate_userid(data))
    {
      $('.error').hide();
    }
```

```
    else
    {
      $('.error').show();
      event.preventDefault();
    }
  });
});

function validate_userid(uid)
{
  var pattern= new RegExp(/^[a-zA-Z0-9_]+$/);
  return pattern.test(uid);
}
```

How It Works

You can see in this jQuery code that the error message is made invisible at the beginning. The click event is attached to the Submit button. In the event handling function of the click event, the user id entered by the user in the text field (that is enclosed in the span element of class name infobox) is retrieved and stored in the data variable. The data variable is passed to the validate_userid() function for validation. The contents of the data variable are assigned to the uid parameter of the validate_userid() method.

In validate_userid(), an instance of the RegExp class is created. The regular expression passed to the RegExp constructor is /^[a-zA-Z0-9_]+$/ which means the user id entered in the input text field may begin or end (^ means beginning and $ means end) with any character from a to z (uppercase or lowercase) or with a numerical value from 0 to 9 or with a _ sign. The + sign after the closing bracket (]) means that this pattern can repeat for one or more times (i.e., you can enter characters, numerals, or a _ sign any number of times in the input text field).

validate_userid() tests the contents of the uid parameter with the regular expression and returns true if the contents of the uid variable match the regular expression supplied or else it returns false. On the basis of the Boolean value returned by the validate_userid() function, the error message is made visible or invisible. If while entering the user id you use a symbol other than the _ sign, you get the error message **User id can contain only letters, numbers or underscore** as shown in Figure 4-9.

Enter User id   Bintu-Harwani   User id can contain only letters, numbers or underscore

Submit

Figure 4-9. *The error message displayed if any symbol other than _ is used in the user id field*

If the user id consists of characters, numbers or _, it is considered a valid user id and is accepted without any error message displayed, as shown in Figure 4-10.

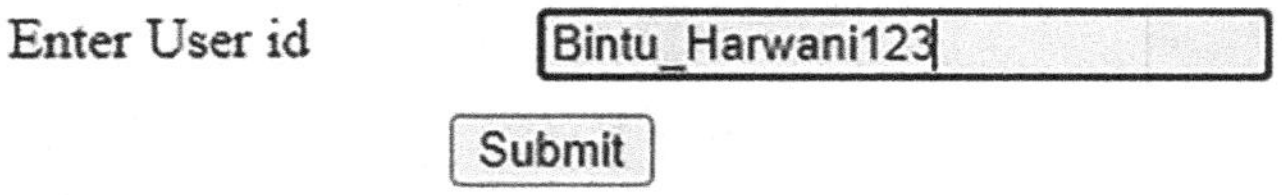

Enter User id   Bintu_Harwani123

Submit

Figure 4-10. *The user id is considered valid if it consists of characters, numerals, and the _ symbol*

4-5. Validating a Date

Problem

You want to validate a date in the format mm/dd/yyyy or mm-dd-yyyy. If the date entered does not match with either format, you want to display an error message.

Solution

Make an HTML file that displays a form that contains a label, an input text field, an error message, and a Submit button. The text of the label is set to **Enter Date of Birth** and the error message is set to **Invalid Date**. The four items are assigned the class names label, infobox, error, and submit, respectively. For the class names, the respective class selectors are written in the external style sheet. The HTML file is as follows:

Validatedate.html

```
<!DOCTYPE html PUBLIC "-//W3C//DTD XHTML 1.0 Transitional//EN"
        "http://www.w3.org/TR/xhtml1/DTD/xhtml1-transitional.dtd">

<html xmlns="http://www.w3.org/1999/xhtml" xml:lang="en" lang="en">
  <head>
    <meta http-equiv="Content-Type" content="text/html; charset=utf-8"/>
    <title></title>
    <link rel="stylesheet" href="style.css" type="text/css" media="screen" />
    <script src="jquery-3.5.1.js" type="text/javascript"></script>
    <script src="validatedatejq.js" type="text/javascript"></script>
  </head>
  <body>
    <form id="signup" method="post" action="">
        <div><span class="label">Enter Date of Birth </span><input
        type="text"  class="infobox" name="dob" /><span class="error">
        Invalid Date. Correct format is mm/dd/yyyy or mm-dd -yyyy
        </span></div>
        <input class="submit" type="submit" value="Submit">
    </form>
  </body>
</html>
```

The class selectors consist of style properties that are automatically applied to the HTML elements and are defined in the style sheet **style.css**. Use the same style sheet file (style.css) from Recipe 4-3.

The jQuery code to accept the date in the format mm/dd/yyyy or mm-dd -yyyy is as follows:

Validatedatejq.js

```
$(document).ready(function() {
  $('.error').hide();
  $('.submit').click(function(event){
    var data=$('.infobox').val();
    if(validate_date(data))
```

```
   {
     $('.error').hide();
   }
   else
   {
     $('.error').show();
     event.preventDefault();
   }
 });
});
function validate_date(date)
{
  var pattern= new RegExp(/\b\d{1,2}[\/-]\d{1,2}[\/-]\d{4}\b/);
  return pattern.test(date);
}
```

How It Works

The error message is made invisible at the beginning in the jQuery code. Then, a click event is attached to the Submit button. In the event handling function of the click event, the date entered by the user in the input text field (that is enclosed in the span element of class name infobox) is retrieved and stored in the data variable. The data variable is passed to the validate_date() function for validation. The contents of the data variable are assigned to the date parameter of the validate_date() function. In the validate_date() function, an instance of the RegExp class is created. The regular expression passed to the RegExp constructor is /\b\d{1,2}[\/-]\d{1,2}[\/-]\d{4}\b/.

The regular expression is explained as follows:

- The \b at the beginning and at the end of a regular expression denotes the word boundary (i.e., the pattern must exactly match the same pattern).

- \d{1,2} means there can be 1 to 2 digits.

- [\/-] means there can be the symbols / or –.

- \d{1,2} means there can be 1 to 2 digits.

- [\/-]means there can be the symbols / or –.

- \d{4} means there must be exactly 4 digits.

Hence, the date entered in the input text field must begin with 1 or 2 digits (month) followed by the / or – symbol. Again there can be 1 or 2 digits (day), followed by the / or – symbol, and finally there must be exactly 4 digits (year). The validate_date() function tests the contents of the date parameter with the regular expression and returns true if the contents of the date variable match with the regular expression supplied or else it returns false. On the basis of the Boolean value returned by the validate_date() function, the error message is made visible or invisible.

Suppose you enter the date incorrectly. Instead of 4 digits, you enter the year in 2 digits. You will get an error message of Invalid Date as shown in Figure 4-11.

Enter Date of Birth | 07-15-90 | Invalid Date. Correct format is mm/dd/yyyy or mm-dd -yyyy
Submit

Figure 4-11. *The error message Invalid Date is displayed if the date is entered incorrectly*

If the date is entered correctly with either the / or – delimiter used between the day, month, and year, it will be accepted without any error message as shown in Figure 4-12.

Enter Date of Birth | 07-15-1990 |
Submit

Figure 4-12. *The date is accepted without any error message if it follows the specified pattern*

4-6. Validating an Email Address

Problem

You want to validate an email address (i.e., you want to confirm that the email address consists of characters and numbers along with the @ and . symbols).

Solution

Make an HTML file that displays a form that contains a label, an input text field, an error message, and a Submit button. The text of the label is set to **Enter Email Id** and the error message is set to **Invalid Email Address**. The four items are assigned the class names `label`, `infobox`, `error`, and `submit`, respectively. For these class names, the respective class selectors are written in the external style sheet. The HTML file is as follows:

Validateemail.html

```
<!DOCTYPE html PUBLIC "-//W3C//DTD XHTML 1.0 Transitional//EN"
        "http://www.w3.org/TR/xhtml1/DTD/xhtml1-transitional.dtd">

<html xmlns="http://www.w3.org/1999/xhtml" xml:lang="en" lang="en">
  <head>
    <meta http-equiv="Content-Type" content="text/html; charset=utf-8"/>
    <title></title>
    <link rel="stylesheet" href="style.css" type="text/css" media="screen" />
    <script src="jquery-3.5.1.js" type="text/javascript"></script>
    <script src="validateemailjq.js" type="text/javascript"></script>
  </head>
  <body>
    <form id="signup" method="post" action="">
      <div><span class="label">Enter Email Id </span><input type="text"
      class="infobox" name="email" /><span class="error"> Invalid Email
      Address. Correct email address is the one that essentially has @ sign
      and a . (period) after  @ sign. It should not have any other special
      symbol except hyphen or underscore and must be termnated by any
      letter only </span></div>
      <input class="submit" type="submit" value="Submit">
    </form>
  </body>
</html>
```

The class selectors consist of style properties that are automatically applied to the HTML elements and are defined in the style sheet `style.css,` the same style sheet file used in Recipe 4-3.

The jQuery code to accept the email address and validate it is as follows:

Validateemailjq.js

```
$(document).ready(function() {
  $('.error').hide();
  $('.submit').click(function(event){
    var data=$('.infobox').val();
    if(valid_email(data))
    {
      $('.error').hide();
    }
    else
    {
      $('.error').show();
    event.preventDefault();
    }
  });
});

function valid_email(email)
{
  var pattern= new RegExp(/^[\w-]+(\.[\w-]+)*@([\w-]+\.)+[a-zA-Z]+$/);
  return pattern.test(email);
}
```

How It Works

The error message is made invisible at the beginning in the jQuery code. Then, a click event is attached to the Submit button. In the event handling function of the click event, the email address entered by the user in the input text field (that is enclosed in the span element of class name infobox) is retrieved and is stored in the data variable. The data variable is passed to the validate_email() function for validation. The contents of the data variable are assigned to the email parameter of the validate_email() function. In the validate_email() function, an instance of the RegExp class is created. The regular expression passed to the RegExp constructor is /^[\w-]+(\.[\w-]+)*@([\w-]+\.)+[a-zA-Z]+$/.

The regular expression is explained as follows:

- * /^[\w-]+ means there can be a letter, number, underscore, or hyphen at the beginning of the email address. ^ means at the beginning. \w refers to letter, number, and underscore. The + sign after the closing bracket (]) means one or more times.

- (\.[\w-]+)* means the pattern consisting of a . (period) followed by a letter, numeral, underscore, and hyphen for 1 or more times can occur for zero or more times. The symbol * at the end of the pattern means 0 or more times.

- @ means the symbol @ must occur after the above said pattern.

- ([\w-]+\.)+ means the letter, numeral, underscore, and hyphen can occur for one or more times followed by a . (period). And this combined thing (character, numeral, underscore, hyphen, and .) can occur for one or more times.

- [a-zA-Z]+$/ means at the end of the email address or in other words, the email address must be terminated by any uppercase or lowercase letter that may occur for one or more times. The $ means the end.

Hence, the email address entered in the input text field must begin with letter(s), number(s), underscore(s), or hyphen(s) followed by a . (period) and again followed by letter(s), number(s), underscore(s), or hyphen(s) for one or more times. After that, there has to be the symbol @ (at) which is followed by letter(s), number(s), underscore(s), or hyphen(s) followed by a . (period). The email address must be terminated by any uppercase or lowercase letter.

The `validate_email()` function tests the contents of the `email` parameter with the regular expression and returns `true` if the contents of the email parameter match the regular expression supplied or else it returns `false`. On the basis of the Boolean value returned by the `validate_email()` function, the error message is made visible or invisible.

Suppose in the email address you don't enter a . (period). You will get the error message **Invalid Email Address** shown in Figure 4-13.

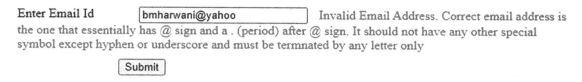

Enter Email Id [bmharwani@yahoo] Invalid Email Address. Correct email address is the one that essentially has @ sign and a . (period) after @ sign. It should not have any other special symbol except hyphen or underscore and must be termnated by any letter only

[Submit]

Figure 4-13. *The error message displayed in case of an invalid email address*

If the email address is correctly entered because it contains @ and . (period), it will be accepted without any error message, as shown in Figure 4-14.

Enter Email Id [bmharwani@yahoo.com]

[Submit]

Figure 4-14. *The email address is accepted if it contains the . and @ symbols*

4-7. Checking Whether a Checkbox Is Checked or Not

Problem

You have several checkboxes where each designates an item being sold at a fast food counter. You want to confirm that at least one of the checkboxes is checked when selecting the Submit button. If none of the checkboxes is selected, you want to display an error message.

Solution

Make an HTML file that displays four checkboxes, an error message, and an empty paragraph element for displaying the result (the total bill of the food items selected). The HTML file is as follows:

Checkcheckbox.html

```
<!DOCTYPE html PUBLIC "-//W3C//DTD XHTML 1.0 Transitional//EN"
        "http://www.w3.org/TR/xhtml1/DTD/xhtml1-transitional.dtd">
```

```
<html xmlns="http://www.w3.org/1999/xhtml" xml:lang="en" lang="en">
  <head>
    <meta http-equiv="Content-Type" content="text/html; charset=utf-8"/>
    <title></title>
    <link rel="stylesheet" href="style1.css" type="text/css" media="screen" />
    <script src="jquery-3.5.1.js" type="text/javascript"></script>
    <script src="checkcheckboxjq.js" type="text/javascript"></script>
  </head>
  <body>
    <form>
      <input type="checkbox"  id="pizza" name="pizza" value=5
      class="infobox">Pizza $5 <br>
      <input type="checkbox"  id="hotdog" name="hotdog" value=2
      class="infobox">HotDog $2<br>
      <input type="checkbox"  id="coke" name="coke" value=1
      class="infobox">Coke $1<br>
      <input type="checkbox"  id="fries" name="fries" value=3
      class="infobox">French Fries $3<br>
      <p class="error">Select at least one checkbox </p>
      <p class="result"></p>
      <input class="submit" type="submit" value="Submit">
    </form>
  </body>
</html>
```

The class selectors to apply the style properties automatically to the HTML elements are defined in the external style sheet **style1.css**, as follows:

Style1.css

```
.infobox { margin-top: 15px; }
.error { color: red; }
```

The jQuery code to see whether a checkbox is checked or not is as follows:

Checkcheckboxjq.js

```
$(document).ready(function() {
    $('.error').hide();
    $('.submit').click(function(event){
        var count=0;
        var amt=0;
        $('form').find(':checkbox').each(function(){
            if($(this).is(':checked'))
            {
                count++;
                amt=amt+parseInt($(this).val());
            }
        });
        if(count==0)
        {
            $('p.result').hide();
            $('.error').show();
         }
        else
        {
            $('.error').hide();
            $('p.result').show();
            $('p.result').text('Your bill is $ '+amt);
        }
        event.preventDefault();
    });
});
```

Checking with the length Method

In the following jQuery code, you confirm whether any of the checkboxes are checked or not before using the loop to inspect each of them individually:

Checkinglengthjq.js

```javascript
$(document).ready(function() {
    $('.error').hide();
    $('.submit').click(function(event){
        var amt=0;
        var count=$('input:checked').length;
        if(count==0)
        {
            $('p.result').hide();
            $('.error').show();
        }
        else
        {
            $('form').find(':checkbox').each(function(){
                if($(this).is(':checked'))
                {
                    amt=amt+parseInt($(this).val());
                }
            });
            $('.error').hide();
            $('p.result').show();
            $('p.result').text('Your bill is $ '+amt);
        }
        event.preventDefault();
    });
});
```

How It Works

In the HTML file, you can see that the four checkboxes are assigned the class name infobox and represent the four items sold at a fast food counter: Pizza, HotDog, Coke, and French Fries, along with their prices. The paragraph element to display an error message is assigned the class name error and its text displays the error message **Select at least one checkbox**. There is one more paragraph element to display the bill of the food items selected via the checkboxes and it is assigned the class name result and is currently empty. It will be assigned the text to display the bill via jQuery code.

The style sheet defines two class selectors: .infobox to be applied to the checkboxes and .error to be applied to the paragraph element that is meant for displaying error message. The .infobox class selector contains a property called margin-top set to 15px to create a sufficient vertical gap among the checkboxes displayed. The class selector .error contains the style property color set to red so that the error message appears in red (so that it appears highlighted).

In the first jQuery code, the error message is set to be invisible. Then, you attach a click event to the Submit button. On selecting the Submit button, its event handling function is executed and does several tasks. In the event handling function, you first initialize a counter count set to 0 (it will be used to count the number of checkboxes that are checked) and another variable called amt set to 0 that will be used to total the bill of the food items selected. Using the .each() function, you check all the checkboxes of the form one by one, and if any check box is found checked, you increment the value of the counter variable count by 1 and also the amount of that food item is added to the amt variable. That is, you set the count of the checked checkboxes in the count variable and the total amount of the selected checkboxes in amt variable. After inspecting all of the checkboxes, if you find that the value of the count variable is 0, meaning none of the checkboxes are selected, you make the paragraph element meant for displaying the error message visible to display the error message **Select at least one checkbox** on the screen. If the value of the count variable is not 0 (meaning at least one of the checkboxes is selected), you make the paragraph element of class result visible (and hide the paragraph of class error)and assign it the text **Your bill is $+amt** where amt is the variable where the total amount for the food items selected is stored.

If you select none of the checkboxes and press the Submit button, an error message of **Select at least one checkbox** will appear on the screen as shown in Figure 4-15.

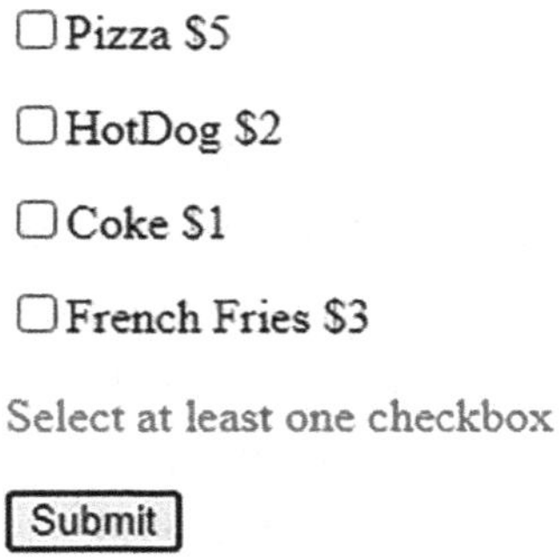

☐ Pizza $5

☐ HotDog $2

☐ Coke $1

☐ French Fries $3

Select at least one checkbox

[Submit]

Figure 4-15. *The error message is displayed if no checkbox is selected*

If you select one checkbox, the error message will become invisible and the bill of the selected food item will appear as shown in Figure 4-16.

☐ Pizza $5

☐ HotDog $2

☑ Coke $1

☐ French Fries $3

Your bill is $ 1

[Submit]

Figure 4-16. *The bill for the one selected food item is displayed*

If you select more than one checkbox, the total amount of the selected food items will be displayed in the form of bill as shown in Figure 4-17.

☑ Pizza $5

☐ HotDog $2

☑ Coke $1

☑ French Fries $3

Your bill is $ 9

Submit

Figure 4-17. *The total bill amount of the three food items is displayed*

In the jQuery code from the *Checking with the Length Method* section, you make use of the statement

```
var count=$('input:checked').length;
```

to find the count of the total number of checkboxes checked. If the count is zero, there is no point of inspecting all the checkboxes one by one to compute the total of the items selected. When the value of the count variable is non zero, you make use of the .each() function to inspect each checkbox one by one to compute the total amount of the food items selected. The output of this jQuery code will be exactly the same as shown in Figures 4-15 through 4-17.

4-8. Checking If a Radio Button Is Selected
Problem

You have several radio buttons and each designates the credit card that the visitor may use to make payments. You want to confirm that one of the radio buttons is selected by the user when selecting the Submit button. If no radio button is selected, you want to display an error message.

Solution

The following HTML file displays three radio buttons. Each radio button is assigned the class name infobox to be used for validation checks and to apply styles. The error message is displayed via a paragraph element with the class name error and the Submit button is of class name submit.

Checkradio.html

```
<!DOCTYPE html PUBLIC "-//W3C//DTD XHTML 1.0 Transitional//EN"
        "http://www.w3.org/TR/xhtml1/DTD/xhtml1-transitional.dtd">

<html xmlns="http://www.w3.org/1999/xhtml" xml:lang="en" lang="en">
  <head>
    <meta http-equiv="Content-Type" content="text/html; charset=utf-8"/>
    <title></title>
    <link rel="stylesheet" href="style1.css" type="text/css" media="screen" />
    <script src="jquery-3.5.1.js" type="text/javascript"></script>
    <script src="checkradiojq.js" type="text/javascript"></script>
  </head>
  <body>
    <form>
          <input type="radio"  name="paymode" class="infobox"
          value="Master Card">Master Card <br>
          <input type="radio"  name="paymode" class="infobox"
          value="ANZ Grindlay Card">ANZ Grindlay Card<br>
          <input type="radio"  name="paymode" class="infobox"
          value="Visa Card">Visa Card<br>
          <p class="error">Select at least one Option </p>
          <p class="result"></p>
          <input class="submit" type="submit" value="Submit">
    </form>
  </body>
</html>
```

The external style sheet contains the following class selectors:

Style1.css

```
.infobox { margin-top: 15px; }
.error { color: red; }
```

The jQuery code to confirm that at least one radio button is selected is as follows:

Checkradiojq.js

```
1.      $(document).ready(function() {
2.           $('.error').hide();
3.           $('.submit').click(function(event){
4.                var amt=0;
5.                var count=$('input:checked').length;
6.                if(count==0)
7.                {
8.                     $('p.result').hide();
9.                     $('.error').show();
10.          }
11.          else
12.          {
13.               $('.error').hide();
14.               $('p.result').show();
15.               $('p.result').text('You have selected
                  '+$('input:checked').attr("value"));
16.          }
17.          event.preventDefault();
18.      });
19. });
```

How It Works

In the style sheet file, the class selector .infobox contains the margin-top property set to 15px to keep spacing among the radio buttons and the class selector .error assigns the red color to the error messages.

The explanation of the jQuery code statement is as follows:

2. The error message in the paragraph element of class error is made hidden.

3. The click event is attached to the Submit button.

5. Find out the count of the radio button that is checked (if any) and store it in the count variable.

8. If no radio button is selected, hide the paragraph element of class result (meant to display the name of the credit card selected).

9. The error message in the paragraph element of class error is displayed if no radio button is selected.

15. Assign the text **You have selected n** where n is the value of the radio button selected.

On execution, if you select the Submit button without selecting any of the radio buttons, you get the error message **Select at least one Option** shown in Figure 4-18.

Figure 4-18. *The error message displayed if no radio button is selected*

If you select a radio button and select the Submit button as shown in Figure 4-19, the message is displayed confirming the name of the credit card selected.

○ Master Card

○ ANZ Grindlay Card

◉ Visa Card

You have selected Visa Card

Submit

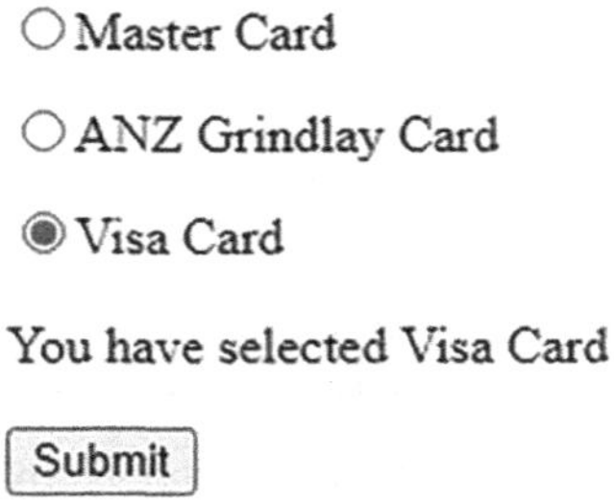

Figure 4-19. *The text of the selected radio button is displayed*

4-9. Checking That an Option in a Select Element is Selected

Problem

You have a dropdown list (select element) showing some food items. You want to confirm that the user selected an option from the dropdown list before pressing the Submit button or else an error message is displayed.

Solution

The following HTML file displays a dropdown list box containing a few food items. The select element with the help of which the dropdown list is displayed is assigned the class name infobox so as to apply the style properties defined in the class selector .infobox (written in the style sheet file style.css) directly to it. The label message **Select the Food Item** is displayed via a span element with the class name label. The error message is displayed via a paragraph element with the class name error and the Submit button is assigned the class name submit.

Checkselect.html

```
<!DOCTYPE html PUBLIC "-//W3C//DTD XHTML 1.0 Transitional//EN"
        "http://www.w3.org/TR/xhtml1/DTD/xhtml1-transitional.dtd">

<html xmlns="http://www.w3.org/1999/xhtml" xml:lang="en" lang="en">
  <head>
    <meta http-equiv="Content-Type" content="text/html; charset=utf-8"/>
    <title></title>
    <link rel="stylesheet" href="style.css" type="text/css" media="screen" />
    <script src="jquery-3.5.1.js" type="text/javascript"></script>
    <script src="checkselectjq.js" type="text/javascript"></script>
  </head>
  <body>
   <form>
      <span class="label">Select the Food Item </span>
      <select id="food" class="infobox">
         <option value="0">Select a Food</option>
```

```
        <option value="Pizza $5">Pizza $5</option>
        <option value="HotDog $2">HotDog $2</option>
<option value="Coke $1">Coke $1</option>
<option value="French Fries $3">French Fries $3</option>
</select>
<p class="error">You have not selected any Option</p>
<p class="result"></p>
<input class="submit" type="submit" value="Submit">
</form>
  </body>
</html>
```

The external style sheet contains the following class selectors that will be automatically applied to the respective HTML element of the specified class:

style.css

```
.label {float: left; width: 150px; }
.infobox {width: 150px; }
.error { color: red; padding-left: 10px; }
.submit { margin-left: 150px; margin-top: 10px;}
```

The jQuery code to confirm that the option from the dropdown list is selected is as follows:

Checkselectjq.js

```
$(document).ready(function() {
    $('.error').hide();
    $('.submit').click(function(event){
        var count=$('select option:selected').val();
        if(count==0)
        {
            $('p.result').hide();
            $('.error').show();
        }
        else
        {
```

```
            $('.error').hide();
            $('p.result').show();
            $('p.result').text('You have selected '+$('select
            option:selected').text());
        }
        event.preventDefault();
    });
});
```

How It Works

In the style sheet file, the class selector .label contains the float property set to the value left to make the label appear on its left (creating space for the dropdown list to appear on its right) and the width property is set to 150px to define the width that the label can consume. The class selector .infobox contains the width property set to 150px to specify the width for the dropdown list and the class selector .error assigns red to the error message and makes the error message appear at the distance of 10px from the left side of the browser window. The class selector submit contains the margin-left property set to value 150px to make the Submit button appear at the distance of 150px from the left side of the browser window (so that it appears below the dropdown list) and the margin-top property is set to 10px to keep some spacing from the above element that may appear (the error or result message).

In the jQuery code, you initially hide the paragraph element of class error meant to display the error message. Then you attach a click event to the Submit button. The statement

```
var count=$('select option:selected').val();
```

retrieves the value of the option selected from the select element and stores it in the variable count. If the value of count is 0, meaning the user has not selected any option, you make the error message appear on the screen by making the paragraph element of class .error visible, and if the value of count variable is non zero, you make the paragraph element of class result display the result using the following statement:

You have selected '+$('select option:selected').text());

which displays the text of the option that is selected from the select element.

On execution, if you press the Submit button without selecting any option from the select element, you get the error message **You have not selected any Option** shown in Figure 4-20.

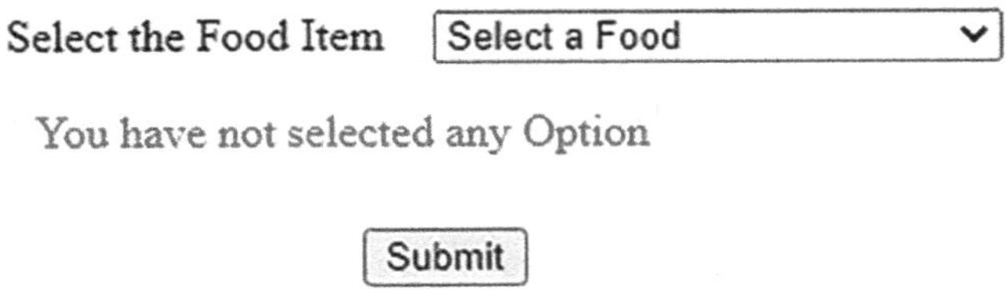

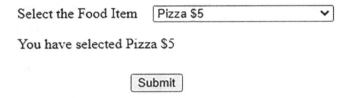

Figure 4-20. *The error message is displayed if no option is selected from the select element*

If you select any option from the list and press the Submit button, you get the message showing the option selected as shown in Figure 4-21.

Select the Food Item   Pizza $5 ⌄

You have selected Pizza $5

Submit

Figure 4-21. *The text of the selected option of the select element is displayed*

Multiple Select

Let's modify the above solution to allow visitors to select more than one option from the select element. To select more than one option from the select element, use the MULTIPLE attribute along with the select element as follows:

Multiselect.html

```
<!DOCTYPE html PUBLIC "-//W3C//DTD XHTML 1.0 Transitional//EN"
        "http://www.w3.org/TR/xhtml1/DTD/xhtml1-transitional.dtd">

<html xmlns="http://www.w3.org/1999/xhtml" xml:lang="en" lang="en">
  <head>
    <meta http-equiv="Content-Type" content="text/html; charset=utf-8"/>
    <title></title>
    <link rel="stylesheet" href="style.css" type="text/css" media="screen" />
```

```
    <script src="jquery-3.5.1.js" type="text/javascript"></script>
    <script src="multiselectjq.js" type="text/javascript"></script>
  </head>
  <body>
    <form>
        <span class="label">Select the Food Item </span>
        <select id="food" class="infobox" MULTIPLE>
            <option value="0" selected="0">Select a Food</option>
            <option value="Pizza $5">Pizza $5</option>
            <option value="HotDog $2">HotDog $2</option>
            <option value="Coke $1">Coke $1</option>
            <option value="French Fries $3">French Fries $3</option>
        </select>
        <p class="error">You have not selected any Option </p>
        <p class="result"></p>
        <input class="submit" type="submit" value="Submit">
    </form>
  </body>
</html>
```

The MULTIPLE attribute when attached to select element will allow you to select more than one option (making use of the Ctrl or Shift key). Using the same jQuery code and style sheet (style.css), you will get the message displaying all the options selected by the user from the select element as shown in Figure 4-22.

Figure 4-22. *All selected options of the select element are displayed without a space in between*

You can see that the options selected are displayed without any space in between. To separate the options with a comma (,) modify the jQuery code as follows:

Multiselectjq.js

```
$(document).ready(function() {
  $('.error').hide();
  $('.submit').click(function(event){
    var selectedopts="";
    var count=$('select option:selected').val();
    if(count==0)
    {
      $('p.result').hide();
      $('.error').show();
    }
    else
    {
      $('select option:selected').each(function(){
        selectedopts+=$(this).text()+",";
      });
      $('.error').hide();
      $('p.result').show();
      $('p.result').text('You have selected '+ selectedopts);
    }
    event.preventDefault();
  });
});
```

You have defined a string variable called selectedopts in the above jQuery code and all of the options selected from the select element are picked up by using the .each() method and you concatenate them to the selectedopts variables along with a comma (,). When the text of all the selected options is added to the selectedopts variable, you display its contents via the paragraph element of class result. See Figure 4-23.

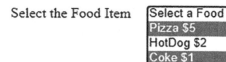

You have selected Pizza $5,Coke $1,

Submit

Figure 4-23. *All selected options of the select element are displayed with a comma in between*

If you don't select any option from the select element and yet press the Submit button, you get the error message shown in Figure 4-24.

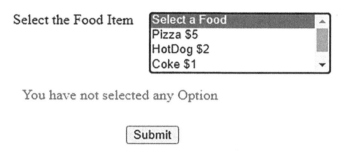

You have not selected any Option

Submit

Figure 4-24. *The error message is displayed if no option is selected*

4-10. Applying Styles to Options and a Form Button

Problem

You have a dropdown list (select element) showing food items and you want to apply styles to the options of the select element.

Solution

For this recipe, use the same HTML file from Recipe 4-9. Rename that HTML file as multiselectstyle.html. You need to add the reference of the style sheet as well. In the style sheet, you need to add one type selector called option to apply its style properties

to all of the options of the select element automatically and also a CSS class named
.meal to apply a style to the odd numbered options of the select element. The style sheet
is as follows:

styleoption.css

```
.label {float: left; width: 150px; }
.infobox {width: 150px; }
.error { color: red; padding-left: 10px; }
.submit { margin-left: 150px; margin-top: 10px;}

option{
    background-color:red;
    color:white;
}

.meal{
    background-color:cyan;
    color:blue;
}
```

To make the options appear colorful, you will be applying different styles to even
numbered and odd numbered options of the select element. The type selector option
will apply style properties to all even options of the select element, setting their
background color to red and their foreground color to white whereas the style rule .meal
will be applied to only odd numbered options of the select elements via the jQuery code,
setting their background color to cyan and their foreground color to blue.

To apply the style rule meal to the odd numbered options of the select element, add
following statement to the jQuery code:

```
$('option:odd').addClass('meal');
```

The overall jQuery code is as follows (for details of the validation logic, see Recipe 4-9).
In the HTML file, modify the reference to the jQuery file.

Optionsjq.js

```
$(document).ready(function() {
  $('.error').hide();
  $('option:odd').addClass('meal');
```

```
$('.submit').click(function(event){
  var selectedopts="";
  var count=$('select option:selected').val();
  if(count==0)
  {
    $('p.result').hide();
    $('.error').show();
  }
  else
  {
    $('select option:selected').each(function(){
      selectedopts+=$(this).text()+",";
    });
    $('.error').hide();
    $('p.result').show();
    $('p.result').text('You have selected '+ selectedopts);
  }
  event.preventDefault();
});
});
```

How It Works

On execution of the above jQuery code, you find that even numbered and odd numbered options of the select elements appear in different foreground and background colors, as shown in Figure 4-25.

Figure 4-25. *Styles applied to options of the select element*

Styling a Form Button

Let's apply styles to the Submit button shown in Figure 4-24 to make it appear attractive. For this, you need to modify the style properties of the class selector `.submit` defined in the style sheet `style.css` as follows:

Styleoption2.css

```
.label {float: left; width: 150px; }
.infobox {width: 150px; }
.error { color: red; padding-left: 10px; }
.submit { margin-left: 150px; margin-top: 10px;font-size:1.5em;
background-color:green;color:blue;}

option{
    background-color:red;
    color:white;
}

.meal{
    background-color:cyan;
    color:blue;
}
```

You can see that the class selector `.submit` contains several properties:

- The `margin-left` property set to 150px to make it appear at the distance of 150px from the left boundary of the browser window (to make it appear below the select element).

- The `margin-top` property set to 10px to create some spacing from the select element at its top.

- The `font-size` property set to 1.5em to increase the font size to 150% of the default font size.

- The `background-color` and `color` properties set to values green and blue, respectively, to set a blue color over a green background.

The Submit button appears as shown in Figure 4-26.

Select the Food Item

Figure 4-26. *Styles applied to the Submit button*

Creating an Image Submit Button

Let's now replace the Submit button with an image that will act as a submit button. First you need to have an image file: submit.jpg as shown in Figure 4-27. You also need to modify the class selector .submit as follows in the style sheet file:

Styleoption3.css

```
.label {float: left; width: 150px; }
.infobox {width: 150px; }
.error { color: red; padding-left: 10px; }
.submit { margin-left: 150px; margin-top: 10px;width:150px;height:40px;}

option{
    background-color:red;
    color:white;
}

.meal{
    background-color:cyan;
    color:blue;
}
```

The class selector .submit defines the space of the image (of the Submit button) from the left boundary of the browser window as 150px, the distance from the top element as 10px, and the width and height of the image itself to be 150px and 40px, respectively.

To apply the image in submit.jpg in place of the Submit button, modify the HTML code as follows:

Multiselectstyle2.html

```
<!DOCTYPE html PUBLIC "-//W3C//DTD XHTML 1.0 Transitional//EN"
        "http://www.w3.org/TR/xhtml1/DTD/xhtml1-transitional.dtd">

<html xmlns="http://www.w3.org/1999/xhtml" xml:lang="en" lang="en">
  <head>
    <meta http-equiv="Content-Type" content="text/html; charset=utf-8"/>
    <title></title>
    <link rel="stylesheet" href="styleoption3.css" type="text/css"
    media="screen" />
    <script src="jquery-3.5.1.js" type="text/javascript"></script>
    <script src="optionsjq.js" type="text/javascript"></script>
  </head>
  <body>
    <form>
        <span class="label">Select the Food Item </span>
        <select id="food" class="infobox" MULTIPLE>
            <option value="0">Select a Food</option>
            <option value="Pizza $5">Pizza $5</option>
            <option value="HotDog $2">HotDog $2</option>
            <option value="Coke $1">Coke $1</option>
            <option value="French Fries $3">French Fries $3</option>
        </select>
        <p class="error">You have not selected any Option </p>
        <p class="result"></p>
        <input class="submit" type="image" value="Submit" src="submit.jpg">
    </form>
</body>
</html>
```

You can see in the above code (marked in bold) that specifying the type attribute to image and specifying the image file name in the src attribute makes the Submit button appear in the form of an image as shown in Figure 4-27.

Select the Food Item

Figure 4-27. *Image applied to Submit button*

4-11. Checking and Unchecking All Checkboxes Together

Problem

You have several checkboxes where each designates an item being sold at a fast food counter. You want a **Check All** checkbox which if checked should check all the other checkboxes. If this checkbox is unchecked, it must uncheck all other checkboxes.

Solution

Make an HTML file that displays five checkboxes (four for the food items and one for collectively checking and unchecking them). The HTML file is as follows:

Allcheckbox.html

```
<!DOCTYPE html PUBLIC "-//W3C//DTD XHTML 1.0 Transitional//EN"
        "http://www.w3.org/TR/xhtml1/DTD/xhtml1-transitional.dtd">

<html xmlns="http://www.w3.org/1999/xhtml" xml:lang="en" lang="en">
  <head>
    <meta http-equiv="Content-Type" content="text/html; charset=utf-8"/>
    <title></title>
    <link rel="stylesheet" href="style2.css" type="text/css" media="screen" />
    <script src="jquery-3.5.1.js" type="text/javascript"></script>
    <script src="allcheckboxjq.js" type="text/javascript"></script>
  </head>
```

```
<body>
    <form>
        <div class="infobox"><input type="checkbox" id="checkall">Check/
        Uncheck all Checkboxes</div>
        <div class="infobox"><input type="checkbox"  id="pizza"
        name="pizza" value=5>Pizza $5</div>
         <div class="infobox"> <input type="checkbox"  id="hotdog"
         name="hotdog" value=2>HotDog $2</div>
        <div class="infobox"><input type="checkbox"  id="coke" name="coke"
        value=1>Coke $1</div>
        <div class="infobox"><input type="checkbox"  id="fries"
        name="fries" value=3>French Fries $3</div>
    </form>
 </body>
</html>
```

In the style sheet, define the class selector .infobox as follows:

Style2.css

```
.infobox{ padding: 5px; }
```

The padding property is set to 5px to create spacing among the checkboxes.

The jQuery code to check and uncheck all the checkboxes on selecting the **Check All** checkbox and display the bill of the selected food items is as follows:

Allcheckboxjq.js

```
$(document).ready(function() {
    $('#checkall').click(function(){
        $("input[type='checkbox']").attr('checked', $('#checkall').
        is(':checked'));
    });
    $('form').find(':checkbox').click(function(){
        var amt=0;
        $('div').filter(':gt(0)').find(':checkbox').each(function(){
            if($('div:gt(0)'))
            {
                if($(this).is(':checked'))
```

```
            {
                    amt=amt+parseInt($(this).val());
            }
        }
    });
    $('p').remove();
    $('<p>').insertAfter('div:eq(4)');
    $('p').text('Your bill is $ '+amt);
    });
});
```

How It Works

In the HTML file, you can see that the five checkboxes are assigned the class name
infobox, out of which four checkboxes represent the four items sold at a fast food
counter: Pizza, HotDog, Coke, and French Fries, along with their prices.

In the jQuery code, you attach a click event to the **Check All** checkbox (element of id
checkall). The statement is

```
$("input[type='checkbox']").attr('checked', $('#checkall').is(':checked'));
```

To understand this statement, let's get a small introduction to the .attr() and .is()
methods that are used in this statement.

.attr( )

The .attr() method is used to set the attributes of the selected element(s).

Syntax:

```
.attr(attribute, value)
```

.is( )

The .is() method checks the selected element(s) with a selector and returns true if the
any of the selected elements match with the selector or else it returns false.

Syntax:

```
.is(selector)
```

The part of the above statement, $('#checkall').is(':checked'), checks if the checkbox of checkall is checked or not. If the checkbox (of id checkall) is checked, the .is() method will return true. If the .is() method returns true, all the input elements of checkbox (i.e., all the checkboxes) will be set to checked mode, and obviously all of them will be set to unchecked mode if the .is() method returns false. Since the user is also allowed to check any individual check box, you check the status of each checkbox that has an index value greater than 0 (because the checkbox with the index value 0 is the **Check All** checkbox). The value of all the checkboxes is added to the amt variable. To display the bill, you create a paragraph element and add the text **Your bill is amt** (where amt is the number value contained in the amt variable) and insert this paragraph element after the div element of index value 4 (i.e., after the last checkbox).

If you select the **Check All** checkbox, all the checkboxes will be checked and the sum of their value is displayed in the form of bill, as shown in Figure 4-28.

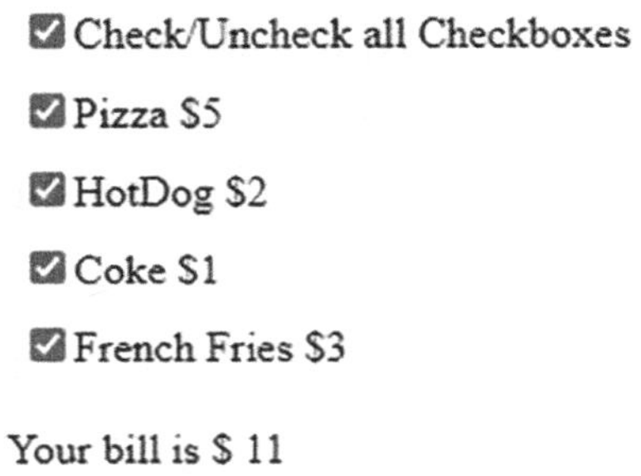

☑ Check/Uncheck all Checkboxes

☑ Pizza $5

☑ HotDog $2

☑ Coke $1

☑ French Fries $3

Your bill is $ 11

Figure 4-28. *All checkboxes are selected by selecting the Check/Uncheck all Checkboxes checkbox*

If the **Check All** checkbox is unchecked, all the checkboxes will be unchecked and hence a bill of $0 will be displayed, as shown in Figure 4-29.

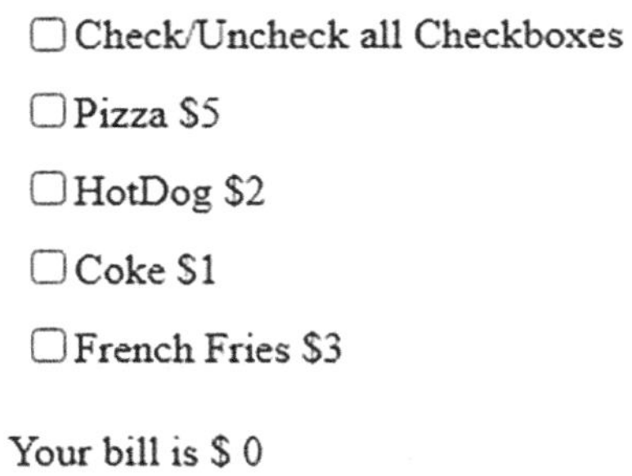

☐ Check/Uncheck all Checkboxes

☐ Pizza $5

☐ HotDog $2

☐ Coke $1

☐ French Fries $3

Your bill is $ 0

Figure 4-29. *All checkboxes are unselected by unchecking the Check/Uncheck all Checkboxes checkbox*

The user can also select any of the individual checkboxes. The total amount of the selected checkboxes will appear as shown in Figure 4-30.

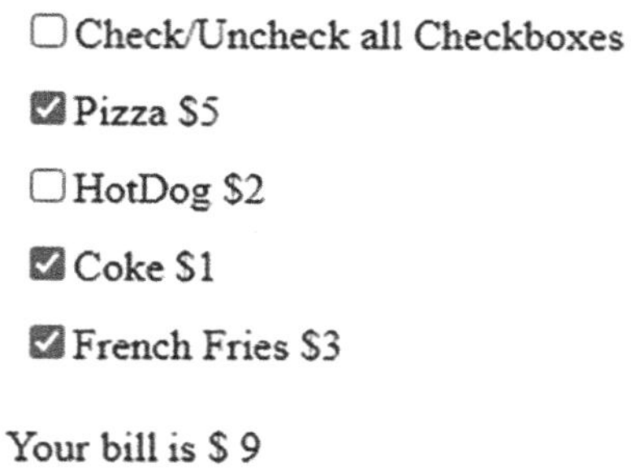

☐ Check/Uncheck all Checkboxes

☑ Pizza $5

☐ HotDog $2

☑ Coke $1

☑ French Fries $3

Your bill is $ 9

Figure 4-30. *Bill of the individually selected food items displayed*

4-12. Validating Two Fields

Problem

You have two fields, **User Id** and **Password**, and you want to confirm that none of the fields are left blank. If any are left blank, you want the respective error message to appear on the screen.

Solution

Make an HTML file that displays two labels and two text fields:

Validatetwo.html

```
<!DOCTYPE html PUBLIC "-//W3C//DTD XHTML 1.0 Transitional//EN"
        "http://www.w3.org/TR/xhtml1/DTD/xhtml1-transitional.dtd">

<html xmlns="http://www.w3.org/1999/xhtml" xml:lang="en" lang="en">
  <head>
    <meta http-equiv="Content-Type" content="text/html; charset=utf-8"/>
    <title></title>
    <link rel="stylesheet" href="stylevalidate.css" type="text/css"
    media="screen" />
    <script src="jquery-3.5.1.js" type="text/javascript"></script>
```

```
    <script src="validatetwojq.js" type="text/javascript"></script>
  </head>
  <body>
    <div><span class="label">User Id *</span><input type="text"
    class="infobox" name="userid" /><span class="error"> This field cannot
    be blank</span></div>
    <div><span class="label">Password *</span><input type="password"
    class="infobox" name="password" /><span class="error"> This field
    cannot be blank</span></div>
  </body>
</html>
```

The style sheet with the respective class selectors is as follows:

stylevalidate.css

```
.label {float: left; width: 120px; }
.infobox {width: 200px; }
.error { color: red; padding-left: 10px; }
div{padding: 5px; }
```

The jQuery code to test that no field is left blank is as follows:

Validatetwojq.js

```
$(document).ready(function() {
  $('.error').hide();
  $('.infobox').each(function(){
    $(this).blur(function(){
      var data=$(this).val();
      var len=data.length;
      if(len<1)
      {
        $(this).parent().find('.error').show();
      }
      else
      {
        $(this).parent().find('.error').hide();
      }
```

```
    });
  });
});
```

How It Works

In the HTML file, the label messages **User Id *** and **Password *** are enclosed in span elements that are assigned the class name `label`. The input text fields are assigned the class name `infobox` and the error message (**This field cannot be blank**) is stored as a span element of class `error`. The reasons for assigning classes to all three items (label, input text field, and error message) is to automatically apply the properties defined in the class selectors `.label`, `.infobox`, and `.error` (defined in the style sheet `style.css`).

In the style sheet file, the class selector `.label` contains the `float` property set to `left` to make the label appear on its left (creating space for the input text field to appear on its right) and the `width` property set to value `120px` to define the width that the label can consume. The class selector `.infobox` contains the `width` property set to value `200px` to specify the width for the dropdown list, and the class selector `.error` is for assigning the red color to the error messages and for making the error messages appear at the distance of 10px from the element on its left. The type selector `div` has the `padding` property set to 5px for creating some space among the two `div` elements where each `div` element contains a combination of label, input text field, and error message.

In the jQuery code, initially you hide all the error messages (span elements of class `error`), then with the use of `.each()` method, you test that if blur event occurs on any of the text fields (i.e., the user loses focus on that field), the value in that input text field is retrieved and stored into the variable `data`. If the `data` variable is empty (i.e., its length is less than 1), you display the error message related to that field.

If you leave the focus from the first text field (User Id) and move on to the next field, you get the error message on first field as shown in Figure 4-31.

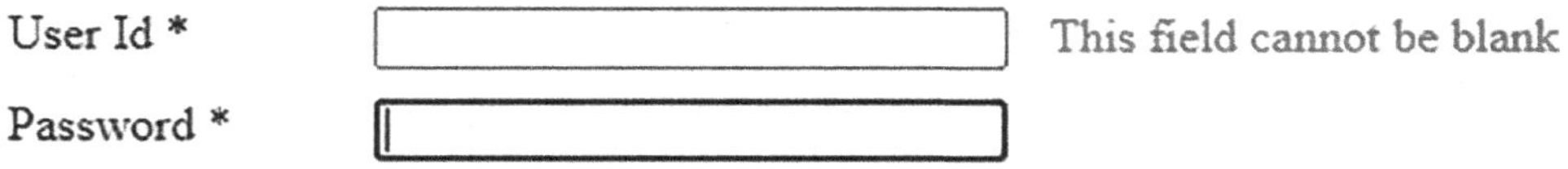

Figure 4-31. *An error message is displayed if the first field is left blank*

And if the second text field is left blank and the focus is lost on it, the error message for it is shown in Figure 4-32.

User Id *	Bintu	
Password *		This field cannot be blank

Figure 4-32. *An error message is displayed if the second field is left blank*

No error appears if data is provided in both input text fields as shown in Figure 4-33.

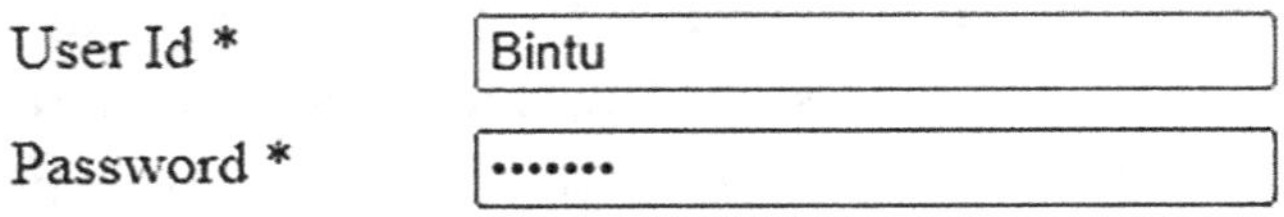

User Id *	Bintu
Password *	••••••••

Figure 4-33. *No error message appears if data is provided in both input text fields*

Adding a Submit Button

In the above solution, you didn't add a Submit button. Let's add a Submit button and validate the input text field one by one when the user selects the Submit button. Add a Submit button to the HTML file as follows:

Addsubmit.html

```
<!DOCTYPE html PUBLIC "-//W3C//DTD XHTML 1.0 Transitional//EN"
        "http://www.w3.org/TR/xhtml1/DTD/xhtml1-transitional.dtd">

<html xmlns="http://www.w3.org/1999/xhtml" xml:lang="en" lang="en">
  <head>
    <meta http-equiv="Content-Type" content="text/html; charset=utf-8"/>
    <title></title>
    <link rel="stylesheet" href="stylevalidate.css" type="text/css"
    media="screen" />
    <script src="jquery-3.5.1.js" type="text/javascript"></script>
    <script src="addsubmitjq.js" type="text/javascript"></script>
  </head>
  <body>
    <form>
        <div><span class="label">User Id *</span><input
        type="text"  class="infobox" name="userid" /><span class="error">
        This field cannot be blank</span></div>
```

```
      <div><span class="label">Password *</span><input type="password"
      class="infobox" name="password" /><span class="error"> This field
      cannot be blank</span></div>
      <input class="submit" type="submit" value="Submit">
   </form>
  </body>
</html>
```

You need to add a class selector .submit in the style sheet file (style.css) to apply the style properties to the Submit button automatically to make it appear below the input text fields with a small spacing from the element just above it.

stylevalidate.css

```
.label {float: left; width: 120px; }
.infobox {width: 200px; }
.error { color: red; padding-left: 10px; }
.submit { margin-left: 125px; margin-top: 10px;}
div{padding: 5px; }
```

The jQuery code is modified to perform validation on the occurrence of a click event on the Submit button as follows:

Addsubmitjq.js

```
$(document).ready(function() {
  $('.error').hide();
  $('.submit').click(function(event){
    $('.infobox').each(function(){
      var data=$(this).val();
      var len=data.length;
      if(len<1)
      {
      $(this).parent().find('.error').show();
      }
```

```
    else
    {
      $(this).parent().find('.error').hide();
    }
  });
  event.preventDefault();
 });
});
```

Since you are interested in performing validation and not in sending the data entered in the input text field to the server on selecting the Submit button, you invoke the `.preventDefault()` method of the event object to stop sending the data to the server. The event object is automatically sent by JavaScript to the event handling function of the click event.

If you leave both fields blank and select the Submit button, you get the two error messages displayed in Figure 4-34.

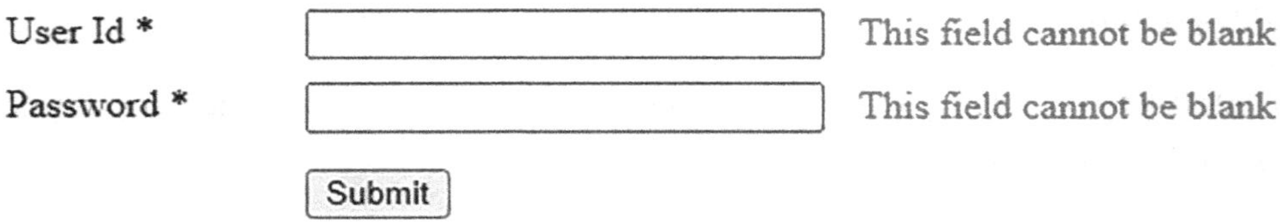

User Id *		This field cannot be blank
Password *		This field cannot be blank
	Submit	

Figure 4-34. *Error messages for both fields appear if they are left blank*

If one of the fields is left blank, the respective error message will be displayed on selecting the Submit button, as shown in Figure 4-35.

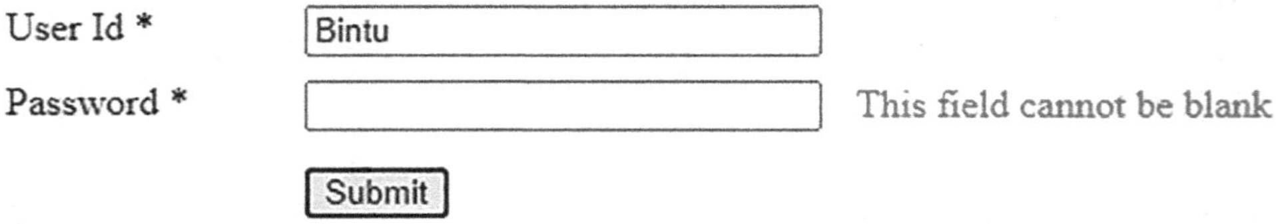

User Id *	Bintu	
Password *		This field cannot be blank
	Submit	

Figure 4-35. *The error message for the first input text field appears if it is left blank*

4-13. Matching the Password and Confirming Password Fields

Problem

You want to assure that the password entered in the Password and Confirm Password fields exactly match.

Solution

Make an HTML file that displays three labels and three text fields for **User Id, Password,** and **Confirm Password**:

Matchingpasswords.html

```
<!DOCTYPE html PUBLIC "-//W3C//DTD XHTML 1.0 Transitional//EN"
        "http://www.w3.org/TR/xhtml1/DTD/xhtml1-transitional.dtd">

<html xmlns="http://www.w3.org/1999/xhtml" xml:lang="en" lang="en">
  <head>
    <meta http-equiv="Content-Type" content="text/html; charset=utf-8"/>
    <title></title>
    <link rel="stylesheet" href="stylevalidate.css" type="text/css"
    media="screen" />
    <script src="jquery-3.5.1.js" type="text/javascript"></script>
    <script src="matchingpasswordsjq.js" type="text/javascript"></script>
  </head>
  <body>
      <form>
          <div ><span class="label">User Id </span><input type="text"
          class="userid" name="userid" /></div>
          <div ><span class="label">Password </span><input type="password"
          class="password" name="password" /><span class="error"> Password
          cannot be blank</span></div>
          <div ><span class="label">Confirm Password </span><input type=
          "password" class="confpass" name="confpass" /><span class="error">
          Password and Confirm Password don't match</span></div>
          <input class="submit" type="submit" value="Submit">
```

229

```
      </form>
    </body>
</html>
```

The style sheet with the respective class selectors is as follows:

stylevalidate.css

```
.label {float: left; width: 120px; }
.error { color: red; padding-left: 10px; }
.submit { margin-left: 125px; margin-top: 10px;}
div{padding: 5px; }
```

The jQuery code to test that the data entered in the **Password** and **Confirm Password** fields are exactly same is as follows:

Matchingpasswordsjq.js

```
$(document).ready(function() {
  $('.error').hide();
  $('.submit').click(function(event){
    data=$('.password').val();
    var len=data.length;
    if(len<1)
    {
      $('.password').next().show();
    }
    else
    {
      $('.password').next().hide();
    }
    if($('.password').val() !=$('.confpass').val())
    {
      $('.confpass').next().show();
    }
```

```
   else
   {
     $('.confpass').next().hide();
   }
   event.preventDefault();
 });
});
```

How It Works

In the HTML file, the label messages **User Id, Password**, and **Confirm Password** are enclosed in span elements that are assigned the class label. The input text fields are assigned the respective classes userid, password, and confpass for retrieving the data entered in them via jQuery. Finally, all input text fields are followed by the error messages nested inside the span element of class error.

The reasons for assigning classes to all items (labels, error messages, and the Submit button) is to automatically apply the properties defined in the class selectors .label, .error, and .submit (defined in style.css). Also, the combination of label, input text field, and error are nested inside the div element so that you can apply a style property to the div element to create spacing among each combination of label, input text field, and error message.

In the style sheet file, the class selector .label contains the float property set to left to make the label appear on the left side of the browser window (creating space for the input text field to appear on its right) and the width property is set to 120px to define the width that the label can consume. The class selector .error assigns the red color to the error messages and makes the error messages appear at the distance of 10px from the element on its left. The class selector .submit contains the margin-left property set to 125px and the margin-top property set to 10px to make it appear at the distance of 125px from the left border of the browser window (to appear below the input text fields) and at a gap of 10px from the element just above it. The type selector div has the padding property set to 5px to create some space among the div elements where each div element contains a combination of a label, an input text field, and an error message.

Before you understand the jQuery code, let's understand the usage of the .next() method that is used in it.

.next( )

This method retrieves the next following sibling in the specified element. Remember, this method returns the very next sibling for each element—and not all next siblings, like the nextAll() method does.

Syntax:

.next(selector)

where selector is an optional parameter used for specifying the selector expression for matching with the specified elements .

In the jQuery code, initially you hide the error messages (elements nested inside the span element of class error). Thereafter, you attach a click event to the Submit button. In the event handling function of the click event, you retrieve the data in the **Password** field (input text field of class password) and store it in the variable data. If the length of the contents in variable data is less than 1 (i.e., if the user has not entered anything in the Password field, you make the element next to the password field (which is the span element of the class error) appear on the screen), you display the error message **Password cannot be blank** on the screen.

If the user has not left the password empty, you check whether the data entered in the **Password** field and the **Confirm Password** field (data in elements of class .password and .confpass) are exactly the same. If the two don't match, you display the error message (which is the element next to the **Confirm Password** field) **Password and Confirm Password don't match** on the screen. You also invoke the preventDefault() method of the event object to prevent the data entered by the user from sending it to the server as you are mainly interested in just confirming that the data entered in the **Password** and **Confirm Password** fields match.

On execution of the jQuery code, if you leave the **Password** field blank and select the Submit button, you get the error message **Password cannot be blank** on the screen as shown in Figure 4-36.

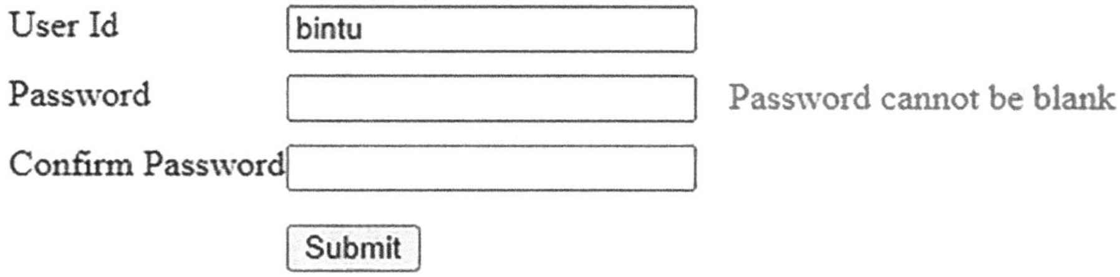

User Id [bintu]

Password [   ]   Password cannot be blank

Confirm Password [   ]

[Submit]

Figure 4-36. *The error message appears if the password is not entered*

If the contents of the **Password** and **Confirm Password** fields don't match, you get the error message **Password and Confirm Password don't match** as shown in Figure 4-37.

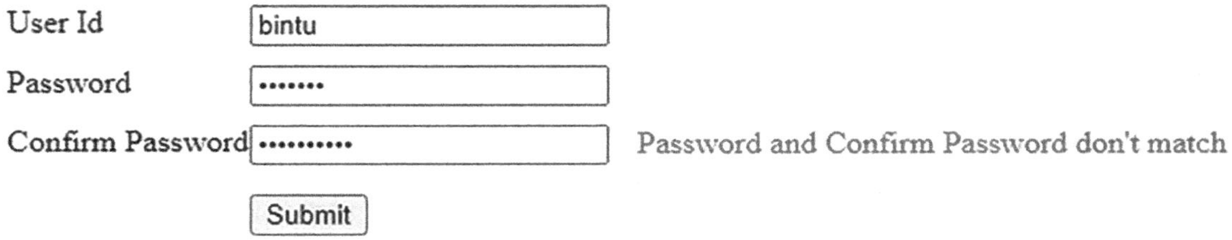

User Id [bintu]

Password [••••••••]

Confirm Password [••••••••••]   Password and Confirm Password don't match

[Submit]

Figure 4-37. *The error message appears if the Password and Confirm Password fields don't match*

4-14. Disabling Certain Fields

Problem

You want the user to fill in the **User Id, Password**, and **Confirm Password** fields and if the user enters invalid data or leaves any field blank, you want not only to display the error message but also to disable the rest of the fields until the error is corrected.

Solution

Use the same HTML and style sheet file (`style.css`) that you used in Recipe 4-13. The only change you will make in that HTML file is that you will remove the Submit button since you are going to validate fields in this example by using a `blur()` event and not the `click()` event. The HTML code is provided below for reference:

Disablefields.html

```
<!DOCTYPE html PUBLIC "-//W3C//DTD XHTML 1.0 Transitional//EN"
        "http://www.w3.org/TR/xhtml1/DTD/xhtml1-transitional.dtd">

<html xmlns="http://www.w3.org/1999/xhtml" xml:lang="en" lang="en">
  <head>
    <meta http-equiv="Content-Type" content="text/html; charset=utf-8"/>
    <title></title>
    <link rel="stylesheet" href="stylevalidate.css" type="text/css"
    media="screen" />
    <script src="jquery-3.5.1.js" type="text/javascript"></script>
    <script src="disablefieldsjq.js" type="text/javascript"></script>
  </head>
  <body>
    <form>
        <div ><span class="label">User Id </span><input type="text"
        class="userid" name="userid" /><span class="error"> User id
        cannot be blank</span></div>
        <div ><span class="label">Password </span><input type="password"
        class="password" name="password" /><span class="error"> Password
        cannot be blank</span></div>
        <div ><span class="label">Confirm Password </span><input type=
        "password" class="confpass" name="confpass" /><span class="error">
        Password and Confirm Password don't match</span></div>
    </form>
  </body>
</html>
```

The style sheet file **stylevalidate.css** will be exactly same as used in Recipe 4-13. The following jQuery code

- Validates the data entered by the user

- Displays the error messages

- Disables the rest of the fields if the data is skipped or some invalid data is entered in any field

Disablefieldsjq.js

```
$(document).ready(function() {
  $('.error').hide();
  $('.userid').blur(function(){
    data=$('.userid').val();
    var len=data.length;
    if(len<1)
    {
      $('.userid').next().show();
      $('.password').attr('disabled',true);
      $('.confpass').attr('disabled',true);
    }
    else
    {
      $('.userid').next().hide();
      $('.password').removeAttr('disabled');
      $('.confpass').removeAttr('disabled');
    }
  });

  $('.password').blur(function(){
    data=$('.password').val();
    var len=data.length;
    if(len<1)
    {
      $('.password').next().show();
      $('.confpass').attr('disabled',true);
    }
    else
    {
      $('.password').next().hide();
      $('.confpass').removeAttr('disabled');
    }
  });
```

```
$('.confpass').blur(function(){
  if($('.password').val() !=$('.confpass').val())
  {
    $('.confpass').next().show();
  }
  else
  {
    $('.confpass').next().hide();
  }
});
});
```

How It Works

Initially, you hide the error messages (elements nested inside the span element of class error). Thereafter, you check if the blur() event has occurred on the input text field of class userid (i.e., whether the focus is lost on the **User Id** field). If yes, you retrieve the data entered by the user in that field and store it in the variable data. If the length of the contents in the variable data is less than 1 (i.e., if the **User Id** field is left blank), you make the element next to the **User Id** field (which is a span element of class error) appear on the screen (i.e., you display the error message **Userid cannot be blank** on the screen). Beside this, you also use these two statements

```
$('.password').attr('disabled',true);
$('.confpass').attr('disabled',true);
```

to disable the **Password** and **Confirm Passwords** fields (two input fields of class password and confpass), so until and unless the user enters a user id, both fields will be disabled. If the user enters some data in the **User Id** field, both of the disabled fields will be enabled by making use of the following two statements:

```
$('.password').removeAttr('disabled');
$('.confpass').removeAttr('disabled');
```

Similarly, you check if the password field is left empty. If yes, again the error message **Password cannot be blank** will be displayed and the **Confirm Password** field will be disabled until the user enters some data in the **Password** field.

Finally, you check if the data entered in the two fields **Password** and **Confirm Password** (data in elements of class `.password` and `.confpass`) are exactly same. If the two don't match, you display the error message (which is the element next to the **Confirm Password** field) **Password and Confirm Password don't match** on the screen.

On execution of jQuery code, if you leave the **User Id** field blank and lose focus from it, you get the error message **User id cannot be blank** as shown in Figure 4-38. Also, both fields, **Password** and **Confirm Password**, will be disabled (i.e., the user will not be able to enter anything in them until the user enters something in the **User Id** field).

User Id   [   ]   User id cannot be blank

Password   [   ]

Confirm Password [   ]

Figure 4-38. *The error message appears if a user id is not provided and the other fields are disabled*

If the **Password** field is left blank and you lose focus on it, you get the error message **Password cannot be blank** on the screen and also the **Confirm Password** field is disabled until something is entered in the **Password** field, as shown in Figure 4-39.

User Id   [bintu   ]

Password   [   ]   Password cannot be blank

Confirm Password [   ]

Figure 4-39. *The error message appears if a password is not entered and the Confirm Password field is disabled*

4-15. Validating a Complete Form

Problem

You have a form where the user is supposed to provide lot of information that includes user id, password, and email address. Also, the user is supposed to select the food items they want to purchase and select the mode of payment (specify the credit card) and to which country they belong. Each field must be validated in the following ways:

- The user id should consist of only characters, numbers, and underscores(_).

- The password cannot be left blank

- The email address must contain the symbols . and @.

- At least one check box (food item) must be selected.

- The user must select one of the modes of payment.

- The country to which user belongs must be selected.

Solution

Let's make an HTML file that displays labels and fields as shown in Figure 4-40. You can see that there are six labels, three input text fields, four check boxes, three radio buttons, and one select element. The HTML code is as follows:

Validateform.html

```
<!DOCTYPE html PUBLIC "-//W3C//DTD XHTML 1.0 Transitional//EN"
        "http://www.w3.org/TR/xhtml1/DTD/xhtml1-transitional.dtd">

<html xmlns="http://www.w3.org/1999/xhtml" xml:lang="en" lang="en">
  <head>
    <meta http-equiv="Content-Type" content="text/html; charset=utf-8"/>
    <title></title>
    <link rel="stylesheet" href="styleform.css" type="text/css"
    media="screen" />
    <script src="jquery-3.5.1.js" type="text/javascript"></script>
    <script src="validateformjq.js" type="text/javascript"></script>
  </head>
```

```
<body>
  <form>
    <div>    <span class="label">User Id </span><input
             type="text"   class="userid" name="userid" /><span
             class="error">User id can contain only numerical,
             character or _(underscore)</span></div>
    <div><span class="label">Password </span><input type="password"
    class="password" name="password" /><span class="error"> Password
    cannot be blank</span></div>
    <div><span class="label">Email Address </span><input type="text"
    class="emailadd" name="emailid" /><span class="error"> Invalid
    email address</span></div>
    <div><span class="label">Select Food items</span><br>
    <input type="checkbox"  id="pizza" name="pizza"
    value=5  class="chkb">Pizza $5 <br>
            <input type="checkbox"  id="hotdog" name="hotdog"
            value=2  class="chkb">HotDog $2<br>
        <input type="checkbox"  id="coke" name="coke"
        value=1  class="chkb">Coke $1<br>
            <input type="checkbox"  id="fries" name="fries" value=3
            class="chkb">French Fries $3<br>
            <span class="fooderror">You have not selected any food
            item</span></div>
    <div><span class="label">Mode of  Payment</span><br>
    <input type="radio"  name="paymode" class="radiobtn"
    value="Master Card">Master Card <br>
        <input type="radio"  name="paymode" class="radiobtn"
        value="ANZ Grindlay Card">ANZ Grindlay Card<br>
        <input type="radio"  name="paymode" class="radiobtn"
        value="Visa Card">Visa Card<br>
        <span class="payerror">You have not selected any payment method
        </span></div>
    <div><span class="label">Country</span>
    <select id="country" class="infobox">
        <option value="0">Select a Country</option>
        <option value="USA">USA</option>
```

```
            <option value="United Kingdom">United Kingdom</option>
            <option value="India">India</option>
            <option value="China">China</option>
        </select>
        <span class="error"> Please select the country</span></div>
        <input class="submit" type="submit" value="Submit">
    </form>
  </body>
</html>
```

The style sheet file to apply style properties to the HTML elements is as follows:

styleform.css

```
.label {float: left; width: 120px; }
.infobox {width: 120px; }
.error { color: red; padding-left: 10px; }
.submit { margin-left: 125px; margin-top: 10px;}
div{padding: 5px; }
.chkb { margin-left: 125px; margin-top: 10px;}
.radiobtn { margin-left: 125px; margin-top: 10px;}
```

The jQuery code to validate all of the fields is as follows:

Validateformjq.js

```
1.      $(document).ready(function() {
2.        $('.error').hide();
3.        $('.fooderror').addClass('error');
4.        $('.fooderror').hide();
5.        $('.payerror').addClass('error');
6.        $('.payerror').hide();

7.        $('.submit').click(function(event){
8.          var data=$('.userid').val();
9.          if(validate_userid(data))
10.          {
11.            $('.userid').next().hide();
12.          }
```

```
13.        else
14.        {
15.          $('.userid').next().show();
16.        }

17.        data=$('.password').val();
18.        var len=data.length;
19.        if(len<1)
20.        {
21.          $('.password').next().show();
22.        }
23.        else
24.        {
25.          $('.password').next().hide();
26.        }

27.        data=$('.emailadd').val();
28.        if(valid_email(data))
29.        {
30.          $('.emailadd').next().hide();
31.        }
32.        else
33.        {
34.          $('.emailadd').next().show();
35.        }

36.        var count=0;
37.        $('div').find(':checkbox').each(function(){
38.          if($(this).is(':checked'))
39.          {
40.            count++;
41.          }
42.        });
43.        if(count==0)
44.        {
45.          $('.fooderror').css({'margin-left':250}).show();
46.        }
```

```
47.          else
48.          {
49.            $('.fooderror').hide();
50.          }

51.          count=0;
52.          $('div').find(':radio').each(function(){
53.            if($(this).is(':checked'))
54.            {
55.              count++;
56.            }
57.          });
58.          if(count==0)
59.          {
60.            $('.payerror').css({'margin-left':250}).show();
61.          }
62.          else
63.          {
64.            $('.payerror').hide();
65.          }

66.          count=$('select option:selected').val();
67.          if(count==0)
68.          {
69.            $('.infobox').next().show();
70.          }
71.          else
72.          {
73.            $('.infobox').next().hide();
74.          }

75.          event.preventDefault();
76.        });
77.      });
```

```
78.     function valid_email(email)
79.     {
80.       var pattern= new RegExp(/^[\w-]+(\.[\w-]+)*@([\w-]+\.)+
          [a-zA-Z]+$/);
81.       return pattern.test(email);
82.     }

83.     function validate_userid(uid)
84.     {
85.       var pattern= new RegExp(/^[a-z0-9_]+$/);
86.       return pattern.test(uid);
87.     }
```

How It Works

The meaning of the jQuery code is as follows:

2. Hiding all errors related to user id, password, email address, and country. All error messages are nested inside the span element of class error.

3-4. Applying the style properties contained in the class selector .error to the error message related to the checkboxes displaying different food items. The style properties in class selector .error apply a red color to the error message. The error message is made hidden for the time being.

5-6. Applying the style properties of the class selector .error to the errors related to the radio buttons displaying different modes of payment (it will appear in red). The error message is made invisible at the beginning.

7. Attaching the click event to the Submit button.

8. Retrieving the data entered in the **User Id** field (input text field of class userid) and storing it in the variable data.

9-16. Validating the user id in the data variable by passing it to the validate_ userid() function to compare it with the regular expression that tests to see that the user id consists only of characters, numerals, or underscores and nothing else. If the user id matches with the regular expression supplied, no error message will be displayed; otherwise the error message (which is the element next to the input text field) **User id can contain only numerals, character or _ (underscore)** will be displayed on the screen.

243

17-26. Retrieving the data entered in the password field (input text field of class `password`) and storing it in the variable `data`. You find out the length of the contents in the `data` variable. If the length is less than 1 (i.e., if the **Password** field is left empty), the error message (which is the element next to the input text field) **Password cannot be blank** will be displayed on the screen; otherwise the error message is kept in hidden mode.

27-35. Retrieving the data entered in the **Email Address** field (input text field of class `emailadd`) and storing it in the variable `data`. Then, you validate the email address in the `data` variable by passing it to the `validate_email()` function to compare it with the regular expression that tests to see that the email address begins with alpha numerals and essentially contains . and @ symbol in it. If the email address matches with the regular expression supplied, no error message will be displayed; otherwise the error message (which is the element next to the input text field) **Invalid email address** will be displayed on the screen.

36-42. Initializing the variable `count` to 0. Finding out if all the checkboxes in the `div` element are checked by making use of the `.each()` function. The value of the variable `count` is incremented by 1 on finding any checked checkbox. In other words, you are counting the number of checked checkboxes.

43-50. If the value in the `count` variable is 0, meaning none of the checkboxes are selected, the error message defined by the span element of class `fooderror` is displayed and the `margin-left` property is applied to it with a value of `250px` using the `.css()` method to make it appear at the distance of 250px from the left border of the browser window (below the other error messages if any). If the value in the `count` variable is not 0, the error message is kept in hidden mode.

51-57. Initializing the variable `count` to 0. Finding out all the radio buttons in the `div` element that are checked (selected) by making use of the `.each()` function. The value of the variable `count` is incremented by 1 on finding any checked radio button.

58-65. If the value in the `count` variable is 0, meaning no radio button is selected, the error message defined by the span element of class `payerror` is displayed and the `margin-left` property is applied to it with `250px` using the `.css()` method to make it appear at the distance of 250px from the left border of the browser window (below the other error messages if any). If the value in the `count` variable is not 0, the error message is kept in hidden mode.

66-74. Finding out the number of options that are selected in the select element. The count of the selected options is stored in the variable count. If the value in the count variable is 0 (i.e., if no option is selected from the select element) then the error message (which is the element next to the select element of class infobox) **Please select the country** is displayed on the screen; otherwise the error message is kept in hidden mode.

75. The preventDefault() method of the event object is invoked to prevent the data entered or selected by the user from being sent to the server as you are only interested here in validation of data.

78-82. Function for validating the email address

83-87. Function for validating the user id

On execution of the jQuery code, if you leave all the fields blank and select the Submit button, you get the error messages shown in Figure 4-40.

User Id		User id can contain only numerical, character or _(underscore)
Password		Password cannot be blank
Email Address		Invalid email address
Select Food items		
	☐ Pizza $5	
	☐ HotDog $2	
	☐ Coke $1	
	☐ French Fries $3	
	You have not selected any food item	
Mode of Payment		
	○ Master Card	
	○ ANZ Grindlay Card	
	○ Visa Card	
	You have not selected any payment method	
Country	Select a Country ⌄ Please select the country	
	Submit	

Figure 4-40. *Error messages appear if no field is filled*

If you enter an invalid user id or email address and don't select any checkbox or any option from the select element, you get the error messages shown in Figure 4-41.

245

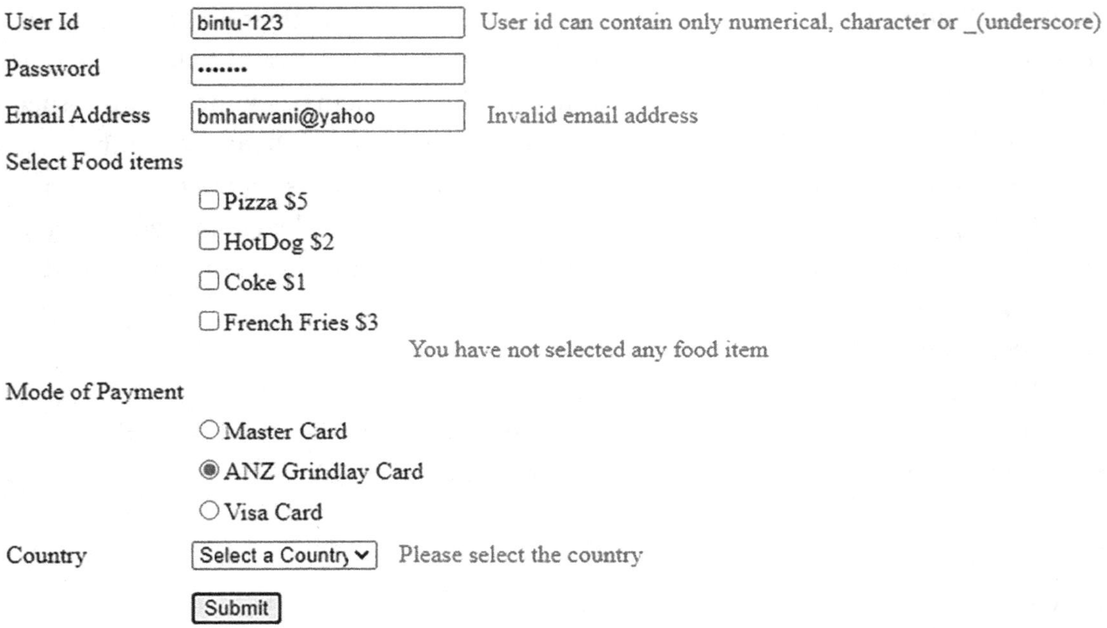

User Id | bintu-123 | User id can contain only numerical, character or _(underscore)

Password | ••••••• |

Email Address | bmharwani@yahoo | Invalid email address

Select Food items

      ☐ Pizza $5

      ☐ HotDog $2

      ☐ Coke $1

      ☐ French Fries $3

           You have not selected any food item

Mode of Payment

      ○ Master Card

      ◉ ANZ Grindlay Card

      ○ Visa Card

Country | Select a Country ∨ | Please select the country

       | Submit |

Figure 4-41. *Error messages are shown if no data or invalid data is provided*

On entering all valid data and selecting all the essential options, the data will be accepted without displaying any error messages, as shown in Figure 4-42.

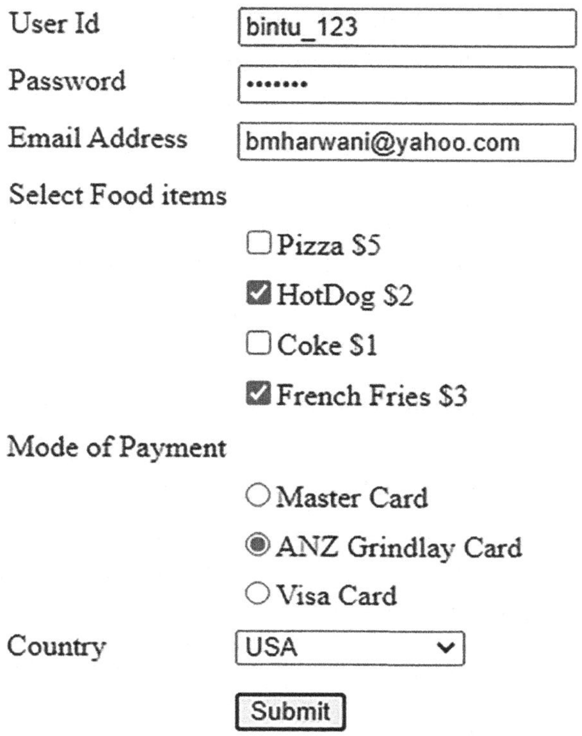

User Id | bintu_123 |

Password | ••••••• |

Email Address | bmharwani@yahoo.com |

Select Food items

☐ Pizza $5

☑ HotDog $2

☐ Coke $1

☑ French Fries $3

Mode of Payment

○ Master Card

◉ ANZ Grindlay Card

○ Visa Card

Country | USA ▾ |

| Submit |

Figure 4-42. *Valid data is accepted*

Highlighting the Input Fields and Grouping Common Form Elements

Let's now group some related elements of the form and also highlight the input fields when they receive focus. To group the form elements and apply a caption to them, you need to use two HTML elements, fieldset and legend:

- The <fieldset> tag is used to group a few form elements together. It draws a box around the grouped elements.

- The <legend> tag is used to define a caption for the form elements that are grouped by the fieldset element.

Let's apply the fieldset elements to make three groups of the above form and apply the legend element to add a caption of **Enter Your Information** to the form. The modified HTML form is as follows:

Highlightgroup.html

```
<!DOCTYPE html PUBLIC "-//W3C//DTD XHTML 1.0 Transitional//EN"
        "http://www.w3.org/TR/xhtml1/DTD/xhtml1-transitional.dtd">

<html xmlns="http://www.w3.org/1999/xhtml" xml:lang="en" lang="en">
  <head>
    <meta http-equiv="Content-Type" content="text/html; charset=utf-8"/>
    <title></title>
    <link rel="stylesheet" href="stylehighlight.css" type="text/css"
    media="screen" />
    <script src="jquery-3.5.1.js" type="text/javascript"></script>
    <script src="highlightgroupjq.js" type="text/javascript"></script>
  </head>
  <body>
    <form>
      <fieldset>
          <legend>Enter Your Information</legend>
          <div id="u">    <span class="label">User Id </span><input type=
          "text"  class="userid" name="userid" /><span class="error">
          User id can contain only numerical, character or _(underscore)
          </span></div>
          <div  id="p"><span class="label">Password </span><input
          type="password" class="password" name="password" /><span
          class="error"> Password cannot be blank</span></div>
          <div><span class="label">Email Address </span><input type="text"
          class="emailadd" name="emailid" /><span class="error"> Invalid
          email address</span></div>
      </fieldset>
      <fieldset>
          <div><span class="label">Select Food items</span><br>
          <input type="checkbox"  id="pizza" name="pizza" value=5
          class="chkb">Pizza $5 <br>
```

```
        <input type="checkbox"  id="hotdog" name="hotdog"
        value=2  class="chkb">HotDog $2<br>
        <input type="checkbox"  id="coke" name="coke"
        value=1  class="chkb">Coke $1<br>
        <input type="checkbox"  id="fries" name="fries"
        value=3  class="chkb">French Fries $3<br>
        <span class="fooderror">You have not selected any food item</
        span></div>
    <div><span class="label">Mode of  Payment</span><br><input type=
    "radio"  name="paymode" class="radiobtn" value="Master Card">
    Master Card <br>
        <input type="radio"  name="paymode" class="radiobtn"
        value="ANZ Grindlay Card">ANZ Grindlay Card<br>
        <input type="radio"  name="paymode" class="radiobtn"
        value="Visa Card">Visa Card<br>
        <span class="payerror">You have not selected any payment
        method</span></div>
</fieldset>
<fieldset>
    <div><span class="label">Country</span>
    <select id="country" class="infobox">
        <option value="0">Select a Country</option>
        <option value="USA">USA</option>
        <option value="United Kingdom">United Kingdom</option>
        <option value="India">India</option>
        <option value="China">China</option>
    </select>
</fieldset>
<span class="error"> Please select the country</span></div>
<input class="submit" type="submit" value="Submit">
    </form>
  </body>
</html>
```

<fieldset> marks the beginning of the group and </fieldset> marks the ending of the group.

To define the border to the grouped elements, you define the style property for the type selector `fieldset`, and to apply border, foreground, and background color to the caption and to make it appear bold, you define style properties for the type selector legend. To highlight the input text field on gaining focus, you define a style rule called `.inputs` in the style sheet. The style sheet is as follows:

stylehighlight.css

```
.submit { margin-left: 125px; margin-top: 10px;}
.label {float: left; width: 120px; }
.infobox {width: 120px; }
.error { color: red; padding-left: 10px; }
div{padding: 5px; }
.chkb { margin-left: 125px; margin-top: 10px;}
.radiobtn { margin-left: 125px; margin-top: 10px;}
.inputs{background-color:cyan}

fieldset{
      border:1px solid #888;
}

legend{
     border:1px solid #888;
     background-color:cyan;
     color:blue;
     font-weight:bold;
     padding:.5em
}
```

To apply the style properties defined in the style rule inputs to the input text fields **User Id, Password**, and **Email address**, you add few statements to the above jQuery code. Those statements are shown in bold in the below jQuery code. The rest of the code is exactly the same.

Highlightgroupjq.js

```
$(document).ready(function() {
  $('.error').hide();
  $('.userid').focus(function(){
    $(this).addClass('inputs');
  });

  $('.password').focus(function(){
    $(this).addClass('inputs');
  });

  $('.emailadd').focus(function(){
    $(this).addClass('inputs');
  });

  $('.fooderror').addClass('error');
  $('.fooderror').hide();
  $('.payerror').addClass('error');
  $('.payerror').hide();

  $('.submit').click(function(event){
    var data=$('.userid').val();
    if(validate_userid(data))
    {
      $('.userid').next().hide();
    }
    else
    {
      $('.userid').next().show();
    }

    data=$('.password').val();
    var len=data.length;
    if(len<1)
    {
      $('.password').next().show();
    }
```

```
else
{
  $('.password').next().hide();
}

data=$('.emailadd').val();
if(valid_email(data))
{
  $('.emailadd').next().hide();
}
else
{
  $('.emailadd').next().show();
}

var count=0;
$('div').find(':checkbox').each(function(){
  if($(this).is(':checked'))
  {
    count++;
  }
});
if(count==0)
{
  $('.fooderror').css({'margin-left':250}).show();
}
else
{
$('.fooderror').hide();
}

count=0;
$('div').find(':radio').each(function(){
  if($(this).is(':checked'))
  {
    count++;
  }
```

```
    });
    if(count==0)
    {
      $('.payerror').css({'margin-left':250}).show();
    }
    else
    {
      $('.payerror').hide();
    }

    count=$('select option:selected').val();
    if(count==0)
    {
      $('.infobox').next().show();
    }
    else
    {
      $('.infobox').next().hide();
    }

    event.preventDefault();
  });
});

function valid_email(email)
{
  var pattern= new RegExp(/^[\w-]+(\.[\w-]+)*@([\w-]+\.)+[a-zA-Z]+$/);
  return pattern.test(email);
}

function validate_userid(uid)
{
  var pattern= new RegExp(/^[a-z0-9_]+$/);
  return pattern.test(uid);
}
```

On execution of this jQuery code, you get the output shown in Figure 4-43.

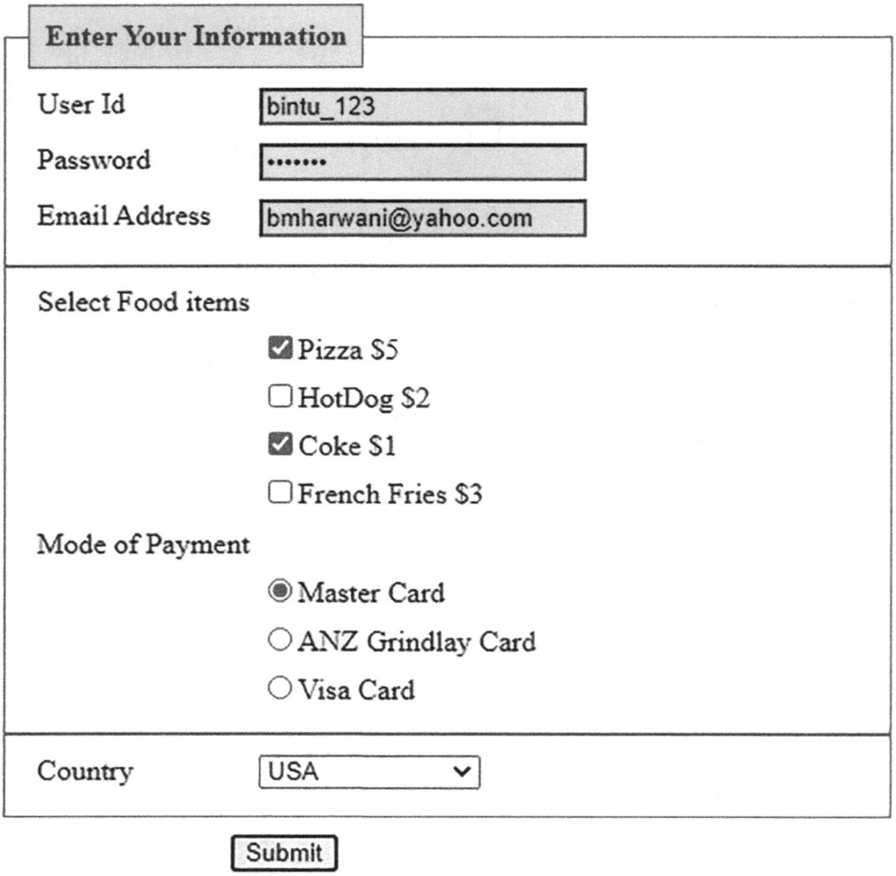

Figure 4-43. *Grouping common elements of the form*

4-16. Summary

In this chapter, you learned about simple validation checks like a field is not left blank, a numeral is entered within a given range, etc. You also learned how to confirm the validity of a phone number, date, email address, etc. You learned the technique of knowing whether a checkbox or radio box is selected or not. Finally, you learned how a complete form is validated.

In the next chapter, you will learn how to make different types of menus for navigation. You will learn to represent links in the form of breadcrumbs and make a menu with hovering menu items. You will create a contextual menu, a navigation menu with access keys, menus with respective menu items and submenu items, an accordion menu, and a dynamic visual menu.

CHAPTER 5

Page Navigation

In this chapter, you will be learning how to make different types of menus for navigating to the target web site. The recipes you will be learning in this chapter are

- Representing links in the form of breadcrumbs

- A menu with hovering menu items

- Creating a contextual menu

- Creating a navigation menu with access keys

- Creating a context menu on right-click

- Two menus with respective menu items

- Two menus with respective menu items and submenu items

- Making an accordion menu

- Making a dynamic visual menu

5-1. Writing a Breadcrumb Menu
Problem

You want to represent a menu of links in the form of breadcrumbs.

© Bintu Harwani 2022
B. Harwani, *jQuery Recipes*, https://doi.org/10.1007/978-1-4842-7304-3_5

Solution

Let's represent a few menu items, **Web Development**, **Programming**, and **RDBMS** of the menu **Books**, in the form of an unordered list element. The HTML file is as follows:

Breadcrumb.html

```
<!DOCTYPE html PUBLIC "-//W3C//DTD XHTML 1.0 Transitional//EN"
        "http://www.w3.org/TR/xhtml1/DTD/xhtml1-transitional.dtd">

<html xmlns="http://www.w3.org/1999/xhtml" xml:lang="en" lang="en">
  <head>
    <meta http-equiv="Content-Type" content="text/html; charset=utf-8"/>
    <title></title>
    <link rel="stylesheet" href="style.css" type="text/css" media="screen" />
    <script src="jquery-3.5.1.js" type="text/javascript"></script>
    <script src="breadcrumbjq.js" type="text/javascript"></script>
  </head>
  <body>
    <ul id="menu">
        <li><a href="http://example.com">Books</a>
            <ul>
                    <li><a href="http://example.com">Web Development
                    </a></li>
                    <li><a href="http://example.com">Programming</a></li>
                    <li><a href="http://example.com">RDBMS</a></li>
            </ul>
        </li>
    </ul>
  </body>
</html>
```

To give the shape of breadcrumbs to the list items, you define two style rules, .liststyle and .ulistyle, with a few style properties as shown in the following style sheet file, style.css:

style.css

```
.liststyle {
    background-image:url(arrow.jpg);
    background-repeat:no-repeat;
    background-position:left;
    padding-left:30px;
    display: inline;
}

.uliststyle {
    list-style:none;
    margin:0;
    padding:0;
    display: inline;
}
```

The jQuery code to apply the two style rules, .ulistyle and .liststyle, to the unordered list and its elements, respectively, is as follows:

Breadcrumbjq.js

```
$(document).ready(function() {
  $('ul').addClass('ulistyle');
  $('ul li ul li').addClass('liststyle');
});
```

How It Works

In the HTML file, you can see that the unordered list is assigned the id menu and consists of a single list item, **Books**, which in turn itself is an unordered list of three elements, **Web Development**, **Programming**, and **RDBMS**. Also, all of the menu items point at a hypothetical web site, example.com, which is the target website where the user will be sent upon clicking any link in the breadcrumb.

In the style sheet file, the .liststyle rule contains the background-image property set to value url(arrow.jpg) to display the arrow images (refer to Figure 5-1). The background-repeat property is set to no-repeat to make the image appear only once. The background-position property is set to left to make the image appear on the left side of the element to which it is applied. The padding-left property is set to 30px to create the distance of 30px on the left and the display property is set to a value of inline to remove any space in the block elements to make them appear in a row (without spaces).

The style rule uliststyle contains the list-style property set to a value of none to remove the traditional bullets from the unordered list. The margin and padding properties are set to 0 to remove the traditional white spaces created by default in the list items and the display property is set to inline to make the block element appear on the same line.

In the jQuery code, the style rule .ulistyle is applied to the unordered list element and the .liststyle is applied to the list items of the unordered list that is nested inside the first list item of the unordered list.

On execution of the jQuery code, you get the output shown in Figure 5-1.

Books ▶▶ Web Development ▶▶ Programming ▶▶ RDBMS

Figure 5-1. *Anchor elements in the form of breadcrumbs*

5-2. Adding a Hover Effect to Menu Items
Problem

You want to display a menu with a few menu items in it. You also want to have a hover effect over the menu and its items.

Solution

Make an HTML file to represent the menu heading and its menu items. You do so with the help of two unordered lists, one nested inside the other.

Addinghover.html

```
<!DOCTYPE html PUBLIC "-//W3C//DTD XHTML 1.0 Transitional//EN"
        "http://www.w3.org/TR/xhtml1/DTD/xhtml1-transitional.dtd">

<html xmlns="http://www.w3.org/1999/xhtml" xml:lang="en" lang="en">
  <head>
    <meta http-equiv="Content-Type" content="text/html; charset=utf-8"/>
    <title></title>
    <link rel="stylesheet" href="stylehover.css" type="text/css"
    media="screen" />
    <script src="jquery-3.5.1.js" type="text/javascript"></script>
    <script src="addinghoverjq.js" type="text/javascript"></script>
  </head>
  <body>
    <ul>
        <li><a href="http://example.com">Books</a>
            <ul>
                    <li><a href="http://example.com">Web
                    Development</a></li>
                     <li><a href="http://example.com">Programming
                     </a></li>
                     <li><a href="http://example.com">RDBMS</a></li>
            </ul>
        </li>
    </ul>
  </body>
</html>
```

You can see in the HTML file an unordered list element with a list item of **Books**, which itself is an unordered list element of three list items to represent the hyperlinks of **Web Development**, **Programming**, and **RDBMS**. These hyperlinks point at a hypothetical web site called http://example.com where the user is sent if any of the menu items are clicked.

To give the appearance of a menu to the unordered list element, you need to apply certain styles to all three elements: `<u>`, `<li>`, and `<a>`. You write their type selectors in the style sheet file so that the properties in it can be automatically applied to these three elements. The style sheet file may appear as follows:

stylehover.css

```css
ul {
  width: 200px;
}

ul li ul {
  list-style-type:none;
  margin: 5;
  width: 200px;
}

a {
  display:block;
  border-bottom: 1px solid #fff;
  text-decoration: none;
  background: #00f;
  color: #fff;
  padding: 0.5em;
}

li {
    display:inline;
}

.hover {
  background: #000;
}
```

The jQuery code to apply the hover event to anchor elements is as follows:

Addinghoverjq.js

```js
$(document).ready(function() {
  $('a').hover(
```

```
    function(event){
      $(this).addClass('hover');
    },
    function(){
      $(this).removeClass('hover');
    }
  );
});
```

How It Works

The type selector `ul` contains the width property set to 200px to define the width of the menu heading **Books**. The type selector `ul li ul` will be applied to the menu items. It contains the `list-style-type` property set to the value of `none` to remove the traditional bullets from the unordered list elements. The `margin` property is set to a value of 5 to make the menu items appear a bit indented as compared to the menu heading. The `width` property is set to 200px to define the width of the menu item to accommodate everything.

The type selector `a` contains the `display` property set to a value of `block` to make the anchor elements appear as a block and not as individual elements. The `border-bottom` property is set to `1px solid #fff` to make a solid white border 1px thick appear below every anchor element (to act as a separator). The `text-decoration` property is set to `none` to remove the traditional underline that usually appears below hyperlinks. The background color is set to blue and the foreground color is set to white for all of the anchor elements. The `padding` property is set to `.5em` (i.e. 50% of the default font size) to define the spacing between the anchor text and its border

The type selector `li` is set to value `inline` to remove any white space between the list items. The CSS class `.hover` contains the background property to set the background color of the menu item (anchor element) to black when a user hovers on any anchor element.

In the jQuery code, you can see that the hover event is applied to the anchor elements. Recall that the hover event contains the two event handling functions, one that is invoked when the mouse pointer is moved over any anchor element and the other when the mouse pointer is moved away from the anchor element. In the event handling function that is invoked when the mouse is moved over the anchor element, you apply the CSS class hover (defined in the style sheet file), making the background color of the anchor element turn to black. In the event handling function that is invoked when the mouse pointer is moved away from the anchor element, you remove the CSS class hover from the anchor element to make it appear as it was initially.

On execution of the jQuery code, the menu will appear as shown in Figure 5-2.

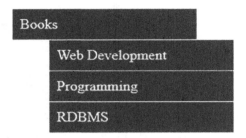

Figure 5-2. *Books menu with three menu items*

When you hover on any menu item, its background color changes to black, as shown in Figure 5-3.

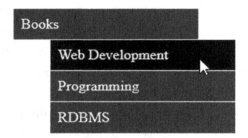

Figure 5-3. *The menu item gets highlighted when being hovered over*

5-3. Creating a Contextual Menu
Problem

You want to display a menu with a few menu items in it. When any menu item is hovered over (the mouse pointer is moved over it), you want to display the information related to it and you also want that menu item to be highlighted. When the menu item is clicked, the user is sent to the related web site.

Solution

Make an HTML file to represent the menu heading **Books** along with three menu items. You create the menu and its three menu items with the help of two unordered lists, one nested inside the other. The list items contain the anchor elements to represent menu items and refer to the target web site http://example.com where user is sent upon selecting any menu item (it is a hypothetical web site). Also, you write information about the three menu items in three paragraphs. The HTML file is as follows:

Contextualmenu.html

```
<!DOCTYPE html PUBLIC "-//W3C//DTD XHTML 1.0 Transitional//EN"
        "http://www.w3.org/TR/xhtml1/DTD/xhtml1-transitional.dtd">

<html xmlns="http://www.w3.org/1999/xhtml" xml:lang="en" lang="en">
  <head>
    <meta http-equiv="Content-Type" content="text/html; charset=utf-8"/>
    <title></title>
    <link rel="stylesheet" href="stylehover.css" type="text/css"
    media="screen" />
    <script src="jquery-3.5.1.js" type="text/javascript"></script>
    <script src="contextualjq.js" type="text/javascript"></script>
  </head>
  <body>
    <table>
        <td>
            <ul>
                    <li><a href="http://example.com">Books</a>
                    <ul>
                            <li><a href="http://example.com" id="webd">
                            Web Development</a></li>
                            <li><a href="http://example.com"
                            id="pgmng">Programming</a></li>
                            <li><a href="http://example.com"
                            id="datab">RDBMS</a></li>
                    </ul>
                </li>
            </ul>
```

```
        </td>
        <td valign="top">
                <p class="web" >The wide range of books that includes how
                Web development can be done with ASP.NET, PHP, JSP etc.</p>
                <p class="prog" >The wide range of books that includes
                developing Programming skills in C, C++, Java etc.</p>
                <p class="rdbms" >The wide range of books that includes how
                Data Base Management is done via Oracle, MySQL, SQL Server
                etc.</p>
        </td>
    </table>
</body>
```

To make the menus appear on the left side and the content on the right side, you make a table and place the menu in the first column and the paragraphs containing the information of the related menu items in the second column of the table.

To give the appearance of a menu to the unordered list element, you need to apply certain styles to all three elements: <ul>, <li>, and <a>. You write their type selectors in the style sheet file so that the properties in it can be automatically applied to these three elements. The style sheet file is as follows:

stylehover.css

```
ul {
    width: 200px;
}

ul li ul {
    list-style-type:none;
    margin: 5;
    width: 200px;
}

a {
    display:block;
    border-bottom: 1px solid #fff;
    text-decoration: none;
```

```
        background: #00f;
        color: #fff;
        padding: 0.5em;
}

li {
        display:inline;
}

.hover {
        background: #000;
}
```

The jQuery code to display the information of the hovered menu item is as follows:

Contextualjq.js

```
$(document).ready(function() {
    $('.web').hide();
      $('.prog').hide();
      $('.rdbms').hide();

    $('#webd').hover(function(event){
        $('.web').show();
            $('.prog').hide();
            $('.rdbms').hide();
            $('#webd').addClass('hover');
    }, function(){
            $('#webd').removeClass('hover');
      });

      $('#pgmng').hover(function(event){
            $('.web').hide();
            $('.prog').show();
            $('.rdbms').hide();
            $('#pgmng').addClass('hover');
    }, function(){
        $('#pgmng').removeClass('hover');
      });
```

```
    $('#datab').hover(function(event){
        $('.web').hide();
        $('.prog').hide();
        $('.rdbms').show();
        $('#datab').addClass('hover');
    }, function(){
        $('#datab').removeClass('hover');
    });
});
```

How It Works

In the style sheet file, the type selector ul contains the width property set to 200px to define the width of the menu heading **Books**. The type selector ul li ul is applied to the menu items. It contains the list-style-type property set to none to remove the traditional bullets from the unordered list elements. The margin property is set to 5 to make the menu items appear a bit indented as compared to the menu heading. The width property is set to 200px to define the width of the menu item to accommodate everything. The type selector a contains the display property set to block to make the anchor elements appear as a block and not as individual elements. The border-bottom property is set to 1px solid #fff to make a solid white border of 1px appear below every anchor element (to act as a separator). The text-decoration property is set to none to remove the traditional underline that usually appears below hyperlinks. The background color is set to blue and the foreground color is set to white for all anchor elements. The padding property is set to .5em (i.e. 50% of the default font size) to define the spacing between the anchor text and its border.

The type selector li is set to inline to remove any white space between the list items.

The CSS class .hover contains the background property to set the background color of the menu item (the anchor element) to black when the user clicks it.

Meaning of the jQuery Code

Initially, you hide the information stored in all three paragraphs (of the respective menu items). That is, you hide the information stored in the three paragraphs of classes web, prog, and rdbms since you will display them only when the related menu item is hovered.

You then attach a hover event to the first menu item, **Web Development** (i.e., to the anchor element of id webd). In the first event handling function of the hover event (that is executed when this menu items is hovered), you set the paragraph of class web (which contains the information on **Web Development**) to visible mode, displaying information related to the books on web development to the user. You keep the rest of the paragraph elements hidden. That is, the paragraph elements of classes prog and rdbms are kept hidden. Also, you apply the properties defined in the style rule .hover (defined in the style sheet) to the hovered menu item to highlight it and remove the hover style rule in the second event handling function of the hover event that is executed when the mouse pointer is moved away from the menu item.

You attach a hover event to the second menu item, **Programming** (i.e., to the anchor element of id pgmng). In the first event handling function of the hover event (that is executed when this menu items is hovered), you set the paragraph of class prog (which contains the information on the **Programming** subject) to visible mode, displaying information related to books on programming to the user. You keep the rest of the paragraph elements hidden. That is, the paragraph elements of classes web and rdbms are kept hidden. Also, you apply the properties defined in the style rule .hover (defined in the style sheet) to the hovered menu item to highlight it and remove the hover style rule in the second event handling function of the hover event that is executed when the mouse pointer is moved away from the menu item.

Finally, you attach a hover event to the third menu item **RDBMS** (i.e. ,to the anchor element of id datab). In the first event handling function of the hover event (that is executed when this menu items is hovered), you set the paragraph of class rdbms (which contains information on the **RDBMS** subject) to visible mode, displaying information related to books on RDBMS to the user. You keep the rest of the paragraph elements hidden. That is, the paragraph elements of classes web and prog are kept hidden. Also you apply the properties defined in the style rule .hover (defined in the style sheet) to the hovered menu item to highlight it and remove the .hover style rule in the second event handling function of the hover event that is executed when the mouse pointer is moved away from the menu item.

On execution of the above jQuery code, you will get a menu along with three menu items in it. When you hover over any menu item, that menu item will be highlighted and the information related to it will be displayed as shown in Figure 5-4.

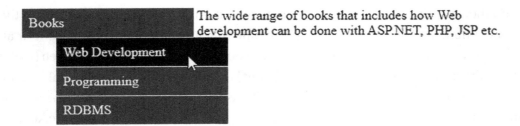

Figure 5-4. *The menu item remains highlighted on being hovered over and related information is displayed*

5-4. Creating a Navigation Menu with Access Keys

Problem

You want to display a menu with a few menu items in it. You want to display the access keys of the menu items. Access keys represent the shortcut keys to a menu item. Also, you want that when any menu item is hovered, the information related to it is displayed. The information must be displayed in both cases, when the menu item is hovered as well as when the access key of any menu item is pressed. When a user clicks on a menu item, they should be sent to the related web site.

Solution

Make an HTML file to represent the menu heading **Books** along with three menu items. You create the menu and its three menu items with the help of an unordered list. The list items contain the anchor elements to represent menu items. Also, you write the information of the three menu items in three paragraphs. To make the character of the menu item (that you want to represent as the access key) appear as underlined, you nest it inside a span element of class hot. The HTML file may appear as follows:

Navigationmenu.html

```
<!DOCTYPE html PUBLIC "-//W3C//DTD XHTML 1.0 Transitional//EN"
        "http://www.w3.org/TR/xhtml1/DTD/xhtml1-transitional.dtd">

<html xmlns="http://www.w3.org/1999/xhtml" xml:lang="en" lang="en">
  <head>
    <meta http-equiv="Content-Type" content="text/html; charset=utf-8"/>
    <title></title>
```

```
<link rel="stylesheet" href="stylehover.css" type="text/css"
media="screen" />
<script src="jquery-3.5.1.js" type="text/javascript"></script>
<script src="navigationjq.js" type="text/javascript"></script>
</head>
<body>
    <table>
        <td>
            <ul>
                <li><a href="http://example.com">Books</a>
                    <ul>
                        <li><a href="http://example.com"
                        id="webd"><span class="hot">W</span>eb
                            Development</a></li>
                        <li><a href="http://example.com"
                        id="pgmng"><span class="hot">P</span>
                            rogramming</a></li>
                        <li><a href="http://example.com" id="datab" >
                        <span class="hot">R</span>DBMS</a></li>
                    </ul>
                </li>
            </ul>
        </td>
        <td valign=top>
            <p class='web' >The wide range of books that includes how
            Web development can be done with ASP.NET, PHP, JSP etc.</p>
            <p class='prog' >The wide range of books that includes
            developing Programming skills in C, C++, Java etc.</p>
            <p class='rdbms' >The wide range of books that includes how
            Data Base Managemenet is done via Oracle, MySQL, Sql Server
            etc.</p>
        </td>
    </table>
</body>
</html>
```

To give the appearance of a menu to the unordered list element, you need to apply certain styles to all three elements: `<u>`, `<li>`, and `<a>`. You write their type selectors in the style sheet file so that the properties in it can be automatically applied to these three elements. The style sheet file may appear as follows:

stylehover.css

```
ul {
        width: 200px;
}

ul li ul {
        list-style-type:none;
        margin: 5;
        width: 200px;
}

a {
    display:block;
      border-bottom: 1px solid #fff;
      text-decoration: none;
    background: #00f;
      color: #fff;
    padding: 0.5em;
}

li {
    display:inline;
}

.hover {
        background: #000;
}

.hot{
    text-decoration:underline;
}
```

The following jQuery code displays the information of the menu item whose access key is pressed or when it is hovered. Also, the hovered menu item is highlighted by the application of certain style rules.

Navigationjq.js

```
$(document).ready(function() {
    $('.web').hide();
    $('.prog').hide();
    $('.rdbms').hide();

    $('body').keypress(function(event){
    if(String.fromCharCode(event.keyCode)=="w" || String.fromCharCode
    (event.keyCode)=="W")
    {
        $('#webd').hover();
    }
    if(String.fromCharCode(event.keyCode)=="p" || String.fromCharCode
    (event.keyCode)=="P")
    {
            $('#pgmng').hover();
    }
    if(String.fromCharCode(event.keyCode)=="r" || String.fromCharCode
    (event.keyCode)=="R")
    {
            $('#datab').hover();
    }
});

    $('#webd').hover(function(event){
        $('.web').show();
            $('.prog').hide();
            $('.rdbms').hide();
            $('#webd').addClass('hover');
    }, function(){
        $('#webd').removeClass('hover');
    });
```

```
    $('#pgmng').hover(function(event){
      $('.web').hide();
            $('.prog').show();
            $('.rdbms').hide();
            $('#pgmng').addClass('hover');
      }, function(){
            $('#pgmng').removeClass('hover');
    });

  $('#datab').hover(function(event){
        $('.web').hide();
            $('.prog').hide();
            $('.rdbms').show();
            $('#datab').addClass('hover');
      }, function(){
            $('#datab').removeClass('hover');
    });
});
```

How It Works

In the HTML file, observe that the first character of the anchor element is highlighted and acts as an access key. Thus the access key for the anchor element **Web Development** is set to the character w so that this menu item can be directly accessed by just pressing the character w (or W). To make the user know that w is the access key, it needs to be underlined. To underline the W of the menu item **Web Development**, you nest it inside the span element and assign the class name hot to the span element to identify it in the style sheet file. Similarly, all characters that you want to be represented as access keys are nested inside the span element of class hot.

Also, to make menus appear on the left side and content on the right side, you make a table and place the menu in the first column and the paragraphs containing the information on the related menu items in the second column of the table.

In the style sheet file, the type selector ul contains the width property set to 200px to define the width of the menu heading **Books**. The type selector ul li ul is applied to the menu items. It contains the list-style-type property set to a value of none to remove the traditional bullets from the unordered list elements. The margin property is set to 5 to make the menu items appear bit indented as compared to the menu heading. The `width` property is set to `200px` to define the width of the menu item to accommodate everything.

The type selector `a` contains the display property set to value `block` to make the anchor elements appear as a block and not as individual elements. The `border-bottom` property is set to value `1px solid #fff` to make a solid white 1px border appear below every anchor element (to act as a separator). The `text-decoration` property is set to `none` to remove the traditional underline that usually appears below hyperlinks. The background color is set to blue and the foreground color is set to white for all anchor elements. The `padding` property is set to `.5em` (i.e. 50% of the default font size) to define the spacing between the anchor text and its border.

The type selector `li` is set to `inline` to remove any white space between the list items.

The CSS class `.hover` contains the background property to set the background color of the menu item (anchor element) to black when user clicks it.

The CSS class `.hot` contains the `text-decorate` property set to `underline` to make all the access characters of each menu item (nested inside the span element of class `hot`) appear as underlined.

In the jQuery code, initially all three paragraph elements are made hidden since you want to display the related information only when any access key is pressed or when any menu item is hovered over. You also attach a keypress event on the body of the HTML file to sense if any key is pressed. If any keypress event occurs, you use conditional statements to check if the pressed key is any of the following characters: w, W, p, P, r, or R. If the any of the said characters are pressed, you invoke the hover event on the respective anchor element. So, if characters w or W are pressed, the hover event on the anchor element **Web Development** (anchor element of id `webd`) is invoked to display the related information. You also attach a hover event to all three menu items. You know that the hover event includes two event handling functions. In the first event handling function of the hover event (which is executed when this menu item is hovered), you set the paragraph that contains the related information to `visible` mode, displaying the desired information. You keep the rest of the paragraph elements hidden. Also, you apply the properties defined in the style rule `.hover` (defined in the style sheet) to the hovered menu item to highlight it and remove the `hover` style rule in the second event handling function of the hover event that is executed when the mouse pointer is moved away from the menu item.

On execution, each of the three menu items appears along with their respective access keys (highlighted as underlined), as shown in Figure 5-5. On pressing the access key or on hovering over the menu item, the information related to it will be displayed, as shown in Figure 5-4.

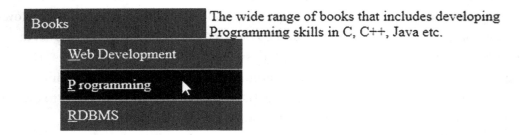

Figure 5-5. *Menu items with access keys displayed as underlined*

5-5. Creating a Context Menu on Right Click

Problem

You want to display a paragraph of text and when you right click on it, you want a context menu to appear on the screen. Also, you want the menu items of the context menu to have a hovering effect (i.e., the menu items get highlighted when the mouse pointer is moved over them). On pressing the Esc key, you want the context menu to disappear.

Solution

Make an HTML file that contains a paragraph element and an unordered list for the menu. The list items of the unordered list represent the menu heading and the menu items. The menu items are written in the form of the anchor elements nested inside the list items. The anchor elements point at some hypothetical web site called http://example.com where the user will be navigated if any menu item is clicked. The HTML file may appear as follows:

Contextrightclick.html

```
<!DOCTYPE html PUBLIC "-//W3C//DTD XHTML 1.0 Transitional//EN"
        "http://www.w3.org/TR/xhtml1/DTD/xhtml1-transitional.dtd">
```

```
<html xmlns="http://www.w3.org/1999/xhtml" xml:lang="en" lang="en">
  <head>
    <meta http-equiv="Content-Type" content="text/html; charset=utf-8"/>
    <title></title>
    <link rel="stylesheet" href="stylehover.css" type="text/css"
    media="screen" />
    <script src="jquery-3.5.1.js" type="text/javascript"></script>
    <script src="contextrightjq.js" type="text/javascript"></script>
  </head>
  <body oncontextmenu="return false">
    <p class="info">
        Books are the world of information. As said the books are the best
        friends. A wise man always has a library of several books</p>
    <ul id="contextmenu">
        <li><a href="http://example.com">Books</a>
            <ul>
                <li><a href="http://example.com">Web Development
                </a></li>
            <li><a href="http://example.com">Programming</a></li>
            <li><a href="http://example.com">RDBMS</a></li>
                </ul>
        </li>
    </ul>
  </body>
</html>
```

You need to define few style rules in the style sheet to give the unordered list the shape of a menu and also to highlight the menu items when the mouse pointer hovers over them (moves over them). The style rules in the style sheet may appear as follows:

stylehover.css

```
ul {
        width: 200px;
}
```

```css
ul li ul {
        list-style-type:none;
        margin: 5;
        width: 200px;
}

a {
    display:block;
        border-bottom: 1px solid #fff;
        text-decoration: none;
    background: #00f;
        color: #fff;
    padding: 0.5em;
}

li {
    display:inline;
}

.hover {
        background: #000;
}
```

The jQuery code to initially hide the menu and to display it when the user clicks the right mouse button on the paragraph element is shown below. The jQuery code also makes the context menu disappear when the Esc key is pressed.

Contextrightjq.js

```javascript
$(document).ready(function() {
    $('#contextmenu').hide();
    $('.info').mousedown(function(event){
        if(event.button==2){
            $('#contextmenu').show();
    $('#contextmenu').css({'position': 'absolute', 'left':event.screenX,
                'top':event.screenY-70});
        }
    });
```

```
    $('a').hover(function(event){
        $(this).addClass('hover');
        },function(){
            $(this).removeClass('hover');
    });
    $('body').keypress(function(event){
        if(event.keyCode==27)
        {
          $('#contextmenu').hide();
        }
    });
});
```

How It Works

The usual problem when displaying a context menu is that when you right-click the paragraph element to display the context menu, the browser's context menu also appears as the default along with your context menu. In order to disable the default browser context menu, use the attribute oncontextmenu="return false" in the body element. The paragraph element is assigned a class name of info so as to access it in jQuery with the help of selectors. The unordered list that is used to display the context menu is assigned the id contextmenu. You can see that the first list item of the unordered list represents the text **Books** (which will act as the menu heading). This list item will contain an unordered list in itself which will represent the menu items.

In the style sheet file, the type selector ul contains the width property set to 200px to define the width of the menu heading **Books**. The type selector ul li ul is applied to the menu items. It contains the list-style-type property set to none to remove the traditional bullets from the unordered list elements. The margin property is set to 5 to make the menu items appear a bit indented as compared to the menu heading. The width property is set to 200px to define the width of the menu item to accommodate everything.

The type selector a contains the display property set to block to make the anchor elements appear as a block and not as an individual element. The border-bottom property is set to 1px solid #fff to make a 1px solid white border appear below every anchor element (to act as a separator). The text-decoration property is set to none to remove the traditional underline that usually appears below hyperlinks. The background color is set to blue and the foreground color is set to white for all anchor elements. The padding property is set to .5em (i.e. 50% of the default font size) to define the spacing between the anchor text and its border.

The type selector li is set to inline to remove any white space between the list items.

The CSS class .hover contains the background property to set the background color of the menu item (anchor element) to black when the user clicks it.

In the jQuery code, you start by hiding the menu represented by the unordered list of id contextmenu.

You then check if the mouse button is pressed on the paragraph element of class info. Recall that you have assigned the class name info to the paragraph element in the HTML file.

If it has been pressed, you check if the mouse button pressed is the right mouse button. The button attribute of the event object contains the value 1 if the left mouse button is pressed and the value 2 if the right mouse button is pressed.

If it is the right mouse button, you make the menu visible on the screen that is represented by the unordered list element of id contextmenu.

Using the css() method, you make the context menu appear at the location specified by the screenX and screenY attributes of the event object that represents the location where the mouse button is pressed. You subtract 70 from the coordinate values stored in the screenY attribute to make the context menu appear closer to the paragraph (i.e., you reduce the gap between the location of the menu and the paragraph).

Also, you attach the hover() event to the anchor elements (menu and the menu items). You apply the style properties defined in the style rule .hover defined in the style sheet file to the anchor elements when the mouse pointer moves over any menu item (making the background color of the menu item turn black). The style properties in the style rule .hover will be removed from the anchor element, making it as it was initially when the mouse pointer moved away from the menu item.

Finally, you attach a keypress event to the body element to sense if any key is pressed. If any key is pressed, you check if it is the Esc key (the key code of the Esc key is 27). If the Esc key is pressed, you hide the context menu.

On right-clicking the mouse button on the paragraph text, the context menu will appear on the screen. The menu items in the menu will have a hovering effect, as shown in Figure 5-6.

Books are the world of information. As said the books are the best friends. A wise man always has a library of several books

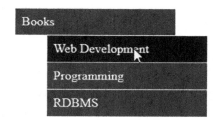

Figure 5-6. *The context menu appears upon right-clicking the paragraph text*

5-6. Creating Two Menus with Separate Menu Items
Problem

You want to display two menus each with respective menu items. You also want to have hovering effects over the menu and its items.

Solution

Make an HTML file to represent two menu headings along with their menu items. You do so with the help of unordered lists, one nested inside the other.

Creatingtwomenu.html

```
<!DOCTYPE html PUBLIC "-//W3C//DTD XHTML 1.0 Transitional//EN"
        "http://www.w3.org/TR/xhtml1/DTD/xhtml1-transitional.dtd">

<html xmlns="http://www.w3.org/1999/xhtml" xml:lang="en" lang="en">
  <head>
    <meta http-equiv="Content-Type" content="text/html; charset=utf-8"/>
    <title></title>
    <link rel="stylesheet" href="styletwomenu.css" type="text/css"
    media="screen" />
    <script src="jquery-3.5.1.js" type="text/javascript"></script>
    <script src="twomenujq.js" type="text/javascript"></script>
  </head>
```

```
<body>
    <ul id="dropdownmenu">
        <li class="mainmenu">
          <a href="example.com">Books</a>
            <ul>
                <li><a href="example.com">Web Development</a></li>
                <li><a href="example.com">Programming</a></li>
                <li><a href="example.com">RDBMS</a></li>
            </ul>
        </li>
         <li class="mainmenu">
           <a href="example.com">Movies</a>
             <ul>
                <li><a href="example.com">Latest Movie Trailers</a></li>
                <li><a href="example.com">Movie Reviews</a></li>
                <li><a href="example.com">Celebrity Interviews</a></li>
             </ul>
         </li>
    </ul>
</body>
</html>
```

You can see in this code that there is an unordered list of id dropdownmenu with two list items that are assigned the class name mainmenu. These two list items represent the menus **Books** and **Movies**. Both list items in turn consist of unordered lists with three elements each. The **Books** menu has three list items: **Web Development**, **Programming**, and **RDBMS**. Similarly, the list item **Movies** consists of an unordered list of three elements: **Latest Movie Trailers**, **Movie Reviews**, and **Celebrity Interviews**.

To apply the styles to the unordered list to give them the appearance of two menus along with menu items, see the following style sheet file:

Styletwomenu.css

```
.mainmenu {float:left; width:220px; list-style-type:none; margin-
right:5px;}
li.mainmenu ul {margin: 0;   }
```

```
a   {width: 200px;display:block; text-decoration: none; background:
#00f;   color: #fff;padding: 0.5em;    border-bottom: 1px solid #fff; }
ul#dropdownmenu li a:hover {   background: #000;}
ul{ margin: 0; list-style: none; }
```

The jQuery code to display one set of menu items out of the two when the mouse pointer moves over the respective menu heading is as follows:

Twomenujq.js

```
$(document).ready(function(){
  $('li.mainmenu').hover(
    function() {
      $('ul', this).show();
    },
    function() {
      $('ul', this).hide();
    }
  );
});
```

How It Works

In the style sheet file, the class selector `.mainmenu` contains the properties that are to be automatically applied to the two menu headings, **Books** and **Movies**. It contains the `float` property set to `left` to make first menu heading float to the left in the browser window (making space for the second menu heading to appear on its right). The `width` property is set to `220px` to make the menu headings 220px wide. The `margin-right` property is set to `5px` to create spacing of 5px among the two menu headings.

The type selector `li.mainmenu ul` contains the style property to be applied automatically to the unordered list that is nested inside the list items of class `.mainmenu` (i.e., to the unordered lists that act as menu items of the list items with text **Books** and **Movies**). The property that it contains is a `margin` property set to value 0 to make the list items of the unordered list (menu items like **Web Development**, **Programming**, etc. of both menu headings, **Books** as well as **Books**) appear one below the other (without any hierarchical gap on the left side).

The type selector a contains the properties that are to be applied to all anchor elements (i.e., to the menus as well as to all menu items). The width property is set to 200px to specify the width of each menu item. The display property is set to block to make the anchor element act as an independent block, the text-decoration property is set to none to remove the traditional underline from the hyperlinks, the background property sets the background color of the menu headings and menu items to blue, and the color property sets the foreground color of the text on the menus (menu headings and menu items) to white. The padding property is set to .5em to create the spacing of 50% of the default font size between the menu text and its border. The border-bottom property is set to 1px solid #fff to create a 1px solid white line of thickness below every anchor element to act as a separator among the menu items.

The type selector ul#dropdownmenu li a:hover contains the style property that will be automatically applied to the menu headings as well as the menu items upon hovering over them. It contains the background property that changes the background color of the menu headings and the menu items to black when the mouse pointer moves over them.

You can see in the jQuery code that when the mouse pointer moves over the list item of class mainmenu (i.e., on any menu heading), the unordered list (containing the menu items) nested in that list item will be displayed. Moving the mouse pointer away from a menu heading will make its menu items invisible because the unordered list of that list item is set to hidden mode.

Initially the two menu headings will appear as shown in Figure 5-7.

Figure 5-7. *Two menu headings, Books and Movies*

Upon moving the mouse pointer over the menu heading **Books**, its menu items (the unordered list that is nested inside the list item with text **Books**) will be displayed as shown in Figure 5-8.

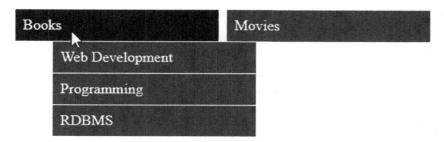

Figure 5-8. *The menu items of the Books menu are displayed with a hovering effect*

Upon moving the mouse pointer over the menu heading **Movies**, its menu items will be displayed and those of the menu heading **Books** will become invisible as shown in Figure 5-9.

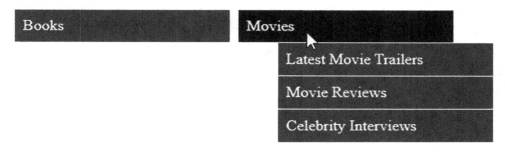

Figure 5-9. *Menu items of the Movies menu with a hovering effect*

5-7. Creating Two Menus with Submenu Items

Problem

You want to display two menus each with menu items and attach submenu items to a few of the menu items. You also want to have a hovering effect over the menu, its items, and the submenu items.

Solution

Make an HTML file to represent two menu headings along with their menu items. You will also define the submenu items. You do so with the help of unordered lists, one nested inside the other. The HTML file may appear as follows:

Twomenuwithsub.html

```
<!DOCTYPE html PUBLIC "-//W3C//DTD XHTML 1.0 Transitional//EN"
        "http://www.w3.org/TR/xhtml1/DTD/xhtml1-transitional.dtd">

<html xmlns="http://www.w3.org/1999/xhtml" xml:lang="en" lang="en">
  <head>
    <meta http-equiv="Content-Type" content="text/html; charset=utf-8"/>
    <title></title>
    <link rel="stylesheet" href="styletwomenusub.css" type="text/css"
    media="screen" />
    <script src="jquery-3.5.1.js" type="text/javascript"></script>
    <script src="twomenuwithsubjq.js" type="text/javascript"></script>
  </head>
<body>
    <ul class="dropdown">
        <li><a href="http://example.com">Books</a>
            <ul>
                <li><a href="http://example.com">Programming</a></li>
                <li><a href="http://example.com">Web Development</a>
                    <ul>
                        <li><a href="http://example.com">.Net</a>
                        </li>
                        <li><a href="http://example.com">JSP</a></li>
                    </ul>
                </li>
                <li><a href="http://example.com">RDBMS</a></li>
                <li><a href="http://example.com">Web Services</a></li>
                <li><a href="http://example.com">Open Source</a></li>
            </ul>
        </li>
```

```
        <li><a href="http://example.com">Movies</a>
            <ul>
                <li><a href="http://example.com">Movie Reviews</a></li>
                <li><a href="http://example.com">Celebrity Interviews
                </a></li>
                <li><a href="http://example.com">Latest Hollywood
                Movies</a>
                    <ul>
                        <li><a href="http://example.com">Arnold
                        Schwarzenegger</a></li>
                        <li><a href="http://example.com">Sylvester
                        Stallone</a></li>
                        <li><a href="http://example.com">Bruce
                        Willis</a></li>
                    </ul>
                </li>
                <li><a href="http://example.com">Action Movies</a>
                    <ul>
                        <li><a href="http://example.com">Casino
                        Royale</a></li>
                        <li><a href="http://example.com">Rambo III
                        </a></li>
                    </ul>
                </li>
                <li><a href="http://example.com">Comedy Movies</a></li>
            </ul>
        </li>
    </ul>
  </body>
</html>
```

The style properties to be assigned to the unordered list to make them appear in the form of menu headings, menu items, and submenu items are as follows:

styletwomenusub.css

```
a{ text-decoration: none; color:#000;}
ul{margin:0; list-style: none; }
ul.dropdown li {float: left;  background: cyan; }
ul.dropdown a:hover {background: #0f0; color: #00f; }
ul.dropdown li a {display: block; padding: 4px; border-right: 1px solid #000; }
ul.dropdown ul {width:150px; visibility: hidden; position: absolute;  }
ul.dropdown ul li {background: yellow; border-bottom: 1px solid #000;
width:100%; }
ul.dropdown ul li a { border-right: none; width:100%; }
ul.dropdown ul ul {left:100%; width:100%;top: 0; }
.hover {position: relative; }
```

The jQuery code to apply to make the menu items and submenus appear on the screen is as follows:

Twomenuwithsubjq.js

```
$(document).ready(function(){
    $("ul.dropdown li").hover(function(){
      $(this).addClass("hover");
              $('ul:first',this).css('visibility', 'visible');
        }, function(){
              $(this).removeClass("hover");
              $('ul:first',this).css('visibility', 'hidden');
    });
     $("ul.dropdown li ul li:has(ul)").find("a:first").append("  >");
});
```

How It Works

In the HTML file, an unordered list is created and is assigned the class name dropdown. It contains two list items with the text assigned as **Books** and **Movies**. These two list items in turn contain unordered list items that are assigned the class name submenu.

The unordered list of the **Books** list item contains five list items: **Programming, Web Development, RDBMS, Web Services,** and **Open Source**. Out of these list items, the **Web Development** one contains an unordered list to represent submenu items called **.Net** and **JSP**.

Similarly, the unordered list contained in the **Movies** list item contains four list items: **Movie Reviews, Celebrity Interviews, Latest Hollywood Movies**, and **Action Movies**. Out of these list items, **Latest Hollywood Movies** contains an unordered list to represent submenu items called **Arnold Schwarzenegger, Sylvester Stallone**, and **Bruce Willis**. Also, the list item **Action Movies** contains an unordered list to represent submenu items **Casino Royale, Rambo III**, and **Comedy Movies**.

In the style sheet file, the type selector a has the property text-decoration set to value none to remove the traditional underline from all anchor elements (i.e., from the menu headings, menu items, and submenu items) and the color property is set to black to make the text on all menus appear in black.

The type selector ul contains the margin property set to 0 to remove the hierarchical margin from the left side in the list items and to make the menu items appear one below the other. The list-style property is set to value none to remove the traditional bullets from the unordered list.

The styles defined in the type selector ul.dropdown li are automatically applied to the list items that belong to the unordered list of class dropdown (i.e., to the menu headings **Books** and **Movies**). The float property is set to left to make one menu heading appear on the left side of the browser window, creating space for the next menu heading to appear on its right. The background color is set to cyan.

The attribute selector ul.dropdown a:hover contains the background and color property to set the background and foreground colors of the anchor elements (all menu items) that are been hovered over to the colors green and blue, respectively.

The type selector ul.dropdown li a contains the style properties that will be applied to the anchor elements that represent the menu headings **Books** and **Movies**. It contains the display property set to block to make the anchor elements act as an independent block element, the padding property set to 4px to create some spacing between the menu text and its border, and the border-right property set to 1px solid #000 to make a black border of 1px on the right of each menu heading (to show them as separate).

The type selector ul.dropdown ul contains the styles that will be applied to the unordered list containing menu items. The width property set to 150px makes each menu item 150px wide, and the visibility property set to hidden keep the whole menu items block hidden and makes it visible only when the menu headings are hovered over. The `position` property set to `absolute` makes the menu items block appear below their respective menu headings.

The type selector `ul.dropdown ul li` contains the properties that will be applied to all list items representing the menu items. The `background` property sets the background color of all menu items and submenu items to yellow, and the `border-bottom` property is set to `1px solid #000` to make a 1px black border appear below each menu item to separate them.

The type selector `ul.dropdown ul li a` contains the properties that are applied to all anchor elements representing the menu items and submenu items. The `border-right` property is set to `none` to remove the border on the right of the menu items because you will be displaying submenu items on the right of the menu items. The `width` property is set to `100%` to make the anchor element take up all of the 200px width assigned.

The type selector `ul.dropdown ul ul` is applied to the unordered list representing the submenu items. The `left` property is set to `100%` to make the submenu items appear at a distance of 100% from the left (i.e., after the width of the menu items) or else it will overlap with the menu items. The `top` property is set to 0 to make the submenu items at the same distance (from the top border of the browser) as the menu item whose submenu items are being displayed

The style rule `.hover;` is applied via jQuery code to the list items to make the submenu items appear at the location relative to their menu items.

Before you begin to understanding the jQuery code, let's understand what `:first` does since it's used in the above code.

:first

It is the custom selector that returns the first instance of the specified element.

Example:

```
$('p:first)
```

will return the first paragraph element.

In the above jQuery code, when the mouse pointer is moved over any of the menu headings, **Books** or **Movies** (the list items of the unordered list of id `dropdown`), the properties of the CSS class `.hover` defined in the stylesheet file will be applied to it and also the first unordered list (menu items of the respective menu heading) will be in visible mode. Similarly, when any menu item is hovered over (that has unordered list in the form of submenu items), then that unordered list will also be displayed (i.e., the submenu items will be displayed). The menu items or submenu items are made hidden when the mouse pointer is away from the menu item or menu heading, respectively. Also, for all list items that have unordered lists nested in them, the symbol > is appended to its anchor element to designate that it has submenu items attached.

Initially, the two menu headings, **Books** and **Movies**, appear as shown in Figure 5-10.

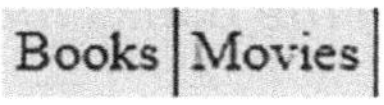

Books │Movies│

Figure 5-10. *Menu headings: Books and Movies*

On moving the mouse pointer to the menu heading **Books**, its menu items will be displayed as shown in Figure 5-11.

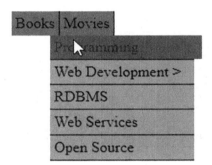

Figure 5-11. *Menu items of the Books menu (the menu items that have submenes items appear with a > symbol)*

On moving the mouse pointer over the menu item that has a submenu attached, the submenu items will be displayed as shown in Figure 5-12.

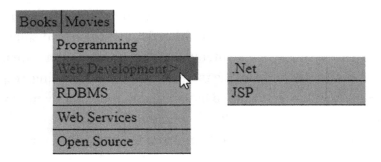

Figure 5-12. *The submenu items of the Books menu being highlighted*

The same thing will be applied to the second menu heading, **Movies**. Its menu items will be made visible when the mouse is hovered over it. Also, the submenu items of the menu item will be displayed when the mouse is hovered over it, as shown in Figure 5-13.

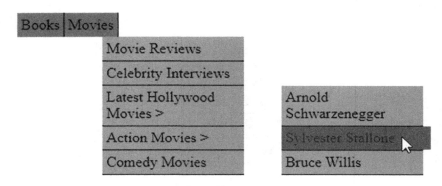

Figure 5-13. *The submenu items of the Movies menu being highlighted*

5-8. Making an Accordion Menu

Problem

You want to display two menus in the form of an accordion menu (i.e., the menu items of the menu that is hovered over will be made visible and the menu items of the other menu heading(s) will be made invisible by using a slide up or slide down technique). You also want the menu items to disappear when the mouse pointer is away from both menus.

Solution

Let's make an HTML file to represent two menu headings along with their menu items. You do so with the help of an unordered list, one nested inside the other. The HTML file may appear as follows:

Makingaccordion.html

```
<!DOCTYPE html PUBLIC "-//W3C//DTD XHTML 1.0 Transitional//EN"
        "http://www.w3.org/TR/xhtml1/DTD/xhtml1-transitional.dtd">

<html xmlns="http://www.w3.org/1999/xhtml" xml:lang="en" lang="en">
  <head>
    <meta http-equiv="Content-Type" content="text/html; charset=utf-8"/>
    <title></title>
    <link rel="stylesheet" href="styleaccordion.css" type="text/css"
    media="screen" />
    <script src="jquery-3.5.1.js" type="text/javascript"></script>
    <script src="makingaccordionjq.js" type="text/javascript"></script>
  </head>
  <body>
      <p class="menus">Books</p>
        <div class="menuitems">
          <ul>
                <li><a href="example.com">Web Development</a></li>
                <li><a href="example.com">Programming</a></li>
                <li><a href="example.com">RDBMS</a></li>
          </ul>
        </div>
      <p class="menus">Movies</p>
        <div class="menuitems">
          <ul>
                <li><a href="example.com">Latest Movie Trailers</a></li>
                <li><a href="example.com">Movie Reviews</a></li>
                <li><a href="example.com">Celebrity Interviews</a></li>
          </ul>
        </div>
  </body>
</html>
```

To apply the styles to the above unordered list to give them the appearance of an accordion menu, use the following file:

styleaccordion.css

```css
.menus{
    width: 200px;
    padding:5px;
    margin:1px;
    font-weight:bold;
    background-color: #0ff;
}

.menuitems{
    display:none;
}
a{
    display:block;
    border-bottom: 1px solid #fff;
    text-decoration: none;
    background: #00f;
    color: #fff;
    padding:10px;
    font-weight:bold;
    width: 190px;
}

.menuitems a:hover {
    background: #000;
}
li {
    display:inline;
}
ul{display:inline;}
```

The jQuery code to display the menu items of the hovered menu headings and to hide the menu items of the other menu heading (where the mouse pointer is moved away) with a sliding effect is as follows:

Makingaccordionjq.js

```
$(document).ready(function() {
    $('p.menus').mouseout(function(){
        $("div.menuitems'").slideUp("slow");
        $('p').css({backgroundImage:""});
    });

      $('p.menus').mouseover(function(){
        $(this).css({'background-image':"url(down.png)", 'background-
        repeat':"no-repeat",
            'background-position':"right"}).next("div.menuitems").
            slideDown(500)
            .siblings("div.menuitems").slideUp("slow");
        $(this).siblings().css({backgroundImage:""});
    });
});
```

How It Works

In the HTML file, there are two paragraph elements of class menus with the text **Books** and **Movies** to represent two menu headings. Each paragraph element is followed by a div element of class menuitems that contains an unordered list with three list items each to represent the menu items of each menu heading. The unordered list (below the paragraph element of the text **Books**) has three list items: **Web Development, Programming**, and **RDBMS**. Similarly, the unordered list that is below the paragraph element called **Movies** has three list items: **Latest Movie Trailers, Movie Reviews**, and **Celebrity Interviews**.

In the style sheet file, the properties defined in the class selector .menus will be automatically applied to the paragraph elements of class .menu to give them the shape of menu headings. The width property is set to 200px to define the menu heading to be 200px wide, and the padding property is set to 5px to keep some space between the border and the menu text. The `margin` property is set to `1px` to keep a space of `1px` between the two menu headings. The `font-weight` property is set to `bold` to make the menu headings appear in bold and the background of the menu heading is set to cyan by applying the code `#0ff` to the `background-color` property.

The properties in the class selector `.menuitems` will be applied to the `div` elements of class `menuitems` automatically. It contains the `display` property set to `none` to hide the menu items initially.

The properties defined in the type selector `a` will be applied to all anchor elements (to all menu items). The `display` property is set to `block` to make the anchor element act as a block. The `border bottom` property is set to `1px solid #fff` to create a 1px solid white line below every anchor element to separate all menu items. The `text-decoration` property is set to `none` to remove the traditional underline from the anchor elements. The background and color properties are used to set the background and foreground colors of the menu items to blue and white, respectively. The `padding` property is set to `10px` to define the spacing between the menu items text and the border. The `font-weight` property is set to `bold` to make the menu items appear in bold and the `width` property is set to `190px` to make the menu items 190px wide.

The properties defined in the attribute selector `.menuitems a:hover` will be automatically applied to the anchor elements nested inside the `div` element of class `menu` element when the mouse pointer hovers over the menu items. It contains the background property that makes the background color of the hovered menu items turn black.

The type selector `li` contains the display property set to `inline` to remove any spacing among the list items. Similarly, the type selector `ul` has the display property set to `inline` to remove the spacing above and below the unordered list

The meaning of above jQuery code statement-wise is as follows:

You attach the mouseout event to the paragraph elements of class `menus` (i.e., to the menu headings **Books** and **Movies**). The reason for doing so is that you want to hide the menu items if the mouse pointer is away from both menus.

Then you attach the mouseover event to the paragraph element of class `menus` (i.e., to the menu headings **Books** and **Movies**).

You then display an image of a down pointer to the hovered menu heading using the `.css()` method (to show that currently it is in expanded mode). The `background-repeat` property is set to `no-repeat` to make it appear once and the `background-position` property is set to `right` to make the down pointer appear on the right end of the menu heading.

The contents of the next element (that matches the selector), which is nothing but a div element of class menuitems (containing the menu items of the hovered paragraph element), is made visible with a slide-down effect and its siblings that match the selector (i.e., the menu items of another menu heading, like the div element of class menuitems) are made invisible by using a slide-up effect.

Finally, the background image is removed from the menu item that has lost focus.

On execution of the above jQuery code, the menu headings will appear one below the other as shown in Figure 5-14.

Figure 5-14. *Two menu headings, Books and Movies*

On hovering over the first menu heading, **Books**, its menu items will be displayed with a slide-down effect as shown in Figure 5-15. You can see that the menu heading has a down pointer attached to it to designate that it is in expanded mode now. Also, these menu items have hovering effect (i.e., they are highlighted on moving the mouse pointer over them).

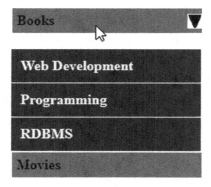

Figure 5-15. *Menu items of the Books menu appear with a slide-down effect*

Similarly, on moving the mouse pointer over another menu heading, like **Movies**, you see that its menu items appear and those of the **Books** menu disappear with a slide-up effect as shown in Figure 5-16.

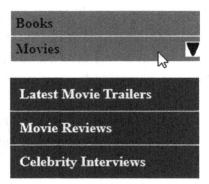

Figure 5-16. *Menu items of the Movies menu appear with slide-down effect*

5-9. Making a Dynamic Visual Menu

Problem

You want to make a curved tab navigation menu that has three menus called **Books**, **Movies**, and **Music**. You want the menu tabs to have a hovering effect (highlighted when the mouse moves over them). You also want related information concerning the menu tab displayed when hovered over.

Solution

Make an HTML file to define the anchor elements with the text **Books, Movies**, and **Music** nested inside the span element of class buttons. The anchor elements are assigned the ids booksbutton, moviesbutton, and musicbutton, respectively (to be accessed via jQuery code) and point at a hypothetical web site called example.com where the user will be sent if the menu item is selected. The HTML file is as follows:

Dynamicvisualmenu.html

```
<!DOCTYPE html PUBLIC "-//W3C//DTD XHTML 1.0 Transitional//EN"
        "http://www.w3.org/TR/xhtml1/DTD/xhtml1-transitional.dtd">

<html xmlns="http://www.w3.org/1999/xhtml" xml:lang="en" lang="en">
  <head>
    <meta http-equiv="Content-Type" content="text/html; charset=utf-8"/>
    <title></title>
```

```
<link rel="stylesheet" href="stylevisualmenu.css" type="text/css"
media="screen" />
<script src="jquery-3.5.1.js" type="text/javascript"></script>
<script src="visualmenujq.js" type="text/javascript"></script>
</head>
<body>
    <span class="buttons"><a href="example.com" id="booksbutton">
    Books </a></span>
    <span class="buttons"><a href="example.com" id="moviesbutton">
    Movies </a> </span>
    <span class="buttons"><a href="example.com" id="musicbutton"> Music
    </a></span><br><br>
    <p class="books">Books of different subjects available at reasonable
    prices. Ranging from web development, programming languages and text
    books all are available at heavy discount. Shipping is free. Also
    available in stock the popular Magazines, E-books and Tutorial CDs
    at affordable prices.</p>
    <p class="movies">Find new movie reviews & latest hollywood movie
    news. Includes new movie trailers, latest hollywood releases, movie
    showtimes, entertainment news, celebrity interviews etc. Also find
    Hollywood actress, actor, videos biography, filmography, photos,
    wallpapers, music, jokes live tv channels at your doorsteps</p>
    <p class="music">Find music videos, internet radio, music downloads
    and all the latest music news and information. We have a large
    collection of music and songs classified by type, language and
    region. All downloads are streamed through RealAudio. You can also
    watch free music videos, tune in to AOL Radio, and search for your
    favorite music artists.</p>
</body>
</html>
```

Below the span elements you find three paragraph elements with three different class names assigned as books, movies, and music, respectively. The paragraphs contain the information related to the three menu tabs.

For this solution, you need two tab images. One tab image is for the left side of the menu tab to give it a curved slope, as shown in Figure 5-17.

Figure 5-17. *Image for the left side of the menu tab*

The image for the left side is saved with the file name tabl.jpg and the image for right side of the menu tab is stored in the file name tabr.jpg and appears as shown in Figure 5-18.

Figure 5-18. *Image for the right side of the menu tab*

The two images in Figures 5-17 and 5-18 are in black. You need the same two images in green, too (which will be used while hovering over the menu tabs). The two images with the left and right slopes respectively as in Figures 5-17 and 5-18 but in green are saved in the files tablselect.jpg and tabrselect.jpg.

The style sheet file style.css contains several style rules to make the span element appear as a tab navigation menu. The style.css file is as follows:

stylevisualmenu.css

```
.buttons{
        background-image:url(tabl.jpg);
        background-repeat:no-repeat;
        background-position: left;
        background-color:#000;
        width: 80px;
        float: left;
        text-align: center;
}

a{
        display:block;
        background-image:url(tabr.jpg);
        background-repeat:no-repeat;
        background-position: right;
        padding:3px;
```

```
        text-decoration:none;
        font-weight:bold;
        color:#fff;
}

.rightselectfig{
        display:block;
        background-image:url(tabrselect.jpg);
        background-repeat:no-repeat;
        background-position: right;
        padding:3px;
        text-decoration:none;
        font-weight:bold;
        color:#fff;
}

.leftselectfig{
        background-image:url(tablselect.jpg);
        background-repeat:no-repeat;
        background-position: left;
        background-color:#0f0;
        width: 80px;
        float: left;
        text-align: center;
}
```

The jQuery code to apply the hovering effect to the menu tabs and to display their related information is as follows:

Visualmenujq.js

```
$(document).ready(function() {
  $('.books').hide();
  $('.movies').hide();
  $('.music').hide();

  $('a').hover(
    function(event){
      $(this).addClass('rightselectfig');
```

```
          $(this).parent().addClass('leftselectfig');
      },
      function(){
        $(this).removeClass('rightselectfig');
        $(this).parent().removeClass('leftselectfig');
      }
    );

    $('#booksbutton').click(function(event){
      event.preventDefault();
      $('.books').show('slow');
      $('.movies').hide();
      $('.music').hide();
    });

    $('#moviesbutton').click(function(event){
      event.preventDefault();
      $('.movies').show('slow');
      $('.books').hide();
      $('.music').hide();
    });

    $('#musicbutton').click(function(event){
      event.preventDefault();
      $('.music').show('slow');
      $('.books').hide();
      $('.movies').hide();
    });
});
```

How It Works

The class selector .buttons contains the style properties that will be automatically applied to the span elements of class buttons (i.e., to all the three texts: **Books, Movies**, and **Music**). The background image property is set to url(tab1.jpg) to make the image shown in Figure 5-17 appear along with the menu text, the background repeat property is set to no-repeat to make the image to appear only once, and the background-position property is set to left to make the image appear on the left side of the menu text to assign it a slope on the left side.

The background color of the menu tab is set to black and the width assigned to the menu tab is 80px. The float property is set to left to make the menu tab appear on the left side of the browser window, making space on its right (for other menu tabs to appear on the right). The text-align property is set to center to make the menu text appear at the center of the defined width of 80px.

The properties defined in the type selector a will be automatically applied to the anchor elements. The display property is set to block to make the anchor elements act as a block element instead of individual elements. The background-image property is set to tabr.jpg to apply the image shown in Figure 5-18 on the right side of the menu tab. The background -repeat property is set to no-repeat to make the image appear only once. The background-position is set to right to make the image appear on the right side to assign it a slope shape on its right. The padding property is set to 3px to have the spacing of 3px between the menu text and its border. The text-decoration property is set to none to remove the traditional underline that usually appears below the anchor elements. The font-weight property is set to bold to make the menu text to appear in bold and the color is set to white to make the menu text appear in white.

The style rule .rightselectfig contains the properties that will be applied to the anchor elements when the mouse pointer is moved over them. It contains the display property set to block to make the anchor element act as a block element instead of an individual element. The background-image property is set to tabrselect.jpg to apply the image shown in Figure 5-18 in the green color on the right side of the menu tab. The background-repeat property is set to no-repeat to make the image appear only once. The background-position is set to right to make the image appear on the right side to assign it a slope shape on its right. The padding property is set to 3px to have the spacing of 3px between the menu text and its border. The text-decoration property is set to none to remove the traditional underline that usually appears below the anchor elements. The font-weight property is set to bold to make the menu text appear in bold and the color is set to white to make the menu text to appear in white.

The style rule .leftselectfig contains the properties that will be applied to the menu tab buttons when the mouse pointer is moved over them. The background image property is set to url(tablselect.jpg) to make the image shown in Figure 5-17 in the green color appear along with the menu text. The background-repeat property is set to no-repeat to make the image to appear only once and the background-position property is set to left to make the image appear on the left side of menu text to assign it a slope on the left side. The background color of the menu tab is set to green to give it a hovering effect. The width assigned to the menu tab is 80px. The float property is set to left to make the menu tab appear on the left side of the browser window, making space on its right (for other menu tabs to appear on the right). The text-align property is set to center to make the menu text appear at the center of the defined width of 80px.

In the jQuery code, all paragraph elements of classes books, movies, and music are made invisible because you will be displaying them only when you hover over the respective menu tab. You then attach the hover event to the anchor element and apply the properties defined in the style rule .rightselectfig to the menu tab (that is being hovered over) to apply green to it and add the image (tabrselect.jpg) on the right side for the right slope of the menu tab. You deal with the left side in the same way.

When the mouse is no longer hovering over the tab, you remove the style properties of the style rules .rightselectfig and .leftselectfig to make the menu tabs appear as they were initially when the mouse moved away from the menu tabs.

Next are the click events for the tabs. In these, you prevent the form from being submitted to the server or being navigated to the target web site on clicking the menu tab. You then display the information associated with the tab that was clicked and hide the contents of the paragraph elements associated with the other tabs.

When you hover over the **Books** menu tab, you find that its background color changes to green and also the information related to books is displayed as shown in Figure 5-19.

Books of different subjects available at reasonable prices. Ranging from web development, programming languages and text books all are available at heavy discount. Shipping is free. Also available in stock the popular Magazines, E-books and Tutorial CDs at affordable prices.

Figure 5-19. *The menu tab gets highlighted upon being hovered over and the respective information is displayed*

In order to give the animation effect to the text being displayed, you can use the slideDown() and slideUp() methods instead of the simple show() and hide() methods as shown in the following jQuery code:

Menuslidejq.js

```
$(document).ready(function() {
  $('.books').hide();
  $('.movies').hide();
  $('.music').hide();

  $('#booksbutton').mouseover(function(){
    $('.books').slideDown('slow');
    $('.movies').slideUp('slow');
    $('.music').slideUp('slow');
  });

  $('#moviesbutton').mouseover(function(){
    $('.movies').slideDown('slow');
    $('.books').slideUp('slow');
    $('.music').slideUp('slow');
  });

  $('#musicbutton').mouseover(function(){
    $('.music').slideDown('slow');
    $('.books').slideUp('slow');
    $('.movies').slideUp('slow');
  });
});
```

5-10. Summary

In this chapter, you saw how to create different types of menus like breadcrumbs, contextual menus, accordion menus, and dynamic visual menus. You also saw how to access menu items using access keys and how to make menus with hovering menu items.

In the next chapter, you will learn how animation is applied to different HTML elements. You will learn to animate an image from right and left, manipulate the jQuery queue, show images one by one upon clicks of buttons, zoom in on an image, display detailed information upon clicking the "read more" link, and expand and collapse a list using animation.

CHAPTER 6

Implementing Animation

In this chapter, you will learn how animation is applied to different HTML elements. You will be making the following recipes in this chapter:

- Animating an image to the right and then the left
- Managing and manipulating the jQuery queue
- Showing images one by one upon clicking the Next and Previous buttons
- Zooming in on the image when the mouse hovers over it
- Displaying detailed information by clicking the **Read more** link
- Expanding and collapsing a list using animation

6-1. Animating an Image to the Right and Then the Left

Problem

You have an image and you want it to animate from left to right and then back to its original location.

Solution

The following is an HTML program that displays the web page heading, a button, and an image:

Animation1.html

```
<!DOCTYPE html PUBLIC "-//W3C//DTD XHTML 1.0 Transitional//EN"
```

© Bintu Harwani 2022
B. Harwani, *jQuery Recipes*, https://doi.org/10.1007/978-1-4842-7304-3_6

```
      "http://www.w3.org/TR/xhtml1/DTD/xhtml1-transitional.dtd">

<html xmlns="http://www.w3.org/1999/xhtml" xml:lang="en" lang="en">
  <head>
    <meta http-equiv="Content-Type" content="text/html; charset=utf-8"/>
    <title></title>
<link rel="stylesheet" href="animation1style.css" type="text/css"
media="screen" />
    <script src="jquery-3.5.1.js" type="text/javascript"></script>
    <script src="animation1bjq.js" type="text/javascript"></script>
  </head>
  <body>
<p>We deal with Electronics Products</p>
<button id="anim">Animate Image</button><br/>
<img class="pic" id="pic1" src="chip.jpg" width="200" height="100">
  </body>
</html>
```

You can see in the above code that a paragraph element is used to display the text **We deal with Electronics Products**. Below the text is a button with the label **Animate Image**. To identify it uniquely, the button is given an ID of anim. Below the button the chip image is displayed at 200px wide and 100px high.

The jQuery code to animate the picture from left to right and then back to its original location is as follows:

Animation1jq.js

```
$(document).ready(function() {
    $("button#anim").click( function() {
        $("img#pic1").animate({ left: '350px'}, 'slow',
        function(){
            $("img#pic1").animate({ left: '0px'}, 'slow');
        });
    });
});
```

This jQuery code uses the left property, so let's have a quick look at it.

left Property

It sets the position of the HTML element in relation to the left border of the browser window. Valid options are

- distance: The element is positioned at the specified distance mentioned in px, cm, etc.

- %: The distance of the element is set at the specified % of the container.

- auto: The browser determines the position of the element from the left border. This is the default option.

- initial: The default value is chosen as the value for this element.

- inherit: The value of this property is inherited from its parent element.

position Property

The position property must be set before using the left property because until and unless the element is positioned, the left property will not work. The following are the valid options of the position property:

- absolute/fixed: The left edge of the element will be set to the specified value.

- relative: The left edge of the element will be set in relation to its current position.

- sticky: It will act as relative or fixed depending on its position. This option will not let the element go off the screen.

- static: The left property will not work.

How It Works

When the button with the ID anim is clicked, the image with the ID pic1 is animated from its current position towards the right direction at a slow speed and it will stop at location 350px from the left boundary of the browser screen (see Figure 6-1). In the callback function of the animate method (i.e., when the image reaches its right destination of 350px from the left border), the callback function will execute, which animates the image back towards left direction at a slow speed and will stop when the image reaches the 0px distance from the left border of the browser screen.

We deal with Electronics Products

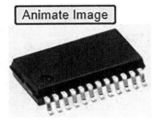

We deal with Electronics Products

Figure 6-1. *On clicking the button, the image animates towards the right direction and then again towards the left direction*

In the callback function, you can paste another picture. Let's modify the above jQuery code so that the chip image animates towards the right and while moving its height and width increases and finally the chip image is replaced by a laptop image. The jQuery file Animation1jq.js shows the code for doing so.

Animation1jq.js

```
$(document).ready(function() {
    $("button#anim").click( function() {
        $("img#pic1").animate({ left: '350px', width: '400px', height:
        '350px'}, 'slow',
        function(){
            $("img#pic1").attr("src", "computer.jpg");
        });
    });
});
```

Initially the chip image and button will appear as shown in Figure 6-2(a). When the button with the ID anim is clicked, the chip image with the ID pic1 is animated from its current position towards the right direction. The chip image will animate until it reaches at the distance of 350px from the left border of the browser screen. While the image is animating, its width will increase to 400px slowly and also its height will increase to 350px slowly (see Figure 6-2(b)). At the end of the animation (i.e., when the chip image becomes 400px wide and 350px high), it will be replaced by the laptop image via the callback function (see Figure 6-2(c)).

We deal with Electronics Products

Animate Image

(a)

We deal with Electronics Products

Animate Image

(b)

We deal with Electronics Products

Animate Image

(c)

Figure 6-2. *(a) The chip image and button appear. (b) The chip image is animated towards the right and its width and height increases with the animation. (c) The chip image is replaced by the laptop image*

6-2. Managing and Manipulating the jQuery Queue

Problem

You execute several animation methods on an image, which are stored in the jQuery queue. You manipulate the methods that are stored in the queue as per your requirement.

Solution

The HTML program to display an image onto which you will be executing different animation methods is as follows:

Animation2.html

```
<!DOCTYPE html PUBLIC "-//W3C//DTD XHTML 1.0 Transitional//EN"
        "http://www.w3.org/TR/xhtml1/DTD/xhtml1-transitional.dtd">

<html xmlns="http://www.w3.org/1999/xhtml" xml:lang="en" lang="en">
  <head>
    <meta http-equiv="Content-Type" content="text/html; charset=utf-8"/>
    <title></title>
    <script src="jquery-3.5.1.js" type="text/javascript"></script>
    <script src="animation2jq.js" type="text/javascript"></script>
  </head>
  <body>
<img class="pic" id="pic1" src="chip.jpg" width="200" height="100">
  </body>
</html>
```

You can see in the above program that an image that is 200px wide and 100px high is displayed. The image is assigned the class pic and ID pic1.

The jQuery code to apply certain animation tasks on the image and to display the jQuery queue length is as follows:

Animation2jq.js

```
$(document).ready(function() {
 $("img#pic1")
 .animate({ "height" : 300 })
```

```
 .fadeOut()
 .fadeIn()
 .animate({ "width" : 400 })
    .slideToggle( 3000 )
  var n =$("img#pic1").queue( "fx" ).length;
alert("The queue length is "+n);
});
```

In this jQuery code, the `slideToggle()` and `queue()` methods are used, so let's have a quick look at these two methods.

slideToggle()

As the name suggests, the `slideToggle()` method toggles between `slideUp()` and `slideDown()` for the selected elements. If the element is hidden, the `slideDown()` method will execute to make the element visible. Similarly, if the element is visible, the `slideUp()` method will run to make it invisible.

Syntax:

$(selector).slideToggle(speed,easing,callback)

- speed defines the speed of sliding. This parameter is optional and its default value is 400 ms. Valid options are `slow`, `fast`, and milliseconds.

- The `easing` parameter determines the speed of animation at different stages. The following are valid options:

  - `swing`: It makes the transition slower at the beginning and end but faster in the middle. This is the default option.

  - `linear`: It makes the transition happen at a constant speed.

.queue()

As the name suggests, the queue contains the functions that are supposed to be run on the selected element(s). These functions can be manipulated if required. The queue enables a series of functions to be executed asynchronously on an element. It is basically an array of functions handled in First-In-First-Out (FIFO) order.

Syntax:

`$(selector).queue(queue_name)`

where the parameter `queue_name` represents the name of the queue. The default jQuery queue name is `fx`.

To retrieve a reference to a jQuery queue, you can call the `.queue()` method without a function argument.

The following methods are used to manipulate the queue:

- `push`: Used to add a function at the end of the queue

- `pop`: Used to remove the last function from the queue

- `unshift`: Used to insert a function at the beginning of the queue

- `shift`: Used to remove a function from the beginning of the queue

- `dequeue()`: When invoked, this method indicates that you want to move to the next item in the queue (i.e., you want to remove the top function from the queue and execute it).

- `clearQueue()`: The method removes all functions in the queue that are not yet executed. The function that is currently being executed will have no effect.

How It Works

The image with ID `pic1` is animated (i.e., its height will increase slowly from its current height until it becomes 300px high). Then the image will become invisible slowly and will reappear again slowly. Thereafter, the image will animate, increasing its width to 400px gradually. Then the `slideToggle()` method will make the image invisible slowly. Because five actions are queued up on the selected element (i.e., on the image), you get the queue length of 5 via the alert dialog box, as shown in Figure 6-3.

Figure 6-3. The alert dialog displays the queue length (i.e., the count of the actions that are queued up on the image)

Popping the Last Function from the Queue

You can make use of the pop() function to remove the last function from the jQuery queue. The jQuery file Animation2jq.js can be modified as follows:

Animation2jq.js

```
$(document).ready(function() {
 $("img#pic1")
 .animate({ "height" : 300 })
 .fadeOut()
 .fadeIn()
 .animate({ "width" : 400 })
    .slideToggle( 3000 )
var queue = $("img#pic1").queue();
var popped_func = queue.pop();
});
```

You retrieve the reference to a jQuery queue from the <img> element and assign it to the variable queue. The last method, slideToggle(3000), will be removed from the queue and assigned to the variable popped_func because the last method is no longer in the queue, so it will not execute. As a result, the chip image will not become invisible (after its height and width is increased) but will remain there.

You can even remove the last function in the queue and insert it at the beginning by making use of the unshift() method as follows:

```
var queue = $("img#pic1").queue();
var popped_func = queue.pop();
queue.unshift(popped_func);
```

The first `animate` method that increases the height of the image executes upon running the application. Then the last method, `slideToggle(3000)`, is removed from the end of the queue by using the `pop()` method and is assigned to the `popped_func` variable. Then the last method in the `popped_func` variable is added at the beginning of the queue. After increasing the height of the image, the `slideToggle(3000)` method executes, making the image invisible.

You can stop the animation by clearing all methods that are stored in the queue by adding the following statement in the jQuery code:

```
$("img#pic1").clearQueue();
```

Because all methods from the queue will be deleted by the above statement, animation will immediately stop after finishing the current executing method. You can even invoke the `clearQueue()` method on clicking a button, allowing the user to stop the animation whenever required.

You can also run the desired methods that are in the queue by redefining the queue with the desired range of methods as shown in following code:

```
$("img#pic1").queue(queue.slice(3,4));
```

Here the statements from the third index location until the fourth index location will be used to make a new queue. The statement at the specified index location is `.animate({ "width" : 400 })` so the new queue will have this statement only. As a result, the width of the chip image will increase to 400px slowly. That's it. Nothing else will happen because the queue has nothing else.

6-3. Showing Images One by One by Clicking the Next and Previous buttons

Problem

You have a few images and you want to display one image at a time. When the user clicks the Next button, the next image in the sequence is displayed. Similarly, by clicking the previous button, the image that was shown previously should appear again.

Solution

The following HTML program displays five images and left and right arrow keys. To manage margin spacing and the display format, the images are enclosed in an unordered list which in turn is enclosed inside a `<div>` element.

animation3.html

```
<!DOCTYPE html PUBLIC "-//W3C//DTD XHTML 1.0 Transitional//EN"
        "http://www.w3.org/TR/xhtml1/DTD/xhtml1-transitional.dtd">

<html xmlns="http://www.w3.org/1999/xhtml" xml:lang="en" lang="en">
  <head>
    <meta http-equiv="Content-Type" content="text/html; charset=utf-8"/>
    <title></title>
<link rel="stylesheet" href="animation3style.css" type="text/css"
media="screen" />
    <script src="jquery-3.5.1.js" type="text/javascript"></script>
    <script src="animation3jq.js" type="text/javascript"></script>
  </head>
 <body>
 <div id="image_slider">
 <ul>
 <li><img src="chip.jpg" width="200" height="150" /></li>
 <li><img src="chip2.jpg" width="200" height="150" /></li>
 <li><img src="chip3.jpg" width="200" height="150" /></li>
 <li><img src="chip4.jpg" width="200" height="150" /></li>
 <li><img src="chip5.jpg" width="200" height="150" /></li>
 </ul>
<img src="leftarrow.png" class="leftarrow" />
<img src="rightarrow.png" class="rightarrow" />
 </div>
 </body>
</html>
```

You can see in the above code that a `<div>` element is defined with the ID `image_slider`. Within the `<div>` element is defined an unordered list element. And within the unordered list element five list items are defined, and within each list item an image is defined.

Below the unordered list element a left arrow image is displayed on the left side to represent the Previous button and a right arrow image on the right side represents the Next button.

In order to display only one image at a time and hide the rest of the images, and to apply padding and other display formats to the <ul> and <div> elements, certain styles are written into the CSS style sheet.

Animation3style.css

```
body {
 padding: 10px;
}

#image_slider {
 width: 210px;
 height: 230px;
 overflow: hidden;
  margin: auto;
  display: block;
}

#image_slider ul {
 list-style: none;
 width: 1200px;
 height: 210px;
 margin: 0;
 padding: 0;
}

#image_slider li {
 width: 210px;
 height: 200px;
 float: left;
}

.leftarrow {
 float: left;
 width: 20px;
 height: 20px;
}
```

```
.rightarrow {
 float: right;
 width: 20px;
 height: 20px;
}
```

In this CSS style sheet, the properties padding, overflow, display, and float are used so let's have a quick look at them.

padding Property

The padding property is used to create spacing among an element's content. To insert spacing on each side of the element, there are variants of the padding property that include padding-top, padding-right, padding-bottom, and padding-left to manage the spacing at the top, right, bottom, and left sides, respectively, of the element.

The valid values for the padding property are

- value: A value that specifies the spacing in units like px, pt, cm, etc.

- %: Spacing is specified in terms of % of the width of the container.

- inherit: Spacing is inherited from the parent element.

overflow Property

The overflow property determines the action to perform on the content that is too big to fit into a container (i.e., it determines whether to display the full element by applying scrollbars or crop the content as per the container size). Valid options are

- visible: The element will be shown fully.

- hidden: The region outside the container's boundary will be cropped and only the region inside the container will be visible.

- scroll: The region within the container's boundary will be visible and the scroll bars will be added, which can be used to see the hidden content.

- auto: Similar to scroll, but it adds scrollbars to the element only when they are required.

display Property

The `display` property determines how the element has to be rendered. A few of the valid values of this property are

- `inline`: The element is displayed as an inline element. The height and width of the element are not considered.

- `block`: The element is displayed as a block element (i.e., the element is displayed on a new line and covers up the whole width of the browser screen).

- `contents`: The container is removed and the child elements become the children of the element that is higher in the DOM.

float Property

The `float` property is used for positioning and formatting content in relation to another component in the same container. It's popularly used to arrange text around images. The following are valid options:

- `left`: The element floats to the left of its container.

- `right`: The element floats to the right of its container.

- `none`: The element does not float. This is the default value.

- `inherit`: The element inherits the float value from its parent.

The padding space of 10px is set around the `<body>` element on all four sides.

The width and height of the `<div>` element whose ID is `image_slider` are set to 210px and 230px, respectively. By using the `overflow` property, the images that cannot be accommodated within the specified width and height region are made hidden. The idea is to make only one image visible at a time. The whole `<div>` element is displayed as a block (i.e., it will be displayed on the new line and will cover the entire width of the browser screen).

The usual bullets from the unordered list items will be removed and the width and height of the unordered list are set to 1200px and 210px so as to accommodate all of the images. The margin and padding spacing are set to 0 in an unordered list.

The width and height of the list items are set to 210px and 200px because an image will be displayed via a list item only. Using the `float` property, the list items (i.e., the images) are set to float towards the left in its container. The left and right arrow images are displayed as 20px wide and 20px high. The left arrow is set to be positioned at the left side and the right arrow image is set to display on the right.

Animation3jq.js

```
$(document).ready(function() {
$('img.leftarrow').click(function() {
    if($("ul").css("marginLeft") == "0px"){
        alert("You are at the first image");
    } else {

     $("#image_slider").children("ul").animate({
        "margin-left" : "+=210px"
        }, 2000);
};
});

$('img.rightarrow').click(function() {
    if($("ul").css("marginLeft") == "-840px"){
        alert("You are at the last image");
    } else {
     $("#image_slider").children("ul").animate({
        "margin-left" : "-=210px"
        }, 2000);
};
});
});
```

In this jQuery code, the css() method and the margin-left property are used, so let's understand them first.

css()

The css() method sets or returns the desired style properties of the selected elements.
Syntax:
The following syntax returns the value of the specified property:

```
css("property");
```

The following syntax sets the value for the specified CSS property:

```
css("property","value");
```

margin-left Property

This property sets the margin of the element from the left boundary of the browser window. The following are the valid options:

- `length`: The distance from the left margin is specified in px, pt, cm, etc. The default value is 0px.

- `%`: The margin from the left boundary is specified in terms of a percentage of the width of the container.

- `auto`: The distance from the left boundary is decided by the browser.

- `initial`: The default value is picked up for this property.

- `inherit`: The value is inherited from the parent element.

How It Works

On running the program, the first image will be displayed initially (see Figure 6-4(a)). When the left arrow image is clicked, it is first checked whether the left margin value is 0px. If the left margin's value is 0px, it means the first picture is being displayed and there is no image on the left of the current image, so the **You are at the first image and no other action will take place** message is displayed. But if the left margin's value is not 0px, it means some other image, not the first image, is being displayed. In that case, the left margin value is increased by 210 px, making the next image visible and hiding the earlier image. The left margin's value is increased in the form of slow animation so the next image will appear as sliding in.

Similarly, when the right arrow image is clicked, it is first checked whether the left margin's value is equal to -840px. Because the left margin's value is decremented by 210px value on every click of the right arrow, the left margin's value will be equal to -840px when the last image is being displayed, hence the message **You are at last image** is displayed (see Figure 6-4(c)). If the value of the left margin is greater than -840px, the value of left margin is decremented by 210px to make the second image visible and make the previous image invisible as shown in Figure 6-4(b).

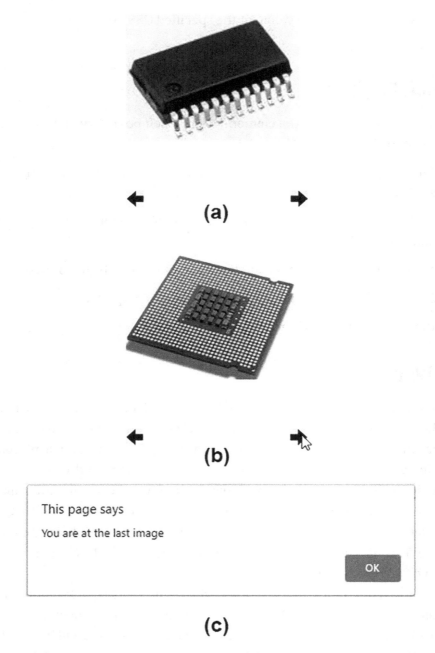

Figure 6-4. (a) The first image is displayed. (b) On clicking the right arrow image, the second image becomes visible, hiding the first image. (c) The alert dialog informing "You are at last image" appears when the right arrow image is clicked on the last image

Displaying All Hidden Images One by One When Any Arrow Key Is Pressed

Instead of stopping after displaying one image, as in the earlier jQuery code, in this code, when you press a right arrow image, all images will slide left one by one and the sliding will stop after displaying the last image. Similarly, on clicking the left arrow image, all the images will slide right one by one and the sliding will stop after displaying the first image.

The jQuery code to do so is as follows:

animation3bjq.js

```
$(document).ready(function() {
    $('img.leftarrow').click(function() {
        if($("ul").css("marginLeft") == "0px"){
            alert("You are at the first image");
        } else {
            for(i=0;i<4;i++){
                    $("#image_slider").children("ul").animate({
                    "margin-left" : "+=210px"
                    }, 2000);
            }
        };
    });

    $('img.rightarrow').click(function() {
        if($("ul").css("marginLeft") == "-840px"){
            alert("You are at the last image");
        } else {
            for(i=0;i<4;i++){
                    $("#image_slider").children("ul").animate({
                    "margin-left" : "-=210px"
                    }, 2000);
            }
        };
    });
});
```

You can see in the above code that upon clicking the left arrow image, a `for` loop is used, which will perform its four iterations, and within each iteration, the left margin of the unordered list element gets incremented by 210px, thus hiding the current image and unhiding the image on the right. Recall that the images are represented via list items of the unordered list element. The `for` loop will slide the images towards the left direction one by one and will stop on the last image, as shown in Figure 6-5(a).

The procedure is repeated when the right arrow image is clicked. Again a `for` loop will iterate four times, decrementing the left margin of the unordered list element by 210px in each iteration. As a result, the current image will be made hidden and one image on the left will be made visible. The `for` loop will give the sliding effect as if the images are sliding towards the right direction one by one and will stop on the first image, as shown in Figure 6-5(b).

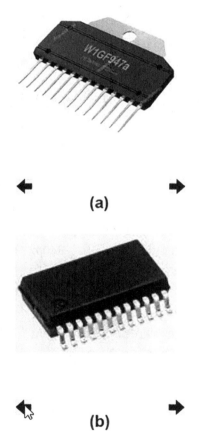

(a)

(b)

Figure 6-5. *(a) Clicking the left arrow makes all of the images side towards the left direction and stop on the last image. (b) Clicking the right arrow makes all of the images slide towards the right direction and stop at the first image*

Making the Images Slide Continuously

Let's modify the jQuery code to make an image slider (i.e., the images will slide continuously towards the left direction one by one). That is, an image will be displayed and then it will move towards the left and will disappear and will be replaced by the next image in the sequence. The jQuery code for an image slider is as follows:

animation3cjq.js

```
$(document).ready(function() {

    $.leftrotate = function(){
        $("#image_slider").children("ul").animate({
            "margin-left" : "-=210px"
            }, 2000,
            function(){
                if($("ul").css("marginLeft") == "-1050px"){
                    $("ul").css( {"marginLeft" : "0px" });
                }
            });
        $.leftrotate();
    }
    $.leftrotate();
});
```

You can see in the above code that a function called leftrotate is defined in which the left margin of the unordered list elements within the <div> element is decremented by 210px slowly. As a result, the current image will become invisible and the image on the right will become visible slowly, giving an animation effect. After an image is displayed, it is checked if the last image is reached or not (i.e., whether the left margin has become equal to -1050px or not). If yes, then the left margin is set to 0px, making the first image visible again. If the last image is not yet reached, the leftrotate function is called again to reduce the left margin by 210px, making the current image invisible and making the next image on the right visible. Because of the recursion, the leftrotate function will be invoked repetitively, making the images slide infinitely, as shown in Figure 6-6.

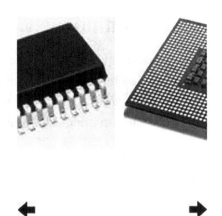

◀   ▶

Figure 6-6. *Images sliding infinitely*

6-4. Zooming In on an Image When the Mouse Hovers Over It

Problem

You have some images that are smaller in size and are displayed one below the other. You want the image to get enlarged when the mouse hovers over it and have the image go back to its previous size when mouse moves out of it.

Solution

The HTML code to display a few images is as follows:

Zoomonhover.html

```
<!DOCTYPE html PUBLIC "-//W3C//DTD XHTML 1.0 Transitional//EN"
        "http://www.w3.org/TR/xhtml1/DTD/xhtml1-transitional.dtd">

<html xmlns="http://www.w3.org/1999/xhtml" xml:lang="en" lang="en">
  <head>
    <meta http-equiv="Content-Type" content="text/html; charset=utf-8"/>
    <title></title>
```

```
<link rel="stylesheet" href="zoomonhoverstyle.css" type="text/css"
media="screen" />
    <script src="jquery-3.5.1.js" type="text/javascript"></script>
    <script src="zoomonhoverjq.js" type="text/javascript"></script>
  </head>
 <body>
<ul id="image_hover">
 <li><img src="chip.jpg"  /></li>
 <li><img src="chip2.jpg"  /></li>
 <li><img src="chip3.jpg"  /></li>
 <li><img src="chip4.jpg"  /></li>
 <li><img src="chip5.jpg" /></li>
 </ul>
</body>
</html>
```

You can see in the above code that an unordered list element is created with the id image_hover. The unordered list element contains five list items and each list item displays an image via the <img> element.

The CSS style sheet to apply styles to the HTML elements is as follows:

Zoomonhoverstyle.css

```
#image_hover {
 list-style: none;
}

img {
 width: 100px;
 height: 75px;
}
```

In order to avoid displaying the default bullets in the list items, the list_style: none property is applied to the unordered list item of ID image_hover. Also, the images are by default set to display at 100px wide and 75px high.

The jQuery code to enlarge the image when the mouse is over it and to reduce it to its previous size when the mouse pointer is moved away from it is as follows:

Zoomonhoverjq.js

```
$(document).ready(function() {
        $("#image_hover").children("li").find("img").on("mouseenter",
        function() {
            $(this).css( {"width" : "350px" });
            $(this).css( {"height" : "250px" });
            }).on("mouseleave", function() {
            $(this).css( {"width" : "100px" });
            $(this).css( {"height" : "75px" });
    });
});
```

How It Works

On running the program, initially the images will appear one below the other in a small size (i.e., 100px wide and 75px high, as shown in Figure 6-7 left side). When the mouse pointer hovers over the list item (i.e., over the images wrapped inside the list items), by making use of the css() method the width and height of the image are increased to 350px and 250px, respectively (see Figure 6-7 right side). And when the mouse pointer moves away from the image, again the css() method is used to reduce the image to its previous size.

(left)   **(right)**

Figure 6-7. *(left) The images appear one below the other in a small size. (right) The width and height of the image are increased when the mouse pointer hovers over it*

6-5. Displaying Detailed Information on Clicking the "Read More" Link

Problem

You want to display a small introduction of a topic, along with a **read more** link below it. You want the hidden content to be displayed when the user clicks the **read more** link. Also, you want the **read more** link to be converted to a **read less** link when hidden content is displayed. You also want the content that recently became visible to get hidden if the **read less** link is clicked.

Solution

The HTML program to display two paragraph elements and one hyperlink is shown below. The second paragraph contains detailed information and will be hidden initially, but will become visible when the hyperlink is clicked.

Readmore.html

```
<!DOCTYPE html PUBLIC "-//W3C//DTD XHTML 1.0 Transitional//EN"
        "http://www.w3.org/TR/xhtml1/DTD/xhtml1-transitional.dtd">

<html xmlns="http://www.w3.org/1999/xhtml" xml:lang="en" lang="en">
  <head>
    <meta http-equiv="Content-Type" content="text/html; charset=utf-8"/>
    <title></title>
    <script src="jquery-3.5.1.js" type="text/javascript"></script>
    <script src="readmorejq.js" type="text/javascript"></script>
  </head>
  <body>
      <p>jQuery is a lightweight cross-platform JavaScript library. Because
      of its easy to use syntax, jQuery has made it quite easy to include
      JavaScript on any web site.  </p>
      <p>It has not only simplified the complex coding but also has reduced
      the size of code as well. Below are the features of jQuery. To use
      jQuery, no installation is required. You need to simply download jQuery
      from its official jQuery website, http://jquery.com/ which has several
      versions of jQuery. You can download the most stable version out of
      them. After downloading jQuery on your local file system, you simply
      refer to the file's location using the HTML script element. </p>
      <a href="#" id="expand">read more</a>
  </body>
</html>
```

You can see in the above code that two <p> elements are made with certain text in them. Below the second paragraph, a hyperlink is defined with default text of **read more**. To access it in jQuery code, the hyperlink is assigned the ID expand.

The jQuery code to display the hidden paragraph when the hyperlink is clicked is shown below. The code also changes the text of hyperlink to **read less** from **read more** when it is clicked. This code also hides the paragraph when the **read less** link is clicked.

Readmorejq.js

```
$(document).ready(function() {
      $('p').eq(1).hide();
      $('a#expand').click(function(event) {
          event.preventDefault();
          if ($('a#expand').text() == 'read more') {
        $('p').eq(1).hide().slideToggle('slow');
              $('a#expand').text('read less');
          } else {
              $('p').eq(1).show().slideToggle('slow');
              $('a#expand').text('read more');
          }
      });
});
```

In the above jQuery code, the preventDefault() method is used, so let's understand this method first.

event.preventDefault() Method

As the name suggest, the event.preventDefault() method avoids the element to take the default action. For example, using this method, you can stop the user from navigating to the target URL on clicking a link.

Syntax:

event.preventDefault()

where the parameter event is provided by the event binding function and it can be anything; it can be any character or word.

How It Works

On running the HTML program, you find that the first paragraph (i.e., the paragraph with the index location 0) is visible and the paragraph element with the index location 1 (i.e., the second paragraph) is hidden. Below the paragraph a hyperlink is displayed with the text **read more**, as shown in Figure 6-8(a). The hyperlink element is assigned the ID expand and when it is clicked (i.e., if the **read more** link is clicked), the preventDefault() method is invoked to avoid the default action of the hyperlink to keep it from navigating to the destination web page. Also, if the text of the hyperlink with the ID expand is **read more**, the second paragraph, which is currently hidden, is made visible slowly by invoking the slideToggle() method. That is, the hidden paragraph is displayed to show the text that was hidden and the text of hyperlink is changed to **read less** to inform the user that the detailed information is already visible (see Figure 6-8(b)).

If the text of the hyperlink is **read less** and is clicked, the visible paragraph is made invisible slowly by invoking the slideToggle() method and the text of hyperlink is changed to **read more**.

jQuery is a lightweight cross-platform JavaScript library. Because of its easy to use syntax, jQuery has made it quite easy to include JavaScript on any web site.

read more

(a)

jQuery is a lightweight cross-platform JavaScript library. Because of its easy to use syntax, jQuery has made it quite easy to include JavaScript on any web site.

It has not only simplified the complex coding but also has reduced the size of code as well. Below are the features of jQuery. To use jQuery, no installation is required. You need to simply download jQuery from its official jQuery website, http://jquery.com/ which has several versions of jQuery. You can download the most stable version out of them. After downloading jQuery on your local file system, you simply refer to the file's location using the HTML script element.

read less

(b)

Figure 6-8. *(a) Below the paragraph, an hyperlink is displayed with the text "read more." (b) The hidden paragraph is displayed after clicking the "read more" link*

6-6. Expanding and Collapsing a List Using Animation

Problem

You want to display certain electronic items like cameras and laptops in the form of expandable list items. Whenever the user clicks a list item, it expands to display detailed information. The expanded list item if clicked again will shrink.

Solution

The HTML code to display an unordered list containing a few list items where the list item itself is an unordered list is shown below. The list will begin with the node **Electronic Products**, which will show two electronic products, **Cameras** and **Laptops**. The **Cameras** list item will show two cameras called **Sony** and **Canon**. Similarly the **Laptops** list item will show only one laptop by name, **Acer**. The **Sony** and **Canon** list items can be expanded to show their respective configuration and price. Also, the **Acer** list item can be expanded to show its configuration and price.

Explandlistanim.html

```
<!DOCTYPE html PUBLIC "-//W3C//DTD XHTML 1.0 Transitional//EN"
        "http://www.w3.org/TR/xhtml1/DTD/xhtml1-transitional.dtd">

<html xmlns="http://www.w3.org/1999/xhtml" xml:lang="en" lang="en">
  <head>
    <meta http-equiv="Content-Type" content="text/html; charset=utf-8"/>
    <title></title>
    <script src="jquery-3.5.1.js" type="text/javascript"></script>
    <script src="expandlistanimjq.js" type="text/javascript"></script>
  </head>
  <body>
<ul id="list">
  <li class="electronics">Electronic Products
    <ul>
      <li class="electronics">Cameras
        <ul>
```

```html
        <li class="electronics">Sony
          <ul>
            <li>Digital Camera w/ 16-50mm and 55-210mm Power Zoom
            Lenses</li>
            <li>Monitor Type: 7.5 cm</li>
            <li>$698</li>
          </ul>
        </li>
        <li class="electronics">Canon
          <ul>
            <li>Digital Camera w/ 50x Optical Zoom</li>
            <li>Wi-Fi & NFC Enabled</li>
            <li>$279</li>
          </ul>
        </li>
      </ul>
    </li>
    <li class="electronics">Laptops
      <ul>
        <li class="electronics">Acer
          <ul>
            <li>14" Full HD Touch</li>
            <li>Intel Core i7-1165G7</li>
            <li>Intel Iris Xe Graphics</li>
            <li>16GB LPDDR4X</li>
            <li>$1292</li>
          </ul>
        </li>
      </ul>
    </li>
  </ul>
  </li>
</ul>
</body>
</html>
```

You can see that an unordered list is created with the ID list, which has a single list item, **Electronics Products.** For access via jQuery code, the list items are assigned the class electronics. The **Electronic Products** list item consists of an unordered list which consists of two list items, **Cameras** and **Laptops.** All the list items are assigned the class electronics. Again, the list item **Cameras** consists of an unordered list which consists of two list items, **Sony** and **Canon.** Similarly, the list item **Laptops** consists of an unordered list which in turn consists of a single list item, **Acer.** The list item **Sony** contains an unordered list of three list items showing the configuration and price of the Sony camera.

Similarly, the **Canon** list items wraps an unordered list consisting of three list items showing the detailed features of the Canon camera. The **Acer** list item contains an unordered list of five list items where each list item displays the features of the Acer laptop with its price.

The jQuery code to expand a list item when clicked once and collapse it if it is again clicked is as follows:

Expanlistanimjq.js

```
$(document).ready(function() {
    $('#list ul').hide();
    $('.electronics').click(function() {
        $(this).children("ul").slideToggle();
            return false;
    });
});
```

How It Works

You can see that the unordered list wrapped inside the unordered list with the ID list is made hidden, hence no child unordered list will appear except the text of the parent unordered list (i.e., **Electronic Products** will be displayed initially). If the user clicks any of the list items, the unordered list wrapped inside that list item will be displayed. Because the slideToggle() method is used, it means that if the unordered list (that is, the child of the list item that is clicked) is visible, it will be made invisible and vice versa. So the list item if clicked will either expand if it is in collapsed mode currently or will get collapsed if it is already expanded.

On running the program, you get the text of the list item of the parent unordered list, **Electronic Products**, on the screen. On clicking the list item, it will expand to show the unordered list within it. The unordered list within has two list items, **Cameras** and **Laptops**, so they are displayed on the screen. On clicking the list item **Cameras**, again it will expand and the unordered list inside this list item will be displayed (i.e., the **Sony** and **Canon** list items will be displayed on the screen; see Figure 6-9(a)). Similarly, on clicking any of the list items, the unordered list hidden inside it will be displayed, showing the information within it. On clicking all of the list items, the information will be displayed as shown in Figure 6-9(b).

- Electronic Products
  - Cameras
    - Sony
    - Canon
  - Laptops

(a)

- Electronic Products
  - Cameras
    - Sony
      - Digital Camera w/ 16-50mm and 55-210mm Power Zoom Lenses
      - Monitor Type: 7.5 cm
      - $698
    - Canon
      - Digital Camera w/ 50x Optical Zoom
      - Wi-Fi & NFC Enabled
      - $279
  - Laptops
    - Acer
      - 14" Full HD Touch
      - Intel Core i7-1165G7
      - Intel Iris Xe Graphics
      - 16GB LPDDR4X
      - $1292

(b)

Figure 6-9. *(a) The text of the parent unordered list, Electronic Products, appears. (b) On clicking any list item, it will expand to show the unordered list within it*

6-7. Summary

In this chapter, you learned how to implement animation on HTML elements. You learned to animate an image to the right and then the left. You learned to manage and manipulate the jQuery queue. You saw how to show images one by one by clicking the Next and Previous buttons and how to zoom in on an image when the mouse hovers over it. You also learned to expand text and display the detailed information when a "read more" link is clicked and finally, you learned to expand and collapse a list using animation.

The next chapter will demonstrate sliding and visual effects. You will learn how to display sliding images in an infinite loop. You will also learn how to make a ball bounce, make images scroll vertically upward within a box, display images vertically where each image is replaced by the next in a sequence, and how to make a news scroller.

CHAPTER 7

Sliding and Visual Effects

In this chapter, you will learn how to apply different sliding and visual effects to different HTML elements. You will be making following recipes in this chapter:

- Displaying images, one at a time infinitely
- Making a ball bounce
- Making images scroll vertically upward within a box
- Displaying images vertically, each replaced by the next in the sequence
- Making a news scroller
- Showing images one after the other on hover
- Showing images pagewise
- Shuffling images in either direction
- Writing a pendulum scroller
- Scrolling images using arrays

The image scrolling and sliding recipes can be used on any web site to display products or services. The news scroller recipe can be used to display the latest activities of an organization. The bouncing ball recipe is to explain how the speed and distance of an animation can be managed.

© Bintu Harwani 2022
B. Harwani, *jQuery Recipes*, https://doi.org/10.1007/978-1-4842-7304-3_7

7-1. Displaying Images, One at a Time Infinitely

Problem

You have several images and you want the images to be displayed one by one at the center top of the page. An image appears slowly and then it fades away and is replaced by the next image slowly and that too fades away and so on. After displaying the last image, again the first image will appear and it goes on endlessly.

Solution

The HTML code to display five images via the list items of an unordered list which in turn is enclosed within a `<div>` element is as follows:

animation1.html

```
<!DOCTYPE html PUBLIC "-//W3C//DTD XHTML 1.0 Transitional//EN"
        "http://www.w3.org/TR/xhtml1/DTD/xhtml1-transitional.dtd">

<html xmlns="http://www.w3.org/1999/xhtml" xml:lang="en" lang="en">
  <head>
    <meta http-equiv="Content-Type" content="text/html; charset=utf-8"/>
    <title></title>
     <link rel="stylesheet" href="animation1style.css" type="text/css"
     media="screen" />
    <script src="jquery-3.5.1.js" type="text/javascript"></script>
    <script src="animation1jq.js" type="text/javascript"></script>
  </head>
  <body>
    <div id="slideshow">
          <ul>
              <li><img src="chip.jpg"></li>
              <li><img src="chip2.jpg"></li>
              <li><img src="chip3.jpg"></li>
              <li><img src="chip4.jpg"></li>
              <li> <img src="chip5.jpg"></li>
          </ul>
```

```
</div>
  </body>
</html>
```

You can see in the above code that a `<div>` element is defined with the ID of `slideshow`. Within the `<div>` element is defined an unordered list and five of the images are displayed via list items of the unordered list.

To apply styles to the `<div>`, `<p>`, and `<img>` elements, certain style classes are defined in a cascade style sheet:

Animation1style.css

```
img{
        width: 300px;
        height: 200px;
        border: 5px solid red;
     padding: 10px;
     margin: 10px;
}

#slideshow {
       margin: 30px auto;
     position: relative;
     width: 350px;
     height: 250px;
     padding: 10px;
}

#slideshow ul li {
     position: absolute;
}
```

In this style sheet file, a property called `position` is used, so let's understand it first.

position Property

The position property defines the positioning of an element. Valid options are

- static: It's the default property. The elements are positioned as static (i.e., the top, bottom, left, and right properties will not affect the HTML element).

- relative: As the name suggests, the element will be positioned in relation to its normal position. The top, right, bottom, and left properties can be added to the element for more precise positions.

- fixed: The element will always remain at the same location even if the page is scrolled.

- absolute: The element is positioned relative to the nearest positioned ancestor or the document body if there is no ancestor to the element.

- sticky: The element toggles between relative and fixed positions depending on the scroll position.

In the CSS file, you can see that the image element is set to appear as 300px wide and 200px high. Also, a border in red of 5px thickness is displayed around the image and 10px padding (i.e., spacing) is created around the image within the border (between the border and the image). Also, a 10px margin is created outside the border.

The margin of the <div> element with the id slideshow is set to 30px. The position of the <div> element is set to relative and its width and height are set to 350px and 250px, respectively. The width and height of the <div> element are set so that only one image is visible at a time. The padding space is set to 10px (i.e., the spacing between the image and the <div> element's border is set to 10px).

The position of the <li> element is set to absolute (i.e., these list items are set in relation to their ancestor, the <div> element).

The following jQuery code will make only one image appear at the top center location of the browser window. The code will then make it disappear in a while and get replaced by the next image in the sequence.

Animation1jq.js

```
$(document).ready(function() {
    $("#slideshow ul li").slice(1).hide();

    setInterval(function() {
            $('#slideshow ul li:first')
                .fadeOut(500)
                .next()
                .fadeIn(500)
                .end()
                .appendTo('#slideshow ul');
}, 2000);

});
```

This jQuery code uses the methods slice(), next(), end(), setInterval(), and appendTo(), so let's have a quick look at them first.

slice()

Extracts a set of elements from the selected element beginning from the specified index location.

Syntax:

$(selector).slice(starting_index_location,stop_index_locatin)

- starting_index_location represents the index location from where to start extracting. The index location begins from 0. If a negative value is used, it means the extraction has to be done from the end.

- stop_index_location is the index location up to where the extraction has to be done. If it is omitted, the extraction is done until the end of the set.

next()

Fetches the immediately following sibling of the selected element(s). Siblings are those elements who have the same parent.

Syntax:

`$(selector).next(filter)`

where `filter` represents the expression to find the next sibling.

end()

Ends the most recent operation and returns the matched element(s) to its previous state.
Syntax:

`recent_operation(s).end( )`

setInterval()

Used for invoking a function or performing certain operations at specified intervals. The time for reinvoking the function or performing the operation is specified in milliseconds. This method will keep invoking the desired function or operation until the method `clearInterval()` is called or the window is closed.

appendTo()

Inserts the specified element(s) at the end of the selected elements.
Syntax:

`$(required_elements).appendTo(selected_element)`

- `required_elements` represents the content to be inserted.
- `selected_element` represents the selected elements to which the element(s) has to be appended.

If the `required_element(s)` already exists, then it will be removed from its current location and will be appended to the selected elements.

In the jQuery code, initially all of the list items from index location 1 until the end are made hidden (i.e., except for the first image, all images displayed via list items are made invisible). Thereafter a function is set to execute after every 2000 milliseconds. Within that function, the first image that is displayed via the first list item is made invisible slowly in 500ms (see Figure 7-1(a)). Thereafter, the second image is made visible slowly in 500ms (see Figure 7-1(b)). The first image is then appended at the end in the unordered list. This function will keep executing after every 2000 ms. Again, the second image, which has now become the first list item, is made invisible gradually and the next list item (i.e., the third image) is made visible slowly. The second image is added at the end in the unordered list (after the first image, which was previously appended). The procedure keeps repeating endlessly.

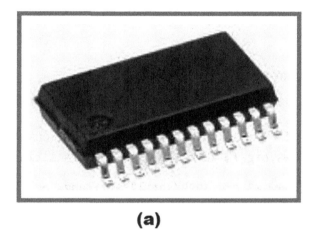

(a)

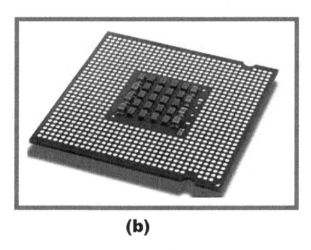

(b)

Figure 7-1. *(a) The first image is visible. (b) The first image becomes invisible and is replaced by the second image*

7-2. Making a Ball Bounce

Problem

You want a ball to bounce using animation. With every bounce, the height that the ball rises to is reduced by half and finally the ball stops.

Solution

The HTML code to display a ball image is as follows:

Animation2.html

```
<!DOCTYPE html PUBLIC "-//W3C//DTD XHTML 1.0 Transitional//EN"
        "http://www.w3.org/TR/xhtml1/DTD/xhtml1-transitional.dtd">

<html xmlns="http://www.w3.org/1999/xhtml" xml:lang="en" lang="en">
  <head>
    <meta http-equiv="Content-Type" content="text/html; charset=utf-8"/>
    <title></title>
    <link rel="stylesheet" href="animation2style.css" type="text/css"
    media="screen" />
    <script src="jquery-3.5.1.js" type="text/javascript"></script>
    <script src="animation2jq.js" type="text/javascript"></script>
  </head>
  <body>
        <img id="ball" src="ball.jpg"></img>
  </body>
</html>
```

You can see in this code that a ball is displayed by making use of an `<img>` element. To apply a style to the ball image, a .css file is created with the following code:

Animation2style.css

```
#ball {
    position: absolute;
}
```

The position of the ball is set to `absolute` that is relative to the body element. Now the ball can be easily bounced by applying the `bottom` property via the jQuery code.

The jQuery code to make the ball bounce is as follows:

Animation2jq.js

```
$(document).ready(function() {
    function bounce() {
        var height = 250;
        var speed=1000;
        for (var i = 1; i <= 6; i++) {
            $('#ball').animate({
                'bottom' : height}, speed);
            $('#ball').animate({'bottom' : 0}, speed);
            height = height/2;
        }
    }
    bounce();
});
```

A function named `bounce` is defined. Within the function, the `height` and `speed` are initialized to values 250 and 1000, respectively. Because you want your ball to bounce six times before stopping, a `for` loop is set to run six times. You can make the ball bounce for any number of times as desired. With every iteration of the `for` loop, the height of the ball will be reduced to half (i.e., the height of the ball will be divided by a value of 2). First, the ball is made to rise high at a certain height gradually in animated form and then the ball is set to come to the bottom (i.e., the ball is set to touch the ground). The height of the ball is reduced (divided by 2) before repeating the next iteration of the `for` loop. The `bounce` function is called once the document is ready and the ball will appear to be bouncing and its height is reduced to half on every bounce before it finally comes to a stop (see Figure 7-2).

Figure 7-2. *A bouncing ball. The ball will bounce vertically up and down*

7-3. Making Images Scroll Vertically Upward Within a Box

Problem

You have several images and you want the images to keep scrolling continuously within a box located at the center top of the browser window. After the last image, the scrolling will continue from the first image onwards.

Solution

The HTML code to display five images through the list items of an unordered list is as follows. The unordered list is nested within the <div> element.

Animation3.html

```
<!DOCTYPE html PUBLIC "-//W3C//DTD XHTML 1.0 Transitional//EN"
        "http://www.w3.org/TR/xhtml1/DTD/xhtml1-transitional.dtd">

<html xmlns="http://www.w3.org/1999/xhtml" xml:lang="en" lang="en">
  <head>
    <meta http-equiv="Content-Type" content="text/html; charset=utf-8"/>
    <title></title>
    <link rel="stylesheet" href="animation3style.css" type="text/css"
    media="screen" />
    <script src="jquery-3.5.1.js" type="text/javascript"></script>
    <script src="animation3jq.js" type="text/javascript"></script>
  </head>
  <body>
        <div id="slideshow">
            <ul id="scroll">
                <li><img src="chip.jpg"></li>
                <li><img src="chip2.jpg"></li>
                <li><img src="chip3.jpg"></li>
                <li><img src="chip4.jpg"></li>
                <li> <img src="chip5.jpg"></li>
            </ul>
        </div>
  </body>
</html>
```

A <div> element is created with the id slideshow. Within the <div> element an unordered list element is defined with the id scroll. The ids are assigned to the <div> and <ul> elements to make them accessible in the jQuery code. Five images are displayed via the five list items within the <ul> element.

To apply styles to the images, the unordered list, and the <div> element, certain style classes are defined as follows:

Animation3style.css

```
img{
        width: 300px;
         height: 200px;
      padding: 10px;
      margin: 10px;
}

#scroll{
      list-style: none;
      width: 320px;
      height: 1000px;
      margin: 0;
      padding: 0;
}

#slideshow {
      width: 320px;
      height: 220px;
       border: 5px solid red;
      overflow: hidden;
       margin: auto;
       display: block;
}
```

The images are set to display at 300px wide and 200px high. The padding and margin spacing of the images is set to 10px. Recall that the padding is the spacing between the element and its border whereas the margin is the spacing around an element (i.e., between the borders of the two elements).

In the unordered list with the id scroll, the list item marker, which by default is disc, is set to none (i.e., no marker will be displayed with list items). Although the image is set to display within the width of 300px, to make the image display along with its padding space the width of the `<ul>` element is set to 320px. There are five images, each 200px high, so the height of the `<ul>` element is set to 1000px. The margin and padding spaces are set to 0px of the unordered list.

The width and height of the `<div>` element enclosing the `<ul>` list is set to 320px and 220px, respectively. It is so because you want only one image to be displayed at a time. A border of 5px thickness in red is displayed around the images. Using the `overflow` property, only one image at a time is set to be displayed and any images that are outside the given width and height will be clipped. The `<div>` element is set to display as a block (i.e., the images within it will be displayed on a fresh line and will take up the whole width assigned to it).

The jQuery code to make the images scroll one after the other in a box is as follows:

animation3jq

```
$(document).ready(function() {

var imageslide = function() {
        $("#slideshow").children("ul").animate({
                "margin-top": -1000}, 4000, function() {
                $('#slideshow').append($('#scroll').clone());
                $('#scroll').css({ "margin-top": 0 });
            });
        imageslide();
    }
    imageslide();
});
```

A function named `imageslide` is defined. The function makes all list items within the unordered list (i.e., all of the images) scroll upwards slowly in animation form until the top margin reaches -1000px. Recall that every image has a height of 200px, so all of the images will scroll up one by one until the top margin becomes -1000px (i.e., when the last, fifth image is scrolled up). After that, the clone (i.e., a copy of all of the list items within the `<ul>` element of id `scroll`) is made and is appended to the `<div>` element of id `slideshow`. The copy of the list items is appended so that the images keep scrolling upwards endlessly. The top margin of the `<ul>` element is set to 0px. The function is recursively called so that again the images within the `<ul>` element will scroll upwards until the top margin becomes -1000px. The function will keep calling recursively, making the images scroll upwards continuously (see Figure 7-3).

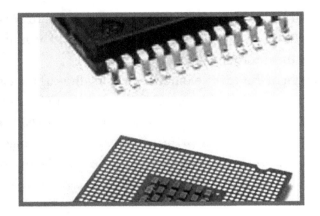

Figure 7-3. *Images scrolling upwards continuously*

7-4. Displaying Images Vertically, Each Replaced by the Next in Sequence

Problem

You have a few images and you want all of them to be displayed vertically. Besides this, you want them to keep changing their location after every few seconds. That is, all of the images are displayed and each image is replaced by the next in the sequence.

Solution

The HTML code to define the images through list items of an unordered list is shown below. To give a scrolling effect and to apply styles, the unordered list is enclosed in a `<div>` element.

Animation4.html

```
<!DOCTYPE html PUBLIC "-//W3C//DTD XHTML 1.0 Transitional//EN"
        "http://www.w3.org/TR/xhtml1/DTD/xhtml1-transitional.dtd">

<html xmlns="http://www.w3.org/1999/xhtml" xml:lang="en" lang="en">
  <head>
    <meta http-equiv="Content-Type" content="text/html; charset=utf-8"/>
    <title></title>
```

```
<link rel="stylesheet" href="animation4style.css" type="text/css"
media="screen" />
<script src="jquery-3.5.1.js" type="text/javascript"></script>
<script src="animation4jq.js" type="text/javascript"></script>
</head>
<body>
    <div id="slideshow">
        <ul id="scroll">
            <li><img src="chip.jpg"></li>
          <li><img src="chip2.jpg"></li>
          <li><img src="chip3.jpg"></li>
          <li><img src="chip4.jpg"></li>
          <li> <img src="chip5.jpg"></li>
        </ul>
    </div>
  </body>
</html>
```

A <div> element is defined with the id slideshow. Within the <div> element is
defined a <ul> element with the id scroll. Several list items are defined within the
unordered list where each list item encloses an image. That is, the five images are
displayed via five list items in an unordered list.

The following is the cascade style sheet file to apply styles to the images, the
unordered list, and the <div> element:

Animation4style.css

```
img{
        width: 300px;
        height: 200px;
       padding: 10px;
       margin: 10px;
}

#scroll{
      list-style: none;
      width: 320px;
      height: 1000px;
```

```
        margin: 0;
        padding: 0;
}

#slideshow {
        width: 320px;
        height: 1000px;
         border: 5px solid red;
        overflow: hidden;
         margin: auto;
         display: block;
}
```

The images are set to be displayed at 300px wide and 200px high. For proper spacing among the images, the padding and margin are set to 10px. Because you want to display all of the images, the width and height of the unordered list are set to 320px and 1000px, respectively. No spacing is set in the unordered list as there is already enough spacing among the images. The width and height of the <div> element are set to 320px and 1000px, respectively. Also, a 5px thick solid border in red is drawn around the <div> element (i.e., around the images). The <div> element is set to display as a block that will take up the entire available width.

The jQuery code to display all the images vertically and to keep them being replaced by the next image in sequence is as follows:

Animation4jq.js

```
$(document).ready(function() {
     setInterval(function() {
         $("#slideshow ul li:first").animate({
             "scrollTop": 200}, 400, function(){
                     $("#scroll").find('li:last').after($('li:first',
                     "#scroll"));
             });
     },1000);
});
```

In this jQuery code, the scrollTop property and the after() method are used, so before understanding the jQuery code, let's understand them quickly.

scrollTop Property

Used to specify the number of pixels the element is supposed to scroll vertically. Also, this property can be used to return the number of pixels that the element is scrolled vertically.

Syntax:

element.scrollTop

This code returns the scrollTop property (i.e., the number of pixels the element is scrolled vertically).

```
element.scrollTop = pixels
```

This code sets the scrollTop property.

after()

Used to insert the specified element(s) after the selected element.
Syntax:

$(selector).after(element,function(index))

- element represents the element to be inserted.

- function(index) represents the function that returns the content to insert. The index position represents the element in the set.

You can see in the jQuery code that a function is defined and set to execute after every 1000 ms. The first image, which is enclosed within the first list element, is set to scroll vertically upward by 200px. And when the first image is scrolled up, it is added after the last list item. Now the second image becomes the first image because the first image is scrolled up, made invisible from the top, and is appended at the bottom. The function is invoked again and the image that is currently at the top is scrolled up and is appended at the last item. The last list item currently is the first image, hence the second image is appended after the first image. The process continues infinitely (see Figure 7-4).

Figure 7-4. *Images scrolling upwards. The scrolled up image is added after the last image*

7-5. Making a News Scroller
Problem

You have certain text that you want to be displayed in a scrolling form like a news scroll on the screen. The scrolling of news will stop when the mouse hovers over the text and the news will again start scrolling when the mouse is moved away.

Solution

You will be using a `<p>` element to display text. To make it scroll it will be nested inside a `<div>` element. Here is the HTML code to do so:

Scrollingnews.html

```
<!DOCTYPE html PUBLIC "-//W3C//DTD XHTML 1.0 Transitional//EN"
        "http://www.w3.org/TR/xhtml1/DTD/xhtml1-transitional.dtd">

<html xmlns="http://www.w3.org/1999/xhtml" xml:lang="en" lang="en">
  <head>
    <meta http-equiv="Content-Type" content="text/html; charset=utf-8"/>
    <title></title>
    <link rel="stylesheet" href="scrollingnewsstyle.css" type="text/css"
    media="screen" />
    <script src="jquery-3.5.1.js" type="text/javascript"></script>
    <script src="scrollingnewsjq.js" type="text/javascript"></script>
  </head>
  <body>
     <div class="scroller">
          <p class="scroll">
jQuery is an open source project that is licensed under the MIT License to
permit its free use on any site and if required, it can be relicensed under
the GNU Public License for inclusion in other GNU-licensed open source
projects.
               It has a large community of users and contributors making it
               better every day. Huge numbers of posts are published by its
               community on its bug fixes and enhancements
```

```
            It has huge number of plug-in enabling you to add additional
            features to your web page and develop the apps compatible to
            different platforms.
            Its API is fully documented making it easy to use and access its
            full features
        </p>
        </div>
    </body>
</html>
```

A `<div>` element is defined and is assigned a class named `scroller`. Within the `<div>` element is the `<p>` element containing certain text that is considered the news that you want to scroll. The `<p>` element is assigned the class `scroll`.

In order to apply styles to the paragraph and the `<div>` element, some style classes are defined in a cascade style sheet file, `scrollingnewsstyle.css`, as follows:

Scrollingnewsstyle.css

```
.scroller {
        width: 200px;
        height: 400px;
        overflow: hidden;
        margin: auto;
        padding:10px;
        position: relative;
border: 1px solid;
}

.scroll {
        position: relative;
}
```

The width and height of the `<div>` element are set to 200px and 400px, respectively. The content outside the given width and height will be clipped. The `margin` space between the `<div>` element and the browser window is set to `auto` (i.e., the browser will decide the spacing). A border of 1px thickness is drawn around the <div> element. The position property of the <div> and <p> elements is set to relative so that the impact of the top property (which is applied through jQuery code) can be seen.

The jQuery code to make the news scroll and stop it when a mouse hovers over it is as follows:

Scrollingnewsjq.js

```
$(document).ready(function() {
    $('.scroller').append($('.scroll').clone());

    var scroll = function(content) {
            $('.scroll').animate({
                    top: -400
                }, 4000, function() {
                        $('.scroll').css({
                                top: 0
                        });
                        scroll($(this));
            });

            $('.scroll').hover(function() {
                        $('.scroll').stop(true, false);
            });

            $(".scroll").mouseleave(function(){
                        scroll();
            });
    }

    scroll();
});
```

In this jQuery code, the stop() method is used, so let's understand its usage first.

stop()

Stops the currently running animation of the selected elements.

Syntax:

$(selector).stop(stop_queued,complete_all)

- stop_queued is a Boolean value. true is supplied here to stop the queued animations. The default value is false.

- complete_all is a Boolean value. true is supplied here to complete all animations immediately. The default value is false.

On running the application, all text in the <p> element is displayed as shown in Figure 7-5(a). A clone (i.e., a copy of the <p> element of class scroll) is made and is appended to the <div> element of class scroller. A function is defined by the name scroll. Within the function, the <p> element of class scroll is set to animate (i.e., to scroll upwards until its position is at 400px above the top edge of the <div> element). This scrolling upwards will happen in animation form of 4000ms duration (see Figure 7-5(b)). Thereafter the position of the <p> element is set at 0px from the top edge of the <div> element.

This function is recursively called so that the process continues (i.e. whatever text is visible in the <div> element is scrolled up so that its top edge reaches at 400px above the top edge of the <div> element). The scrolled up text is appended at the bottom and the process continues.

When the mouse pointer hovers over the <p> element, the stop() method is invoked, which stops the currently running animation on the <p> element.

When the mouse pointer moves away from the <p> element, the scroll() function is again invoked to continue scrolling the <p> element.

jQuery is an open source
project that is licensed under
the MIT License to permit its
free use on any site and if
required, it can be relicensed
under the GNU Public License
for inclusion in other GNU-
licensed open source projects.
It has a large community of
users and contributors making
it better every day. Huge
number of posts are published
by its community on its bug
fixes and enhancements It has
huge number of plug-in
enabling you to add additional
features to your web page and
develop the apps compatible to
different platforms. Its API is
fully documented making it
easy to use and access its full
features

(a)

features to your web page and
develop the apps compatible to
different platforms. Its API is
fully documented making it
easy to use and access its full
features

jQuery is an open source
project that is licensed under
the MIT License to permit its
free use on any site and if
required, it can be relicensed
under the GNU Public License
for inclusion in other GNU-
licensed open source projects.
It has a large community of
users and contributors making
it better every day. Huge
number of posts are published
by its community on its bug
fixes and enhancements It has
huge number of plug-in
enabling you to add additional

(b)

Figure 7-5. *(a) All of the text in the <p> element is displayed. (b) The text scrolls upwards*

7-6. Showing Images One After the Other on Hover

Problem

You have several images to be displayed and you want to display them one by one. The first image is displayed and when you hover over it, you want it to fade out and another image to fade in. Then you want the second image to fade out on hover and the third image to fade in, and so on. After the last image, you want the first image to reappear.

Solution

Make an HTML file to display all five images in the form of a hyperlink, so that if a visitor clicks on the image, they will be navigated to the target web site displaying complete information about the object that the image represents. Currently you assume the target web site as any hypothetical web site. The HTML file is as follows:

showimageonhover.html

```
<!DOCTYPE html PUBLIC "-//W3C//DTD XHTML 1.0 Transitional//EN"
        "http://www.w3.org/TR/xhtml1/DTD/xhtml1-transitional.dtd">
<html xmlns="http://www.w3.org/1999/xhtml" xml:lang="en" lang="en">
  <head>
    <meta http-equiv="Content-Type" content="text/html; charset=utf-8"/>
    <title></title>
    <link rel="stylesheet" href="stylesliding.css" type="text/css"
    media="screen" />
    <script src="jquery-3.5.1.js" type="text/javascript"></script>
    <script src="showimageonhoverjq.js" type="text/javascript"></script>
  </head>
  <body>
    <a class="image" href="http://example.com" ><img src="chip.jpg"
    width=300px
height=300px></a>
    <a class="image" href="http://example.com"><img src="chip2.jpg"
    width=300px
height=300px></a>
```

```
    <a class="imge" href="http://example.com"><img src="chip3.jpg"
    width=300px
height=300px></a>
    <a class="imge" href="http://example.com" ><img src="chip4.jpg"
    width=300px
height=300px></a>
    <a class="imge" href="http://example.com" ><img src="chip5.jpg"
    width=300px
height=300px></a>
  </body>
</html>
```

All the anchor elements are assigned the class name `imge` to automatically apply to them the style properties that are defined in the class selector `.imge` defined in the external style sheet (`style.css`).

The class names are also used to identify the elements to which you want to apply jQuery code. Also, all images are assigned an identical width and height of 300px to give them a uniform appearance. The style sheet code is as follows:

stylesliding.css

```
.imge{
    position:absolute;
    top:10px;
    left:10px;
}
```

The jQuery code to make an image fade out (become invisible) slowly and replace it with another image that fades in (becomes visible) slowly is as follows:

showimageonhoverjq.js

```
$(document).ready(function() {
    $(".imge").hide();
    $('.imge:first').fadeIn('slow');
    $('.imge').hover(
    function(){
        $(this).fadeIn('slow');
    },
```

```
    function(){
        var next = ($(this).next().length) ? $(this).next()
        :$('.imge:first');
        $(this).fadeOut('slow');
        next.fadeIn('slow');
    }
    );
})
```

How It Works

You want it so that when you hover on one image, it will be replaced by another image at the same place, so you use the position property and set the class selector .imge to absolute to define the exact location of the image to appear on the web page. Also, the top and left properties are set to 10px to assure that the image appears at the distance of 10px from the top and left boundaries of the browser window.

Now looking at the jQuery code itself, you make all the images disappear initially, since you want them to appear one by one. You then make the first element of all the HTML elements of the class imge appear slowly on the web page. That is, the first image (of all the images) will appear slowly upon opening the web page. This is the initial image that will appear first on the web page. Once this is complete, you attach the hover event to all images (all HTML elements of the class imge).

In the hover event, you make the current image appear slowly when the mouse is over the image. When the mouse pointer is moved away from the image being displayed, you see the next image to be displayed. You first check that you are not on the last image (of the elements of the class imge) and then you assign the next image in the sequence to the variable next. And if you are at the last image, the first image (of the HTML elements of the class imge) is assigned to the variable next. In other words, the variable next is set to refer either to the next image in the sequence or to the first image (if you have reached the last image of the class imge).

Once you have decided on the image to display next, the image that is currently visible is made to fade out slowly. Finally, the image in the variable next (referring to the next image in the sequence) is set to appear slowly on the web page (fade in). Initially, you get the first image of the five images on the screen, as shown in Figure 7-6.

Figure 7-6. *The first image displayed on loading the web page*

On hovering over the image (that is, on moving the mouse over the image and taking it away), the next image in the sequence will appear slowly, as shown in Figure 7-7. Similarly, all the images will be displayed one by one. When the last image is reached, the first image will reappear.

Figure 7-7. *The first image is replaced by the next image in the sequence on hover*

Making a Slide Show

So let's make a slide show. You'll display an image that, when clicked, will be replaced by another image in the sequence, and so on. The only modification that you will make to the preceding jQuery code is that instead of the hover event, you attach the click event (i.e., mousedown event) to the images. The jQuery code is as follows:

slideshowjq.js

```
$(document).ready(function() {
    $(".imge").hide();
    var next;
    $('.imge:first').fadeIn('slow');
    $('.imge').on("mousedown", function(event) {
        $(this).fadeIn('slow');
        next = ($(this).next().length) ? $(this).next()
        :$('.imge:first');
        $(this).fadeOut('slow');
        next.fadeIn('slow');
        event.preventDefault();
    });
});
```

You can see that all of the images are initially made invisible. The first image is made visible by a fadein effect. A mousedown event is attached to the images and if the click event occurs on any of the images, the next image in the sequence is retrieved and stored in the variable next. The image that was visible earlier is made invisible slowly with a fadeout effect, and the next image in the sequence (which is retrieved in the next variable) is made visible with the fade-in effect. To stop from migrating to the target web page on clicking the image, the preventDefault method of the event object (that is automatically passed to the event-handling function by JavaScript) is used.

7-7. Showing Images Pagewise

Problem

You have several images on the web page and you want to display them pagewise, where a page may contain one or more images (depending on the space on the web page). At the top of the image, you want the numbers to represent the page numbers. You want the image of the selected page number to be displayed on the screen.

Solution

Create an HTML file to define five images that you want to be displayed. Also, since you want the images to act as hyperlinks that navigate the visitor to the target web page (one that will display more detailed information about the image that's been selected) you need to nest the image elements inside the anchor elements. The HTML file is as follows:

imagespagewise.html

```
<!DOCTYPE html PUBLIC "-//W3C//DTD XHTML 1.0 Transitional//EN"
        "http://www.w3.org/TR/xhtml1/DTD/xhtml1-transitional.dtd">
<html xmlns="http://www.w3.org/1999/xhtml" xml:lang="en" lang="en">
  <head>
    <meta http-equiv="Content-Type" content="text/html; charset=utf-8"/>
    <title></title>
    <link rel="stylesheet" href="stylepagewise.css" type="text/css"
    media="screen" />
    <script src="jquery-3.5.1.js" type="text/javascript"></script>
    <script src="imagespagewisejq.js" type="text/javascript"></script>
  </head>
  <body>
    <div id="images">
        <a href="http://example.com" ><img src="chip.jpg" width=150px
        height=150px /></a>
        <a href="http://example.com"><img src="chip2.jpg" width=150px
        height=150px /></a>
        <a href="http://example.com"><img src="chip3.jpg" width=150px
        height=150px /></a>
```

```
        <a href="http://example.com" ><img src="chip4.jpg" width=150px
        height=150px /></a>
        <a href="http://example.com" ><img src="chip5.jpg" width=150px
        height=150px /></a>
    </div>
  </body>
</html>
```

You can see in the HTML page that all img elements are assigned the same width and height of 150px to give them a uniform appearance and the anchor elements target some hypothetical website to which the visitor will be navigated on selecting any image.

Now let's define the CSS classes in the external style sheet file stylepagewise.css:

stylepagewise.css

```
.page{
    margin:5px;
}
.hover{
    color: blue ;
    background-color:cyan
}
```

The jQuery code to divide the images into pages and display the image of the selected pages is as follows:

imagespagewisejq.js

```
$(document).ready(function() {
    var $pic = $('#images a');
    $pic.hide();
    var imgs = $pic.length;
    var next=$pic.eq(0);
    next.css({'position': 'absolute','left':10});
    next.show();
    var $pagenumbers=$('<div id="pages"></div>');
```

```
for(i=0;i<imgs;i++)
{
    $('<span class="page">'+(i+1)+'</span>').appendTo($pagenumbers);
}
$pagenumbers.insertBefore(next);
$('.page').hover(
function(){
    $(this).addClass('hover');
},
function(){
    $(this).removeClass('hover');
}
);
$('span').on("mousedown", function(event){
    $pic.hide();
    next=$pic.eq($(this).text()-1);
    next.show();
});
});
```

How It Works

The CSS class page contains the style property margin set to 5px to define the space between the page numbers and the class hover contains two properties, color and background-color, set to blue and cyan, respectively, to change the background and foreground colors of the page numbers when the mouse pointer moves over them.

Now let's look at the jQuery code itself. First, all anchor elements (that is, all of the images enclosed in the anchor elements) nested in the div element of ID images are retrieved and stored in the variable $pic. The object $pic contains all the images. You then hide all the images and set some variables; the count of the images is stored in the variable imgs, and the first image in the $pic object is stored in the variable next.

To the first image stored in variable next, some style properties are applied using the .css() method.

The position property is set to absolute and the left property is set to 10px to make the image stored in the variable next appear at the distance of 10px from the left

369

boundary of the browser window. With that done, the image in the next variable is made visible on the screen and you define a variable $pagenumbers and a div element of ID pages is assigned to it.

A for loop is then used to create several span elements (equal to the number of images) of the class pages. The text in the span element is 1,2... (to serve as page numbers). The span elements are assigned the class name pages so that the properties defined in the class selector .pages (in the style.css file) can be applied to them automatically. The span elements are appended to the div element of ID pages that you assigned to the variable $pagenumbers.

The whole div element of ID pages containing the span elements (which contain the page numbers) is inserted before the first image displayed via the variable next, and you apply and remove the CSS class hover to the page numbers (span elements of the class page) when the mouse pointer is moved over the page numbers. You then need to attach the mousedown event to the span elements (that is, to the page numbers).

Here you make all of the images invisible, including the current one that is displayed if the user selects any of the page numbers. Finally, you retrieve the image from the $pic object (containing an array of images), depending on the value of the page number selected; you store it in the variable next and display the image retrieved in the variable next.

On execution of the jQuery code, initially the first image is displayed with page numbers at its top, as shown in Figure 7-8.

Figure 7-8. *The first image, along with the page number list above it*

On selecting the page number, the image of that page number will be displayed as shown in Figure 7-9.

Figure 7-9. *The image that appears on clicking page number 4*

7-8. Shuffling Images in Either Direction

Problem

You want to display a few images on the web page within an invisible window, along with left and right arrow buttons below them. You want it to work so that when the left arrow button is pressed, the images shuffle toward the left side (making the images that were hidden scroll left), and when the right arrow button is selected, all the images scroll right to display any hidden images.

Solution

Create an HTML file to define the images that you want to be displayed. The images are nested inside the div element of ID images (to apply styles and codes via jQuery code), which in turn is nested inside the div element of ID scroller. The HTML file you want to create is shown here:

shufflingeither.html

```
<!DOCTYPE html PUBLIC "-//W3C//DTD XHTML 1.0 Transitional//EN"
        "http://www.w3.org/TR/xhtml1/DTD/xhtml1-transitional.dtd">
<html xmlns="http://www.w3.org/1999/xhtml" xml:lang="en" lang="en">
  <head>
    <meta http-equiv="Content-Type" content="text/html; charset=utf-8"/>
    <title></title>
```

```
    <link rel="stylesheet" href="styleshufflingeither.css" type="text/css"
    media="screen" />
    <script src="jquery-3.5.1.js" type="text/javascript"></script>
    <script src="shufflingeitherjq.js" type="text/javascript"></script>
  </head>
  <body>
    <div id="scroller">
        <div id="images">
            <a href="http://example.com" ><img src="chip.jpg"
            width=150px height=150px /></a>
            <a href="http://example.com"><img src="chip2.jpg"
            width=150px height=150px /></a>
            <a href="http://example.com"><img src="chip3.jpg"
            width=150px height=150px /></a>
            <a href="http://example.com" ><img src="chip4.jpg"
            width=150px height=150px /></a>
            <a href="http://example.com" ><img src="chip5.jpg"
            width=150px height=150px /></a>
        </div>
    </div>
    <div id="direction">
        <img src="leftarrow.png" class="leftarrow"/>
        <img src="rightarrow.png" class="rightarrow"/>
    </div>
  </body>
</html>
```

The images are enclosed within the anchor elements so as to navigate the visitor to the target web page to display the detailed information about the image that's been selected. For the time being, assume the target web site as some hypothetical web site. The anchor elements containing the img elements are enclosed within the two div elements, one inside the other. The outer div element is assigned the ID scroller and the inner div element is assigned the ID images. To the outer div element, you apply the style properties to define the width of the invisible window; that is, it decides how many images you want to see at a time. To the inner div element, you apply the style properties that decide the total width of the complete image block. All images are assigned an identical width and height of 150px to give them a uniform appearance. Also, you make use of the img element to display the left and right arrow buttons. These img elements are assigned the class names leftarrow and rightarrow, respectively, so that the style properties defined in the class selectors can be applied to them. The two arrows are nested inside the div element that is assigned the ID direction. You define the style properties for the div elements and the img elements in the style sheet **styleshufflingeither.css**, as follows:

styleshufflingeither.css

```css
#scroller {
    position: relative;
    height:150px;
    width: 460px;
    overflow:hidden;
    margin:auto;
}
#images{
    width: 770px;
}
#images a img { border:0; position:relative;}
#direction
{
    width: 460px;
    margin:auto;
}
.leftarrow{margin-top:10px;}
.rightarrow{margin-left:300px;margin-top:10px;}
```

The jQuery code to make the images scroll on selecting the left and right arrow images is shown here:

shufflingeitherjq.js

```javascript
$(document).ready(function() {
    var $wrapper=$('#scroller a img');
    var leftanimator = function(imgblock) {
        imgblock.animate({left:-310 }, 2000);
    }
```

```
    var rightanimator = function(imgblock) {
        imgblock.animate({left:0 }, 2000);
    }
    $('.leftarrow').on("mousedown", function(event){
        leftanimator($wrapper);
        event.preventDefault();
    });
    $('.rightarrow').on("mousedown", function(event){
        rightanimator($wrapper);
        event.preventDefault();
    });
});
```

How It Works

You can see in the style.css file that the ID selector #scroller contains the position property set to relative, a necessary condition to make the image scroll (images scroll when you assign them some position relative to their current location). The height and width are set to 150px and 460px, respectively.

The width of 460px is required to display at most three images at a time (the width includes the width of three images of 150px each, with some space in between). The overflow property is set to hidden to make invisible the region of the images that fall outside the width of this invisible window. The margin property is set to auto to make the horizontal scroller appear at the center of the width of the browser window.

The ID selector #images contains the width property that will be applied to the inner div element.

The width property is set to 770px, which is the total of the width of all of the images that you want to be displayed in the scroller (with some distance between the images). The width property here decides the number of images that you want to see in the horizontal scroller. Also, the style sheet contains a type selector #images a img to apply the style properties to the img element nested inside the anchor element, which in turn is enclosed with an HTML element of ID images. As you'll notice, images contains the border property set to 0 (to make the borders of the images invisible) and the position property is set to relative to make the images scroll.

The ID selector `#direction` contains the style properties that will be applied to the block of left and right arrow images. The `width` property set to 460px assigns the maximum width that this block (of the two arrow images) can occupy, and the `margin` value set to `auto` makes the block (of two images) appear at the center of the browser window, just below the images block.

The class selector `.leftarrow` contains the properties that are automatically applied to the left arrow image. It has the `margin-top` property set to `10px` to keep the left arrow at a distance of 10px from the images block at its top. Meanwhile, the class selector `.rightarrow` contains the style properties that are automatically applied to the right arrow image. It contains the `margin-left` property set to `300px` to make the right arrow image be right-justified in the assigned width of 460px, and the `margin-top` property is set to `10px` to keep it 10px from the images block at its top.

Now turning to the jQuery code in this solution, you'll notice that all of the images that are nested inside the anchor element of the `div` element of ID `scroller` are retrieved and stored in a variable named `$wrapper`.

You continue by defining a function named `leftanimator` that takes in the parameter `imgblock`, which it animates toward the left slowly and stops at the distance of -310px from the left border (310px inside the left border). As a result, the two images on the left of the image block disappear inside the left border of the invisible window, making two images on the right (which were hidden earlier) become visible.

The `rightanimator` method takes in the parameter `imgblock`, which it animates toward the right slowly and stops at the distance of 0px from the left border. That is, it makes the image block scroll toward the right border and stop when the first image of the block becomes visible. The scrolling stops when the first three images are visible in the invisible window. It makes the two images on the right side become invisible.

Next you attach a mousedown event to the left arrow image, and when the mousedown (i.e., the mouse click event) occurs on it, the `leftanimator` function is invoked and the `$wrapper` variable containing the block of all five images is sent to it, which will be assigned to its parameter `imgblock`. The function makes the image block scroll to the left, displaying the last three images. The `preventDefault` method is invoked for the event object to avoid navigating to the target web site to which the image (nested inside the anchor element) is pointing.

Finally, you attach a mousedown event to the right arrow image, and when the mouse click event occurs on it, the `rightanimator` function is invoked and the `$wrapper` variable containing the block of all five images is sent to it and will be assigned to its parameter `imgblock`. The function makes the image block scroll toward the right, making the first three images reappear on the screen. The `preventDefault` method of the event object is invoked to avoid navigating to the target web site to which the image (nested inside the anchor element) is pointing. Initially, the first three images are displayed along with the left and right arrows below them, as shown in Figure 7-10.

Figure 7-10. *Three images appear initially, along with the left and right arrows at the bottom. On selecting the left arrow button, the images will scroll left and you will be able to see the last three images (of the five-image block), as shown in Figure 7-11*

Figure 7-11. *Images scrolled to the left on selecting the left arrow*

Similarly, if you select the right arrow button, the images will scroll right, making the first three images reappear.

7-9. Writing a Pendulum Scroller
Problem

You have a block of five images and you want it to work so that initially three of the five images appear in an invisible window. Then these images should scroll left and disappear out of the window, as if they're swinging on a pendulum. When the last image also disappears, you want the images to appear from the left border and scroll toward the right border (making the last image appear first, followed by the fourth, and so on). All of the images will scroll toward the right border and disappear from the window. When the first image disappears, you want the images to again scroll toward the left border, and the process continues.

Solution

Let's set up an HTML file to define the images that you want to be displayed. The images are nested inside the `div` element of ID `images` (to apply styles and codes via jQuery code), which in turn is nested inside the `div` element of ID `scroller`. The HTML file is as follows:

pendulum.html

```
<!DOCTYPE html PUBLIC "-//W3C//DTD XHTML 1.0 Transitional//EN"
        "http://www.w3.org/TR/xhtml1/DTD/xhtml1-transitional.dtd">
<html xmlns="http://www.w3.org/1999/xhtml" xml:lang="en" lang="en">
  <head>
    <meta http-equiv="Content-Type" content="text/html; charset=utf-8"/>
    <title></title>
    <link rel="stylesheet" href="styleshufflingeither.css" type="text/css"
    media="screen" />
    <script src="jquery-3.5.1.js" type="text/javascript"></script>
    <script src="pendulumjq.js" type="text/javascript"></script>
  </head>
  <body>
    <div id="scroller">
        <div id="images">
```

```
        <a href="http://example.com" ><img src="chip.jpg"
        width=150px height=150px /></a>
        <a href="http://example.com"><img src="chip2.jpg"
        width=150px height=150px /></a>
        <a href="http://example.com"><img src="chip3.jpg"
        width=150px height=150px /></a>
        <a href="http://example.com" ><img src="chip4.jpg"
        width=150px height=150px /></a>
        <a href="http://example.com" ><img src="chip5.jpg"
        width=150px height=150px /></a>
      </div>
    </div>
  </body>
</html>
```

The images are enclosed within the anchor elements so as to navigate the visitor to the target web page to display the detailed information of the image that's been selected. For the time being, assume the target web site as some hypothetical web site.

The anchor elements containing the img elements are enclosed within the two div elements, one inside the other. The outer div element is assigned the ID scroller and the inner div element is assigned the ID images. To the outer div element, you apply the style properties to define the width of the invisible window; that is, it decides how many images you want to see at a time. To the inner div element, you apply the style properties that decide the total width of the complete image block. All images are assigned an identical width and height of 150px to give them a uniform appearance.

In this recipe, you will use the same style sheet, **styleshufflingeither.css**, that you used in Recipe 7-8 to apply the style properties to the div elements and the img elements.

The jQuery code to make the images scroll as if on a pendulum is shown here:

pendulumjq.js

```
$(document).ready(function() {
    var $wrapper=$('#scroller a img');
    var left_rightanimator = function() {
    $wrapper.animate(
        {left:-770}, 5000,
```

```
        function() {
        $wrapper.animate({left:465 }, 5000);
        left_rightanimator();
        }
    );
    }
    left_rightanimator();
});
```

How It Works

You can see in the `style.css` file that the ID selector `#scroller` contains a `position` property set to `relative`—a necessary condition to make the image scroll (images scroll when you assign them some position relative to their current location). The height and width are set to 150px and 460px, respectively.

The width of 460px is required to display at most three images at a time (the width includes the width of three images of 150px width, with some space in between). The `overflow` property is set to `hidden` to make invisible the region of the images that falls outside the width of this invisible window. The `margin` property is set to `auto` to make the horizontal scroller appear at the center of the width of browser window.

The ID selector `#images` contains the `width` property that is applied to the inner `div` element.

The width property is set to 770px, which is the total of the width of all of the images that you want to be displayed in the scroller (with some distance between the images). The width property here decides the number of images that you want to see in the horizontal scroller.

Also, the style sheet contains a type selector `#images a img` to apply the style properties to the `img` element nested inside the anchor element, which in turn is enclosed with an HTML element of ID `images`.

It contains the `border` property set to `0` (to make the borders of the images invisible) and the `position` property set to `relative` to make the images scroll. Looking now at the jQuery code, all images that are nested inside the anchor element and the `div` element of ID `scroller` are retrieved and stored in the `$wrapper` variable. That is, the `$wrapper` variable contains the whole block of five images.

Next you define a function named left_rightanimator, which animates the images block toward the left border (of the invisible window) and stops at the distance of –770px from the left border (that is, 770px inside the left border) which will make the whole block of five images disappear (recall that each image is 150px wide and there is some space between images). So again, the image block is set to appear from the left border and is set to animate towards the right (making the last image appear first), and the scrolling will stop when the first image also disappears out of the window (from the right border) at the distance of 465px from the left border, which is when the first image also disappears in the right border of the invisible window.

The last action of this method is to make a recursive call to the left_rightanimator() function to make the image block keep scrolling left and right. Finally, you invoke the left_rightanimator() function to get the process going.

The images scroll toward the left border, disappear, reappear from the left border, and scroll toward the right border. The last two images appear as shown in Figure 7-12 while scrolling left.

Figure 7-12. *Images scrolling to the left and disappearing*

7-10. Scrolling Images Using Arrays

Problem

You have a block of five images and you want it to work so that initially three of the five images appear in the invisible window. Then these images should scroll toward the left border (making the last two hidden images appear in the invisible window). All the images should disappear out of the left border. You want to do this with the help of arrays.

Solution

You will be making use of the same HTML file and style sheet file,
styleshufflingeither.css, that you used in the Recipe 7-9. The jQuery code to make
each image scroll toward the left border and become invisible one by one is as follows:

scrollingusingarraysjq.js

```
$(document).ready(function() {
    var $pic = $('#scroller a img');
    var imgs = $pic.length;
    var next;
    for (var i=0;i<imgs;i++){
        next=$pic.eq(i);
        scroll(next);
    };
});

function scroll(im)
{
    im.animate({'left': -770}, 5000);
};
```

Here, you start by retrieving all of the images nested inside the anchor elements,
which are in turn nested inside the div element of ID scroller, and storing them in
the variable $pic. $pic is now an array of five images. You then find out the number of
images in the $pic array and store the count in the imgs variable. In the for loop you
get one image from the $pic array and store it in the variable next. That is, all the images
will be assigned to the variable next one by one. To scroll, you invoke the function
scroll, and the image stored in the variable next is passed to it (that is, the variable next
is assigned to its parameter im).

In the scroll() method, the image is set to animate toward the left and stop at a
distance of -770px from the left border (that is, 770px inside the left border) to make even
the last (fifth) image disappear. The image while scrolling may appear as in Figure 7-13.

Figure 7-13. *All images scrolling to the left*

Scrolling an Image Over Other Images

Say you want to adapt the solution above because you want three images to appear
stationary and one image (the fourth) to scroll over this block of three images. The
jQuery code for that solution is as follows:

scrollingimageoverjq.js

```
$(document).ready(function() {
    var $pic = $('#scroller a img');
    var next;
    next=$pic.eq(3);
    scroll(next);
});

function scroll(im)
{
    im.animate({'left': -770}, 5000);
};
```

You can see that the variable next is assigned to the fourth image (at index location 3)
in the $pic array in the fourth statement and is passed to the scroll function to scroll
over the images. Initially, you have three images that appear in the invisible window, as
shown in Figure 7-14.

Figure 7-14. *Initial images on loading the web page*

The fourth image begins from the right border and scrolls toward the left border (of the invisible window) over the three images, as shown in Figure 7-15, where that fourth image is over the second and third images.

Figure 7-15. *An image scrolling to the left on top of the other images*

Scrolling Only the Image That Is Hovered Over

You have three images that appear initially in the invisible window and you want functionality so that any image that is hovered over will scroll toward the left border and disappear. The jQuery code is as follows:

scrollingimagehoveredjq.js

```
$(document).ready(function() {
    var $pic = $('#scroller a img');
    $pic.hover(
    function(){
        $(this).animate({'left': -770}, 5000);
    });
});
```

You can see that the third statement attaches the hover event to the block of images (stored in the $pic array) and in its event-handling function you animate the hovered image toward the left border and make it stop at the distance of –770px from the left border (that is, 770px inside the left border) to make it completely invisible. If you hover over the middle image, it will start scrolling toward the left, as shown in Figure 7-16.

Figure 7-16. *An image that is hovered over starts scrolling left*

When the middle image is completely scrolled into the left border, you're left with a blank space in the middle of the image block, as shown in Figure 7-17.

Figure 7-17. *The middle image scrolled to the left, creating an empty space*

Fading Out and Replacing an Image

You have three images that appear initially in the invisible window, and you want any image that is hovered over to slowly become invisible with a fadeout effect and its space to be filled by the next image (making a hidden image visible). The jQuery code is as follows:

fadingoutreplacingjq.js

```
$(document).ready(function() {
    var $pic = $('#scroller a img');
    $pic.hover(
        function(){
            $(this).fadeOut(5000);
        });
});
```

A hover event is attached to the $pic variable, which is nothing but the array of five images. In the event-handling function of the hover event, you make the image that is being hovered on fade out in 500 milliseconds. The moment the image becomes completely invisible, the next image in the $pic array will fill up the vacant space.

Initially, you have three images visible in the window, as was shown in Figure 7-16. When the first image is hovered over, it will fade out slowly and its place will be occupied by the next image in sequence.

Scrolling One Image Left and One Image Right, and Fading Out the Middle

Let's end this set of recipes with a final, rather fancy modification of the current recipe, just to give you more ideas of what's possible now that you have the core solutions around scrolling and fading!

Let's say you have three images that appear initially in the invisible window, and you want the first image to scroll toward the left border and disappear, the third image to scroll toward the right border of the invisible window and disappear, and the middle image to remain at its position and slowly fade out. This time, the jQuery code is as follows:

scrollingleftrightjq.js

```
$(document).ready(function() {
    var $pic = $('#scroller a img');
    $pic.eq(0).animate(
    {'left': -155}, 5000,
    function(){
        $pic.eq(2).animate(
```

```
        {'right': -155}, 5000,
        function(){
            $pic.fadeOut(5000);
        }
        );
        }
    );
});
```

All of the image elements that are nested inside the anchor elements of ID `scroller` are retrieved and stored in the variable `$pic`. The first image (the image at the index location 0 in the `$pic` array) is set to animate toward the left border and stop at a distance of -155px from the left border (that is, 155px inside the left border), which is sufficient for the image of 150px width to disappear. Similarly, the third image is set to animate toward the right border and stop at a distance of -155px from the right border (that is, 155px inside the right border) to make the image disappear. The middle image that is left behind is set to fade out slowly, in 5000 milliseconds.

7-11. Summary

In this chapter, you learned to display images that slide from left to right infinitely. You also learned to make a ball bounce. You learned to slide the images horizontally as well as vertically within a box. Finally, you learned to make a news scroller.

In the next chapter, you will learn about Tables. You will learn how to sort tables, filter desired information, paginate table content etc.

CHAPTER 8

Dealing with Tables

In this chapter, you will try the following recipes that will be performed on tables:

- Hovering over table rows
- Highlighting alternate columns
- Filtering out a selected row
- Erasing a selected column
- Paginating the table
- Expanding and collapsing list items
- Expanding and collapsing rows of the table
- Sorting list items
- Sorting a table
- Filtering rows from a table

8-1. Hovering Over Table Rows
Problem

You have a table consisting of a few rows and columns. You want that when you hover over any of the rows (the mouse pointer is moved over it), the row should get highlighted.

© Bintu Harwani 2022
B. Harwani, *jQuery Recipes*, https://doi.org/10.1007/978-1-4842-7304-3_8

Solution

Make an HTML file that contains a table element with some row and column elements (th, td, tr) defined in it. The HTML file is as follows:

Hoverrows.html

```
<!DOCTYPE html PUBLIC "-//W3C//DTD XHTML 1.0 Transitional//EN"
        "http://www.w3.org/TR/xhtml1/DTD/xhtml1-transitional.dtd">

<html xmlns="http://www.w3.org/1999/xhtml" xml:lang="en" lang="en">
  <head>
    <meta http-equiv="Content-Type" content="text/html; charset=utf-8"/>
    <title></title>
    <link rel="stylesheet" href="style.css" type="text/css" media="screen" />
    <script src="jquery-3.5.1.js" type="text/javascript"></script>
    <script src="hoverrowsjq.js" type="text/javascript"></script>
  </head>
  <body>
    <table border="1">
      <thead>
          <tr><th>Roll</th><th>Name</th><th>Marks</th></tr>
      </thead>
      <tbody>
          <tr><td>101</td><td>John</td><td>87</td></tr>
          <tr><td>102</td><td>Naman</td><td>90</td></tr>
          <tr><td>103</td><td>Chirag</td><td>85</td></tr>
      </tbody>
    </table>
  </body>
</html>
```

Define a style rule named .hover in the style sheet file style.css to apply the style properties to the hovered row:

style.css

```
.hover { background-color: #00f; color: #fff; }
```

The jQuery code to apply a hovering effect to the table rows is as follows:

Hoverrowsjq.js

```
$(document).ready(function() {
  $('tbody tr').hover(
    function(){
      $(this).find('td').addClass('hover');
    },
    function(){
      $(this).find('td').removeClass('hover');
    }
  );
});
```

How It Works

In the HTML file you see that a table with a border of 1px is defined. It has three column headings (defined using the th element): **Roll, Name**, and **Marks**. Also, it contains three rows of student records. The table headings are nested inside the thead element and the body of the table (the rows that contain information) is nested inside the tbody element.

In the style sheet file, the .hover style rule contains the background-color property set to #00f and the color property set to value #fff to change the background and foreground color of the hovered row to blue and white, respectively.

In the jQuery code, you attach the hover() event to the tr (row elements) that are nested inside the tbody element since you want only the rows that contain student information to be hovered over and not the row that contains the column headings. In the event handling function of the hover event, you search for the td elements of the hovered row and apply the properties defined in the style rule .hover (which exists in the style sheet file style.css) to change their background and foreground color to blue and white, respectively, so as to highlight them.

Initially, the table appears as shown in Figure 8-1.

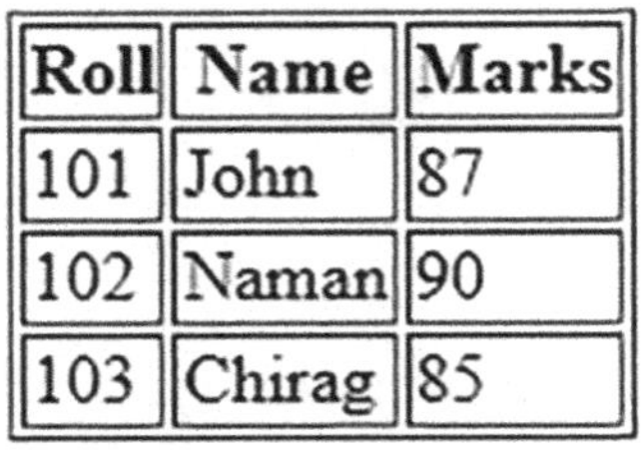

Roll	Name	Marks
101	John	87
102	Naman	90
103	Chirag	85

Figure 8-1. *Table consisting of a few rows and columns*

On moving the mouse pointer over any of the rows, they will be highlighted as shown in Figure 8-2.

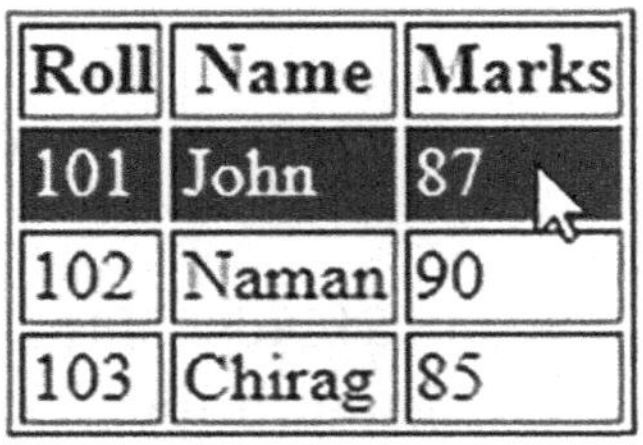

Roll	Name	Marks
101	John	87
102	Naman	90
103	Chirag	85

Figure 8-2. *The highlighted row on being hovered over*

8-2. Highlighting Alternate Columns

Problem

You have a table consisting of a few rows and columns. You want alternate columns of the table to be highlighted (i.e., some styles are applied on them).

Solution

For this solution, you will make use of the same HTML and style sheet file (`style.css`) that you used in the Recipe 8-1.

The jQuery code to apply the style properties defined in the style rule `.hover` to the alternate columns of the table is as follows:

Highlightaltcolsjq.js

```
$(document).ready(function() {
  $('td:nth-child(odd)').addClass('hover');
});
```

How It Works

Since you are using the :nth-child() method in the above jQuery code, let's first understand what it does.

:nth-child()

This method is used to retrieve all elements that are the nth child of their parent. This method is 1-based (i.e., it begins counting from 1 and not 0). This method is different from the :eq() method in the following two ways:

- The :eq() method matches only a single element whereas the :nth-child() method matches more than one (i.e., one for each parent with the specified index).

- The :eq() method is 0-based (i.e., it begins counting from 0) whereas :nth-child() is 1-based (i.e., it begins counting from 1).

For example,

```
$('tr:nth-child(3)');
```

selects all tr elements that are the third child of their parent (which may be a tbody or table element), so it will select the third row of the table.

Similarly, the statement

```
$('tr:nth-child(even)');
```

selects all of the even rows of the table.

In the above jQuery code, the statement

```
$('td:nth-child(odd)').addClass('hover');
```

selects the odd columns of the table (in other words, each td that is an odd child of its parent) and applies the style properties defined in the style rule hover to them, changing their background color to blue and foreground color to white, as shown in Figure 8-3.

Roll	Name	Marks
101	John	87
102	Naman	90
103	Chirag	85

***Figure 8-3.** Table with odd numbered columns highlighted*

Highlighting Alternate Rows

To highlight alternate rows of the table, modify the jQuery code as follows:

Highlightaltrowsjq.js

```
$(document).ready(function() {
  $('table tr:odd').addClass('hover');
});
```

This jQuery code will select all the odd rows of the table and apply the style properties defined in the style rule `.hover` to them so as to highlight them as shown in Figure 8-4.

Roll	Name	Marks
101	John	87
102	Naman	90
103	Chirag	85

***Figure 8-4.** Table with alternate rows highlighted*

Highlighting the Column That Is Hovered Over

You want to highlight only those columns whose column headings are hovered over (i.e., when the mouse pointer moves over any column heading, you want that column to be highlighted). The jQuery code is as follows:

Highlightcolumjq.js

```
$(document).ready(function() {
  $('th').hover(
    function(){
      var colindex=$(this).parent().children().index(this);
      $('table td:nth-child('+(colindex+1)+')').addClass('hover');
    },
    function(){
      $('table tr').children().removeClass('hover');
    }
  );
});
```

Before you begin to understand the jQuery code, let's learn about the `.index()` method that is used in this code.

.index()

This method searches every matched element for the passed element and returns the ordinal index of the element, if found, starting with 0. It returns -1 if the passed element is not found in the matched set. If a jQuery object is passed in this method, only the first element is checked.

Syntax:

`.index(element)`

The meaning of the above jQuery code is as follows. You first attach the hover event to the table heading (`th`) elements.

When the user hovers over a table heading, you find out the index (column number) of its column and store that index location in the variable `colindex`. The `.index()` method uses 0-based counting, which means it begins counting from 0. So an index of 0 means the first column heading is hovered over, a 1 means the second column heading is hovered over, and so on.

You can then apply the style properties defined in the style rule `.hover` to the column whose index location is stored in variable `colindex`. Since the `:nth-child()` method is 1-based (i.e., it begins counting from 1 as compared to the `.index()` method which begins from 0), you need to increment the value stored in the variable `colindex` by 1 before applying the style rule `.hover` to the column represented by `colindex` in the event handling function of the `hover` event.

In the event handling function, which is invoked when the mouse pointer is moved away from the column heading, you remove the style properties defined in the style rule `.hover` from all rows of the table.

The contents of the column whose heading is hovered over are highlighted as shown in Figure 8-5.

Roll	Name	Marks
101	John	87
102	Naman	90
103	Chirag	85

Figure 8-5. *Highlighted column contents of the hovered-over column heading*

Highlighting the Column Heading Also While Hovering

In above example, the column contents are highlighted when its column heading is hovered over but the column heading is not highlighted. It appears as it was initially. You need to add one more statement (shown in bold) in the jQuery code to highlight the column heading as well:

Highlightcolheadjq.js

```
$(document).ready(function() {
  $('th').hover(
    function(){
      var colindex=$(this).parent().children().index(this);
      $(this).addClass('hover');
      $('table td:nth-child('+(colindex+1)+')').addClass('hover');
    },
```

```
function(){
    $('table tr').children().removeClass('hover');
    }
  );
});
```

The statement

```
$(this).addClass('hover');
```

applies the style properties defined in the style rule .hover to the column heading too when it is hovered over as shown in Figure 8-6.

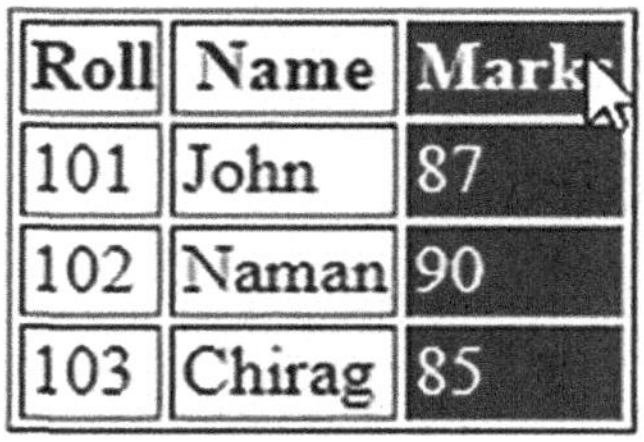

Roll	Name	Mark
101	John	87
102	Naman	90
103	Chirag	85

Figure 8-6. *Highlighted column contents and column heading of the hovered-over column heading*

Highlighting Individual Cells of the Table When Hovered Over

You want that when any of the cells of the table except the column headings are hovered over, it must be highlighted. The jQuery code for doing this is as follows:

Highlightcellhoveredjq.js

```
$(document).ready(function() {
  $('td').hover(
    function(){
      $(this).addClass('hover');
    },
    function(){
      $('table tr').children().removeClass('hover');
    }
  );
});
```

You can see that this time the hover event is attached to the td elements so that if any of the cells are hovered over (except the column headings), the properties defined in the style rule .hover are applied to it to highlight it as shown in Figure 8-7.

Roll	Name	Marks
101	John	87
102	Naman	90
103	Chirag	85

Figure 8-7. *Table cell highlighted on being hovered over*

8-3. Filtering Rows
Problem

You have a table consisting of a few rows and columns. You want that when the mouse pointer moves on any row, it must be highlighted, and when the user clicks on any part of the row, all the rows of the table should disappear except the one that is clicked.

Solution

For this solution, you will make use of the same HTML and style sheet files (style.css) you used in Recipe 8-1.

The jQuery code to highlight the row that is hovered over and to make all the rows to become invisible except the one that is clicked is as follows:

Filterrowsjq.js

```
$(document).ready(function() {
  $('tbody tr').hover(
    function(){
      $(this).find('td').addClass('hover');
    },
```

```
    function(){
      $(this).find('td').removeClass('hover');
    }
  );
  $('tbody tr').click(function(){
    $('table').find('tbody tr').hide();
    $(this).show();
  });
});
```

How It Works

In the first half of the jQuery code, you attach the hover() event to the tr (row elements) that are nested inside the tbody element since you want only the rows that contain student information to be hovered over and not the row that contains the column headings. In the event handling function of the hover event, you search for the td elements of the hovered row and apply the properties defined in the style rule .hover (which exists in the style sheet file style.css) to change their background and foreground colors to blue and white, respectively, so as to highlight them.

In the second half of the jQuery code, you attach the click event to all of the tr elements (nested inside the tbody element), and in its event handling function, you search for all the tr elements (that are nested inside the tbody element) and make all of them invisible (i.e., all the rows of the table except the column headings will be invisible). Thereafter, you make the contents of the row that was clicked visible, hence making only the clicked row appear in the table.

On hovering over any row of the table, the table will appear as shown in Figure 8-8.

Roll	Name	Marks
101	John	87
102	Naman	90
103	Chirag	85

Figure 8-8. *The row gets highlighted on being hovered over*

On clicking any row, all rows will become invisible except for the one that was clicked as shown in Figure 8-9.

Roll	Name	Marks
103	Chirag	85

Figure 8-9. *The selected row is left behind in the table*

Hiding the Selected Row

You can modify above jQuery code to reverse the process (i.e., instead of keeping the selected row, you can hide the selected row). The jQuery code is as follows:

Hidingrowsjq.js

```
$(document).ready(function() {

  $('tbody tr').hover(
    function(){
      $(this).find('td').addClass('hover');
    },
    function(){
      $(this).find('td').removeClass('hover');
    }
  );

  $('tbody tr').click(function(){
    $(this).hide();
  });
});
```

You can see in this jQuery code that the selected row is hidden by making it invisible by using the `.hide()` method. On hovering over the last row, the table may appear as shown in Figure 8-8. On clicking on that row, you find that it is erased and the remaining table may appear as shown in Figure 8-10.

Roll	Name	Marks
101	John	87
102	Naman	90

Figure 8-10. *The selected row is erased from the table*

8-4. Hiding the Selected Column
Problem

You have a table consisting of a few rows and columns. You want that when the mouse pointer moves on any column heading, that column, including the column heading, gets highlighted. Also, when a user clicks on any column heading, the complete column along with its heading should become hidden.

Solution

For this solution, you will make use of the same HTML and style sheet files (`style.css`) you used in Recipe 8-1.

The jQuery code to highlight the column (when its column heading is hovered over) and to make its contents become invisible on being clicked is as follows:

Hidingcolumnsjq.js

```
$(document).ready(function() {
  $('th').hover(
    function(){
      var colindex=$(this).parent().children().index(this);
      $(this).addClass('hover');
      $('table td:nth-child('+(colindex+1)+')').addClass('hover');
    },
    function(){
      $('table tr').children().removeClass('hover');
    }
  );
```

```
$('th').click(function(){
  $(this).hide();
  colindex=$(this).parent().children().index(this);
  $('table td:nth-child('+(colindex+1)+')').hide();
});
});
```

How It Works

The meaning of the jQuery code is as follows. You start by attaching the hover event to all of the column headings of the table. In the event handler, you finding out the index location of the column heading that is been hovered over and store it in the variable colindex. The .index() method uses 0-based counting (i.e., begins from value 0).

You then apply the style properties defined in the style rule .hover to the highlighted column heading and to the column whose index location is stored in the colindex variable (the one that is hovered over) to highlight them. Since the :nth-child() method is 1-based (i.e., begins counting from 1 instead of 0), you increment the value of colindex by 1 before highlighting it.

When the mouse pointer is moved away from the column heading, you remove the properties defined in the style rule .hover from all rows of the table.

In the click event handler, you hide the column heading that has been clicked and find out its index, which you store in the colindex variable.

Finally, you hide the column contents whose value is stored in the colindex variable (the index location of the column heading that is clicked). Hence, the column heading along with the complete column contents will be made invisible when any of the column heading is clicked.

On hovering over the column heading, it will be highlighted along with the contents of the complete column as shown in Figure 8-11.

Roll	Name	Marks
101	John	87
102	Naman	90
103	Chirag	85

Figure 8-11. *The column contents and the column heading get highlighted when the column heading is hovered over*

On clicking the column heading, it will be erased along with the contents of the column as shown in Figure 8-12.

Name	Marks
John	87
Naman	90
Chirag	85

Figure 8-12. *The selected column is erased from the table*

Filtering Out Columns

You want to make all columns of the table invisible except the one whose column heading is clicked. That is, you want to keep the selected column (along with its heading) that is been clicked, making the rest of the columns invisible.

The modified jQuery code to highlight the column (when its column heading is hovered over) and to hide all of the columns except the one that has been clicked is as follows:

Filteringcolumnsjq.js

```
$(document).ready(function() {
  $('th').hover(
    function(){
      var colindex=$(this).parent().children().index(this);
      $(this).addClass('hover');
      $('table td:nth-child('+(colindex+1)+')').addClass('hover');
    },
    function(){
      $('table tr').children().removeClass('hover');
    }
  );

  $('th').click(function(){
    colindex=$(this).parent().children().index(this);
    $('table th:not(:nth-child('+(colindex+1)+'))').hide();
    $('table td:not(:nth-child('+(colindex+1)+'))').hide();
  });
});
```

How It Works

Let's look at the `:not()` selector used in this jQuery code.

:not()

This selector selects all of the elements that do not match the specified selector. For example,

```
$('table :not(.student)')
```

selects all of the elements of the table that do not belong to class `student`.

The meaning of the jQuery code is as follows. In the hover event handler, you find the index location of the column heading that is being hovered over and store it in the variable `colindex`. The `.index()` method use 0-based counting (i.e., it begins from the value 0). You then apply the style properties defined in the style rule `.hover` to the highlighted column heading and to the column whose index location is stored in the `colindex` variable (the one that is hovered over) to highlight it. Since the `:nth-child()` method is 1-based (i.e., begins counting from 1 instead of 0), you increment the value of `colindex` by 1 before highlighting it.

When the mouse pointer is moved away from the column heading, you remove the properties defined in the style rule `.hover` from all of the rows of the table.

In the click event handler, you find out the index of the column heading that has been clicked and store the value in the `colindex` variable.

You then hide all of the column headings that are not clicked using the `:not` selector (i.e., keeping the column heading whose index location is stored in the `colindex` variable). The rest of the column headings are made invisible.

Finally, you hide all of the column contents whose value is not equal to the index location stored in the `colindex` variable (the index location of the column heading that is clicked). That is, all the columns whose column heading is not clicked are hidden. In other words, the only column to remain visible is the one whose column heading is clicked.

On hovering over the column heading, it will be highlighted along with the contents of the complete column as shown in Figure 8-13.

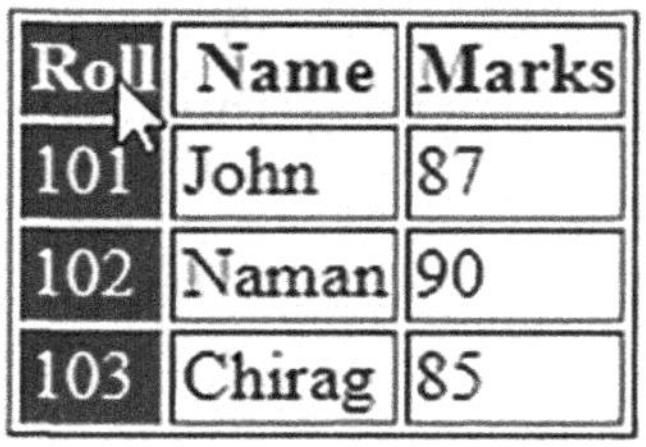

Roll	Name	Marks
101	John	87
102	Naman	90
103	Chirag	85

Figure 8-13. *The column heading and the column contents get highlighted when the column heading is hovered over*

On clicking on any column heading, that heading along with its column contents will be filtered out, making the rest of the columns of the table invisible as shown in Figure 8-14.

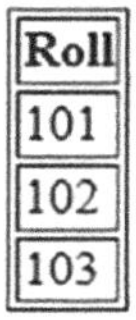

Roll
101
102
103

Figure 8-14. *The selected column is filtered out*

8-5. Paginating the Table

Problem

You have a table consisting of a few rows and columns. You want the rows of the table to be displayed page-wise. That is, at the top of the table, you want the page numbers to appear and when any page number is clicked, the rows that belong to that page number be displayed.

Solution

For this solution, you will make use of the same HTML file that you used in Recipe 8-1. You need to define style rules to highlight the page numbers (when being hovered over) and to keep some spacing among the page numbers. The two style rules that you define are .hover and .page as shown in the following style sheet file:

stylepaginating.css

```
.hover { background-color: #00f; color: #fff; }
.page{ margin:5px; }
```

The jQuery code to divide the rows of the table into pages (depending on the numbers of rows that you want to see per page) and to display the respective rows when a page number is clicked is as follows:

Paginatingtablejq.js

```
$(document).ready(function() {
  var rows=$('table').find('tbody tr').length;
  var no_rec_per_page=1;
  var no_pages= Math.ceil(rows/no_rec_per_page);
  var $pagenumbers=$('<div id="pages"></div>');
  for(i=0;i<no_pages;i++)
  {
    $('<span class="page">'+(i+1)+'</span>').appendTo($pagenumbers);
  }
  $pagenumbers.insertBefore('table');

  $('.page').hover(
    function(){
      $(this).addClass('hover');
    },
    function(){
      $(this).removeClass('hover');
    }
  );

  $('table').find('tbody tr').hide();
  var tr=$('table tbody tr');

  $('span').click(function(event){
    $('table').find('tbody tr').hide();
    for(var i=($(this).text()-1)*no_rec_per_page;
        i<=$(this).text()*no_rec_per_page-1;
        i++)
    {
      $(tr[i]).show();
    }
  });
});
```

How It Works

The style rule `.hover` contains the `background-color` and `color` properties set to values #00f and #fff, respectively, to turn the background color of the hovered page number to blue and its foreground color to white. The style rule `.page` contains the `margin` property set to 5px to create the space of 5px among the page numbers.

The jQuery code is doing the following tasks. You start by counting the number of rows (`tr` elements nested inside the `tbody` element) and storing the count in the variable `rows`. For this example, you want to see only one row per page, so you initialize the value of the variable `no_rec_per_page` equal to 1. You next have to find out the total number of pages by dividing the total count of the rows by the number of records that you want to see per page. The count of the pages is assigned to the variable `no_pages`. The final action to take before you start on the event handlers is to set up the page number display. You start this by defining a `div` element of id `pages` and assigning it to the variable `$pagenumbers`.

With the help of a `for` loop, you create a few span elements (equal to the number of pages) that contain the sequence of page numbers 1,2,... and the span element is assigned the class named `page` so that the style properties defined in the class selector `.page` can be automatically applied to all of the page numbers. Finally, all span elements containing the page numbers are appended to the `div` element of id `pages`. To finish the job, you insert the `div` element of id `pages` that was stored in variable `$pagenumbers` before the table element. This makes the page numbers appear above the table.

Next, you attach the `hover()` event to the page numbers (span element of class `.pages`). In the event handler, you highlight the page numbers when the mouse pointer moves over them (the properties defined in the style rule `.hover` are applied to the page numbers, changing their background and foreground color to blue and white, respectively). Conversely, when the mouse pointer moves away from them, you remove the style properties (of the style rule `.hover`).

After the hover event handler, because you don't want to see any of the data when the page first loads, you hide all of the rows (`tr` elements nested inside the `tbody` element) of the table, keeping only the column headings visible. Only when the user selects a page number will the rows (that belong to that page number) be displayed. You then retrieve all of the rows of the table and store them in the variable `tr` (i.e., now `tr` is an array containing all the rows of the table).

In the click event handler of the page numbers, you hide all of the rows of the table (keeping only the column visible). You then display the rows that fall within the clicked page number using the `tr` array.

Initially, you get a blank table with only column headings and page numbers at the top, as shown in Figure 8-15.

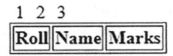

Figure 8-15. *Table with column headings and page numbers*

On hovering on any page number, it will be highlighted, and on clicking on it, the rows of that page number will be displayed as shown in Figure 8-16.

Roll	Name	Marks
101	John	87

Figure 8-16. *Displaying rows of page number 1 (assuming 1 row per page)*

You get only one row displayed because you have set the value of the variable no_ rec_per_page (which decides the number of rows to be displayed per page) equal to 1 (refer to statement number 3). Let's set its value equal to 5. Assuming that the HTML file has some more rows added in its table element, you will now get five rows on selecting any page number as shown in Figure 8-17.

Roll	Name	Marks
101	John	87
102	Naman	90
103	Chirag	85
104	David	92
105	Kelly	81

Figure 8-17. *Displaying the rows of page number 1 (assuming five rows per page)*

Also, you can modify the jQuery code to display the rows that belong to page number 1 at the beginning (instead of just showing only the column headings; refer to Figure 8-15). The jQuery code that displays the rows of the first page number by default is as follows:

Rowsfirstpagejq.js

```
$(document).ready(function() {
  var rows=$('table').find('tbody tr').length;
  var no_rec_per_page=1;
  var no_pages= Math.ceil(rows/no_rec_per_page);
  var $pagenumbers=$('<div id="pages"></div>');
  for(i=0;i<no_pages;i++)
  {
    $('<span class="page">'+(i+1)+'</span>').appendTo($pagenumbers);
  }
  $pagenumbers.insertBefore('table');

  $('.page').hover(
    function(){
      $(this).addClass('hover');
    },
    function(){
      $(this).removeClass('hover');
    }
  );

  $('table').find('tbody tr').hide();
  var tr=$('table tbody tr');

  for(var i=0;i<=no_rec_per_page-1;i++)
  {
    $(tr[i]).show();
  }

  $('span').click(function(event){
    $('table').find('tbody tr').hide();
    for(i=($(this).text()-1)*no_rec_per_page;i<=$(this).text()*no_rec_per_
    page-1;i++)
    {
```

```
        $(tr[i]).show();
    }
  });
});
```

You can see that a for loop is added to make the rows of the first page number (depending on the value assigned to the variable no_rec_per_page) visible on the screen.

8-6. Expanding and Collapsing List Items

Problem

You have an unordered list with two list items and both of these list items in turn contain a nested unordered list in them. You want the two list items to appear with a plus (+) icon to their left (indicating that some items are hidden in them). When the user selects the plus icon, you want that list item to expand to display all of the elements that were hidden inside it and also you want the plus icon to be replaced with a minus (-) icon when in expanded mode.

Solution

Make an HTML file that contains an unordered list with two list items, **Tea** and **Coffee**. Both list items are assigned the class name drink so as to identify and access them via the jQuery code. The first list item (**Tea**) contains an unordered list of three list items. The text of three list items is **Darjeeling, Assam**, and **Kerala**. The list item **Assam** is assigned the class named drink and it contains an unordered list item with two list items: **Green Leaves** and **Herbal**.

The second list item, **Coffee**, contains an unordered list element with two list items: **Cochin** and **Kerala**. The HTML file is as follows:

Expandingcollapsinglist.html

```
<!DOCTYPE html PUBLIC "-//W3C//DTD XHTML 1.0 Transitional//EN"
        "http://www.w3.org/TR/xhtml1/DTD/xhtml1-transitional.dtd">

<html xmlns="http://www.w3.org/1999/xhtml" xml:lang="en" lang="en">
  <head>
```

```
    <meta http-equiv="Content-Type" content="text/html; charset=utf-8"/>
    <title></title>
    <link rel="stylesheet" href="styleexpandlist.css" type="text/css"
    media="screen" />
    <script src="jquery-3.5.1.js" type="text/javascript"></script>
    <script src="expandcollapselistjq.js" type="text/javascript"></script>
  </head>
  <body>
      <ul>
          <li class="drink">Tea
          <ul>
                  <li>Darjeeling</li>
                  <li class="drink">Assam
                  <ul>
                          <li>Green Leaves</li>
                          <li>Herbal</li>
                  </ul>
                  </li>
                  <li>Kerala</li>
          </ul>
          </li>
          <li class="drink">Coffee
          <ul>
                  <li>Cochin</li>
                  <li>Kerala</li>
          </ul>
          </li>
      </ul>
  </body>
</html>
```

Without applying any style or jQuery code, the above HTML file on execution displays the unordered list with its respective list items as shown in Figure 8-18.

- Tea
  - Darjeeling
  - Assam
    - Green Leaves
    - Herbal
  - Kerala
- Coffee
  - Cochin
  - Kerala

Figure 8-18. *Unordered list element with its list items*

To add the plus and minus icons to the list items, you need to apply certain style rules. The style sheet file style.css contains the following style rules:

styleexpandlist.css

```
.plusimageapply{list-style-image:url(plus.jpg);}
.minusimageapply{list-style-image:url(minus.jpg);}
.noimage{list-style-image:none;}
```

In order to apply these style rules to the list items and to make them expand and collapse on selecting the plus and minus icons on their left, you need to use the following jQuery code:

Expandcollapselistjq.js

```
$(document).ready(function() {
  $('li.drink').addClass('plusimageapply');
  $('li.drink').children().addClass('noimage');
  $('li.drink').children().hide();
  $('li.drink').each(
    function(column) {
      $(this).click(function(event){
        if (this == event.target) {
          if($(this).is('.plusimageapply')) {
            $(this).children().show();
            $(this).removeClass('plusimageapply');
            $(this).addClass('minusimageapply');
          }
```

```
        else
        {
          $(this).children().hide();
          $(this).removeClass('minusimageapply');
          $(this).addClass('plusimageapply');
        }
      }
    });
  }
);
});
```

How It Works

The style rule plusimageapply is applied to all of the list items (in collapsed mode) that have a nested unordered list in them and it contains the list-style-image property set to value url(plus.jpg) to replace the traditional bullet symbol with a plus icon (which exists in the image file plus.jpg). Similarly, the style rule minusimageapply is applied to all the list items in expanded mode and it contains the list-style-image property set to value url(minus.jpg) to display a minus icon on the left of the list items. (The image file minus.jpg contains a minus icon in it.) The style rule noimage is applied to all of the list items that do not have unordered lists nested in them and it contains the list-style-image property set to value none to display them with the traditional bullet symbols.

The meaning of the jQuery code is as follows. To the list items of class drink (those that have unordered list items nested in them) the style rule plusimageapply is applied, making a plus icon to appear on their left. To the rest of the list items (that do not have nested list items in them), the style rule noimage is applied to make them appear with the traditional bullet symbols. You initially make all nested elements of the list items (that have unordered list items in them) invisible. That is, you make all list items (that have unordered list items in them) appear in collapsed mode.

To apply the expansion functionality, you attach a click event to each of the list items (that has an unordered list item in them), one by one. In the event handler, you check whether the list item on which the click event has occurred has the style rule plusimageapply applied on it or not. That is, you test whether that list item has a plus icon attached to it or not. If it has, you display the hidden contents of the list item.

You then remove the style properties of the style rule plusimageapply and apply the style properties of the style rule minusimageapply to replace the plus icon with the minus icon for the expanded list items.

If the list item that was clicked has a minus icon on its left (i.e., the style rule plusimageapply is not applied to it), you hide the nested contents.

You also remove the style properties of style rule minusimageapply and apply the style properties of the style rule plusimageapply to replace the minus icon with the plus icon for the list items that are in collapsed mode (you need to collapse the list item that has the minusimageapply style rule applied on it and is clicked).

Initially, the list items will appear in collapsed mode with a plus icon on their left as shown in Figure 8-19.

Figure 8-19. *Two list items in collapsed mode*

On selecting the plus icon (or the list item itself), it will be expanded showing the nested unordered list in it and replacing the plus icon with the minus icon as shown in **Figure** 8-20. The **Assam** list item has an unordered list item in it and that is why it has a plus icon on its left.

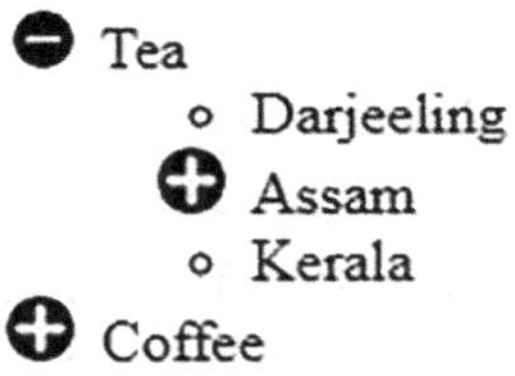

Figure 8-20. *Contents of first list item displayed when clicked*

On selecting the plus icon of the **Assam** list item, it will expand to show the hidden list items in it and the plus icon will be replaced with the minus icon, as shown in Figure 8-21.

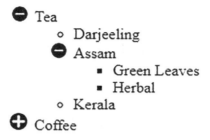

Figure 8-21. *Contents of the nested list item (collpased list item) of the first list item displayed when clicked*

On selecting the plus icon (or the list item itself) of the **Coffee** list item, it will expand to show the list items in it and the plus icon will be replaced with the minus icon as shown in Figure 8-22.

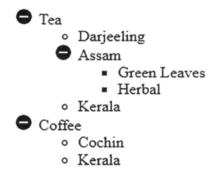

Figure 8-22. *Contents of the second list item displayed when clicked*

8-7. Expanding and Collapsing Rows of the Table

Problem

You have a table consisting of say 15 rows where each row has three columns. The table represents students' records. The table initially displays three rows: **Roll 101-105, Roll 106-110**, and **Roll 111-115**. You want to see at most five records of the students at a time, so if you hover over row **Roll 101-105**, it expands to show the student records with roll numbers between 101 and 105. Similarly, if you hover over row **Roll 106-110**, it expands to show the student records with the given range of roll number and so on.

Solution

Make an HTML file with a table element that has table headings and a table body consisting of 15 row (`tr`) elements as follows:

Expandcollapserows.html

```
<!DOCTYPE html PUBLIC "-//W3C//DTD XHTML 1.0 Transitional//EN"
        "http://www.w3.org/TR/xhtml1/DTD/xhtml1-transitional.dtd">

<html xmlns="http://www.w3.org/1999/xhtml" xml:lang="en" lang="en">
  <head>
    <meta http-equiv="Content-Type" content="text/html; charset=utf-8"/>
    <title></title>
    <link rel="stylesheet" href="style.css" type="text/css" media="screen" />
    <script src="jquery-3.5.1.js" type="text/javascript"></script>
    <script src="expandcollapserowsjq.js" type="text/javascript"></script>
  </head>
  <body>
    <table border="1">
        <thead>
            <tr><th>Roll</th><th>Name</th><th>Marks</th></tr>
        </thead>
        <tbody>
            <tr><td colspan=3 class="studgroup" align="center">Roll
            101-105</td></tr>
            <tr><td>101</td><td>John</td><td>87</td></tr>
            <tr><td>102</td><td>Naman</td><td>90</td></tr>
            <tr><td>103</td><td>Chirag</td><td>85</td></tr>
            <tr><td>104</td><td>David</td><td>92</td></tr>
            <tr><td>105</td><td>Kelly</td><td>81</td></tr>
            <tr><td colspan=3 class="studgroup"  align="center">Roll
            106-110</td></tr>
            <tr><td>106</td><td>Charles</td><td>77</td></tr>
            <tr><td>107</td><td>Jerry</td><td>91</td></tr>
            <tr><td>108</td><td>Beth</td><td>75</td></tr>
            <tr><td>109</td><td>Caroline</td><td>82</td></tr>
            <tr><td>110</td><td>Hanen</td><td>71</td></tr>
```

```
    <tr><td colspan=3 class="studgroup"  align="center">Roll
    111-115</td></tr>
    <tr><td>111</td><td>Douglas</td><td>57</td></tr>
    <tr><td>112</td><td>Tim</td><td>86</td></tr>
    <tr><td>113</td><td>Michael</td><td>68</td></tr>
    <tr><td>114</td><td>Kimbley</td><td>88</td></tr>
    <tr><td>115</td><td>Christina</td><td>72</td></tr>
  </tbody>
  </table>
 </body>
</html>
```

The table headings are represented by th elements nested inside the thead element and the students' records are represented by tr elements nested inside the tbody element. To designate a block of five rows, you define three rows (consisting of a td element spanning three columns) called **Roll 101-105, Roll 106-110**, and **Roll 111-115**. These rows (td element spanning three columns) are assigned the class studgroup so as to identify and use them in jQuery.

To highlight the rows, you define a style rule .hover in the style sheet file, style.css, as follows:

style.css

```
.hover { background-color: #00f; color: #fff; }
```

The jQuery code to expand the hidden rows when the respective row (designating the respective block of rows) is hovered over is as follows:

Expandcollapserowsjq.js

```
$(document).ready(function() {
    $('table tbody tr').hide();
    $('table tbody').find('.studgroup').parent().show();
  $('tbody tr').hover(
      function(){
          var tr=$('table tbody tr');
            var rindex=$(this).parent().children().index(this);
          for(var i=rindex;i<=rindex+5;i++)
          {
```

```
        $(tr[i]).show();
      }
        $(this).addClass('hover');
    },
    function(){
        $('table tbody tr').hide();
        $('table tbody').find('.studgroup').parent().show();
        $(this).removeClass('hover');
    }
  );
});
```

How It Works

The .hover style rule contains the background-color property set to #00f and the color property set to #fff to change the background and foreground colors of the hovered row to blue and white, respectively.

The meaning of the jQuery code is as follows. You begin by hiding all rows that are nested inside the tbody element of the table (i.e., except for the table headings, you hide all of the rows).

Then you display the three rows that represent blocks of five rows (consisting of a td element spanning three columns): **Roll 101-105, Roll 106-110**, and **Roll 111-115**. These three rows are assigned the class name studgroup.

You then attach the hover event to the visible rows of the table. In the event handler, you highlight the row when mouse pointer moves over it (the properties defined in the style rule .hover are applied to that row, changing its background and foreground colors to blue and white, respectively). Conversely, when the mouse pointer moves away from the row, you remove the style properties (of the style rule .hover). Also, in the hover event handler, you retrieve all rows of the table and store them in variable tr (i.e., now tr is an array containing all the rows of the table and you find out the index number of the row that is hovered over by the user and store it in variable rindex). Thereafter, with the help of a for loop you display the next five rows (i.e., the rows under the row heading (of class name studgroup) are displayed).

In the event handler of the hover event that is executed when the mouse pointer is moved away from the rows, besides removing the properties of the hover style rule, you hide all of the rows of the table except the heading rows.

On execution of the above jQuery code, you find three rows with text **Roll 101-105, Roll 106-110,** and **Roll 111-115** that designate the group of records underneath them as shown in Figure 8-23.

Roll	Name	Marks
Roll 101-105		
Roll 106-110		
Roll 111-115		

Figure 8-23. *Table with rows designating groups of rows undeneath them*

On hovering over any row, the group of five records nested inside the row of the class name studgroup will be displayed. So if you're hovering over the row **Roll 101-105**, you will get the rows shown in Figure 8-24 and also the hovered row will be highlighted.

Roll	Name	Marks
Roll 101-105		
101	John	87
102	Naman	90
103	Chirag	85
104	David	92
105	Kelly	81
Roll 106-110		
Roll 111-115		

Figure 8-24. *Records of the students displayed when the row designating their group is hovered over*

Similarly, when the row **Roll 111-115** is hovered over, not only the row will be highlighted but also the student records that belong to that range of roll numbers will be displayed as shown in Figure 8-25.

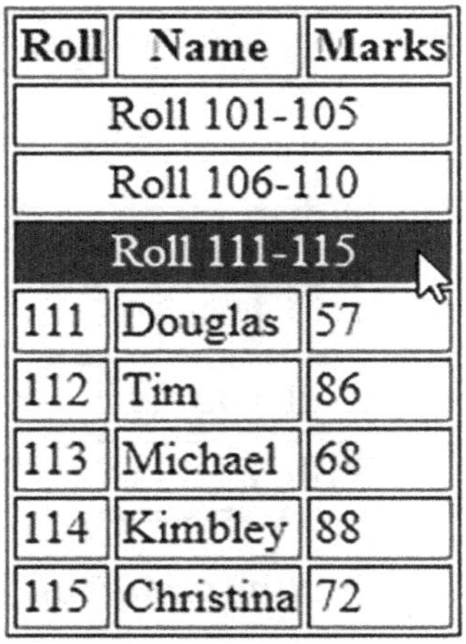

Roll	Name	Marks
Roll 101-105		
Roll 106-110		
Roll 111-115		
111	Douglas	57
112	Tim	86
113	Michael	68
114	Kimbley	88
115	Christina	72

Figure 8-25. *Respective student records displayed on hovering over their row group*

Rows with Plus and Minus Icons

For the rows (shown in Figure 8-23) you want a plus icon be displayed on their left. When these rows are hovered over, it should expand to display the records in the respective range and the plus icon should be replaced with a minus icon.

The jQuery code may be modified as follows:

Rowswithiconsjq.js

```
$(document).ready(function() {
    $('.studgroup').css(
            {'background-image':"url(plus.jpg)",
             'background-repeat':"no-repeat",
             'background-position':"left"}
    );
    $('table tbody tr').hide();
    $('table tbody').find('.studgroup').parent().show();
      $('tbody tr').hover(
```

```
function(){
    $(this).find('.studgroup').css(
        {'background-image':"url(minus.jpg)",
                'background-repeat':"no-repeat",
                'background-position':"left"}
    );
      var tr=$('table tbody tr');
    var rindex=$(this).parent().children().index(this);
      for(var i=rindex;i<=rindex+5;i++)
      {
            $(tr[i]).show();
      }
        $(this).addClass('hover');
    },
    function(){
            $(this).find('.studgroup').css(
                    {'background-image':"url(plus.jpg)",
                    'background-repeat':"no-repeat",
                    'background-position':"left"}
            );
      $('table tbody tr').hide();
      $('table tbody').find('.studgroup').parent().show();
      $(this).removeClass('hover');
      }
    );
});
```

The meaning of the jQuery code is as follows. In the rows that display the range
of roll numbers (the td element spanning three columns and assigned the class
.studgroup), you display a plus icon that exist in the image file plus.jpg. Also, you
make use of the background-repeat and background-position properties in the .css()
method to make the icon appear only once and on the left side of the row.

You then hide all the rows that are nested inside the tbody element of the table. That
is, you hide all of the students' records (except the table headings) since you want to
display them only when the plus icon of the respective row is hovered over. Then you
display the three rows that display the range of roll numbers (rows that are assigned the
class studgroup and that have a plus icon attached).

419

When any row is hovered over, its plus icon is replaced with a minus icon using the .css() method and the background-repeat and background-position properties are set to values no-repeat and left, respectively, to make the minus appear only once and on the left side of the row. Also, in the hover event handler, you retrieve all of the rows of the table and store them in variable tr (i.e., now tr is an array containing all of the rows of the table and you find out the index number of the row that is hovered over by the user and store it in variable rindex). Thereafter, with the help of a for loop you display the next five rows (i.e., the rows under the row heading (of class name studgroup) are displayed). Finally, for the hover event, you apply the properties defined in the style rule hover to highlight the hovered row.

When the mouse pointer is moved away from the hovered row, its minus icon is replaced with a plus icon using the .css() method and the background-repeat and background-position properties are set to values no-repeat and left, respectively, to make the plus icon appear only once and on the left side of the row. You then hide all of the rows of the table except the rows that show the range of roll numbers along with a plus icon (this is what you want when mouse pointer is moved away from the hovered row).

Finally, you remove the properties defined in the .hover style rule to make the row appear as it was initially when the mouse pointer moves away from the row.

On execution of this jQuery code, you find three rows with text **Roll 101-105, Roll 106-110,** and **Roll 111-115** that designate a group of records underneath them. Also, you find that on left of each row is a plus icon representing that the rows are currently in collapsed mode as shown in Figure 8-26.

Roll	Name	Marks
⊕ Roll 101-105		
⊕ Roll 106-110		
⊕ Roll 111-115		

Figure 8-26. *Rows designating a group of records underneath them along with a plus icon on the left*

When you hover on any row, say **Roll 101-105**, that row will be highlighted and the records of the students having a roll number in the range of 101-105 will be displayed and also the plus icon will be replaced by a minus icon in the hovered row as shown in Figure 8-27.

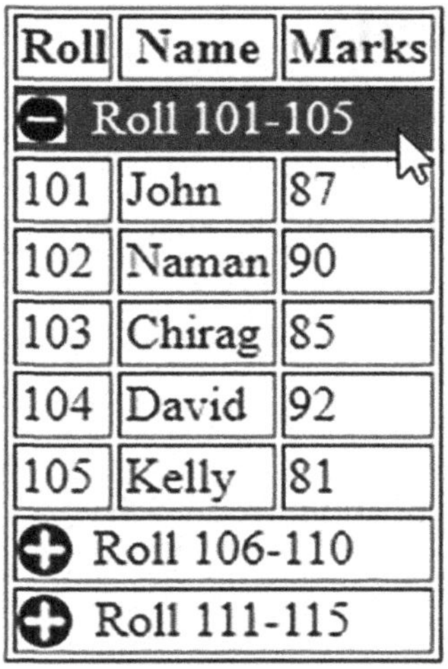

Roll	Name	Marks
⊖ Roll 101-105		
101	John	87
102	Naman	90
103	Chirag	85
104	David	92
105	Kelly	81
⊕ Roll 106-110		
⊕ Roll 111-115		

Figure 8-27. *Hovered row group displays records in its range with the plus icon replaced by minus icon*

Similarly, if you hover over the row **Roll 106-110**, it will be highlighted and the students' records having roll numbers in the range of 106-110 will be displayed. Also the plus icon of the hovered row will be replaced by a minus icon and at the same time the row that has lost focus (which was hovered over earlier) will get the plus icon back and will appear as it was initially as shown in Figure 8-28.

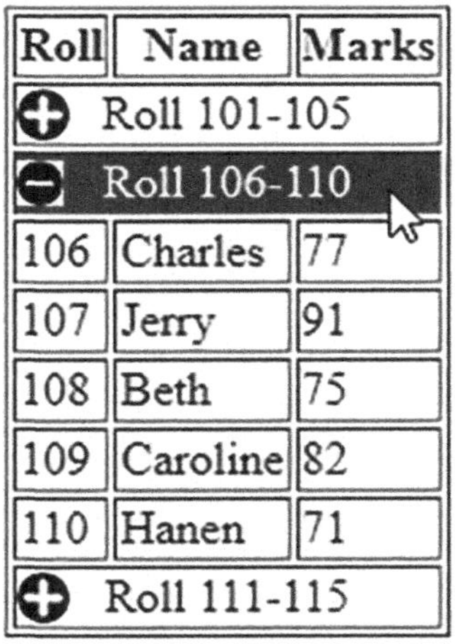

Roll	Name	Marks
⊕ Roll 101-105		
⊖ Roll 106-110		
106	Charles	77
107	Jerry	91
108	Beth	75
109	Caroline	82
110	Hanen	71
⊕ Roll 111-115		

Figure 8-28. *The row group gets the plus icon back to represent the collapsed mode when focus is lost on it*

8-8. Sorting List Items

Problem

You have an unordered list consisting of a few list items and you want to sort these list items.

Solution

Make an HTML file that consists of an unordered list:

Sortinglist.html

```
<!DOCTYPE html PUBLIC "-//W3C//DTD XHTML 1.0 Transitional//EN"
        "http://www.w3.org/TR/xhtml1/DTD/xhtml1-transitional.dtd">

<html xmlns="http://www.w3.org/1999/xhtml" xml:lang="en" lang="en">
  <head>
    <meta http-equiv="Content-Type" content="text/html; charset=utf-8"/>
    <title></title>
    <script src="jquery-3.5.1.js" type="text/javascript"></script>
    <script src="sortinglistjq.js" type="text/javascript"></script>
  </head>
  <body>
<ul>
        <li>Tea</li>
        <li>Coffee</li>
        <li>Pepsi</li>
        <li>Energy Drink</li>
        <li>Soup</li>
</ul>
  </body>
</html>
```

This HTML file when opened in a browser will show the list items shown in Figure 8-29.

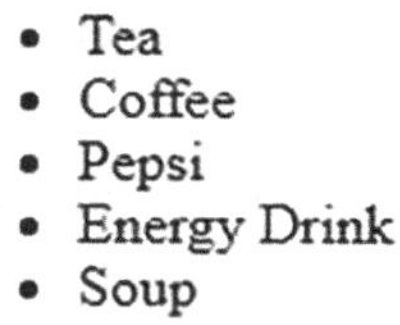

- Tea
- Coffee
- Pepsi
- Energy Drink
- Soup

Figure 8-29. *Original unsorted list items*

The jQuery code to sort the list items of the unordered list element is as follows:

Sortinglistjq.js

```
$(document).ready(function() {
      var drinks = $('ul').children('li').get();
      drinks.sort(function(a, b) {
            var val1 = $(a).text().toUpperCase();
            var val2 = $(b).text().toUpperCase();
            return (val1 < val2) ? -1 : (val1 > val2) ? 1 : 0;
      });

      $.each(drinks, function(index, row) {
            $('ul').append(row);
      });
});
```

How It Works

The meaning of the jQuery code statement is as follows. You get all the list items that are children of an unordered list and store them in the variable `drinks`, which will become an array containing the list item's text.

You then invoke the `.sort()` function on the `drinks` array, which repeatedly takes two elements of the array at a time and assigns them to parameters a and b for comparison. The sort function will return a value depending on the values assigned to parameters a and b. When the function returns

- <0: It means the second value is larger than the first and is hence pushed down.

- =0: Both values are equal and there's no need to change the sort order.

- >0: It means the first value is larger than the second and must be pushed down.

Before you invoke the sort algorithm, you convert the two array elements passed to the sort function to uppercase. You then use the sorting algorithm to return values as explained above, which will sort the list items in alphabetical (ascending order).

Finally, the each() function operates on the array drinks (that contains sorted list items), where you extract each element stored in it and append it to the unordered list element (that is, append the sorted list items to the unordered list element for display).

On execution of the jQuery code, you get the sorted list of items shown in Figure 8-30.

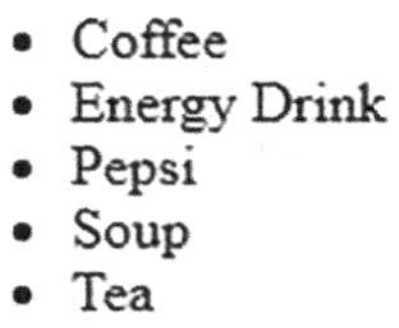

- Coffee
- Energy Drink
- Pepsi
- Soup
- Tea

Figure 8-30. *Sorted list items*

8-9. Sorting a Table

Problem

You have a table consisting of a few rows and columns. You want that when you select any column of the table, its contents are sorted in ascending order of the selected column.

Solution

Make an HTML file that contains a table element with some rows and columns elements defined in it:

Sortingtable.html

```
<!DOCTYPE html PUBLIC "-//W3C//DTD XHTML 1.0 Transitional//EN"
        "http://www.w3.org/TR/xhtml1/DTD/xhtml1-transitional.dtd">

<html xmlns="http://www.w3.org/1999/xhtml" xml:lang="en" lang="en">
  <head>
    <meta http-equiv="Content-Type" content="text/html; charset=utf-8"/>
    <title></title>
```

```
<link rel="stylesheet" href="stylesortingtable.css" type="text/css"
media="screen" />
<script src="jquery-3.5.1.js" type="text/javascript"></script>
<script src="sortingtablejq.js" type="text/javascript"></script>
</head>
<body>
    <table border="1">
        <thead>
            <tr><th>Roll</th><th>Name</th><th>Marks</th></tr>
        </thead>
        <tbody>
            <tr><td>103</td><td>Chirag</td><td>85</td></tr>
            <tr><td>102</td><td>Naman</td><td>90</td></tr>
            <tr><td>101</td><td>John</td><td>87</td></tr>
        </tbody>
    </table>
</body>
</html>
```

In this HTML file you see that a table with a border of 1px is defined with three column headings (defined using the th element): **Roll**, **Name,** and **Marks**. Also, it contains three rows of student records. The table headings are nested inside the thead element and the body of the table (rows that contain information) is nested inside the tbody element.

You will learn this recipe in three steps:

1. Determining which column heading is clicked

2. Sorting the table on the basis of the selected column (only in ascending order)

3. Sorting the table on the basis of the selected column in ascending as well as in descending order

Determining Which Column Heading Is Clicked

Before sorting a table in the ascending or descending order of any column, you need
to know which of the column headings of the table is selected. To highlight the column
heading selected by the user, you need to define a style rule named .hover in the style
sheet file:

stylesortingtable.css

```
.hover{
    cursor: default;
    color: blue ;
    background-color:cyan
}
```

The jQuery code to display which of the column headings is selected by the user is as
follows:

Sortingtablejq.js

```
$(document).ready(function() {
  $('th').each(function() {
    $(this).hover(
      function(){
        $(this).addClass('hover');
      },
      function(){
        $(this).removeClass('hover');
      }
    );

    $(this).click(function(){
      alert($(this).text()+' column is selected');
    });
  });
});
```

How It Works

In the style sheet file, the style rule .hover contains the cursor property set to default to make the mouse pointer appear as it normally appears (in the form of a pointer). The color and background color properties are set to blue and cyan, respectively, to turn the background color of the highlighted column heading to cyan and its foreground color to blue.

You can see in the jQuery code that each table heading is checked to see if it is hovered over. If a table heading is hovered over (the mouse pointer is moved over it), the style properties defined in the style rule .hover are applied to it to highlight it (its background color changes to cyan and its foreground color changes to blue). Also, when the mouse pointer is moved away from the column heading, the style properties of the .hover style rule are removed, making the column heading appear as it was initially. Also, you check if any table heading is clicked. If a table heading is clicked, you display the text of the column heading using the alert() method.

On moving the mouse pointer on any column heading, it gets highlighted and its name is displayed via the alert() method, as shown in Figure 8-31.

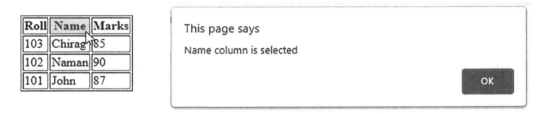

Figure 8-31. *Column name displayed when column heading is hovered*

Sorting the Table on the Basis of a Selected Column (Only in Ascending Order)

The jQuery code to sort the table in ascending order of the selected column is as follows:

Sortingtablecolumjq.js

```
$(document).ready(function() {
  $('th').each(function(column) {
    $(this).hover(
      function(){
```

427

```
      $(this).addClass('hover');
    },
    function(){
      $(this).removeClass('hover');
    }
  );

  $(this).click(function(){
    var rec=$('table').find('tbody >tr').get();
    rec.sort(function(a, b) {
      var val1 = $(a).children('td').eq(column).text().toUpperCase();
      var val2 = $(b).children('td').eq(column).text().toUpperCase();
      return (val1 < val2) ? -1 : (val1 > val2) ? 1 : 0;
    });

    $.each(rec, function(index, row) {
      $('tbody').append(row);
    });
  });
});
});
```

In this code, the > symbol is a selector used for finding the children of the selected element:

>

It is a selector that represents the children of the selected element.

Syntax:

E1>E2

It selects all children of element E1 that are matched by element E2.

The meaning of the jQuery code is as follows. Each table heading is checked to see if it is hovered over. If any table heading is hovered over, the style properties defined in the style rule .hover are applied to it to highlight it. Also, when the mouse pointer is moved away from the column heading, the style properties of the .hover style rule are removed, making the column heading appear as it was initially.

Then you attach a click event to each of the table headings. In the click handler, you retrieve all of the table rows (nested in the tbody element) and store them in variable rec. The rec is now an array containing all of the table rows. By invoking the sort() function on the rec array you repeatedly take two elements (rows) of the array at a time and arrange them in ascending order.

To do so, the column contents of the first and second parameters (rows) passed to the sort() function are extracted and converted to uppercase before comparison.

The sort() function then returns any of the three values <0, =0, or >0, which helps in deciding which column contents should be moved ahead in the sort order and which should be pushed down in the sort order. When this sort function is over, the rec array has all of the rows sorted in ascending order of the selected column.

Finally, the sorted rows from the rec array are retrieved and appended to the tbody element of the table for display.

Initially, the table appears as shown in Figure 8-32.

Roll	Name	Marks
103	Chirag	85
102	Naman	90
101	John	87

Figure 8-32. *Original unsorted table*

On selecting the **Roll** column, it gets highlighted and the table rows are sorted in the ascending order of the roll numbers as shown in Figure 8-33.

Roll	Name	Marks
101	John	87
102	Naman	90
103	Chirag	85

Figure 8-33. *Table sorted in ascending order of roll number*

Similarly, on selecting the **Name** column, it gets highlighted and the table rows are sorted on the ascending order of the names as shown in Figure 8-34.

Roll	Name	Marks
103	Chirag	85
101	John	87
102	Naman	90

Figure 8-34. *Table sorted in ascending order of the names*

Sorting the Table on the Basis of a Selected Column in Ascending as Well as Descending Order

You want that if any of the column headings are clicked for the first time, the table must be sorted in ascending order of that column, and if the column is clicked again, the table must be sorted in descending order of the column. In other words, you want the sort order to toggle on each click. In order to inform the user which sorting order is currently applied on a column, you need to display up or down arrows in the column heading. The up arrow will denote that the table is currently sorted in ascending order of the column and the down arrow will denote that table is sorted in descending order of the column.

To display the up and down arrows in the column headings, you need to define two style rules in the style sheet file, stylesortcolascdesc.css:

stylesortcolascdesc.css

```
.asc{
    background:url('up.png') no-repeat; padding-left:20px;
}

.desc{
    background:url('down.png') no-repeat; padding-left:20px;
}
```

Let's modify the jQuery code to sort the table in ascending as well as descending order of the selected column. The jQuery code is as follows:

Sortcolascdescjq.js

```
$(document).ready(function() {
  $('th').each(function(column) {
    $(this).hover(
      function(){
        $(this).addClass('hover');
      },
      function(){
        $(this).removeClass('hover');
      }
    );

    $(this).click(function(){
      if($(this).is('.asc'))
      {
        $(this).removeClass('asc');
        $(this).addClass('desc');
        sortdir=-1;
      }
      else
      {
        $(this).addClass('asc');
        $(this).removeClass('desc');
        sortdir=1;
      }
      $(this).siblings().removeClass('asc');
      $(this).siblings().removeClass('desc');

      var rec=$('table').find('tbody >tr').get();

      rec.sort(function(a, b) {
        var val1 = $(a).children('td').eq(column).text().toUpperCase();
        var val2 = $(b).children('td').eq(column).text().toUpperCase();
        return (val1 < val2) ? -sortdir : (val1 > val2) ? sortdir : 0;
      });
```

```
    $.each(rec, function(index, row) {
      $('tbody').append(row);
    });
  });
 });
});
```

How It Works

The style rule .asc contains the background property set to url(up.png) to display an up arrow pointer in the column heading. The value no-repeat will make the pointer appear only once in the column heading and the padding-left property is set to 20px to make some space on the left. Similarly, the style rule desc contains the background property to display the down arrow pointer in the column heading.

The jQuery code does the following tasks. Each table heading is checked to see if it is hovered over. If a table heading is hovered over, the style properties defined in the style rule .hover are applied to it to highlight it. Also, when the mouse pointer is moved away from the column heading, the style properties of the .hover style rule are removed, making the column heading appear as it was initially.

You then attach a click event to each of the table headings and check if the selected column heading has the style rule .asc applied on it or not. That is, you check if the table is already sorted in ascending order of the selected column heading or not.

If it is, you remove the style properties defined in the style asc and apply the style properties defined in the style desc (when the column heading already sorted in ascending order is again clicked). As a result, the column heading will display a down arrow pointer on its left. Also, the value of the variable sortdir is set to -1, which is used to manipulate the return values of the sort function to perform sorting in descending order.

If the selected column has the desc style rule already applied to it (i.e., the table is sorted in descending order of the selected column), you remove the style properties defined in the style rule desc and apply the properties defined in the style rule asc, which will make an up arrow pointer appear on the left of the column heading. Also, the value of the variable sortdir is set to 1 to make the sort function perform sorting in an ascending order.

Once you've sorted the column, you need to remove the properties of the style rules `.asc` and `.desc` from the other column headings (which may have been applied on other column headings previously) from all column headings except the one that is selected by the user. You also need to retrieve all table rows (nested in the `tbody` element) and store them in the variable `rec`. The `rec` will be now an array containing all the table rows.

You can then invoke the `sort` function on the `rec` array. The `sort` function will repeatedly take two elements (rows) of the array at a time and arrange them in sort order as decided by the value in the variable `sortdir`. The `sort` function begins by extracting the column contents of the first and second parameters (rows) passed to the `sort` function and converting to uppercase before comparison.

The function returns any of the three values <0, =0, or >0, which helps in deciding which column contents should be moved ahead in the sort order and which should be pushed down in the sort order. When this `sort` function is over, the `rec` array has all the rows sorted in either ascending or descending order of the selected column depending on the value assigned to variable `sortdir`.

Finally, the sorted rows from the `rec` array are retrieved and appended to the `tbody` element of the table for display.

Initially, the table may appear as shown in Figure 8-35.

Roll	Name	Marks
103	Chirag	85
102	Naman	90
101	John	87

Figure 8-35. *Original unsorted table consisting of a few rows and columns*

On selecting the column heading Name once, you will see an up arrow pointer appearing on its left (representing that sorting will be done in ascending order) and the table will be sorted in alphabetical order of the names as shown in Figure 8-36.

Roll	▲ Name	Marks
103	Chirag	85
101	John	87
102	Naman	90

Figure 8-36. *Table sorted in ascending order of the names*

On selecting the Name column heading again, you find a down pointer appearing in the column heading (representing that sorting will be done in descending order) and the table will be sorted in descending order of the names shown in Figure 8-37.

Roll	▼ Name	Marks
102	Naman	90
101	John	87
103	Chirag	85

Figure 8-37. *Table sorted in descending order of the names*

8-10. Filtering Rows from a Table

Problem

You have a table consisting of few rows and columns along with an input text field preceding it. You want to filter the rows of the table on the basis of the character typed by the user in the input text field. So if the user enters the character c, all the rows in the table that have names beginning with the character c will be displayed and the rest of the rows should be filtered out.

Solution

Make an HTML file that contains a table element with some row and column elements. Also, before the table, display the message **Enter the character** followed by an input text field. Below the input text field, display a Submit button, which on being clicked will display the filtered information of the table. The HTML file is as follows:

Filteringrowstable.html

```
<!DOCTYPE html PUBLIC "-//W3C//DTD XHTML 1.0 Transitional//EN"
        "http://www.w3.org/TR/xhtml1/DTD/xhtml1-transitional.dtd">

<html xmlns="http://www.w3.org/1999/xhtml" xml:lang="en" lang="en">
  <head>
    <meta http-equiv="Content-Type" content="text/html; charset=utf-8"/>
    <title></title>
    <link rel="stylesheet" href="stylefilteringrows.css" type="text/css"
    media="screen" />
    <script src="jquery-3.5.1.js" type="text/javascript"></script>
    <script src="filteringrowstablejq.js" type="text/javascript"></script>
  </head>
  <body>
    <div><span class="label">Enter the character </span><input
    type="text"  class="infobox"  /></div>
        <input class="submit" type="submit" value="Submit"/><br/><br/>
            <table border="1">
              <thead>
                    <tr><th>Roll</th><th>Name</th><th>Marks</th></tr>
              </thead>
              <tbody>
                    <tr><td>101</td><td>John</td><td>87</td></tr>
                    <tr><td>102</td><td>Naman</td><td>90</td></tr>
                    <tr><td>103</td><td>Chirag</td><td>85</td></tr>
                    <tr><td>104</td><td>David</td><td>92</td></tr>
                    <tr><td>105</td><td>Kelly</td><td>81</td></tr>
                    <tr><td>106</td><td>Charles</td><td>77</td></tr>
                    <tr><td>107</td><td>Jerry</td><td>91</td></tr>
                    <tr><td>108</td><td>Beth</td><td>75</td></tr>
                    <tr><td>109</td><td>Caroline</td><td>82</td></tr>
                    <tr><td>110</td><td>Hanen</td><td>71</td></tr>
                    <tr><td>111</td><td>Douglas</td><td>57</td></tr>
                    <tr><td>112</td><td>Tim</td><td>86</td></tr>
                    <tr><td>113</td><td>Michael</td><td>68</td></tr>
```

```
                <tr><td>114</td><td>Kimbley</td><td>88</td></tr>
                <tr><td>115</td><td>Christina</td><td>72</td></tr>
            </tbody>
        </table>
    </body>
</html>
```

You can see that the text message is nested inside the span element of class `label`, the input text field is assigned the class name `infobox`, and the Submit button is assigned the class name `submit` so that the style properties defined in the class selectors `.label`, `.infobox`, and `.submit` (defined in the style sheet file) can be applied to them automatically. The style sheet containing the respective class selectors is as follows:

stylefilteringrows.css

```
.label {float: left; width: 120px; }
.infobox {width: 200px; }
.submit { margin-left: 125px; margin-top: 10px;}
```

The jQuery code to filter the table rows to display the names that begin with the character filled in the input text field is as follows:

Filteringrowstablejq.js

```
$(document).ready(function() {
  var rows;
  var coldata;

  $('.submit').click(function(event){
    $('table').find('tbody tr').hide();
    var data=$('.infobox').val();
    var len=data.length;
    if(len>0)
    {
      $('table tbody tr').each(function(){
        coldata=$(this).children().eq(1);
        if(coldata.text().charAt(0).toUpperCase()==data.charAt(0).
        toUpperCase())
        {
```

```
            $(this).show();
        }
      });
    }
    event.preventDefault();
  });
});
```

How It Works

The properties defined in class selector .label include the float property set to value left to make the label appear on the left of the browser window, making space for the next element to appear on its right. The width property is set to 200px to make the label fit within the width of 200px. The class selector .infobox contains the width property set to 200px to make the input text field 200px wide and the class selector .submit contains the margin-left property set to 125px to make the Submit button appear at the distance of 125px from the left border of the browser window (so that it appears below the input text field). The margin-top property is set to 10px to make the Submit button appear at the distance of 10px from the input text field at its top.

The jQuery code does following tasks. You start by attaching a click event to the Submit button where you hide all the rows of the table (tr elements nested inside the tbody element) displaying only the column headings. You then retrieve the contents typed in the input text field (that is assigned the class name infobox) and store them in the variable data.

Next, you find the length of the variable data and scan each row of the table (the tr element nested inside the tbody element).

For each row, you get the contents of the children of the row element with an index value of 1 (i.e., of the Name column) and store them in the variable coldata.

Now you start the filtering by comparing the first character of the column content (in coldata) with that of the character typed in the input text field (after converting both of them into uppercase). If they match, display the row.

Finally, you invoke the .preventDefault() method of the event object so as to avoid the submission of information entered by the user to the server (i.e., avoiding the default behavior of the browser when a button is clicked).

On execution of the jQuery code, you get an input text field with a Submit button. If you enter the character c in the input text field, all the names in the table that begin with the character c will be displayed, filtering out the rest of the rows as shown in Figure 8-38.

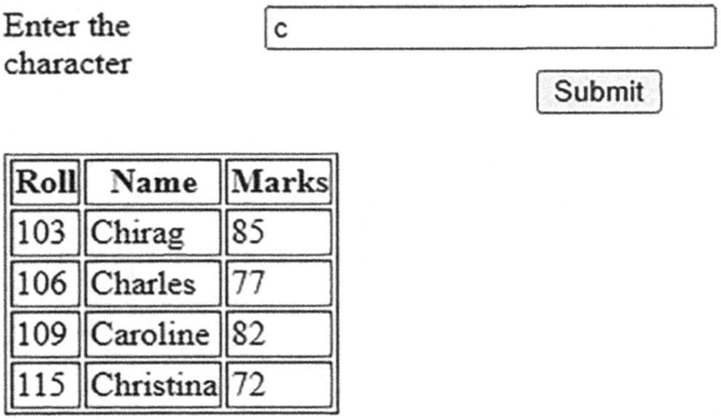

Enter the
character

c

Submit

Roll	Name	Marks
103	Chirag	85
106	Charles	77
109	Caroline	82
115	Christina	72

Figure 8-38. *Table displaying rows with a name beginning with the character entered in the input text field*

8-11. Summary

In this chapter, you saw different recipes that perform different functions on tables, including highlighting rows and columns, filtering out the selected row, erasing the selected column, displaying the rows of the table page-wise, and more. You also saw the method involved in expanding and collapsing rows of a table and you learned how a table can be sorted in the ascending or descending order of the selected column.

In the next chapter, you will learn to use different widgets that are provided with the jQuery UI. You will learn how to make it easy to select a date using a datepicker, how to make use of suggestions by using the autocomplete widget, and how to display large volumes in categories by making use of accordions, dialogs, and tabs.

CHAPTER 9

jQuery UI

In this chapter, you will learn to use different widgets that are provided with the jQuery UI. You will be making the following recipes in this chapter:

- Using the datepicker
- Using the autocomplete widget
- Using an accordion
- Using dialogs
- Using the tabs widget

Download the latest jQuery UI from `https://jqueryui.com/download/`. You'll get the `jquery-ui-1.12.1.zip` file downloaded to your computer. Unzip the file and copy `jquery-ui.js` and `jquery-ui.css` into the folder where you are creating HTML files.

9-1. Using Datepicker

The datepicker widget provides a user friendly interface to select dates. The date widget can be associated to any input box where a date needs to be entered. The moment a user clicks on the input box, the datepicker widget opens up via animation. The user can select a date either by using a mouse or a keyboard. To navigate using a keyboard, you need to press the Ctrl key and use the arrow keys and finally select the day by pressing the Enter key.

Problem

You are making a hotel reservation page and you want the user to select the date of the reservation. Instead of asking the user to enter the date manually, you want a datepicker widget to open up that displays the entire calendar of the month along with the weekdays with a facility to navigate to any desired date.

439

© Bintu Harwani 2022
B. Harwani, *jQuery Recipes*, https://doi.org/10.1007/978-1-4842-7304-3_9

Solution

The first step is to create an interface that asks the user to enter a date. The following HTML file shows an input box prompting the user to enter the date of reserving a hotel room:

Datepicker.html

```
<!doctype html>
<html lang="en">
<head>
  <meta charset="utf-8">
  <meta name="viewport" content="width=device-width, initial-scale=1">
  <title></title>
  <link rel="stylesheet" href="jquery-ui.css" type="text/css"
  media="screen" />
  <script src="jquery-3.5.1.js" type="text/javascript"></script>
  <script src="jquery-ui.js"></script>
  <script>
  $( function() {
        $( "#reserve_date" ).datepicker();
  } );
  </script>
  </head>
  <body>
     Enter Date of reservation: <input type="text" id="reserve_date">
  </body>
</html>
```

You can see in the above HTML program that the text **Enter Date of reservation** is displayed on the screen. Following the text, an input box is displayed and to associate the datepicker to this input box, an id of reserve_date is assigned to this input box.

In the jQuery code, you can see that the input box with the id reserve_date is selected and a datepicker with a default configuration is invoked via the datepicker() method.

On running the HTML program, you get an input box asking the user to enter a date for reserving the hotel room (see Figure 9-1(a)). You might face issues when running the program in the Firefox browser because it doesn't support datepicker. On clicking in the input box, the datepicker opens up using animation and displays the current date, as shown in Figure 9-1(b). The datepicker can be configured with different options but even the default datepicker has lots of features. Using the Previous and Next buttons, you can navigate to the desired month. On selecting a date from the required month, the selected date is added to the input box and the calendar is closed.

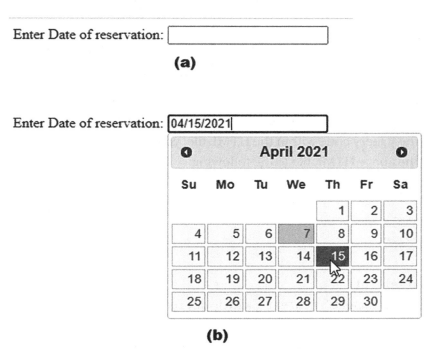

Figure 9-1. *(a) The input box asks the user to enter a date for reserving the hotel room. (b) The datepicker opens up, displaying the current date on clicking in the input box*

Configuring Properties of the Datepicker Widget

The following are the properties that can be set with the datepicker in order to configure it:

- appendText: Adds text after the datepicker <input> box to inform the format of the selected date.

- changeMonth: Set it to true to display the month change dropdown.

- changeYear: Set this option to true to display the year change dropdown.

- isRTL: Set this option to true if you want to set the calendar to right-to-left format.

- duration: Set the value of this option to slow, normal, or fast to determine the speed of animation at which the datepicker opens.

- numberOfMonths: Set the value of this option to 1 or 2 to set the number of months to be displayed on a single datepicker.

- showOtherMonths: Set the value of this option to false if you don't want to show the last and first days of the previous and next months.

In order to configure the datepicker widget to display the calendar in the desired format, you need to modify the jQuery code shown previously. Also, you will not be embedding the jQuery code within the HTML file; you will be making a separate file. So, let's modify the above HTML file to the following:

datepicker1.html

```
<!doctype html>
<html lang="en">
<head>
  <meta charset="utf-8">
  <meta name="viewport" content="width=device-width, initial-scale=1">
  <title></title>
  <link rel="stylesheet" href="jquery-ui.css" type="text/css"
  media="screen" />
  <script src="jquery-3.5.1.js" type="text/javascript"></script>
  <script src="jquery-ui.js"></script>
  <script src="datepicker1jq.js" type="text/javascript"></script>
  </head>
  <body>
      Enter Date of reservation: <input type="text" id="reserve_date">
  </body>
</html>
```

You can see in the above code that an external jQuery file, datepicker1jq.js, is referenced. The HTML code prompts the user to enter the desired date. On clicking the input box, the datepicker will open up, allowing the user to select the desired date.

To configure the datepicker widget, the jQuery code sets the following datepicker properties:

Datepicker1jq.js

```
$(document).ready(function() {
    var datepicker_Options = {
        appendText: " MM/DD/YYYY",
        changeMonth: true,
        changeYear: true,
        isRTL: false,
        showOtherMonths: true,
        numberOfMonths: 2,
        duration: "normal"
    };
        $( "#reserve_date").datepicker(datepicker_Options);
});
```

On running the HTML program, you can see in the above jQuery code that the text MM/DD/YYYY will be appended after the input box, informing the user that this is the format in which the selected date will be displayed (see Figure 9-2(a)). A dropdown will be displayed with the month, enabling the user to jump to any month. Similarly, using the changeYear option, a dropdown is displayed with the year, enabling the user to choose the desired year directly.

The calendar will be set to display from left to right. Using the showOtherMonths option, the last days of the previous month and the starting days of the next month will be displayed. The speed of animation is set to normal using the duration option. The numberOfMonths option is set to 2 to display a calendar of two months (see Figure 9-2(b)).

Enter Date of reservation: [   ] MM/DD/YYYY

(a)

Enter Date of reservation: [04/15/2021|] MM/DD/YYYY

◀	Apr ▾	2021 ▾								**May 2021**			▶
Su	**Mo**	**Tu**	**We**	**Th**	**Fr**	**Sa**	**Su**	**Mo**	**Tu**	**We**	**Th**	**Fr**	**Sa**
28	29	30	31	1	2	3	25	26	27	28	29	30	1
4	5	6	7	8	9	10	2	3	4	5	6	7	8
11	12	13	14	15	16	17	9	10	11	12	13	14	15
18	19	20	21	22	23	24	16	17	18	19	20	21	22
25	26	27	28	29	30	1	23	24	25	26	27	28	29
							30	31	1	2	3	4	5

(b)

Figure 9-2. *(a) The text MM/DD/YYYY is appended after the input box showing the format in which the selected date will be displayed. (b) The calendar for two months is displayed along with dropdowns associated with month and year*

Instead of the default date format of MM/DD/YYYY, you can have the date in another desired format.

Changing the Date Format

The dateFormat property of the datepicker widget is used to set the format of the dates. The following are the valid options that can be combined to get the date in the desired format:

- d: Displays the day of the month in a single digit

- dd: Displays the day of the month in two digits

- m: Displays the month of the year in a single digit

- mm: Displays the month of the year in two digits.

- y: Displays the year in two digits

- yy: Displays the year in four digits

- D: Displays the day in the short format

- DD: Displays the complete day name

- M: Displays the month in the short format

- MM: Displays the month in the long format

Let's create another jQuery file by the name of datepicker2jq.js and write the following jQuery code in it to display the selected date in a specific format:

datepicker2jq.js

```
$(document).ready(function() {
    var datepicker_Options = {
        dateFormat: "dd-mm-yy"
    };
    $( "#reserve_date" ).datepicker(datepicker_Options);
});
```

You can see that the days are set to be displayed in two digits with a dash (-) following them. Thereafter, the month is displayed in a two-digit format followed by a dash (-). Finally, the year is displayed in four digits (see Figure 9-3).

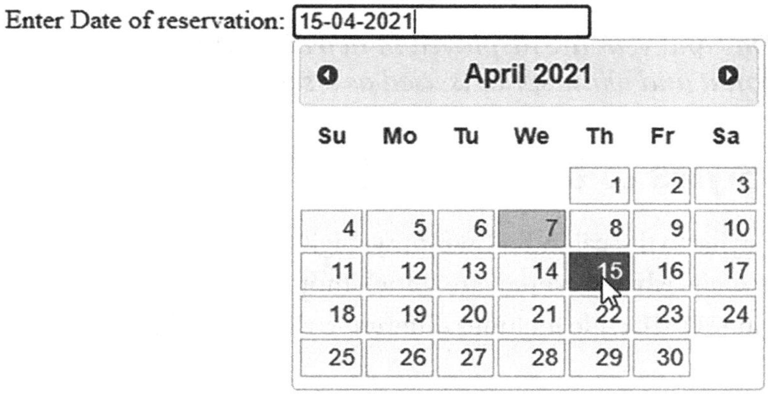

Figure 9-3. *Days and months are displayed in two digits, the year is displayed in four digits, and a dash is used as a separator*

You can also modify the jQuery file to try another date format as follows:

```
$(document).ready(function() {
    var datepicker_Options = {
        dateFormat: "dd MM y"
    };
    $( "#reserve_date" ).datepicker(datepicker_Options);
});
```

The date is formatted so that the day is displayed in two digits followed by a white space. Thereafter, the month is displayed in the long format followed by a white space. Finally, the year is displayed in two digits (see Figure 9-4).

Figure 9-4. *Day and year are displayed in two digits and the month is displayed in the long format and white space is used as a separator among them*

Applying Styles to the Datepicker

You can apply styles to the calendar boundary, digits being displayed, background color, the color of the digits when hovered, and much more.

The following HTML code includes different styles applied to different datepicker components:

Datepicker2.html

```
<!doctype html>
<html lang="en">
<head>
  <meta charset="utf-8">
  <meta name="viewport" content="width=device-width, initial-scale=1">
  <title></title>
  <link rel="stylesheet" href="jquery-ui.css" type="text/css"
  media="screen" />
  <script src="jquery-3.5.1.js" type="text/javascript"></script>
  <script src="jquery-ui.js"></script>
  <script src="datepicker2jq.js" type="text/javascript"></script>
   <style>
     #ui-datepicker-div { border:1px solid #0000ff; }
     #ui-datepicker-div a, .ui-datepicker-inline a {
         color:#ff0000;
     }
     #ui-datepicker-div a:hover, .ui-datepicker-inline a:hover {
         color:#00ff00 ;
     background-color:#000000;
     }
     .ui-datepicker-header { background:#ff0000; }
</style>
</head>
<body>
      Enter Date of reservation: <input type="text" id="reserve_date">
 </body>
</html>
```

In this code, the border of the datepicker is set to solid and blue. The days in the datepicker are set to be displayed in red. On hovering over any day in the datepicker, the background color will be black and the day will appear in green. The header in the datepicker is set to appear in red (see Figure 9-5).

447

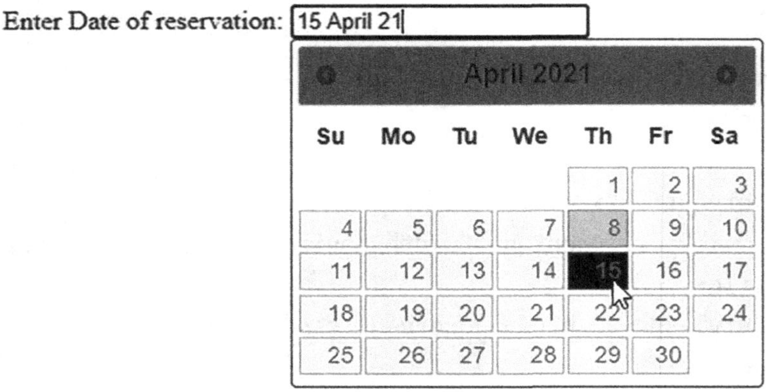

Enter Date of reservation: [15 April 21|

Figure 9-5. *Formatting applied to the border, days, and header of the datepicker*

9-2. Using the Autocomplete Widget

In order for faster data entry and to avoid typing mistakes, autocomplete widgets are used. Autocomplete widgets show suggestions as soon as the user types a few characters and the user is simply supposed to click the desired word from the list of suggestions displayed. The suggested list can be displayed via an array or from another source, including any file or database.

Problem

You want to ask the user to select a food item and display an autocomplete widget for a faster and error-free selection.

Solution

To create a user interface to ask the user to select a food item, a HTML program is created with following code. The HTML code will display an input box prompting the user to choose the desired fast food item.

Autocomplete.html

```
<!DOCTYPE html PUBLIC "-//W3C//DTD XHTML 1.0 Transitional//EN"
        "http://www.w3.org/TR/xhtml1/DTD/xhtml1-transitional.dtd">
```

```
<html xmlns="http://www.w3.org/1999/xhtml" xml:lang="en" lang="en">
  <head>
    <meta http-equiv="Content-Type" content="text/html; charset=utf-8"/>
    <title></title>
    <link rel="stylesheet" href="jquery-ui.css" type="text/css"
    media="screen" />
    <script src="jquery-3.5.1.js" type="text/javascript"></script>
    <script src="jquery-ui.js"></script>
    <script src="autocompletejq.js" type="text/javascript"></script>
  </head>
  <body>
      <div class="ui-widget">
            <label>Select your food item: </label>
            <input id="items">
</div>
</body>
</html>
```

You can see in the above HTML code that a <div> element is defined of the class
ui-widget. It is done so that the CSS style for class ui-widget defined in the jquery-ui.
css style sheet file can be automatically applied to the <div> element. Within the <div>
element a label and input box are defined. The label displays a message telling the user to
select a food item. To access it in the jQuery code, the input box is assigned the id items.

The jQuery code to define the source of food items to be displayed via the
autocomplete widget and to display that source in the form of suggestions when the user
types any character in the input box is as follows:

Autocompletejq.js

```
$(document).ready(function() {
    var foodItems = [
            "Bacon Cheese Burger",
        "Biscuits",
        "Blizzard",
        "Cajun Fries ",
        "Chicken Nuggets",
        "Chicken Sandwich",
```

```
                "Chicken Tenders",
                "Crunch Shell Tacos",
                "Curly Fries",
                "Fries",
                "Frosty",
                "Pretzel",
                "Shack Burger",
                "Tacos",
                "Waffle Fries"    ];
            $( "#items" ).autocomplete({
                    source: foodItems
            });
});
```

You can see in the above code that a string array called fooditems contains the food items that you want to be displayed via the autocomplete widget. Thereafter, the autocomplete widget is associated to the input box and the fooditems array is linked to the autocomplete widget as its source. On running the HTML program, you get an input box asking you to select a food item. The moment you press any key, all suggestions related to the entered key will be displayed via the autocomplete widget as shown in Figure 9-6.

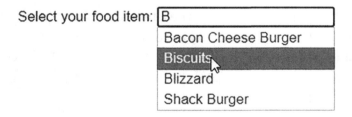

Figure 9-6. *All suggestions related to the entered key are displayed via the autocomplete widget*

Configuring the Autocomplete Widget

The autocomplete widget can be configured as per your requirements. The following are the options that can be used to configure the autocomplete wizard:

- appendTo: Used to append an element to the autocomplete widget. The default value is null.

- autoFocus: The first item will be automatically focused when the options appear. The default value is false.

- delay: For specifying the time delay in milliseconds for finding the matching values. The default value is 300ms.

- disabled: If this option is set to true, the autocomplete widget will be disabled. The default value is false.

- minlength: Used for specifying the minimum number of characters to be pressed for finding the matching values. The default value is 1.

- position: Determines the position of the autocomplete options to pop up. By default its value is { my: "left top", at: "left bottom", collision: "none" }.

- source: For specifying the source of options to display in the autocomplete widget.

In order to configure the autocomplete widget, you need to modify the jQuery code created previously. So, let's create a new jQuery file to configure the autocomplete widget. Modify the HTML code to point at this new jQuery file.

Automcomplete1.html

```
<!DOCTYPE html PUBLIC "-//W3C//DTD XHTML 1.0 Transitional//EN"
        "http://www.w3.org/TR/xhtml1/DTD/xhtml1-transitional.dtd">

<html xmlns="http://www.w3.org/1999/xhtml" xml:lang="en" lang="en">
  <head>
    <meta http-equiv="Content-Type" content="text/html; charset=utf-8"/>
    <title></title>
    <link rel="stylesheet" href="jquery-ui.css" type="text/css"
    media="screen" />
    <script src="jquery-3.5.1.js" type="text/javascript"></script>
    <script src="jquery-ui.js"></script>
    <script src="autocomplete1jq.js" type="text/javascript"></script>
  </head>
```

```
<body>
    <label>Select your food item: </label>
    <input id="items">
</body>
</html>
```

The HTML code shown above simply shows two elements, a label and an input box. The label displays a text message and the input box is assigned an id of items to be accessible to the jQuery code.

The jQuery code to display the autocomplete widget when any character is typed in input box and to configure its different properties is as follows:

Autocomplete1jq.js

```
$(document).ready(function() {
    var foodItems = [
            "Bacon Cheese Burger",
        "Biscuits",
        "Blizzard",
        "Cajun Fries ",
        "Chicken Nuggets",
        "Chicken Sandwich",
        "Chicken Tenders",
        "Crunch Shell Tacos",
        "Curly Fries",
        "Fries",
        "Frosty",
        "Pretzel",
        "Shack Burger",
        "Tacos",
        "Waffle Fries"
    ];
    $( "#items" ).autocomplete({
        autoFocus: true,
        delay: 400,
        minLength: 1,
        position: { my : "left top", at: "right bottom" },
```

```
            //disabled: true,
                source: foodItems
        });
});
```

A string array called fooditems contains certain food items to be used as suggestions in the autocomplete widget. The autocomplete widget automatically opens when the user clicks any character in the input box. The autocomplete widget is configured so that the food items included in the fooditems array are displayed as suggestions and the first food item is automatically focused when the options appear. The time delay of 400ms is set to display the matching options. The options start appearing the moment the user enters one character in the input box. The position of the autocomplete widget is set to appear at the right bottom of the input box. The autocomplete widget can be disabled by setting its disabled property to true, but this is commented out because you want the autocomplete widget to be enabled (see Figure 9-7).

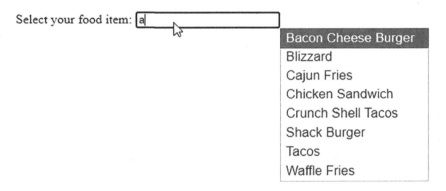

Figure 9-7. *On configuring the autocomplete widget, the first food item is automatically focused. It is positioned to appear at the right bottom of the input box*

9-3. Using an Accordion

An accordion is a combination of collapsible content panels where only one panel can be expanded to display its contents, hence it's very popularly for displaying a lot of information in less space.

Problem

You want to explain about a product and its features in less space. You want to give an introduction of jQuery, explain its features, and about the DOM and selectors in minimum space. An accordion will do this task efficiently.

Solution

To display content about jQuery and its features along with the DOM and selectors, use the following HTML code:

Accordion.html

```
<!DOCTYPE html PUBLIC "-//W3C//DTD XHTML 1.0 Transitional//EN"
        "http://www.w3.org/TR/xhtml1/DTD/xhtml1-transitional.dtd">

<html xmlns="http://www.w3.org/1999/xhtml" xml:lang="en" lang="en">
  <head>
    <meta http-equiv="Content-Type" content="text/html; charset=utf-8"/>
    <title></title>
    <link rel="stylesheet" href="jquery-ui.css" type="text/css"
    media="screen" />
    <script src="jquery-3.5.1.js" type="text/javascript"></script>
    <script src="jquery-ui.js"></script>
    <script src="accordionjq.js" type="text/javascript"></script>
  </head>
  <body>
      <div id="accordion">
          <h3>jQuery Intro</h3>
          <div>
                  <p>jQuery is a lightweight cross-platform JavaScript
                  library. Because of its easy to use syntax, jQuery has
                  made it quite easy to include JavaScript on any web
                  site.  </p>
          </div>
          <h3>Features</h3>
          <div>
```

```
        <p>jQuery has not only simplified the complex coding but
        also has reduced the size of code as well. Below are the
        features of jQuery: </p>
        <ul>
                <li>It has huge number of plug-in enabling you
                to add additional features to your web page
                and develop the apps compatible to different
                platforms.</li>
                <li>Its API is fully documented making it easy to
                use and access its full features</li>
                <li>Its learning curve is very easy. Because it
                uses CSS and HTML, so it is every easy to learn
                its concepts.</li>
        </ul>
    </div>
    <h3>Understanding DOM</h3>
    <div>
        <p>DOM provides a representation of the HTML elements
        as a network of objects i.e. a tree of elements on the
        page.  </p>
        <p>Here, <html> is the ancestor or parent of all the
        elements on the web page. That is, all the elements are
        descendants or children of <html>. </p>
    </div>
    <h3>Selectors</h3>
    <div>
        <p>As the name suggests, the jQuery selectors helps in
        finding a DOM (Document Object Model) element in an
        HTML document based on id, name, types, attributes,
        class  etc.  </p>
     </div>
   </div>
  </body>
</html>
```

A <div> element is assigned the id accordion. It can be any id. It is through this id that the <div> element will be accessed. A <h3> element is used for the title of the content panel and a <div> element is used to define the text of that content panel. The <div> element can have a <p> element or a <ul> element or any other HTML element to represent its text. So, you have four <h3> and <div> element pairs within the outermost <div> element to define the content panel title and its text, respectively. The four <h3> elements contain the text **jQuery Intro, Features, Understanding DOM**, and **Selectors**, which eventually will become the titles of the content panels.

The jQuery code to invoke the accordion (i.e., to make the different <div> elements appear in the form of an accordion in the form of expandable and collapsible content panels) is as follows:

Accordionjq.js

```
$(document).ready(function() {
        $( "#accordion" ).accordion();
});
```

The accordion is invoked on the <div> element with the id accordion. You get the four content panels with the respective text. On clicking a content panel's title, it will expand to show the content within it. The rest of the content panels will be collapsed automatically (see Figure 9-8).

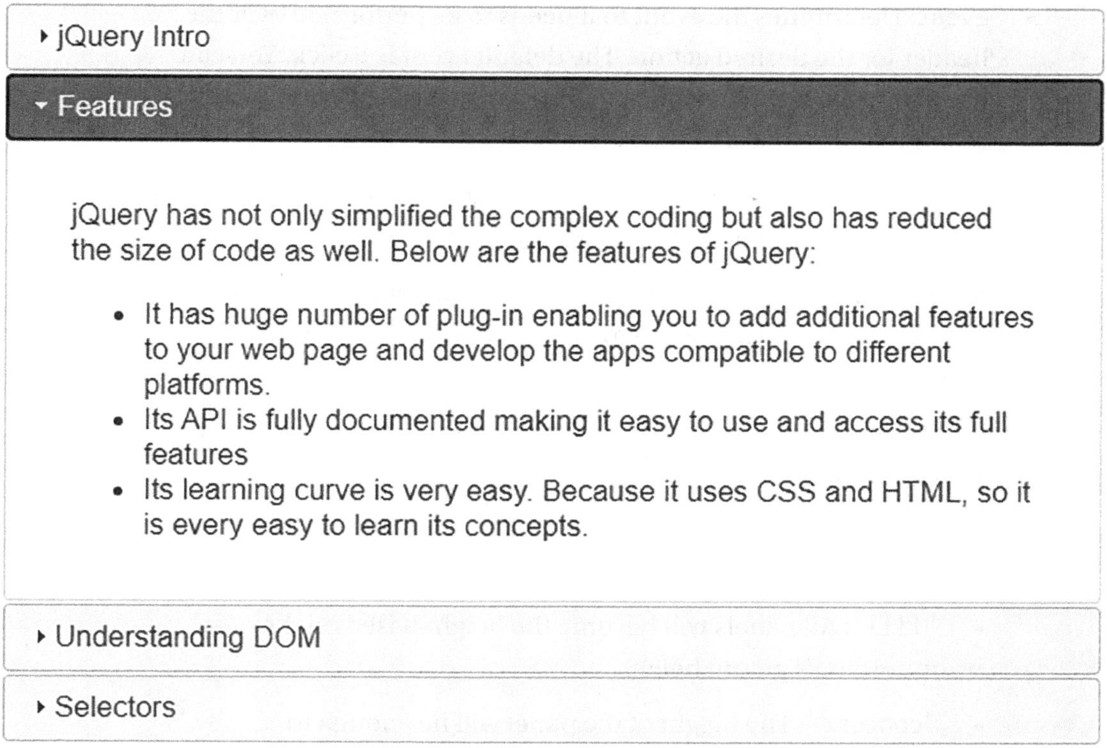

Figure 9-8. *The accordion appears with four content panels, and the active content panel appears in the expanded form*

Configuring an Accordion

The following are the options that can be used to configure an accordion:

- `active`: Determines which panel is to be set as active or open. Panels are zero-based. A negative value is used if you want to select backwards from the last panel. The default value is 0. You can set it to false to collapse all panels, provided the collapsible option is set to `true`.

- `animate`: Used to make the panels animate. You can set this option to `false` to disable animation or you can specify the duration of animation in milliseconds with default easing.

- `disabled`: Used for disabling the accordion by setting a Boolean value of `true`.

- event: Determines the event that needs to be performed over the header for the desired action. The default event is a click. You can use a mouseover, mouseout, etc. You can even use multiple events separated by a space.

- collapsible: Determines if all sections can be closed including the active section. The default value is false.

- header: Represents the selector for the header element. Remember that the content panel needs to be the sibling immediately after the header.

- heightStyle: Determines the height of the accordion and its panels. Valid options are

  - "auto": All panels will be set equal to the height of the tallest panel.

  - "fill": All panels will become the height based on the accordion's parent height.

  - "content": The height of the panel will be enough to accommodate its content.

- icons: Determines the type of icons to be used in the headers. You can set this option to false to have no icons in the headers. The default value is

  ```
  {
  "header": "ui-icon-triangle-1-e",
  "activeHeader": "ui-icon-triangle-1-s"
  }
  ```

To configure the accordion, you need to apply different properties on it as shown in the following jQuery code:

Accordion1jq.js

```
$(document).ready(function() {
     $( "#accordion" ).accordion({
          active: 3,
          animate: 1000,
```

```
            disabled: false,
        event: "mouseover",          .
            collapsible: true,
            heightStyle: "content",
            header: "h3",
          icons: { "header": "ui-icon-arrowthick-1-s", "activeHeader":
          "ui-icon-arrowthick-1-n" }
      });
});
```

By default, you are making the fourth content panel to be active (i.e., on running the HTML program, the fourth content panel, **Selectors**, will appear in expanded form showing its content and the rest of the content panels will appear as collapsed). Whenever any content panel expands or collapses, it will happen in animation form with the delay of 1000ms. The accordion is enabled by setting its disabled property to false. You don't need to click the content panel's title to expand or collapse it; just hovering over the content panel's title with the mouse is enough to expand or collapse it because the event property is set to mousehover. By setting the collapsible property to true, the content panel will expand when its title bar is hovered and will collapse when hovered again. The height of the content panels is set equal to its content (i.e., the height of the content panel will be quite enough to show its content completely). All <h3> elements in the HTML file are set to represent the header (i.e., the content panel's title bar). The icon of the headers (i.e., the content panel title bars) is changed to ui-icon-triangle-1-e when the content panel is in the collapsed form. And the icon of the header changes to ui-icon-triangle-1-s when the content panel is active (i.e., when it is expanded). Visit this URL for available icons: https://api.jqueryui.com/resources/icons-list.html.

On running the HTML program, as expected the fourth content panel will appear as active (see Figure 9-9(a)). You can hover over any content panel to expand it and can hover over it again to collapse it (see Figure 9-9(b)). Also, note the icons when the content panels are expanded and when they are closed. The icons are changed as required.

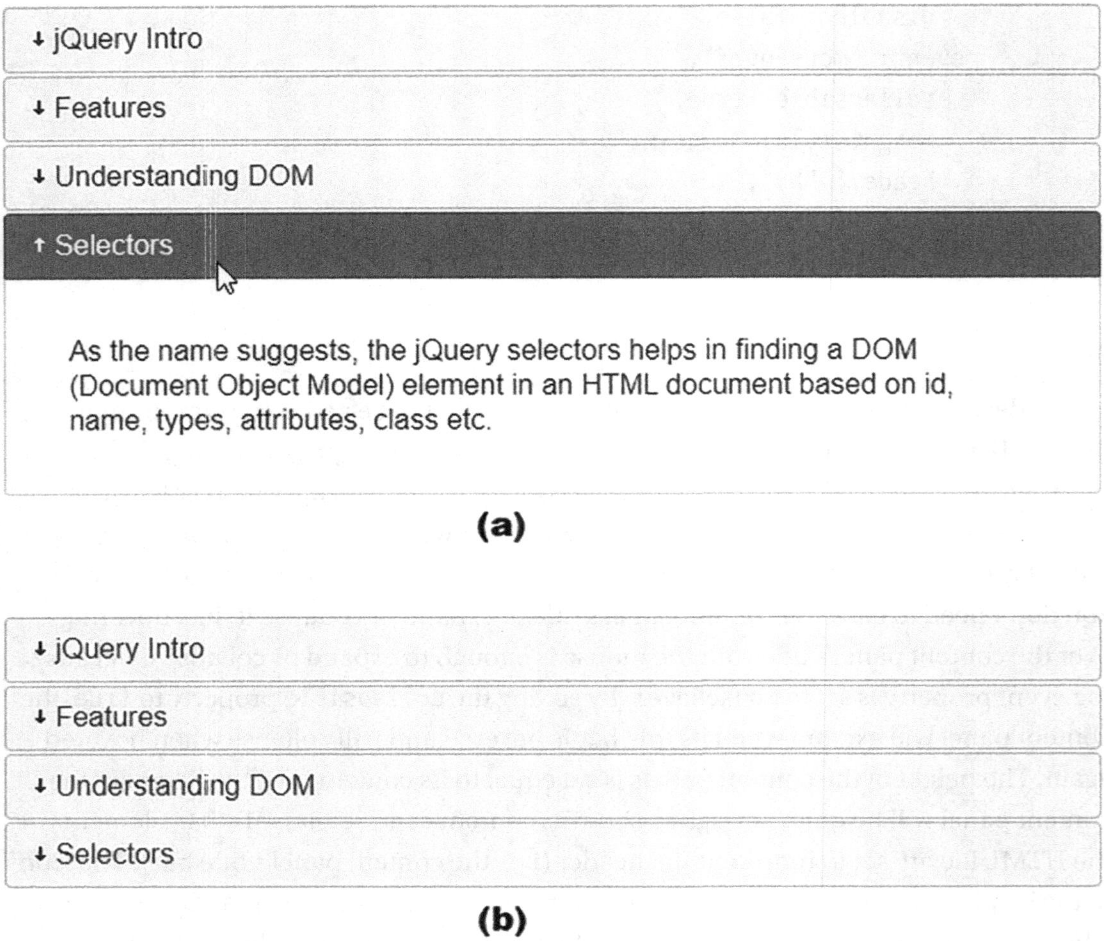

```
↓ jQuery Intro

↓ Features

↓ Understanding DOM

↑ Selectors

        As the name suggests, the jQuery selectors helps in finding a DOM
        (Document Object Model) element in an HTML document based on id,
        name, types, attributes, class etc.
```

(a)

```
↓ jQuery Intro

↓ Features

↓ Understanding DOM

↓ Selectors
```

(b)

Figure 9-9. *(a)The fourth content panel is active and in expanded form. (b)The icons of the active and inactive content panels are changed*

9-4. Using Dialogs

A dialog is a floating box that is used to display certain information to the user. It has a title and an x icon that can be used to close the dialog. The dialog can be moved using its title bar and can be resized by dragging its boundaries. If the dialog box is so much reduced in size that its whole content is not visible, then the scrollbars will automatically appear.

Problem

You want to display some content to the user via a dialog box, which the user can close after reading the information

Solution

To define the title of the dialog and to display the text through it, the HTML code is as follows:

Dialog.html

```
<!DOCTYPE html PUBLIC "-//W3C//DTD XHTML 1.0 Transitional//EN"
        "http://www.w3.org/TR/xhtml1/DTD/xhtml1-transitional.dtd">

<html xmlns="http://www.w3.org/1999/xhtml" xml:lang="en" lang="en">
  <head>
    <meta http-equiv="Content-Type" content="text/html; charset=utf-8"/>
    <title></title>
    <link rel="stylesheet" href="jquery-ui.css" type="text/css"
    media="screen" />
    <script src="jquery-3.5.1.js" type="text/javascript"></script>
    <script src="jquery-ui.js"></script>
    <script src="dialogjq.js" type="text/javascript"></script>
  </head>
  <body>
      <div id="jquery_intro" title="Introduction to jQuery">
          <p>jQuery is a lightweight cross-platform JavaScript library.
          Because of its easy to use syntax, jQuery has made it quite
          easy to include JavaScript on any web site. It has not only
          simplified the complex coding but also has reduced the size of
          code as well. Below are the features of jQuery.</p>
      </div>
  </body>
</html>
```

You can see in the above HTML code that a `<div>` element is defined with the title **Introduction to jQuery**. This title will become the dialog title. To make the `<div>`

element accessible in jQuery code, it is assigned the id `jquery_intro`. Within the `<div>` element is a `<p>` element that contains the text to be displayed via the dialog. To invoke the dialog and to link it with the `<div>` element of id `jquery_intro`, the following jQuery code has to be written:

Dialogjq.js

```
$(document).ready(function() {
      $( "#jquery_intro" ).dialog();
});
```

You can see that the dialog is invoked and is associated with the `<div>` element of id `jquery_intro`. On running the HTML program, you get the dialog displaying the text defined via the `<p>` element that was nested inside the `<div>` element as shown in Figure 9-10. You can close the dialog using its right top icon whenever desired.

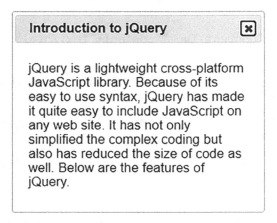

Figure 9-10. *A dialog appears, displaying the assigned text*

Options to Configure a Dialog Box

You can use the following properties to configure the dialog box as per your requirements:

- `appendTo`: Used to append the dialog to the specified element. The dialog needs to be closed while using the `appendTo` option.

- `title`: Used to specify the title of the dialog. Its default value is null. If the title is not specified, the title associated with the selector is used.

- autoOpen: Determines whether the dialog box has to be open or closed on launching of the application. If this option is set to false, the dialog box will remain closed and until the open() method is invoked, it won't be opened. The default value is true.

- buttons: Determines the type of buttons to be displayed on the dialog. You can specify the label of the button, its icon, and the callback function to be fired if any event occurs on that button. You can have more than one button in the form of an array in a dialog.

- closeOnEscape: By default this option is set to true and it means that the dialog will close when the user has focus on it and presses the Esc key. You can set this option to false if you don't want the dialog to close on pressing the Esc key.

- draggable: By default this option is true and it enables the dialog to be dragged by its title bar. To make it non-floating, set this option to false.

- height: Used to specify the height of the dialog. Its default value is auto, which means the height of the dialog will be set to accommodate its content. You can also specify the initial height of the dialog in pixels.

- width: Used to specify the width of the dialog. Its default value is 300 pixels.

- hide: Used to specify the method by which the dialog will hide while closing it. You can specify the type of animation desired while closing along with the specified duration. If you don't specify the duration, the animation will be performed with the default duration. Its default value is true, which means the dialog will fade out with the default duration and with the default easing. If you assign a Boolean value of false to this option, it means the dialog will close immediately without any animation.

- maxHeight: Determines the maximum height that the dialog can achieve when resized. Its default value is false (i.e., the dialog box can be resized to whatever height desired).

- maxWidth: Used to specify the maximum width to which the dialog can be resized. Its default value is false.

- minHeight: Used to specify the minimum height to which the dialog can be resized (i.e., the dialog cannot be made smaller in height than the value specified). Its default value is 150px.

- minWidth: Used to specify the minimum width to which the dialog can be reduced. Its default value is 150px.

- modal: This option can be set to true to make the dialog a modal dialog. A modal dialog is a dialog that stops you from interacting with other parts of the page until the dialog is closed. Its default value is false.

- resizable: This option determines whether the dialog can be resized or not. Its default value is true. If this option is set to false, the height and width of the dialog cannot be changed.

- show: Determines whether the dialog has to be displayed immediately or slowly via animation. If the value of this option is set to false, the dialog will open immediately. If this option is set to true, the dialog will fade in with the default duration and easing. You can also specify the animation, its duration, and easing too. The default animation is considered fadeIn. If the duration and easing are not specified, then the default duration and easing are used.

To configure the dialog, its different properties can be set as shown in the following jQuery code:

Dialog1jq.js

```
$(document).ready(function() {
    $( "#jquery_intro" ).dialog({
        title: "What is jQuery",
          closeOnEscape: false,
          draggable: false,
        height: "auto",
        width: 200,
          minHeight: 200,
          maxHeight: 400,
```

```
            minWidth: 150,
            maxWidth: 300,
        //  hide: "slideUp",
        hide: { effect: "fadeOut", duration: 2000 },
            buttons: [
                {
                    text: "Close",
                    icon: "ui-icon-closethick",
                    click: function() {
                        $( this ).dialog( "close" );
                    }
                }
            ],
            modal: true,
        //show: true
        show: { effect: "slideDown", duration: 1000 }
    });
});
```

The title of the dialog is set to **What is jQuery** and the dialog cannot only be closed by its top right icon but also by pressing the Esc key when the focus is on the dialog. By setting the draggagle property to false, the dialog cannot be dragged by its title bar. The height of the dialog box is set to adjust according to its content. The width of the dialog is set to 200px. The height of the dialog can be increased up to 400px and can be reduced up to 200px. Similarly, the width of the dialog can be increased up to 300px and can be reduced up to 150px. When closing the dialog it can be set to animate with a slideUp effect. It is commented out and it is set to animate with a fadeOut effect of 2000ms duration. A button is set to be displayed in the dialog with text Close with the icon ui-icon-closethick and the dialog will get closed when the click event occurs on that button. Visit this URL for available icons: https://api.jqueryui.com/resources/ icons-list.html. The dialog is set to appear as a modal dialog (i.e., the user cannot interact with any other part of the web page until the dialog is closed). The dialog can be set to appear via animation. The dialog is set to open with a slideDown animation of 1000ms duration (see Figure 9-11).

Figure 9-11. *A Close button is displayed in the dialog and the dialog is set to appear as a modal dialog*

9-5. Using the Tabs Widget

Tabs are used to display categorized information in a limited space. It is a single region with multiple panels where each panel's title or tab when clicked displays the required information.

Problem

You want to display information related to a jQuery introduction, jQuery features, and understanding the DOM using a tab widget where each tab or panel when clicked displays the required information.

Solution

The first step is to define the content to be displayed via the tabs or panels. Here it is important to understand that for using the tabs widgets, the tabs must be in an ordered, <ol>, or unordered, <ul>, list. The tab titles have to be enclosed within each <li> and wrapped with a href attribute. The HTML code to display content via the tab widget is as follows:

Tabs.html

```
<!DOCTYPE html PUBLIC "-//W3C//DTD XHTML 1.0 Transitional//EN"
        "http://www.w3.org/TR/xhtml1/DTD/xhtml1-transitional.dtd">

<html xmlns="http://www.w3.org/1999/xhtml" xml:lang="en" lang="en">
  <head>
    <meta http-equiv="Content-Type" content="text/html; charset=utf-8"/>
    <title></title>
    <link rel="stylesheet" href="jquery-ui.css" type="text/css"
    media="screen" />
    <script src="jquery-3.5.1.js" type="text/javascript"></script>
    <script src="jquery-ui.js"></script>
    <script src="tabsjq.js" type="text/javascript"></script>
  </head>
  <body>
      <div id="showinfo">
          <ul>
                <li><a href="#tab1">jQuery Intro</a></li>
                <li><a href="#tab2">Features</a></li>
                <li><a href="#tab3">Understanding DOM</a></li>
          </ul>
          <div id="tab1">
                <p>jQuery is a lightweight cross-platform JavaScript
                library. Because of its easy to use syntax, jQuery has
                made it quite easy to include JavaScript on any web
                site.</p>
          </div>
          <div id="tab2">
```

467

```
                    <p>jQuery has not only simplified the complex coding but
                    also has reduced the size of code as well. Below are the
                    features of jQuery: </p>
                     <ul>
                            <li>It has huge number of plug-in enabling you
                            to add additional features to your web page
                            and develop the apps compatible to different
                            platforms.</li>
                            <li>Its API is fully documented making it easy to
                            use and access its full features</li>
                            <li>Its learning curve is very easy. Because it
                            uses CSS and HTML, so it is every easy to learn
                            its concepts.</li>
                     </ul>
               </div>
               <div id="tab3">
                       <p>DOM provides a representation of the HTML elements
                       as a network of objects i.e. a tree of elements on the
                       page.  </p>
                       <p>Here, <html> is the ancestor or parent of all the
                       elements on the web page. That is, all the elements are
                       descendants or children of <html>. </p>
               </div>
          </div>
       </body>
</html>
```

You can see in the HTML code that a `<div>` element is defined with the id `showinfo`. It is through this id that the `<div>` element will be accessed in the jQuery code and the tab widget will be associated to it. To define tab or panel titles, an unordered list, `<ul>`, is defined with three `<li>` elements where each `<li>` element has a nested anchor, `<a>`, element with an `href` attribute to link the tab or panel's titles with their respective content. The anchor elements are set to point at the ids `tab1`, `tab2`, and `tab3`, respectively. It means that when any of the anchor elements are clicked, it will search for the element with the specified id and will navigate to it. The three `<li>` elements are set to display the panel's titles, **jQuery Intro**, **Features**, and **Understanding DOM**, respectively.

To define the content to be displayed when any tab or panel's title is clicked, three <div> elements are defined with the ids tab1, tab2, and tab3. That is, when any anchor element with an href attribute is clicked, it will implement navigation to the <div> element whose id matches with the id it is pointing at. The <div> uses <p> elements, <ul> elements, etc. to show its content in the desired format.

To associate the <div> element with the tab widget and to display content via its panels, the following jQuery code is required:

Tabsjq.js

```
$(document).ready(function() {
        $( "#showinfo" ).tabs();
});
```

The <div> element of id showinfo is accessed and the tab widget is set to display the panel's titles via the <ul> elements defined in the <div> element. Also, the anchor element with the href attribute is linked to the respective <div> element to display the information when any panel's title is clicked as shown in Figure 9-12.

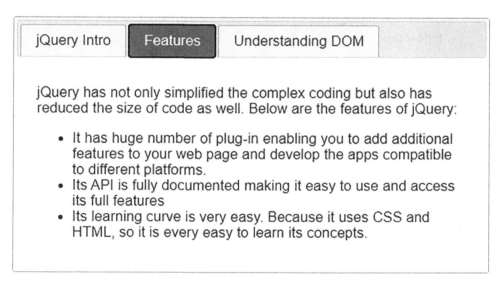

Figure 9-12. *The tab widget is set to display the panel's titles and the information of the clicked panel is displayed*

Options to Configure Tabs

The following are the properties of the tabs widget that can be used to configure it:

- `active`: Determines which tab has to be kept active on startup. The default value is 0.

- `collapsible`: If this option is set to `true`, selecting a selected tab again will make it deselected. If this option is set to `false`, selecting a selected tab does not deselect it. The default value is `false`.

- `disabled`: Used for disabling the desired tabs. For example, if this option is set to `valu, [1,2]`, it will disable the first three tabs. The default value is `false`.

- `event`: You can select the event that activates the tab. The event can be mouseover, mouseout, click, etc. The default event is `click`.

- `heightStyle`: Determines the height of the tab widget. The following are the valid options:

  - `"auto"`: The height of all tabs will be set equal to the height of the tallest tab.

  - `"fill"`: All tabs will become of the height based on the tab's parent height.

  - `"content"`: The height of the tab will be enough to accommodate its content.

- `hide`: Determines the animation for hiding a tab. The default value is `null`.

- `show`: Determines the animation required to display the tab. The default value is `null`.

To configure tab widget as per your requirements, its different properties are set, so the jQuery code is modified to appear as follows:

Tabs1jq.js

```
$(document).ready(function() {
    $( "#showinfo" ).tabs({
        active:1,
```

```
        collapsible: true,
        //disabled: [1,2]
        event: "mouseover",
        heightStyle:"content"
            });
});
```

The second panel is set to be active on startup. On selecting a panel's title, it will get selected, and on selecting the active panel's title again, the panel will get deselected. The second and third panels can be disabled with the `disabled` property as shown in the code above. But because you want all the panels to be active, the `disabled` property is commented out. To select any panel, you don't need to click on that panel; just hovering over its title is enough as the `event` property is set to `mouseover`. The height of the panel is set to be quite enough to display its content. On running the HTML program, you get the tab widget to display the content as shown in Figure 9-13.

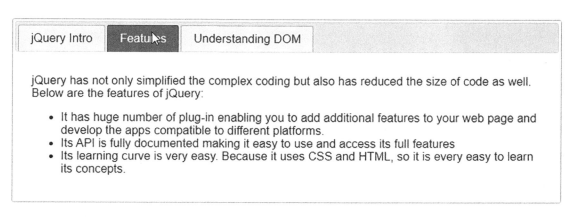

Figure 9-13. *The tab widget is set to display the content*

9-6. Summary

In this chapter, you learned to use different widgets that are provided with jQuery UI. You learned to select a date and format that date using the datepicker widget. Also, you saw how to configure and apply styles to the datepicker widget. Then you learn to make use of the autocomplete widget to display suggestions when any character is typed in the input box. Also, you learned to display large volumes of data in a categorized form by making use of the accordion and tabs widgets. Besides displaying the desired content, you also learned to configure the accordion and tabs widgets. Also, you learned to display information to the user via closable dialogs.

The next chapter will show you the procedure to implement AJAX, making your web pages more responsive. You will learn to return single and multiple lines of text from the server, return name/value pairs using JSON, return a simple JSON object, and return the JSON object from the server that displays images. You will also learn to convert a string into uppercase using AJAX, how to get the price of the selected product through an AJAX request, and also how to authenticate a user using AJAX.

CHAPTER 10

AJAX

In this chapter, you learn to implement AJAX (i.e., exchanging data with a web server in the background) and update the web page asynchronously. This chapter covers the following recipes.

- Returning a single line of text from the server

- Returning multiple lines of text from the server

- Returning a name/value pair using JSON

- Returning a JSON object

- Returning the JSON object that displays images

- Converting a string into uppercase using AJAX

- Displaying price of the selected product through an AJAX request

- Authenticating a user using AJAX

- Validating a user name

- Using autocomplete

- Importing HTML

- Getting XML data

- Paginating tables

You need to install WampServer to run the programs of this chapter. Appendix A includes all the steps to download and install WampServer.

Copy the code in this chapter (with the source code bundle of the book) to WampServer's www folder installed on your computer (i.e., in the C:\wamp64\www folder).

© Bintu Harwani 2022
B. Harwani, *jQuery Recipes*, https://doi.org/10.1007/978-1-4842-7304-3_10

10-1. Returning a Single Line of Text from the Server

Problem

You want to make an AJAX request to the server that returns a single line of text.

Solution

The following is the HTML code to display an H1 element and a Submit button. The H1 element displays the text returned by the server, and the Submit button initiates the request to be sent to the server.

Returnonetext.html

```
<!DOCTYPE html>
<html>
  <head>
    <script src="jquery-3.5.1.js" type="text/javascript"></script>
    <script src="returnonetextjq.js" type="text/javascript"></script>
  </head>
  <body>
        <H1 id="askname">What is your name</H1>
        <button>Submit</button>
  </body>
</html>
```

An H1 element is defined with "askname" and the "What is your name" text. A Submit button is created below the H1 element.

The file on the server is supposed to return a single line of text, so the file on the server, returnname.txt, contains a single line, "My Name is Bintu".

Returnname.txt

```
My Name is Bintu
```

The following is the jQuery code to make an AJAX request to the server and display the line of text returned by the server.

Returnonetextjq.js

```
$(document).ready(function(){
    $("button").click(function(){
            $.ajax({
              url: "/returnname.txt",
              success: function(result){
                        $("#askname").html(result);
            }});
        });
});
```

This jQuery code shows an ajax()method; let's first learn what this method does.

ajax()

The ajax() method implements AJAX in jQuery (i.e., sending asynchronous HTTP requests to the server).

Syntax

$.ajax({name:value, name:value, ... })

- url represents the URL to which the request has to be sent. By default, the current page is considered as the URL

- success represents a callback function that is to be executed run when the request succeeds

- complete represents a callback function that is to be executed when the request is finished (i.e., after success and error functions)

- data represents the data to be sent to the server. The data can be JSON object, string or array.

- error represents a callback function to be executed when the request fails.

Whenever a click event occurs on a button, the ajax() method is invoked. The ajax() method sends the request to the returnname.txt file available on WampServer.

The callback function defined through the success option is invoked when the request succeeds. The callback function displays the content returned by the URL file to the H1 element after replacing its earlier content. When running the HTML program, you get the H1 element and the Submit as shown in Figure 10-1(a). Clicking the Submit button displays the text returned by the URL file via the H1 element, as shown in Figure 10-1(b).

What is your name

Submit

(a)

My Name is Bintu

Submit

(b)

Figure 10-1. *(a) The H1 element and a Submit button appears. (b) The text returned by the URL file will be displayed via the H1 element*

10-2. Returning Multiple Lines of Text from Server

Problem

You want to make an AJAX request to the server, and when the request succeeds, the server returns multiple lines of text.

Solution

The two lines of text returned by the server are displayed via H1 elements, so the HTML code to display two H1 elements and a Submit button is shown next. The Submit button initiates the AJAX request to be made to the server.

Returnmultipletext.html

```
<!DOCTYPE html>
```

```
<html>
  <head>
    <script src="jquery-3.5.1.js" type="text/javascript"></script>
    <script src="returnmultipletextjq.js" type="text/javascript"></script>
  </head>
  <body>
        <H1 id="name">What is your name</H1>
        <H1 id="work">What do you do</H1>
        <button>Submit</button>
  </body>
</html>
```

Two H1 elements are defined with ids, name, and work, respectively. The H1 element with id, name displays the "What is your name" text. The H1 element with the work id displays the" What do you do" text. Below the H1 elements is a Submit button.

Returndata.txt

```
My Name is Bintu <br/>
I am working on jQuery <br/>
```

The file on the server returns two lines of text with a line break in between.

The following is the jQuery code to make an AJAX request to the server and to split the multiple lines returned by the server and display them.

Returnmultipletextjq.js

```
$(document).ready(function(){
    $("button").click(function(){
            $.ajax({
              url: "/returndata.txt",
              success: function(result){
                  var lines=result.split("<br/>");
                  $("#name").html(lines[0]);
                  $("#work").html(lines[1]);
                }});
        });
});
```

On running the HTML program, you get the two H1 elements displaying the "What is your name" and "What do you do" text, along with a Submit button at the bottom (see Figure 10-2(a)). When the user clicks the button, the ajax() method is invoked, sending the request to the returndata.txt file on the server.

The callback function specified with the success option is invoked when the request succeeds. The parameter in the callback function contains the content returned by the file mentioned in the URL on the server. Because the file on the server returns two lines, the lines are split wherever the <br/> line break occurs, and the individual lines are assigned to the lines array. The first and second lines returned from the server are assigned to lines[0] and lines[1] index locations, respectively. The text in lines[0] index location (i.e., My Name is Bintu) is displayed through the H1 element with a name id. The text in lines[1] index location (i.e., I am working on jQuery) is displayed through the H1 element with a work id, as shown in Figure 10-2(b).

What is your name

What do you do

Submit

(a)

My Name is Bintu

I am working on jQuery

Submit

(b)

Figure 10-2. *(a) Two H1 elements with a Submit button appear. (b) The two lines returned by the server are displayed through two H1 elements*

JSON stands for JavaScript Object Notation. It is a lightweight syntax for sending data from the server to the client's browser. JSON maintains data in the form of name/value pairs that are separated by commas. The objects are enclosed within the curly braces, and arrays use square brackets.

10-3. Returning a Name/Value Pair Using JSON

Problem

You want to place an AJAX request to the server that returns the name/value pair in JSON format if the request succeeds.

Solution

Because the content returned by the server is displayed by appending it to the <body> element of the HTML file, the HTML file currently does not have an element to display.

Returnjson1.html

```
<!doctype html>
<html lang="en">
  <head>
    <meta charset="utf-8">
    <title>Returning JSON using jQuery</title>
    <script src="jquery-3.5.1.js" type="text/javascript"></script>
    <script src="returnjson1jq.js" type="text/javascript"></script>
  </head>
  <body>
  </body>
</html>
```

As such, the HTML program does not display anything. It is through the jQuery ajax() method that a request is made to the server, and the data returned by the server is displayed in the body of the HTML program.

The JSON file on the server has some data in name/value pair format. The file contains certain fast-food items along with their prices, as shown.

Jsonsample1.json

```
{
  "Pizza": "20$",
  "Burger": "10$",
  "Hot Dog": "7$"
}
```

Following is the jQuery code to fetch the JSON data from the server and display it on the screen in the desired format.

Returnjson1jq.js

```
$.getJSON( "/jsonsample1.json", function(result ) {
    var items = [];
    $.each(result, function( item, price ) {
        items.push( "<tr><td>" + item + "</td><td>" + price +
        "</td><tr/>" );
    });
    $( "<table/>", {
        html: items.join( "" )
    }).appendTo( "body" );
});
```

This jQuery code makes use of the methods like getJSON(), each(), arr.push(), and join(), so let's have a quick look at these methods first.

getJSON()

As the name suggests, the getJSON() method gets JSON data from the server using GET HTTP requests.

Syntax

$(selector).getJSON(url,data,success(data,status,xhr))

- url represents the URL to which the request is to be sent.
- data represents the data to be sent.
- success represents the callback function that executes if the request succeeds.

The syntax for the success functions is

success(data,status,xhr)

- data represents the data returned from the server.
- status represents the string containing request status. The status can be "success", "notmodified", "error", "timeout", or "parsererror").
- xhr represents the XMLHttpRequest object.

each()

The each() method specifies a function that has to be executed on each matching element.

Syntax

`$(selector).each(function(index,element))`

- `function(index,element)` represents the function to execute on each matching element.
- `index` represents the index location of the selector.
- `element` represents the current element.

arr.push()

The arr.push() method resembles the push operation usually performed with a stack (i.e., it pushes or adds one or more values into the array).

Syntax

`arr.push(element1, element2 ...)`

`element` represents the elements to be inserted into an array.

join()

The join() method returns an array into a string format. The original array is not changed. The specified separator separates all the elements of the arrays. The default separator is a comma (,).

Syntax

`array.join(separator)`

The separator is optional. If not used, the comma separates elements.

The getJSON() method sends the AJAX request to the server, and if the request succeeds, the callback function is executed. The content in the jsonsample1.json file, which is on the server, is returned via the result parameter of the callback function. An items is defined. Using the each() method, the result returned by the file on the server is observed, and a callback function is applied to each of the name/value pairs returned.

The name (i.e., item name) and the value (i.e., its price) are pushed (i.e., added into the items array after enclosing them in the table columns). The table columns arrange the item names and their prices in proper alignment. After adding all the item names and their price values to the items array, the <table> element is closed. The entire table in the items array is converted into string format by invoking the join() method.

Finally, the table in string format containing the item names and their prices is appended to the <body> element of the HTML file for display (see Figure 10-3).

Pizza   20$
Burger   10$
Hot Dog 7$

Figure 10-3. *The result returned by the file on the server is formatted in the form of a table and displayed*

10-4. Returning a JSON Object

Problem

You want to make an AJAX request to the server to get a JSON object in return. The JSON object comprises the name and work of a person—the person's name and the kind of work they do is returned by the server.

Solution

To display name and work of a person via H1 elements, two H1 elements are defined along with a button. The two H1 elements display the name and work attribute of the JSON object returned by the server. The following is the HTML code.

Returnjson2.html

The following is the HTML code to display two H1 elements and a button.

```
<!DOCTYPE html>
<html>
  <head>
    <meta charset="utf-8">
    <title>Returning JSON using jQuery </title>
    <script src="jquery-3.5.1.js" type="text/javascript"></script>
```

```
        <script src="returnjson2jq.js" type="text/javascript"></script>
    </head>
    <body>
<H1 id = "Name">What is your Name</H1>
            <H1 id = "Work">What do you do</H1>
        <div>
                <button type = "button">Enter Info</button>
        </div>
    </body>
</html>
```

The two H1 elements are defined with id, Name, and Work, respectively. Both H1 elements are set to display certain default text. The name attribute returned by the JSON object is displayed through the first H1 element, and the work attribute of the JSON object is displayed through the second H1 element.

The URL file on the server contains a JSON object comprising two attributes: name and work.

Jsonsample2.json

```
{"name": "Bintu Harwani", "work": "I am working with jQuery"}
```

The following is the jQuery code to fetch the JSON object from the server, access the name and work attributes from the object, and display it.

Returnjson2jq.js

```
$(document).ready(function(){
    $("button").click(function(){
        $.getJSON( "/jsonsample2.json", function(jsonObj ) {
            $("#Name").html( jsonObj.name);
            $("#Work").html( jsonObj.work);
        });
    });
});
```

When running the application, the two H1 elements are displayed with default text assigned to them: "What is your Name," and "What do you do," respectively. Below the H1 elements is a button, as shown in Figure 10-4(a). When the click event occurs on the button, the getJSON() method is invoked that send the AJAX request to the server. If the request succeeds, the callback function is invoked, and the JSON object returned by the server is assigned to the jsonObj parameter of the callback function. The name and work of the person are stored in the name and work attributes of the JSON object, jsonObj, which are displayed via the H1 elements of IDs, Name, and Work, respectively (see Figure 10-4(b)).

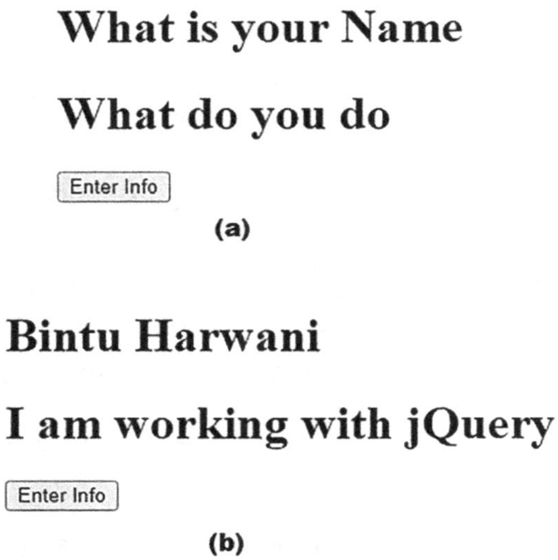

What is your Name

What do you do

Enter Info

(a)

Bintu Harwani

I am working with jQuery

Enter Info

(b)

Figure 10-4. *(a) Two H1 elements with the assigned text and a button appear. (b) Name and work accessed from the JSON object that is returned by the server are displayed through the H1 elements*

10-5. Returning the JSON Object That Displays Images

Problem

You want to place an AJAX request to the server, and if the request succeeds, the server returns the product name and its image file name.

Solution

You want the product name and images to appear on the screen when the user clicks a button. The following is the HTML code to display a button and <div> element.

Returnjsonimages.html

```html
<html>
  <head>
    <title>Returning Images using JSON</title>
    <script src="jquery-3.5.1.js" type="text/javascript"></script>
    <script src="returnjsonimagesjq.js" type="text/javascript"></script>
  </head>
  <body>
    <div>
                  <button type = "button">Show Images</button>
        </div>
        <div id='Images'></div>
  </body>
</html>
```

The id <div> element displays the images returned by the respective attribute in the JSON object.

The following is the file on the server that contains an array of JSON objects where each JSON object comprises two attributes: Name and Image.

Jsonsampleimages.json

```json
[
    {
        "Name": "Intel",
        "Image": "chip.jpg"
    },
    {
        "Name": "AMD",
        "Image": "chip2.jpg"
    },
    {
        "Name": "Cisc",
        "Image": "chip3.jpg"
    },
```

```
{
    "Name": "Risc",
    "Image": "chip4.jpg"
},

{
    "Name": "Dual Core",
    "Image": "chip5.jpg"
}
]
```

The following is the jQuery code that sends the AJAX request to the server, and when the request succeeds, the code access the JSON objects returned by the mentioned URL and displays the image name and the respective image on the screen.

Returnjsonimagesjq.js

```
$(document).ready(function(){
    $("button").click(function(){
            $.getJSON("/jsonsampleimages.json", function (data) {
                    var arrItems = [];
                    $.each(data, function (index, value) {
                arrItems.push(value);
                    });
            var arrImages = [];
            for (var i = 0; i < arrItems.length; i++) {
                arrImages.push( "<tr><td><H1>" + arrItems[i].Name +
                "</H1></td><td><img src=" + arrItems[i].Image + ">
                </td><tr/>" );
            };
            $( "<table/>", {
                    html: arrImages.join( "" )
                }).appendTo( "#Images" );
        });
    });
});
```

When the click event occurs on the button, the getJSON method is invoked that makes an AJAX request to the server; if the request succeeds, the JSON objects in the jsonsampleimages.json file on the server are returned and are accessible through the data parameter in the callback function.

An array, arrItems is defined. Using the each method, each of the JSON objects in the URL file is accessed and pushed into the arrItems array. So, the arrItems array contains the JSON objects fetched from the server.

Now, it's time to separate name and image attributes in the JSON object and insert them into another array, so one more array, arrImages, is created. A for loop is used to access each JSON object in the arrItems array and push the Name and Image attributes of the JSON object into the arrImages array after enclosing them in <td> and </td> elements. The <td> and </td> elements make the JSON object attributes to appear in tabular format. The Name and Image attributes of a JSON object contain the product name and image filename, respectively. All the product name and image file names in tabular format are converted into a string by invoking the join() method and appended to the <div> element of id, Images for display. The Show Images button appears on the screen when the application runs, as shown in Figure 10-5(a). When pressed, the Show Images button displays the product name and corresponding images, as shown in Figure 10-5(b).

(b)

Figure 10-5. *(a) Show Images button appears on the screen. (b) Product names and their corresponding images are displayed by pressing the Show Images button*

10-6. Converting a String to Uppercase Using AJAX

Problem

You have a web page that prompts the user to enter a string. If you click the Submit button, the AJAX request is made to the server that accesses a PHP script on the server. It converts the entered string to uppercase and returns it to the browser.

Solution

The following is the HTML file containing the code that prompts the user to enter a string, which is sent to the server for conversion into uppercase.

Ajaxphp1.html

```
<!DOCTYPE html PUBLIC "-//W3C//DTD XHTML 1.0 Transitional//EN"
        "http://www.w3.org/TR/xhtml1/DTD/xhtml1-transitional.dtd">

<html xmlns="http://www.w3.org/1999/xhtml" xml:lang="en" lang="en">
  <head>
    <meta http-equiv="Content-Type" content="text/html; charset=utf-8"/>
    <title></title>
    <link rel="stylesheet" href="ajax1style.css" type="text/css"
    media="screen" />
    <script src="jquery-3.5.1.js" type="text/javascript"></script>
    <script src="ajaxphp1jq.js" type="text/javascript"></script>
  </head>
  <body>
    <form>
        <label>Enter a string</label>
        <input type="text" size="50" class="enteredStr"/> <br/>
         <input type="submit" id="submit"/>
    </form>
    <div id="response"></div>
  </body>
</html>
```

You can see in the HTML code that a form is defined, and within the form, a label, an input box, and a button are defined. The label is set to display an "Enter a string" message. The input box is supposed to take a string from the user. The box size is defined as 50 characters, but the user can always enter more as the entered text scroll. The button, when clicked, initiates the AJAX request to the server. The response sent by the server is displayed via <div> element of id, response.

The following is the jQuery code to make an AJAX request, send the string entered by the user to the file on the server, and display the response sent back by the server.

Ajaxphp1jq.js

```
$(document).ready(function() {
    $('#submit').click(function () {
        var str = $('.enteredStr').val();
        var data = 'enteredStr=' + str;
         $.ajax({
             type:"POST",
             url:"convertcap.php",
             data: data,
             success: function (html) {
                 $('#response').html(html);
             }
        });
        return false;
    });
});
```

When the click event occurs on the button, the string entered in the input box with the enteredStr class is accessed and assigned to the str variable. A name/value pair comprises the name (enteredStr) and the value as the string that the user entered. This name/value pair is assigned to the data variable.

After that, the ajax request is made to the server, and the data from the server is fetched using an HTTP POST request method. The convertcap.php script on the server is accessed. The name/value pair in the data variable is passed to the file on the server (i.e., to the convertcap.php script). If the AJAX request is successful, the callback function is invoked, and the response sent by the server is assigned to the HTML parameter.

The response sent by the server in HTML parameter is displayed via the <div> element with id, response.

The following is the PHP script file on the server that converts the string to uppercase.

Convertcap.php

```php
<?php
    $str = $_POST['enteredStr'];
    echo "String in upper case is: ".  strtoupper($str);
?>
```

The strtoupper() method is used in the PHP script. Let's discuss what this method does.

strtoupper()

The strtoupper() function converts a string into uppercase.

Syntax

strtoupper(string)

The string parameter represents the string to convert into uppercase.

On running the program, the HTML program displays an input box asking the user to enter a string, as shown in Figure 10-6(a). Let's assume that the user enters some text in the input box and clicks the Submit button. What happens is that using the PHP superglobal variable, $_POST, the string passed to the script file is accessed. Recall, the name/value pair was sent to the PHP script file on the server via data variable where the name was enteredStr and value was the string entered by the user. The string entered by the user is accessed using the $_POST global variable and assigned to the str variable. Finally, by invoking the strtoupper() method, the string is converted to uppercase and returned, which is then displayed on the screen, as shown in Figure 10-6(b).

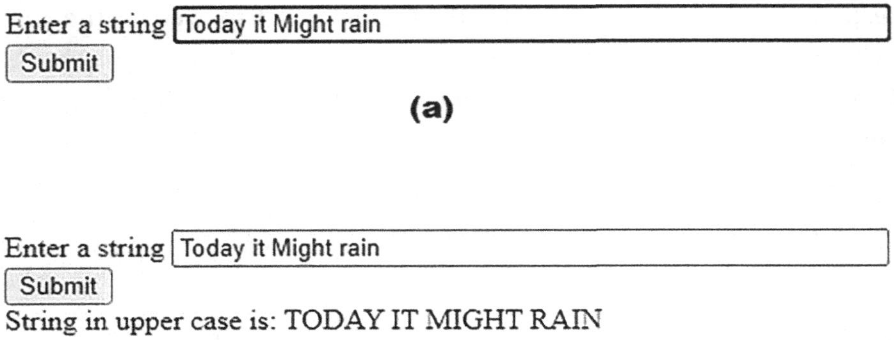

Enter a string [Today it Might rain   ]
[Submit]

(a)

Enter a string [Today it Might rain   ]
[Submit]
String in upper case is: TODAY IT MIGHT RAIN

(b)

Figure 10-6. *(a) Input box appears asking the user to enter a string. (b) The entered string is converted to uppercase and displayed on the screen*

10-7. Displaying the Price of the Selected Product Through an AJAX Request

Problem

You want to display three fast food items using a combo box, and when the user selects any of the food items, the AJAX request is made to the server. The server sends the selected food item's price.

Solution

The following is the HTML code to display a combo box showing three food items.

Ajaxphp2.html

```
<!DOCTYPE html PUBLIC "-//W3C//DTD XHTML 1.0 Transitional//EN"
        "http://www.w3.org/TR/xhtml1/DTD/xhtml1-transitional.dtd">

<html xmlns="http://www.w3.org/1999/xhtml" xml:lang="en" lang="en">
  <head>
    <meta http-equiv="Content-Type" content="text/html; charset=utf-8"/>
    <title></title>
```

```
    <link rel="stylesheet" href="ajax1style.css" type="text/css"
    media="screen" />
    <script src="jquery-3.5.1.js" type="text/javascript"></script>
    <script src="ajaxphp2jq.js" type="text/javascript"></script>
  </head>
  <body>
Select your food item :
            <select class="fooditem" >
<option value="" selected>Select Food Item</option>
                <option value="Pizza">Pizza</option>
                <option value="Burger">Burger</option>
                <option value="Hot Dog">Hot Dog</option>
            </select>
<div id="info"></div>
  </body>
</html>
```

You can see that a text message, "Select your food item," is displayed. Following the text message, a combo box is displayed by making use of HTML select element. Three food items are defined in this combo box. After the combo box, a <div> element is defined with id, "info" to display the result sent by the server when the AJAX request succeeds.

The jQuery code to place an AJAX request sends the selected food item to the file on the server and displays the price of the food returned by the server.

Ajaxphp2jq.js

```
$(document).ready(function() {
    $('.fooditem').on('change', function () {
        var str = $('.fooditem').val();
        var data = 'fooditem=' + str;
        $.ajax({
            type:"GET",
            url:"findprice.php",
            data: data,
            success: function (html) {
                $('#info').html(html);
```

```
            }
        });
          return false;
      });
  });
```

The combo box is assigned to the fooditem class. The callback function is invoked on the "change" event of the combo box (i.e., the moment any of the food items is selected, the callback function is invoked). In the callback function, the food item selected by the user is accessed and assigned to the str variable. A name/value pair is defined by the name and data, where the name is fooditem. The value is the food item selected by the user. An AJAX request is made to the server, and using the HTTP GET method, the name/value pair is passed to the PHP script, findprice.php. If the AJAX request is successful, the content returned by the server (i.e., the price of the food item returned by the server is assigned to the HTML parameter of the callback function associated with the success option of the ajax() method). The price returned by the server is displayed on the screen by using the <div> element of info id.

Findprice.php

```php
<?php
        $product = $_GET['fooditem'];
        if($product == "Pizza")
              $price="15 $";
        if($product == "Burger")
              $price="10 $";
        if($product == "Hot Dog")
              $price="5 $";
        echo "You have chosen " . $product . " and its price is " . $price;
?>
```

Certain food items are displayed using the combo box (see Figure 10-7(a)). When a food item is selected, an AJAX request is made, which invokes the PHP script on the server. In the PHP script, you find that using the PHP superglobal variable, $_GET, the value passed with the name, fooditem is accessed and assigned to the product variable.

Recall that the food item selected by the user is passed to the server along with the name fooditem. When using an if-else statement, the food item is checked, and its price is assigned to the price variable. Finally, the price of the food item in the price variable is returned to the client's browser and displayed, as shown in Figure 10-7(b).

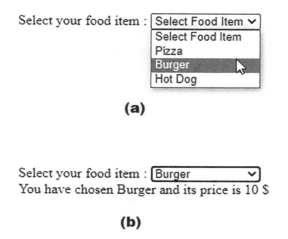

(a)

Select your food item : [Burger   ▾]
You have chosen Burger and its price is 10 $

(b)

Figure 10-7. *(a) Some food items are displayed using the combo box. (b)The price of the selected food item that is returned by the server is displayed*

10-8. Authenticating a User Using AJAX

Problem

You have a MySQL database table containing the user's email address, password, and name. If the user enters a valid email address and password, the user is greeted with a welcome message and the user's name fetched from the MySQL table.

Solution

To do this recipe, you need to create a MySQL database and a table and insert a few rows. Let's take a quick look at the MySQL basic statements.

Create Database

The create database statement creates a new SQL database.

Syntax

`Create database database_name;`

database_name represents the name of the database to be created.

Show Databases

As the name suggests, the show databases statement is to get a list of all the MySQL databases.

Syntax

`Show databases;`

Use Statement

The use statement informs MySQL to use the specified database for performing the subsequent SQL statements.

Syntax

`USE database_name;`

Once the USE statement is used, the specified database remains the current database until another USE statement.

Create Table

As the name suggests, the create table statement creates a database table.

Syntax

```
create table table_name(
        column_name datatype optional_attribute,
        column_name datatype optional_attribute,
................
);
```

A datatype includes varchar, int, and timestamp, which are the type of data stored in that column.

An optional attribute can be any of the following.

- NOT NULL: The column stores a value. A null value is not allowed in this column.

- DEFAULT value: The column stores a specified value when no value is supplied for this column.

- AUTO_INCREMENT: When adding a new row, the value in this column is automatically incremented by 1.

- PRIMARY KEY: The value in this column must be unique. This attribute is usually used with AUTO_INCREMENT. A database table can be efficiently searched if it has a primary key column.

SHOW TABLES Statement

This statement shows the tables in the currently open database.

Syntax

```
Show tables [LIKE 'pattern']
```

Using the LIKE keyword, only the tables that match the specified pattern are displayed.

SELECT Query

The SELECT statement fetches the data from the MySQL database. This statement can be run via the command prompt or written in any scripting, like PHP and Ruby.

Syntax

```
SELECT [DISTINCT|ALL ] [ * | selected fields ] FROM table_name [WHERE condition]
```

- [DISTINCT | ALL] displays unique rows, whereas ALL displays all rows, including duplicate rows. The ALL option is the default.

- [* | selected fields] displays all the fields of the selected table. You can also display selected fields in the output.

- FROM table_name specifies the table or tables from which the selected fields must be chosen. It is mandatory to specify the table name.

- The WHERE condition specifies the logical expression. The rows that satisfy the given condition are displayed. This is optional.

INSERT INTO

The INSERT INTO statement inserts new rows into the specified table.

Syntax

```
INSERT INTO table_name (column1, column2, column3,...)
VALUES (value1, value2, value3,...)
```

You can specify the column name and their respective values in sequence. But if you are specifying values for all the columns of the table, then no need to specify the column names but the values supplied must match the order of the columns in the table.

Open the MySQL command-line client window and run the following command that creates a MySQL database by name, jquerydb, and in that database creates a table called users. The users table has three columns: email address, password, and user name.

```
mysql> create database jquerydb;

mysql> use jquerydb;

mysql> create table users(
    email_address varchar(50) NOT NULL,
    password varchar(15) Not NULL,
    user_name varchar(50),
    primary key(email_address));

mysql> show tables;
mysql> select * from users;
mysql> insert into users values('bintu@yahoo.com', 'gold123', 'bintu');
mysql> insert into users values('chirag@gmail.com', 'chirag123', 'chirag');
mysql> select * from users;
```

```
+------------------+-----------+-----------+
| email_address    | password  | user_name |
+------------------+-----------+-----------+
| bintu@yahoo.com  | gold123   | bintu     |
| chirag@gmail.com | chirag123 | chirag    |
+------------------+-----------+-----------+
2 rows in set (0.00 sec)
```

Screenshots of the execution of MySQL commands are shown in Figures 10-8 and 10-9.

```
mysql> show databases;
+--------------------+
| Database           |
+--------------------+
| information_schema |
| mysql              |
| performance_schema |
| sys                |
+--------------------+
4 rows in set (0.00 sec)

mysql> create database jquerydb;
Query OK, 1 row affected (0.15 sec)

mysql> use jquerydb;
Database changed
mysql> create table users(
    -> email_address varchar(50) NOT NULL,
    -> password varchar(15) NOT NULL,
    -> user_name varchar(50),
    -> primary key(email_address));
Query OK, 0 rows affected (0.68 sec)

mysql> ▄
```

Figure 10-8. *Screenshot for creating database and table*

```
mysql> show tables;
+--------------------+
| Tables_in_jquerydb |
+--------------------+
| users              |
+--------------------+
1 row in set (0.05 sec)

mysql> select * from users;
Empty set (0.04 sec)

mysql> insert into users values('bintu@yahoo.com', 'gold123', 'bintu');
Query OK, 1 row affected (0.12 sec)

mysql> select * from users;
+-----------------+----------+-----------+
| email_address   | password | user_name |
+-----------------+----------+-----------+
| bintu@yahoo.com | gold123  | bintu     |
+-----------------+----------+-----------+
1 row in set (0.00 sec)

mysql> insert into users values('chirag@gmail.com', 'chirag123', 'chirag');
Query OK, 1 row affected (0.16 sec)

mysql> select * from users;
+------------------+-----------+-----------+
| email_address    | password  | user_name |
+------------------+-----------+-----------+
| bintu@yahoo.com  | gold123   | bintu     |
| chirag@gmail.com | chirag123 | chirag    |
+------------------+-----------+-----------+
2 rows in set (0.00 sec)

mysql>
```

Figure 10-9. *Screenshot for showing tables, running Select and Insert SQL statements*

The next step is to create an HTML file for the user interface.

The following is the HTML code that asks the user to enter their email address and password.

Ajaxphp3.html

```
<!DOCTYPE html PUBLIC "-//W3C//DTD XHTML 1.0 Transitional//EN"
        "http://www.w3.org/TR/xhtml1/DTD/xhtml1-transitional.dtd">
```

```
<html xmlns="http://www.w3.org/1999/xhtml" xml:lang="en" lang="en">
  <head>
    <meta http-equiv="Content-Type" content="text/html; charset=utf-8"/>
    <title></title>
    <link rel="stylesheet" href="ajax1style.css" type="text/css"
    media="screen" />
    <script src="jquery-3.5.1.js" type="text/javascript"></script>
    <script src="ajaxphp3jq.js" type="text/javascript"></script>
  </head>
  <body>
      <form>
          <label>Enter your Email Address</label>
          <input type="text" class="email"/> <br/>
          <label>Enter your Password</label>
          <input type="password" name="password" class="passwd"/> <br/>
          <input type="submit" id="submit"/>
      </form>
      <div id="response"></div>
  </body>
</html>
```

You can see in the HTML code that a <form> is defined, and within a form, two labels and two input boxes are defined. The two labels display the text that guides the user to enter the email address and password in the adjacent input boxes. The two input boxes are meant for entering email address and password and are assigned the email class and passwd class, respectively.

Below the two input boxes is a Submit button which, when clicked, initiates the AJAX request. Below the Submit button is a <div> element of id, response which is meant for displaying the result sent by the server when AJAX request succeeds.

The following is the jQuery code to make an AJAX request, invoke the PHP script on the server, and fetch the result sent by the server.

Ajaxphp3jq.js

```
$(document).ready(function() {
    $('#submit').click(function () {
        var emailaddr = $('.email').val();
```

```
        var pwd = $('.passwd').val();
        var data='email='+emailaddr+'&password='+pwd;
        $.ajax({
            type:"GET",
            url:"authenticate.php",
            data:data,
            success:function(html) {
                $("#response").html(html);
            }
        });
        return false;
    });
});
```

When the Submit button is clicked, the email address entered by the user is accessed and assigned to emailaddr variable. The password entered by the user is accessed and is assigned to the pwd variable. The name and password are combined into a name, value pair and assigned to the data variable. An AJAX request is made, and the email address and password in the data variable are passed to the PHP script, authenticate.php on the server. If the AJAX request succeeds, the callback function in the success option is invoked. The result sent by the server is assigned to the HTML parameter of the callback function. The content sent by the server in the HTML parameter is displayed on the screen via <div> element of id, response.

The following is the PHP script that establishes a connection to the MySQL database and compares the email address and password entered by the user with the data present in the MySQL table.

Authenticate.php

```
<?php
    $emailaddr = trim($_GET['email']);
    $pswd = trim($_GET['password']);
    $connect = mysqli_connect("localhost", "root", "gold123", "jquerydb");
    if(!$connect){
            die('Please, check your server connection.');
    }
```

```
$query = "SELECT user_name FROM users WHERE email_address LIKE
'$emailaddr%' and password like '$pswd%'";
$results = mysqli_query($connect, $query);
if($results)
{
    $count = mysqli_num_rows($results);
    if ($count >0)
    {
        while ($row = mysqli_fetch_array($results,MYSQLI_ASSOC)) {
            extract($row);
            echo 'Welcome ' . $user_name. ' !';
        }
    }
    else
    echo "Invalid email address or password";
}
else
    echo "Sorry database table not found or access is denied";
?>
```

The PHP script uses several methods, such as trim(), mysqli_connect(), die(), mysqli_query(), and mysqli_num_rows(). Let's take a quick look at these methods first.

trim()

The trim() function removes whitespace and few predetermined characters from either side of the supplied string.

Syntax

trim(string, char_to_remove)

- string represents the string from which the whitespaces must be removed.

- char_to_remove represents the characters to be removed from the string. This is optional, and if not used, all the following characters are removed.

- "\0" (NULL character)

- "\t" (tab space)

- "\n" (new line character)

- "\x0B" (vertical tab)

- "\r" (carriage return)

- " " (white space)

mysqli_connect()

mysql_connect opens a new connection to the MySQL server.
Syntax

mysqli_connect(host, user_name, password, database, port, socket)

- host represents the hostname. The IP address of the host can also be mentioned. The keyword, localhost can be used if a local server is used. It is optional.

- user_name represents an authentic MySQL username. This parameter is optional, and usually, the root is the username.

- password represents the MySQL password

- database represents the database to which the connection must be made.

- port represents the port number to connect with the MySQL server. It is optional.

- socket represents the socket or named pipe to be used. It is optional.

die()

The die() method prints the error message and exits from the script.
Syntax

die(message)

The message parameter contains the text to be displayed. It is optional.

mysqli_query()

The mysqli_query() method executes the specified query on a database.

Syntax

mysqli_query(connection_link, query_string, result_mode)

- connection_link represents the MySQL connection to use

- query_string represents the SQL query string

- result_mode is optional and determines how the result is returned from the MySQL server. The following constants can be used.

- MYSQLI_STORE_RESULT (default) returns a mysqli_result object with a buffered result set.

- MYSQLI_USE_RESULT returns a mysqli_result object with an unbuffered result set. Until and unless all rows are fetched, the connection line is busy, and all subsequent calls result in an error. So, either all rows must be fetched from the server, or the result set must be discarded by calling mysqli_free_result().

- A MYSQLI_ASYNC query is performed asynchronously, and no result set is immediately returned. The mysqli_poll() function is used to get results.

mysqli_num_rows ()

The mysqli_num_rows() function returns the number of rows in a result set. It is frequently used to determine whether the desired data is available in the database or not.

Syntax

mysqli_num_rows(result_set);

The result_set parameter represents the result set returned by fetch query functions like mysqli_query().

When the HTML program runs, you get a screen that prompts users to enter an email address and password. After entering the email address and password, when the user clicks the Submit button, an AJAX request invokes the PHP script on the server. In the

PHP script, the email address and password send via data variable are accessed using the PHP superglobal variable, $_GET. The email address and password passed to the PHP script are accessed and assigned to the emailaddr and pswd variables.

Connection to the jquerydb MySQL database is established by passing the userid, root, and password. After establishing a connection to the MySQL database, the SQL SELECT statement is executed to find row(s) in the users table that matches the supplied email address and password. If the row is not found in the users table, then a message, Invalid email address, or password is returned to the client's browser (see Figure 10-10(a)). If any row is found in the users table that matches the supplied email address and password, a welcome message along with the user's name (accessed from the users table) is sent back to the client's browser for display, as shown in Figure 10-10(a)).

Enter your Email Address | bintu@yahoo.com
Enter your Password | ••••••
Submit
Invalid email address or password

(a)

Enter your Email Address | bintu@yahoo.com
Enter your Password | •••••••
Submit
Welcome bintu !

(b)

Figure 10-10. (a) Invalid email address or password message appears when the row is not found in the users table. (b) The welcome message is displayed along with the user's name if the matching row is found in the user's table

10-9. Validating a User Name

Problem

You want to ask the user to enter a name, and you want to use a server-side script to confirm that the field is not left blank. If the user does not enter anything in the name field, they should get an error message.

Solution

Let's start by creating an HTML file that displays a label: "Enter your Name" and an input text field and a Submit button. The HTML file may appear as follows.

validateuser.html

```
<!DOCTYPE html PUBLIC "-//W3C//DTD XHTML 1.0 Transitional//EN"
        "http://www.w3.org/TR/xhtml1/DTD/xhtml1-transitional.dtd">

<html xmlns="http://www.w3.org/1999/xhtml" xml:lang="en" lang="en">
  <head>
    <meta http-equiv="Content-Type" content="text/html; charset=utf-8"/>
    <title></title>
    <link rel="stylesheet" href="stylesuservalidate.css" type="text/css"
    media="screen" />
    <script src="jquery-3.5.1.js" type="text/javascript"></script>
    <script src="validateuserjq.js" type="text/javascript"></script>
  </head>
  <body>
    <form>
        <span class="label">Enter your Name</span>
            <input type="text" name="uname" class="uname"/>
            <span class="error">
        </span><br>
        <input type="submit" id="submit"/>
    </form>
  </body>
</html>
```

You can see here that the input text field is assigned the uname class to access it via jQuery code. Following the input text field is an empty span element of the error class. The text to this span element is assigned from the server-generated response—if the user leaves the input text field blank.

In order to specify a width to the input text field label, and a color to the error message, you need to write some style rules in the style sheet file.

stylesuservalidate.css

```
.label {float: left; width: 120px; }
```

507

```
.uname {width: 200px; }
.error { color: red; padding-left: 10px; }
#submit { margin-left: 125px; margin-top: 10px;}
```

The following is the jQuery code to invoke the server side script, which passes to validateuser.php, the name entered by the user as a parameter, and displays an error message if the name is left blank by the user.

validateuserjq.js

```
$(document).ready(function() {
    $('.error').hide();
    $('#submit').click(function () {
        var name = $('.uname').val();
        var data='uname='+name;
        $.ajax({
            type:"POST",
            url:"validateuser.php",
            data:data,
            success:function(html) {
                $('.error').show();
                $('.error').text(html);
            }
        });
        return false;
    });
});
```

The validateuser.php script file is on the server. It checks that the name of the user was not left blank. The following is the code.

validateuser.php

```
<?php
if($_POST['uname'] == '')
{
    echo "This field cannot be blank";
}
?>
```

How It Works

You start the jQuery code, which you see in the preceding, by hiding the span element of the error class and attaching a click event to the Submit button assigned the submit id. You then retrieve the name entered by the user in the input text fields (of uname class) and store it in a name variable.

The variable stores a string, uname=name, where the name holds the name entered by the user.

This data variable is sent to the server to be assigned to the validateuser.php script file (assumed to already exist on the server) to confirm that the name is not left blank.

You invoke the request through the ajax() method, in which you specify that the method of request that you are going to use is POST and that the name of the script file that is executed on the server is validateuser.php. You also specify that the parameter you're passing to the script file is contained in the string data.

After processing the passed data, the code you have in validateuser.php generates the output, which is received by the JavaScript file in the HTML parameter of the callback function. The response returned by the script file (stored in HTML) is then assigned to the span element of the error class to display the error response to the user, which is generated by the script file on the server. Before assigning the response HTML to the span element of error class, however, you first make it visible because you made it hidden at the beginning of the code. Finally, you return false in the click event to suppress the default browser click behavior; that is, you want it to take action that is specified via jQuery code and not its default action.

You can see also how the PHP script retrieves the name passed via the data parameter through the $_POST array and, on finding it blank, responds with an error message. This field cannot be blank, which is displayed in the span element of the error class. No response is generated if the name is not blank.

On leaving the input text field blank, if you select the Submit button, you get the error message displayed, as shown in Figure 10-11.

Enter your Name [   ]   This field cannot be blank
                 [Submit]

Figure 10-11. *Error message displayed when name field is left blank*

If a valid name is entered, the name is accepted without displaying any error message, as shown in Figure 10-12.

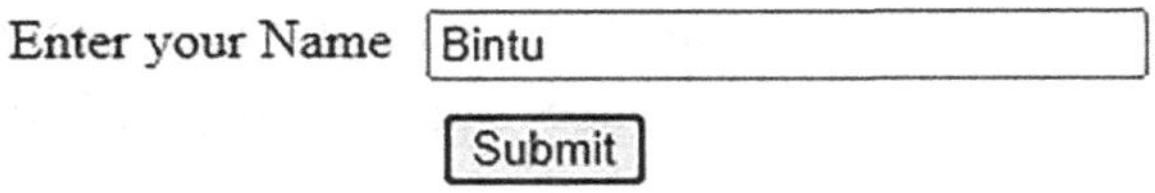

Enter your Name [Bintu   ]

[Submit]

Figure 10-12. *Name accepted and no error message displayed*

10-10. Using Autocomplete

Problem

You want to ask the user to enter a name in the input text field so that the moment the user types the first character of a name, a suggestion box appears that displays all the names beginning with the character typed. You also want the names displayed in the suggestion box to have a hovering effect so that they become highlighted on moving the mouse pointer over them and the clicked name to be inserted in the input text field.

Solution

Let's create an HTML file that displays a label: "Enter userid" and an input text field. Below the input text field, you create two empty div elements that are assigned class names: listbox and nameslist, respectively. The following is the HTML file.

autocomplete.html

```
<!DOCTYPE html PUBLIC "-//W3C//DTD XHTML 1.0 Transitional//EN"
        "http://www.w3.org/TR/xhtml1/DTD/xhtml1-transitional.dtd">
<html xmlns="http://www.w3.org/1999/xhtml" xml:lang="en" lang="en">
  <head>
    <meta http-equiv="Content-Type" content="text/html; charset=utf-8"/>
    <title></title>
    <link rel="stylesheet" href="stylesautocomplete.css" type="text/css"
    media="screen" />
    <script src="jquery-3.5.1.js" type="text/javascript"></script>
    <script src="autocompletejq.js" type="text/javascript"></script>
  </head>
```

```
<body>
    <form>
        <span class="label">Enter user id</span>
        <input type="text" name="userid" class="userid"/>
        <div class="listbox">
            <div class="nameslist">
            </div>
        </div>
    </form>
</body>
</html>
```

The div element of the listbox class displays a box. The nameslist div element displays the names with hovering effect. You define the style rules to be applied to the two div elements in the following style.css file.

stylesautocomplete.css

```
.listbox {
    position: relative;
    left: 10px;
    margin: 10px;
    width: 200px;
    background-color: #000;
    color: #fff;
    border: 2px solid #000;
}
.nameslist {
    margin: 0px;
    padding: 0px;
    list-style:none;
}
.hover {
    background-color: cyan;
    color: blue;
}
```

511

The following is the jQuery code to make the suggestion box appear when the user types the first character in the input text field and make the clicked name (in the suggestion box) appear in the input text field automatically.

autocompletejq.js

```javascript
$(document).ready(function() {
    $('.listbox').hide();
    $('.userid').keyup(function () {
        var uid = $('.userid').val();
        var data='userid='+uid;
        $.ajax({
            type:"POST",
            url:"autocompletescript.php",
            data:data,
            success:function(html) {
                $('.listbox').show();
                $('.nameslist').html(html);
                $('li').hover(function(){
                    $(this).addClass('hover');
                },function(){
                    $(this).removeClass('hover');
                });
                $('li').click(function(){
                    $('.userid').val($(this).text());
                    $('.listbox').hide();
                });
            }
        });
        return false;
    });
});
```

The autocomplete.php script file on the server is designed to send the list of names as response; it should look like the following.

autocompletescript.php

```php
<?php
    echo '<li>Jackub</li>';
    echo '<li>Jenny</li>';
    echo '<li>Jill</li>';
    echo '<li>John</li>';
?>
```

Getting Names Generated from the Database

One drawback in the server-side script is that it only returns the names beginning with the *j* character. Even if the user types any other character, it still generates names beginning with the *j* character. You want to instead generate names beginning with any character typed by the user. For this, you need to create a database and a table containing hundreds of names. I created a database called autofill (using MySQL server) and a table with the name information in it. The table information contains a field name, and you'll insert a few names in it, beginning with the characters a to z.

autocompletedbscript.php

```php
<?php
$name = $_POST['userid'];
$connect = mysqli_connect("localhost", "root", "gold123", "jquerydb");
if(!$connect){
    die('Please, check your server connection.');
}
$query = "SELECT user_name FROM users WHERE user_name LIKE '$name%'";
$results = mysqli_query($connect, $query);
if($results)
{
    while ($row = mysqli_fetch_array($results,MYSQLI_ASSOC)) {
        extract($row);
        echo '<li>' . $user_name. '</li>';
    }
}
?>
```

How It Works

In the style sheet file, the listbox style rule includes the position property set to value relative to assign it a position in relation to its container (which is usually the browser window when not defined). The left property is set to 10px to make the suggestion box appear at the distance of 10px from the left border of the browser window. The Margin property is set to value 10px to keep the distance of 10px from the input text field above it. The Width property is set to 200px to make the names (displayed in this box) occupy 200px. The background-color and color properties are set to value #000 and #fff, respectively, to make the background color of the box turn black and the names appear in white. The border property is set to value 2px solid #000 to make a solid black border of 2px thickness appear around the names displayed in the suggestion box.

Moving along to the jQuery code, you hide the div element of the listbox class at the beginning because you only want to display it when user types a character in the input text field. You attach the keyup() event to the input text field, which is assigned the class name userid, so that its event handling function is fired when the user releases a key on the keyboard. You then retrieve the character typed by the user in the input text field of the userid class and store it the uid variable; then define a data variable that store a string userid=uid where uid holds the first character (of the name) entered by the user. This data variable is sent to the server to be assigned to the autocomplete.php script file (assumed to already exist on the server) to display the suggestion box to the user.

You invoke the actual request through the ajax() method, where you specify that the method of request that you are going to use is POST and the name of the script file executed on the server is autocompletescript.php. The parameter to be passed to the script file is contained in the string data, containing the string userid=uid. After processing the passed data, the script file (autocompletescript.php on the server) generates the output received by the jQuery file in the HTML parameter of the callback function. You then make the div element of the listbox class visible to display the names in it.

You also assign the response returned by the script file (stored in HTML) to the div element of the nameslist class. The script file then returns few names in the form of list items. Next, you attach the hover event to the names returned by the script file (in the form of list items). In this event, you add the style properties defined in the hover style rule to the names (in the form of list items) when the mouse pointer moves over them, making them appear in blue over the cyan background. You also remove the style properties defined in the hover style rule from the names when the mouse pointer moves away.

You attach the click event to the names that exist in the list items, make the clicked name appear in the input text field of the userid class, and hide the suggestion box containing names. Return false in the click event to suppress the default browser click behavior because you want it to take action specified via jQuery code and not its default action.

You can see that the PHP code just generates a few names in the form of list items to be sent back to the jQuery file. The script sends a few names beginning with a *j* character if the user enters only this character (as the first character). To make this script generate names beginning with any character typed by the user (from a to z), you need a database with hundreds of names in it. You'll look at interacting with such a database soon, but for now, upon execution, you find an "Enter user id" input text field. When the user types a character, the names sent by the server are displayed in a suggestion box, as shown in Figure 10-13.

Figure 10-13. *A suggestion box appears on entering a single character in the input text field*

You can hover on any name with the mouse pointer. You might also observe that the hovered name is highlighted, as shown in Figure 10-14.

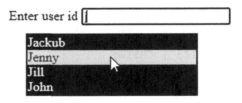

Figure 10-14. *The available options are highlighted when hovering over them*

Clicking a name displays it in the input text field, as shown in Figure 10-15.

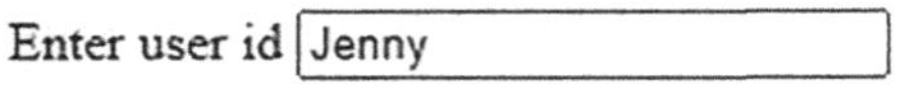

Enter user id `Jenny`

Figure 10-15. *The clicked option appears in the input text field*

Let's examine the database solution. I used the jquerydb and the users table created in the 10-8 recipe. To display user names on entering a character, I inserted a few more rows in the users table in the input box. The following is a list of SQL commands executed to insert few rows in the users table. Before inserting rows, let's look at the SQL statements for selecting the database and showing existing rows in the table.

```
mysql> show databases;
+--------------------+
| Database           |
+--------------------+
| information_schema |
| jquerydb           |
| mysql              |
| performance_schema |
| sys                |
+--------------------+
5 rows in set (1.21 sec)

mysql> use jquerydb;
Database changed
mysql> select * from users;
+-------------------+-----------+-----------+
| email_address     | password  | user_name |
+-------------------+-----------+-----------+
| bintu@yahoo.com   | gold123   | bintu     |
| chirag@gmail.com  | chirag123 | chirag    |
+-------------------+-----------+-----------+
2 rows in set (0.09 sec)

mysql> insert into users values('ben@gmail.com', 'ben777', 'ben');
Query OK, 1 row affected (0.44 sec)

mysql> insert into users values('bekky@yahoo.com', 'bekky123', 'bekky');
Query OK, 1 row affected (0.15 sec)
```

```
mysql> insert into users values('bittu@yahoo.com', 'bitty555', 'bittu');
Query OK, 1 row affected (0.05 sec)

mysql> select * from users;
+------------------+-----------+-----------+
| email_address    | password  | user_name |
+------------------+-----------+-----------+
| bekky@yahoo.com  | bekky123  | bekky     |
| ben@gmail.com    | ben777    | ben       |
| bintu@yahoo.com  | gold123   | bintu     |
| bittu@yahoo.com  | bitty555  | bittu     |
| chirag@gmail.com | chirag123 | chirag    |
+------------------+-----------+-----------+
5 rows in set (0.03 sec)
```

Once rows are inserted in the jquerydb users table, you can understand the code in the PHP script, autocompletedbscript.php.

You start by retrieving the character sent from the JavaScript file (data parameter) with the help of the $_POST array (since the request was sent via HTTP POST method) and storing it in the $name variable. Then, you write a SQL query to retrieve all the user_name from the users table that begins with the character stored in $name (which was typed by the user in the input text field).

You execute the SQL query, and the rows returned by the table as the outcome of the query are stored in the $results array. You then retrieve each name stored in the $results array, one by one, using a while loop and sending each user_name to the jQuery file after enclosing them in <li> tags because you want to generate names in the form of list items.

Note   You can also cache the results and filter on the cache for each user session.

Now, you get the names beginning with any character that you type in the input text field. So, if you type the *b* character, you get all the names beginning with the letter *b*, as shown in Figure 10-16.

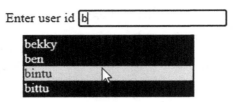

Figure 10-16. *The options in the suggestion box change based on the first character typed in input text field*

10-11. Importing HTML

Problem

You want to import HTML content from another file into the current web page.

Solution

Let's create an HTML file that contains a paragraph element and a hyperlink. You want the contents to be imported only when user selects the hyperlink. The following is the HTML file.

importhtml.html

```
<!DOCTYPE html PUBLIC "-//W3C//DTD XHTML 1.0 Transitional//EN"
        "http://www.w3.org/TR/xhtml1/DTD/xhtml1-transitional.dtd">
<html xmlns="http://www.w3.org/1999/xhtml" xml:lang="en" lang="en">
  <head>
    <meta http-equiv="Content-Type" content="text/html; charset=utf-8"/>
    <title></title>
    <script src="jquery-3.5.1.js" type="text/javascript"></script>
    <script src="importhtmljq.js" type="text/javascript"></script>
  </head>
  <body>
    <p>You are going to organize the Conference on IT on 2nd Feb 2022</p>
    <a href="abc.com" class="list">Participants</a>
    <div id="message"></div>
  </body>
</html>
```

The hyperlink is assigned the list class name so that you can access it via jQuery code. Below that hyperlink is an empty div element called message which you use for displaying the imported HTML contents. The file from where you want to import HTML contents is named, for example, namesinfo.htm and it likely have the following content.

namesinfo.html

```
<p>The list of the persons taking part in conference</p>
<ul>
    <li>Jackub</li>
    <li>Jenny</li>
    <li>Jill</li>
    <li>John</li>
</ul>
<p>We wish them All the Best</p>
```

You can see that the HTML file contains two paragraph elements and a list item. The following is the jQuery code to import the HTML content.

importhtmljq.js

```
$(document).ready(function() {
    $('.list').click(function () {
        $('#message').load('namesinfo.html');
        return false;
    });
});
```

Importing Only Desired Elements

You can also import only the desired HTML elements from the imported file. So, in the following jQuery code, you import only the list items (and no paragraph elements) from the namesinfo.html file.

importdesiredhtmljq.js

```
$(document).ready(function() {
    $('.list').click(function () {
        $('#message').load('namesinfo.html li');
        return false;
    });
});
```

How It Works

Before you begin understanding the jQuery code, let's first see what the load() method does and its use in the preceding code. Essentially, this function adds the specified file from the server and returns its HTML contents, like the following.

Syntax

`.load(url, parameters, callback function)`

- url is the string defining the location of the server-side script file.

- parameters contain the data that you want to be passed to the server-side script file for some processing.

- The callback function is the one that is executed when the request succeeds.

Note   With Internet Explorer, the load() method caches the loaded file.

The jQuery code begins by attaching the click event to the hyperlink of the list class, and in its event handling function, you load the HTML contents of the namesinfo. htm file and assign it to the div element message. You return false in the click event to suppress the default browser click behavior because you want it to take action specified via jQuery code and not its default action.

Initially, the web page contains a paragraph element and a hyperlink with text: Participants (see Figure 10-17).

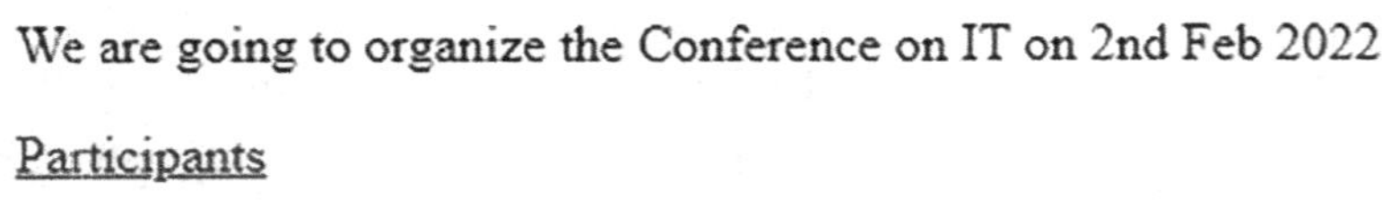

We are going to organize the Conference on IT on 2nd Feb 2022

Participants

Figure 10-17. *Original web page with hyperlink*

On selecting the hyperlink, the contents (consisting of two paragraph elements and list items) are imported from the namesinfo.htm file into the current web page, as shown in Figure 10-18.

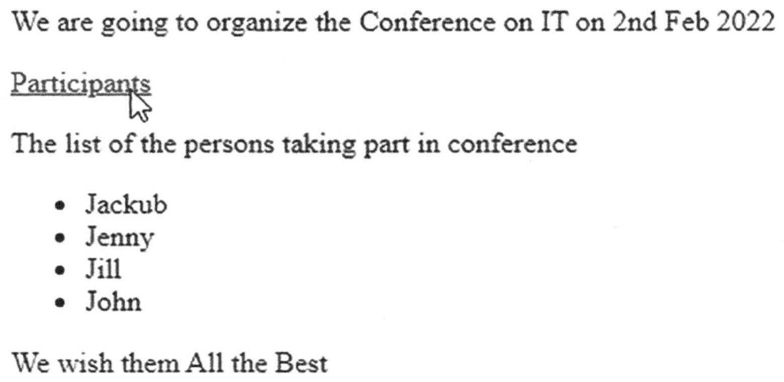

We are going to organize the Conference on IT on 2nd Feb 2022

Participants

The list of the persons taking part in conference

- Jackub
- Jenny
- Jill
- John

We wish them All the Best

Figure 10-18. *Web page after contents imported from other HTML file*

When importing only the desired elements, you can see that in the load() method, the namesinfo.htm file is followed by li to declare that you want to import only the list items present in the file namesinfo.htm. As a result, when you click the Participants hyperlink, only the list items imported in the div element message are shown (see Figure 10-19).

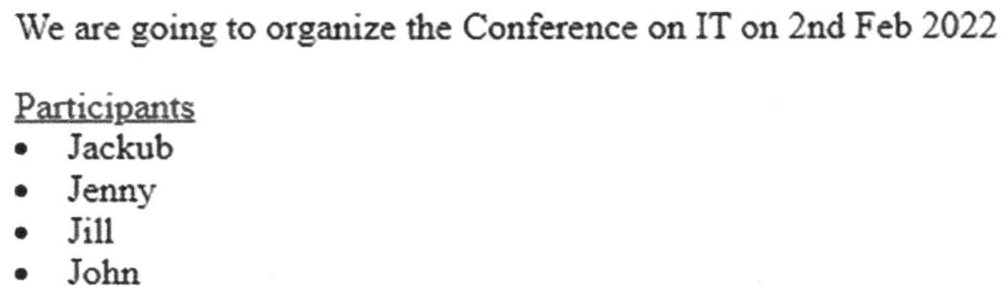

We are going to organize the Conference on IT on 2nd Feb 2022

Participants
- Jackub
- Jenny
- Jill
- John

Figure 10-19. *The web page after list items are imported from another HTML file*

10-12. Getting XML Data
Problem

You have an XML file that contains information about some students. You want to import that information from an XML file into the current web page asynchronously. The XML file contains some user-defined tags to organize its information.

Solution

Let's first create an HTML file that contains a paragraph element, a Submit button, and an empty div element. The HTML file should look like the following.

gettingxml.html

```
<!DOCTYPE html PUBLIC "-//W3C//DTD XHTML 1.0 Transitional//EN"
        "http://www.w3.org/TR/xhtml1/DTD/xhtml1-transitional.dtd">
<html xmlns="http://www.w3.org/1999/xhtml" xml:lang="en" lang="en">
  <head>
    <meta http-equiv="Content-Type" content="text/html; charset=utf-8"/>
    <title></title>
    <script src="jquery-3.5.1.js" type="text/javascript"></script>
    <script src="gettingxmljq.js" type="text/javascript"></script>
  </head>
  <body>
    <p>To see the Names of the students extracted from XML file click the
    button given below: </p>
    <input type="submit" id="submit"/>
    <div id="message"></div>
  </body>
</html>
```

The paragraph element just displays a message to the user in friendly fashion, and you want the user to select the Submit button when they are ready. You then want the information from the XML file to be imported and displayed in the div element message. Assuming the name of XML file be student.xml, its XML content can look like the following.

student.xml

```
<?xml version="1.0" encoding="utf-8" ?>
<school>
    <student>
        <roll>101</roll>
        <name>
            <first-name>Anil</first-name>
            <last-name>Sharma</last-name>
```

```
        </name>
        <address>
            <street>22/10 Sri Nagar Road</street>
            <city>Ajmer</city>
            <state>Rajasthan</state>
        </address>
        <marks>85</marks>
    </student>
    <student>
        <roll>102</roll>
        <name>
            <first-name>Manoj</first-name>
            <last-name>Arora</last-name>
        </name>
        <address>
            <street>H.No 11-B Alwar Gate</street>
            <city>Ajmer</city>
            <state>Rajasthan</state>
        </address>
        <marks>92</marks>
    </student>
</school>
```

The jQuery code to import the information stored in the XML tag first-name and display it in the form of list items, in the current web page, then looks like the following.

gettingxmljq.js

```
$(document).ready(function() {
    $('#submit').on("mousedown", function(event) {
        $.ajax({
            type:"GET",
            url:"student.xml",
            dataType:"xml",
            success: function (sturec) {
                var stud="<ul>";
                $(sturec).find('student').each(function(){
```

```
                              var name = $(this).find('first-name').text()
                              stud+="<li>"+name+"</li>";
                        });
                        stud+="</ul>";
                        $('#message').append(stud);
                  }
            });
            return false;
      });
});
```

Displaying Roll, First Name, and Marks from an XML File

Before you look at how the preceding code works, it's worth noticing briefly that you can modify the jQuery code to retrieve text from other tags very easily. Here's some code that retrieves text from <roll>, <first-name>, <last-name>, and <marks> tags.

retrievespecificjq.js

```
$(document).ready(function() {
      $('#submit').on("mousedown", function(event) {
            $.ajax({
                  type:"GET",
                  url:"student.xml",
                  dataType:"xml",
                  success: function (sturec) {
                        var stud="<table border='1'>";
                        $(sturec).find('student').each(function(){
                              var roll = $(this).find('roll').text()
                              var fname = $(this).find('first-name').text()
                              var lname = $(this).find('last-name').text()
                              var marks = $(this).find('marks').text()
                              stud+="<tr><td>"+roll+"</td><td>"+fname+"
                              "+lname+"</td><td>"+marks+"</td></tr>";
                        });
                        stud+="</table>";
                        $('#message').append(stud);
```

```
            }
        });
        return false;
    });
});
```

How It Works

You start by attaching a mousedown (i.e., the mouse click event to the Submit button), and you then invoke the request through the ajax() method, where you specify that the method of request that you are going to use is GET and the URL of the XML file on the server is student.xml. You also assert that the value of the dataType key is set to XML to signal that the URL contains the data in XML form.

The information loaded from the XML file (which is assumed to be present on the server) is returned to the JavaScript file in the form of response generated from the server, and is received in the parameter of the callback function. Here sturec is an array of objects, where each element contains following tags: <school>, <student>, <roll>, <name>, <first-name>, <last-name>, <address>, <street>, <city>, <state>, and <marks>. These correspond to the tags in an XML file.

You initialize a variable and assign it a <ul> tag because you want to send the response (the students' first names) to the web page in the form of an unordered list. The information received in sturec contains several tags and you want to return only the contents in the <first-name> tag to the web page, in the form of list items.

So, you first find the <student> tag in sturec and use the each() method to parse each student record in sturec one by one. In the <student> tag, search for the <first-name> tag, and its text is retrieved and stored in the name variable. The upshot of this is that the text in the <first-name> tag is extracted for each student. The first name is nested between the <li> and </li> tags to make them appear as list items, having been concatenated in the stud variable. Finally, you assign the contents in the stud variable to the div element of the message for display.

As usual, you return false in the click event to suppress the default browser click behavior. You want that event to take action on specified via the jQuery code and not by its default action. On execution, the web page initially displays the paragraph element and a Submit button, as shown in Figure 10-20.

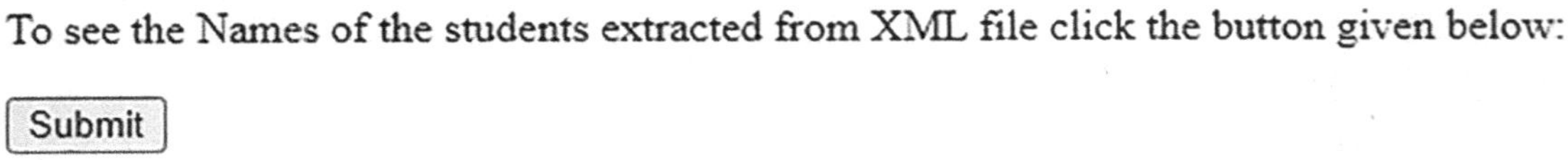

To see the Names of the students extracted from XML file click the button given below:

Submit

Figure 10-20. *Initial web page with text message and a Submit button to import XML contents*

On selecting the Submit button, the first names of all the students (in the XML file) are displayed in the form of list items, as shown in Figure 10-21.

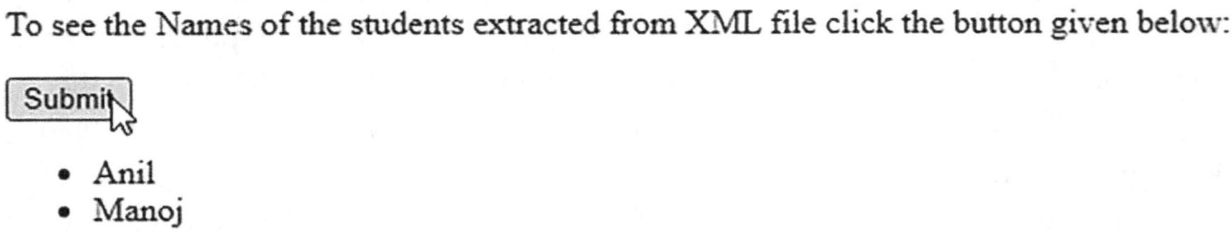

To see the Names of the students extracted from XML file click the button given below:

- Anil
- Manoj

Figure 10-21. *The contents of first-name tag of XML file imported in the form of list items*

When you modified the code, also, the content text from <roll>, <first-name>, <last-name> and <marks> tags are retrieved and nested inside <tr> and <td> tags to make them appear in the form of a table. On execution, you get the roll numbers, first and last names, and marks of all students in the form of a table, as shown in Figure 10-22.

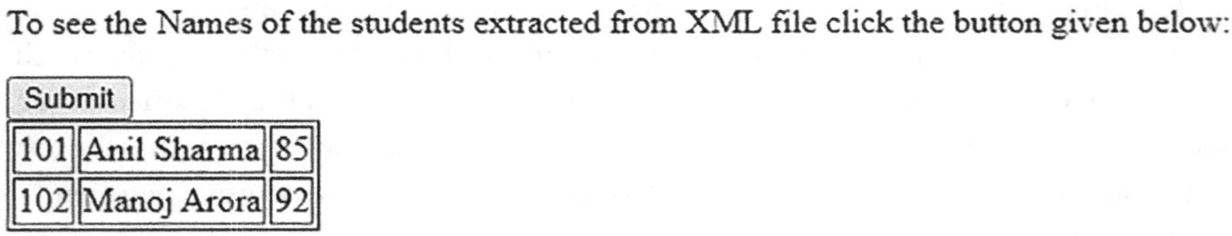

To see the Names of the students extracted from XML file click the button given below:

Submit

| 101 | Anil Sharma | 85 |
| 102 | Manoj Arora | 92 |

Figure 10-22. *The tags: roll, first-name, last-name, and marks imported from XML file in the form of the table*

10-13. Paginating Tables
Problem

You want to retrieve some student information from a table from a MySQL server, and you want to display them pagewise. You've been asked to display five records per page.

Solution

You'll begin by creating an HTML file that contains an empty div element message that displays the student records table pagewise. The HTML file should appear as follows.

paginatingtable.html

```
<!DOCTYPE html PUBLIC "-//W3C//DTD XHTML 1.0 Transitional//EN"
        "http://www.w3.org/TR/xhtml1/DTD/xhtml1-transitional.dtd">
<html xmlns="http://www.w3.org/1999/xhtml" xml:lang="en" lang="en">
  <head>
    <meta http-equiv="Content-Type" content="text/html; charset=utf-8"/>
    <title></title>
    <link rel="stylesheet" href="stylepaginating.css" type="text/css"
    media="screen" />
    <script src="jquery-3.5.1.js" type="text/javascript"></script>
    <script src="paginatingtablejq.js" type="text/javascript"></script>
  </head>
  <body>
    <div id="message"></div>
  </body>
</html>
```

The following is the jQuery code to divide the rows of the table in pages, with five rows per page, and display the respective rows when a page number is clicked.

paginatingtablejq.js

```
$(document).ready(function() {
    $.ajax({
        type:"POST",
        url:"getusersrec.php",
```

```
    success:function(html) {
        $('#message').html(html);
        var rows=$('table').find('tbody tr').length;
        var no_rec_per_page=5;
        var no_pages=Math.ceil(rows/no_rec_per_page);
        var $pagenumbers=$('<div id="pages"></div>');
        for(i=0;i<no_pages;i++)
        {
            $('<span class="page">'+(i+1)+'</span>').
            appendTo($pagenumbers);
        }
        $pagenumbers.insertBefore('table');
        $('.page').hover(function(){
            $(this).addClass('hover');
        }, function(){
            $(this).removeClass('hover');
        });
        $('table').find('tbody tr').hide();
        var tr=$('table tbody tr');
        for(var i=0;i<=no_rec_per_page-1;i++)
        {
            $(tr[i]).show();
        }
        $('span').click(function(event){
            $('table').find('tbody tr').hide();
            for(i=($(this).text()-1)*no_rec_per_page;i<=$(this).
            text()*no_rec_per_page-1;i++)
            {
                $(tr[i]).show();
            }
        });
    }
});
});
```

You can see that you are invoking the request through the ajax() method, in which you specify that the method of request is POST and the URL of the server-side script file is getstudrec.php. The response generated from that server-side script file—all the student records—is returned to the JavaScript file and received in the HTML parameter of the callback function. You then assign the server response (HTML) to the div element message for display. The following is the code for the getusersrec.php script file.

getusersrec.php

```php
<?php
    $connect = mysqli_connect("localhost", "root", "gold123", "jquerydb");
    if(!$connect){
        die('Please, check your server connection.');
    }
    $query = "SELECT user_name, password, email_address from users";
    $results = mysqli_query($connect, $query);
    if($results)
    {
        echo '<table border="1">';
        echo '<thead>';
        echo '<tr><th>User Name</th><th>Password</th><th>Email Address
        </th></tr>';
        echo '</thead>';
        echo '<tbody>';
        while ($row = mysqli_fetch_array($results,MYSQLI_ASSOC)) {
            extract($row);
            echo '<tr><td>' . $user_name . '</td><td>' . $password .
            '</td><td>' . $email_address . '</td></tr>';
        }
        echo '</tbody>';
        echo '</table>';
    }
?>
```

To apply a hover effect to the page numbers and assign spacing around those page numbers, you need to define two style rules in the style sheet file, as follows.

stylepaginating.css

```
.hover { background-color: #00f; color: #fff; }
.page{ margin:5px; }
```

How It Works

In the server-side script, you begin by connecting to the MySQL server and selecting the jquerydb database. You then write an SQL query to retrieve all users' username, password, and email address from the users table. You then execute the SQL query, and the rows returned by the table as an outcome of the query are stored in the $results array.

The hover style rule contains the background-color and color properties set to the #00f and #fff values, respectively, to turn the background color of the hovered page number to blue and its foreground color to white. The page style rule contains the margin property set to value 5px to create the space of 5px among page numbers.

In the jQuery code itself, you invoke the request through the ajax() method, where you specify that the method of request that you are going to use is POST and the URL of the server-side script is getusersrec.php. The response generated by the server-side script file is returned to the JavaScript file and received in the HTML parameter of the callback function. Note here that HTML is an array of users rows, so it is a table of users records (containing user data regarding their user name, password, and email address).

The response generated by the server-side script is assigned to the div element message for displaying the table of records on the screen. To do so, you count the number of rows (tr elements nested inside the tbody element) and store the count in variable rows. Assume that you want to see five rows per page, and you initialize the value of the no_rec_per_page variable equal to 5.

You find out the total count of the page numbers by dividing the total count of the rows by the number of records that you want to see per page. The count of the pages is assigned to the no_pages variable. You define the div element page and assign it to the $pagenumbers variable. Then with the help of a for loop, you create few span elements (equal to the number of pages) that contain the sequence of page numbers (so 1,2,3...), and the span element is assigned the name page class so that the style properties defined in the selector page class be automatically applied to all the page numbers. Finally, all the span elements containing the page numbers are appended to the div element of id pages. You insert the div element pages stored in $pagenumbers variable before the table element so that the page numbers appear above the table.

In the hover event to the page numbers (span element of pages class) you'll see that you highlight the page numbers when the mouse pointer moves over them by manipulating the properties defined in the hover style rule, which apply to the page numbers. Change the background and foreground colors to blue and white, respectively, in that event. When there is no hover, you remove those style properties and the associated visual effect.

You then hide all the rows (that is, tr elements nested inside the tbody element) of the table, keeping only the column headings visible, and retrieve all the rows of the table and store them in tr variable. Remember, tr is an array containing all the table rows, so you use the for loop to display the first five rows of the table.

Attach the click event to the span elements so that all the table's page numbers and hidden rows are displayed, leaving only the column headings. Finally, you display the rows that fall within the page number that the user clicks, using the tr array. On execution, you get the first five rows of the table and page numbers at the top, as shown in Figure 10-23.

1 2		
User Name	Password	Email Address
anu	anu707	anu@gmail.com
bekky	bekky123	bekky@yahoo.com
ben	ben777	ben@gmail.com
bintu	gold123	bintu@yahoo.com
bittu	bitty555	bittu@yahoo.com

Figure 10-23. *A table displayed along with page numbers at the top*

10-14. Summary

In this chapter, you learned how AJAX gets the processing been done asynchronously behind the scene. You learned to return single lines and multiples lines of text from the server. You also learned to return a name/value pair using JSON, return JSON objects from the server that contains the text, and the JSON object that displays images. You also learned to convert the case of a string using AJAX, display the price of the selected product, and authenticate a user using AJAX.

The next chapter focuses on creating a plugin, making a plugin chainable, and passing customization options to a plugin. You also learn to use built-in plugins like the Magnific Popup plugin, iCheck plugin, blueimp Gallery plugin, and the validation plugin to make image sliders, format checkboxes and radio buttons, and validate a form.

CHAPTER 11

Creating and Using jQuery Plugins

jQuery plugins make functions portable and easy to integrate with any number of projects, hence implementing reusability. In this chapter, you learn to create jQuery plugins from scratch and how to use some popular jQuery plugins. You learn how to do the following with the recipes in this chapter.

- Create a plugin that changes the font size, font style, and foreground and background color of an element, and make the plugin chainable

- Enable passing customization options to a plugin

- Modify content using a plugin

- Display an images slider using the Magnific Popup plugin

- Display dynamic checkboxes and radio buttons using the iCheck plugin

- Create an image gallery and carousel using the blueimp Gallery plugin

- Validate a form using the jQuery validation plugin

Creating a Plugin

A plugin is code written in a standard JavaScript file that provides certain jQuery methods that can be directly applied along with the jQuery library methods. The plugin is written so that it can be easily reused in the code. Hence, you write once and benefit multiple times. The following are the rules for creating plugins.

- All the methods inside a plugin must end with a semicolon (;).

533

© Bintu Harwani 2022
B. Harwani, *jQuery Recipes*, https://doi.org/10.1007/978-1-4842-7304-3_11

- The method must return the jQuery object unless explicitly noted otherwise.

- The keyword this.each must iterate over the matching elements.

- The plugin filename must be prefixed with jQuery with extension .js.

The following is the syntax for naming the jQuery plugins.

```
jquery.plugin_name.js
```

Minified versions are represented by adding a min as shown.

```
jquery.plugin_name.min.js
```

Note   Using the jquery prefix while naming the created plugins eliminates the name collisions with other libraries.

You can increase jQuery features by adding functions to the prototype. To do this, you need to expose the jQuery prototype. The jQuery prototype is exposed through jQuery.fn. In other words, the simplest way to create a plugin is by using the fn property. In jQuery, the fn property is a simple alias for the prototype property of the jquery.fn function.

Syntax

```
jQuery.fn = jQuery.prototype = {
        jquery code;
}
```

Adding functions to this prototype enables those functions to be called and used from any constructed jQuery object. A constructed jQuery object holds an array of elements based on the selector that is used. For example, $('p') constructs a jQuery object that holds <p> elements.

11-1. Creating a Plugin That Changes the Font Size, Font Style, and Foreground and Background Color of an Element

Problem

You want to create a plugin that, when applied to any HTML element, must set its font size to 25px, change its font style to italics and change its foreground and background color to red and yellow, respectively.

Solution

To apply and test the plugin, let's create an HTML file that sells few products. The following HTML code displays two products for sale, Mobiles and Laptops, via two <p> elements. Both the <p> elements are wrapped inside the <div> element as follows.

Crplugin1.html

```
<!DOCTYPE html PUBLIC "-//W3C//DTD XHTML 1.0 Transitional//EN"
        "http://www.w3.org/TR/xhtml1/DTD/xhtml1-transitional.dtd">

<html xmlns="http://www.w3.org/1999/xhtml" xml:lang="en" lang="en">
  <head>
    <meta http-equiv="Content-Type" content="text/html; charset=utf-8"/>
    <title></title>
    <script src="jquery-3.5.1.js" type="text/javascript"></script>
    <script src="jquery.crplugin1.js" type="text/javascript"></script>
    <script src="crplugin1jq.js" type="text/javascript"></script>
  </head>
  <body>
    <div> We deal with variety of products:
        <p>Mobiles</p>
        <p>Laptops</p>
    </div>
  </body>
</html>
```

You can see that a <div> element is defined with certain text. Nested inside the <div> elements are the two <p> elements that show the text indicating the product names to which you apply the plugin effect.

The following is the jQuery code that creates a plugin with a function named, style_ products.

Jquery.crplugin1.js

```
$.fn.style_products = function() {
    this.css({ fontSize: "25px",
        color: "red",
    "font-style": "italic",
    background: "yellow" });
};
```

Remember that the "this" keyword within the plugin function represents the constructed jQuery object that the function is called on. The plugin function is applying CSS style attributes to the jQuery object. The object's font size is set to 25 px, its foreground color is set to red, its font style is set to italic, and its background color is set to yellow.

The following is the jQuery code to apply the plugin's method to the <p> elements of the HTML file.

```
Crplugin1jq.js
$(document).ready(function() {
    $("p").style_products();
});
```

When $("p").style_products() is invoked, the value of "this" refers to the jQuery object containing all the <p> elements on the page. As a result, the font size of both product names is 25px, the font style is italic, the background color is yellow, and the color of the text is red, as shown in Figure 11-1.

We deal with variety of products:

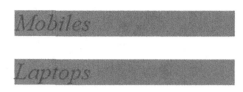

Figure 11-1. *The font size of both the product names has become 25px, font style has become italic, and their background color has turned to yellow, and the foreground color has become red*

11-2. Making a Plugin Chainable

To give a jQuery plugin the ability to be used in real examples, it needs to support *chaining*, which means the capability to apply other functions. To do so, the plugin's function must return the original jQuery object, as follows.

Jquery.crplugin1.js

```
$.fn.style_products = function() {
    this.css({ fontSize: "25px",
        color: "red",
    "font-style": "italic",
    background: "yellow" });
    return this;
};
```

The last statement, "return this;" returns the original jQuery object.

To demonstrate the application of chaining on the selected element, let's create a CSS style sheet containing the enlarge style class called, as follows.

Crplugin1style.css

```
.enlarge{
    width: 100px;
    height: 100px;
}
```

You can see that the enlarge style class contains two properties—width and height, and both the properties are set to a value of 100px.

To apply and see the effect of chaining, modify the jQuery code, crplugin1jq.js as follows.

```
$(document).ready(function() {
    $("p").style_products().addClass("enlarge");
});
```

You can see that because of the application of chaining on the selected <p> element, the style_products() method of the jQuery plugin is applied, and then the enlarge too is applied on the <p> elements. By applying the style_products() method, the font size of both the product names is set to 25px, their font style is set to italics, and the background color of the text is set to yellow text color is set to red. By applying enlarge style class, the width and height of the <p> element containing the product names are set to 100px, as shown in Figure 11-2.

We deal with variety of products:

Figure 11-2. *After setting font size, font style, background and foreground color, the width and height of the product names is set to 100px*

11-3. Enabling Passing Customization Options to a Plugin

Problem

You want to create a plugin and want to pass different customization options to it.

Solution

Sometimes, you want a plugin to be customizable (i.e., the user can change or modify its certain default values). In this recipe, you create a plugin method, define its default options, and overwrite them with the options passed by the user (i.e., passing different customization options to the plugin, making it reusable on different selectors). To create a customizable plugin, jQuery provides an $.extend utility method that creates a plugin and hence helps in enhancing jQuery features.

To apply desired options on HTML element via customizable plugin, let's create an HTML file. The following is the HTML code that defines a <div> element and within the <div> element, two <p> elements are defined as follows.

Crplugin1b.html

```
<!DOCTYPE html PUBLIC "-//W3C//DTD XHTML 1.0 Transitional//EN"
        "http://www.w3.org/TR/xhtml1/DTD/xhtml1-transitional.dtd">

<html xmlns="http://www.w3.org/1999/xhtml" xml:lang="en" lang="en">
  <head>
    <meta http-equiv="Content-Type" content="text/html; charset=utf-8"/>
    <title></title>
    <script src="jquery-3.5.1.js" type="text/javascript"></script>
    <script src="jquery.crplugin1b.js" type="text/javascript"></script>
    <script src="crplugin1bjq.js" type="text/javascript"></script>
  </head>
  <body>
    <div> We deal with variety of products:
        <p id="phone">Mobiles</p>
```

```
      <p id="computer">Laptops</p>
    </div>
  </body>
</html>
```

You can see that a <div> element is defined to display a message, indicating the type of products sold on this site. The two <p> elements are defined to display the two products sold on the site, Mobiles and Laptops. Because, on one <p> element, you want to apply the plugin function with default options, and on another <p> element, you want to apply the plugin function with the options supplied by the user, different ids, "phone" and "computer" are assigned to the two <p> elements.

The following shows the jQuery plugin code with the style_products method. The method contains the default values for the properties and applies the values to the properties if the user provides them.

Jquery.crplugin1b.js

```
(function ($) {
$.fn.style_products = function(custom) {
    var settings = $.extend({
        fontSize: "15px",
        color : "white",
        fontStyle: "bold",
        background : "blue"
    }, custom);
    return this.css({
        fontSize: settings.fontSize,
        color: settings.color,
        fontStyle: settings.fontStyle,
        background: settings.background
    });
};
}(jQuery));
```

You can see in the code that the default settings specify the font size as 15px, the font style as bold, and the background and text color as blue and white, respectively. If the user provides any of the property values (i.e., font size, color, font style, or background color), the default values of the property are overridden by the ones designated by the user.

The following is the jQuery code to invoke the default and customizable function of the plugin.

Crplugin1bjq.js

```
$(document).ready(function() {
    $("#computer").style_products();
    $("#phone").style_products({
        fontSize: "25px",
            color: "red",
        fontStyle: "italic",
        background: "yellow"
    });
});
```

The method can be called to apply the default properties and apply the customized properties as well. The first statement in the code invokes the style_products method of the plugin. The default properties are applied on the elements with the computer id (i.e., the Laptops text appears in bold white with a font size of 15 px, and the background color is blue). To see how the user can supply customized values in the properties, the style_products() method is invoked on the <p> element with the phone id. For the Mobiles text, the properties with values designated by the user are applied. As a result, the Mobiles text is in red italics with a font size of 25px, and the background color is yellow (see Figure 11-3).

Figure 11-3. *By application of properties, the text Mobiles appears in font size 25px, in italic font style and yellow background and the text in red color. Laptops is in font size 15 px, bold style, with blue background and white text color*

Modifying Content Using a Plugin

You can override the style properties of any HTML element using a plugin. For example, you can change or append the text (i.e., the content of the HTML elements can be modified through a plugin).

To append text to any of the HTML element, the plugin's method is modified as follows.

Jquery.crplugin1b.js

```
(function ($) {
$.fn.style_products = function(custom) {
    var settings = $.extend({
        product_name: 'Refrigerators',
        fontSize: "15px",
        color : "white",
        fontStyle: "bold",
        background : "blue"
    }, custom);
    return this.append(", "+settings.product_name).css({
        fontSize: settings.fontSize,
            color: settings.color,
        fontStyle: settings.fontStyle,
        background: settings.background
    });
};
}(jQuery));
```

You can see a user-defined property, product_name is set to a default value, Refrigerators; The user can always change its default value by providing the desired value of this property. When returning the "this" jQuery object, you append a comma (,) and the value assigned to the product_name property. As a result, the "Refrigerators" text is appended to the HTML element to which the plugin method is applied.

You have two <p> elements in the HTML file, so to one <p> element, you apply the plugin method with default values, and to the second <p> element, you apply the plugin method with user's values. By doing so, you can see the effect of the plugin method on the default options and the user's values.

The following is the jQuery code to apply the plugin method with default options and with customized options.

Crplugin1bjq.js

```
$(document).ready(function() {
    $("#computer").style_products();
    $("#phone").style_products({
        product_name:'AirConditioners',
        fontSize: "25px",
            color: "red",
        fontStyle: "italic",
        background: "yellow"
    });
});
```

The style_products method is applied to the <p> element with the computer id without providing the value of any property. As a result, the style_products() method uses the default values for its properties. "Refrigerators" is appended to the text of the <p> element with the computer id (i.e. "Laptops" is modified to "Laptops, Refrigerators"), as shown in Figure 11-4.

The user provided the AirConditioners value as the product_name property. "AirConditioners" is appended to the text of <p> element with the phone id. Consequently, the paragraph text displays as Mobiles, AirConditioners (see Figure 11-4).

We deal with variety of products:

Figure 11-4. *The text is modified to "Laptops, Refrigerators" and the "AirConditioners" is appended to "Mobiles"*

Using Plugins

jQuery has a large repository of plugins at `https://plugins.jquery.com`. Most of these plugins contain links to demos, examples, code, and documentation. The plugins mentioned in this registry are all managed in the GitHub (`http://github.com`) code repository. GitHub tracks the popularity of the plugins. I demonstrate the quickest way of using a few plugins and use a few of their methods. I suggest you refer to the official documentation for the plugin discussed here for complete coverage.

It is quite simple to use a plugin in code: download and unzip it. Copy the plugin's .js and .css files to your site's folder. Once you have the plugin in your site's directory, you can reference it on your web page. Make sure you refer to the plugin after the main jQuery source file and before the jQuery scripts that invoke the plugin.

11-4. Displaying Images Slider Using a Magnific Popup Plugin

The Magnific Popup was developed by Dmitry Semenov. It is a very light and mobile-friendly lightbox and a modal dialog plugin that focuses on optimum performance and the best experience for users with any device (for jQuery or Zepto.js). Images, videos, Google maps, and photo galleries can be displayed with animation effects with this plugin. You can find complete information on the Magnific Popup at `https://plugins.jquery.com/magnific-popup/`. The page shows the links for demo, download, documentation, the home page, and so on. Click the "Download now" link to download the code. A code bundle in zip format is downloaded to your computer. Unzip the file. From the dist folder, copy the jquery.magnific-popup.js and magnific-popup.css files to your site's folder.

Problem

You want to display certain images and videos in the form of an image slider using the Magnific Popup plugin.

Solution

You are learning to make an image slider using the Magnific Popup plugin step by step. First, make a small image popup of a single image, then you increase images. Finally, you learn to make a complete image slider that not only displays images but videos too.

The simplest example of using the Magnific Popup plugin is to display a hyperlink that opens the associated image with animation.

The following is the HTML code to display a hyperlink pointing to an image file.

Usingpopup.html

```
<!DOCTYPE html PUBLIC "-//W3C//DTD XHTML 1.0 Transitional//EN"
        "http://www.w3.org/TR/xhtml1/DTD/xhtml1-transitional.dtd">

<html xmlns="http://www.w3.org/1999/xhtml" xml:lang="en" lang="en">
  <head>
    <meta http-equiv="Content-Type" content="text/html; charset=utf-8"/>
    <title></title>
    <script src="jquery-3.5.1.js" type="text/javascript"></script>
    <link rel="stylesheet" href="magnific-popup.css">
    <script src="jquery.magnific-popup.js"></script>
    <script src="usingpopupjq.js" type="text/javascript"></script>
  </head>
  <body>
<a class="test-popup-link" href="images/chip.jpg">Open popup</a>
  </body>
</html>
```

You can see that the CSS style sheet supplied by the magnific-popup.css plugin is included in the HTML code along with the jquery.magnific-popup.js file. Also, you can see that a "Open popup" hyperlink is created; it points to a chip.jpg in the images folder. The <a> element is assigned the test-popup-link class to be accessible in the jQuery code and auto-apply the CSS styles mentioned in the plugin's magnific-popup.css file.

Note   I used images in this program. Don't forget to copy the images folder supplied with the book's code bundle to your site's folder.

The following is the jQuery code to apply the plugin methods to the hyperlink defined in HTML file.

Usingpopupjq.js

```
$(document).ready(function() {
        $('.test-popup-link').magnificPopup({
            type: 'image'
        });
});
```

You can see that to the hyperlink with the test-popup-link class, the plugin's magnificPopup() method is applied with the "type" property set to the "image" value. As a result, an "Open popup" link appears on the web page, as shown in Figure 11-5(a). When the user clicks the hyperlink, the linked image pops up in a dialog box with a Close button in the top right (see Figure 11-5(b)).

Open popup

(a)

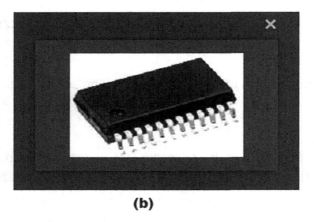

(b)

Figure 11-5. *(a) The Open popup link appears on the web page. (b) The linked image pops up as a dialog box*

If you want to display two or more images, you need to create hyperlinks for each that point to its respective image. The following is the HTML code to do this.

Usingpopup.html

```
<!DOCTYPE html PUBLIC "-//W3C//DTD XHTML 1.0 Transitional//EN"
         "http://www.w3.org/TR/xhtml1/DTD/xhtml1-transitional.dtd">

<html xmlns="http://www.w3.org/1999/xhtml" xml:lang="en" lang="en">
  <head>
    <meta http-equiv="Content-Type" content="text/html; charset=utf-8"/>
    <title></title>
    <script src="jquery-3.5.1.js" type="text/javascript"></script>
    <link rel="stylesheet" href="magnific-popup.css">
    <script src="jquery.magnific-popup.js"></script>
    <script src="usingpopupjq.js" type="text/javascript"></script>
  </head>
  <body>
    <div class="parent-container">
            <a href="images/chip.jpg">Preprocessor Chip</a>
          <a href="images/chip2.jpg">RISC chip</a>
          <a href="images/chip3.jpg">CISC chip</a>
      </div>
  </body>
</html>
```

You can see in the HTML code that three hyperlinks are defined, each pointing to its respective image that is placed in the images folder. All the three hyperlinks are nested inside the <div> element, and to make the <div> element and its hyperlinks accessible by the plugin methods, the <div> element is assigned the parent-container: class.

To apply the plugin's method to the <div> element containing the hyperlinks, the jQuery code is modified as follows.

Usingpopupjq.js

```
$(document).ready(function() {
        $('.parent-container').magnificPopup({
            delegate: 'a', // by clicking on it popup will open
            type: 'image'
        });
});
```

You can see in the jQuery code, that to the <div> element of the parent-container: class, the magnificPopup method is applied with the delegate property set to 'a,' and "type" property set to the "image" value.

As a result, the three hyperlinks appear on the screen at the top left corner of the browser window. Each hyperlink opens the respective image it is pointing at (see Figure 11-6(a)). Clicking a hyperlink displays its image in a popup window with a Close button in the top right, as shown in Figure 11-6(b). On closing the dialog box, the focus is back to the hyperlinks, where you can click any other hyperlink to see the image associated with it.

Preprocessor Chip RISC chip CISC chip

(a)

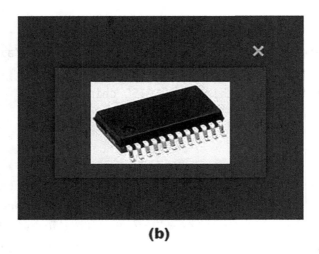

(b)

Figure 11-6. *(a) Three hyperlinks appear at the top left corner of the screen (b) Clicking a hyperlink displays its image in a popup*

In the earlier program, clicking a hyperlink made the associated image display in a popup dialog, which you could close. On closing the dialog, you were able to click another hyperlink to see another image. Now let's look at adding Next and Previous buttons to the popup dialog so that you can navigate to any image easily.

Let's assume that you want to display two image galleries. The first image gallery displays two images. The second image gallery displays two images and a video. The HTML code is modified as follows.

Usingpopup.html

```
<!DOCTYPE html PUBLIC "-//W3C//DTD XHTML 1.0 Transitional//EN"
        "http://www.w3.org/TR/xhtml1/DTD/xhtml1-transitional.dtd">

  <html xmlns="http://www.w3.org/1999/xhtml" xml:lang="en" lang="en">
  <head>
    <meta http-equiv="Content-Type" content="text/html; charset=utf-8"/>
    <title></title>
    <script src="jquery-3.5.1.js" type="text/javascript"></script>
    <link rel="stylesheet" href="magnific-popup.css">
    <script src="jquery.magnific-popup.js"></script>
    <script src="usingpopupjq.js" type="text/javascript"></script>
  </head>
  <body>
    <div class="gallery">
            <a href="images/chip.jpg">Preprocessor Chip (gallery #1)</a>
            <a href="images/chip2.jpg">RISC chip (gallery #1)</a>
    </div>
    <div class="gallery">
            <a href="images/chip3.jpg">CISC chip (gallery #2)</a>
            <a href="images/chip4.jpg">EPIC chip (gallery #2)</a>
            <a href="http://bmharwani.com/videos/01javafirstlecturesample
            inenglish.mp4" class="mfp-iframe">Open my video</a>
    </div>
  </body>
</html>
```

You can see that two <div> elements are defined and each is assigned the gallery class, which is assigned to auto apply the respective CSS styles mentioned in the attached CSS style sheet make to the <div> elements and to make them accessible in jQuery code. The first <div> element encloses the two hyperlinks pointing at the two images to be displayed in the first image gallery. The second <div> element encloses three hyperlinks where the first two hyperlinks point at the two images and the third hyperlink points at the video to be displayed in the image gallery.

The following is the code to display the galleries that show the images and videos that can navigate to the next or previous image or video.

Usingpopjq.js

```
$(document).ready(function() {
        $('.gallery').each(function() { // the containers for all your
                                            galleries
            $(this).magnificPopup({
                    delegate: 'a', // the selector for gallery item
                    type: 'image',
                    gallery: {
                            enabled:true
                    }
            });
    });
});
```

In the jQuery code, you can see that the <div> elements in the gallery class are selected. In each of them, the statements in the callback functions are executed. In the callback function, the magnificPopup method is invoked on the <div> element with the delegate property set to value, 'a', type property set to value, image, and the gallery property with its enabled element set to true. As a result, the hyperlinks in the two div elements appear in two lines on the top left border of the web page, as shown in Figure 11-7(a). You can click any link of any gallery whose image you want to pop up. After clicking an image's hyperlink, it opens as a popup, as shown in Figure 11-7(b). You can see a Close button on the top right corner of the dialog that enables you to close the image gallery and go back to the hyperlinks at the top. Also, you can see the Next and Previous arrows on the right and left sides of the image. Using these arrows, you can navigate to other images in the gallery. Figure 11-7(c) shows the output showing how the video appears in the gallery. Clicking the Next button on the last image/video displays the first image/video. Similarly, clicking the Previous button on the first image/video displays the last image or video.

Preprocessor Chip (gallery #1) RISC chip (gallery #1)

CISC chip (gallery #2) EPIC chip (gallery #2) Open my video

(a)

(b)

(c)

Figure 11-7. *(a) The hyperlinks mentioned in the two div elements appear in two lines at the top left corner. (b) The image opens in the popup by clicking its link in the gallery. (c) The video appears in the gallery*

So far, you've seen images in a popup dialog and a gallery. Next, you learn to zoom an image when it is clicked. To display a thumbnail of an image, the HTML code is modified as follows.

Usingpopup.html

```
<!DOCTYPE html PUBLIC "-//W3C//DTD XHTML 1.0 Transitional//EN"
        "http://www.w3.org/TR/xhtml1/DTD/xhtml1-transitional.dtd">

<html xmlns="http://www.w3.org/1999/xhtml" xml:lang="en" lang="en">
  <head>
    <meta http-equiv="Content-Type" content="text/html; charset=utf-8"/>
```

551

```
<title></title>
<script src="jquery-3.5.1.js" type="text/javascript"></script>
<link rel="stylesheet" href="magnific-popup.css">
<script src="jquery.magnific-popup.js"></script>
<script src="usingpopupjq.js" type="text/javascript"></script>
</head>
<body>
  <a href="images/chip3.jpg" class="image-link">
        <img src="images/chip3thumnail.jpg" />
  </a>
</body>
</html>
```

You can see that a hyperlink is created that shows a thumbnail of an image. The filename of the thumbnail is chip3thumnail.jpg. The hyperlink is linked to the zoomed version of the image via chip3.jpg. To apply CSS styles and make it accessible in jQuery code, the hyperlink is assigned the image-link class.

The following is the jQuery code to display the larger version of an image in a popup when its thumbnail is clicked.

Usingpopupjq.js

```
$(document).ready(function() {
      $('.image-link').magnificPopup({
          type: 'image',
          mainClass: 'mfp-with-zoom', // this class is for CSS animation
                                        below

          zoom: {
                  enabled: true, // By default it's false, so don't forget
                                    to enable it
                  duration: 300, // duration of the effect, in milliseconds
                  easing: 'ease-in-out', // CSS transition easing function
                  opener: function(openerElement) {
                          return openerElement.is('img') ? openerElement :
                          openerElement.find('img');
```

```
                    }
              }
    });
});
```

You can see that the hyperlink with the image-link class is selected, and the plugin method, magnificPopup is applied to it with the type property set to image. The mainClass property is set to mfp-with-zoom to apply animation while zooming the image. The zoom property is set with its enabled element set to true, the animation duration is set to 300ms, the easing transition is set to ease-in-out. The opener property is set to point at a function that returns a Boolean value, true if the operations are applied on an img element.

When the application runs, a thumbnail image is shown (see Figure 11-8(a)). Clicking the thumbnail displays a larger version in a popup, as shown in Figure 11-8(b).

(a)

(b)

Figure 11-8. *(a) A thumbnail image appears. (b) Clicking the thumbnail displays its zoomed version in a popup*

11-5. Displaying Dynamic Checkboxes and Radio Buttons Using an iCheck Plugin

iCheck is a jQuery plugin developed by Damir Sultanov. It provides highly customizable checkboxes and radio buttons. There are identical checkboxes and radio buttons across different browsers and devices, whether mobile or desktop machines. These inputs also work on touch devices like iOS, Android, BlackBerry, Windows Phone, and Amazon Kindle. It supports jQuery and Zepto and provides 32 options to customize checkboxes and radio buttons, 11 callbacks to handle changes, nine methods to make changes programmatically, and much more.

You can find complete information of iCheck plugin at `https://plugins.jquery.com/icheck/`. The page shows the links for demo, download, documentation, the home page, and so on. Click the "Download now" link to download the code. A code bundle in zip format is downloaded to your computer. Unzip the file and copy the icheck.js file to your site's folder. From the skins subfolder, copy the minimal, futurico, and line folders into your site's folder. These folders contain the CSS styles that apply styles to the checkboxes and radio buttons.

Problem

You want to display a web page that displays few food items and the method of payment. Users can select any number of food items and the payment method. Because the user might select more than one food item, so food items are displayed via checkboxes. Because only one of the payment methods is chosen by the user, the payment method is displayed through radio buttons. You make these checkboxes and radio buttons look dynamic by applying the iCheck plugin.

Solution

You want to display three food items and two payment methods options. The following is the HTML code to display three checkboxes and two radio buttons.

Usingicheck.html

```
<!DOCTYPE html PUBLIC "-//W3C//DTD XHTML 1.0 Transitional//EN"
        "http://www.w3.org/TR/xhtml1/DTD/xhtml1-transitional.dtd">
```

```html
<html xmlns="http://www.w3.org/1999/xhtml" xml:lang="en" lang="en">
  <head>
    <meta http-equiv="Content-Type" content="text/html; charset=utf-8"/>
    <title></title>
    <link href="minimal/minimal.css" rel="stylesheet">
    <script src="jquery-3.5.1.js" type="text/javascript"></script>
    <script src="icheck.js" type="text/javascript"></script>
    <script src="usingicheckjq.js" type="text/javascript"></script>
  </head>
  <body>
    <p> Select your fast food item: </p>
      <label><input type="checkbox"  name="food" value="Pizza">Pizza
      </label><br/>
      <label><input type="checkbox" name="food" value="Hot Dog">Hot Dog
      </label><br/>
      <label><input type="checkbox"  name="food" value="Burger"
      checked>Burger</label><br/>
<p> Select the payment method: </p>
<form id="pay">
          <label><input type="radio" name="iCheck"  value="Payment By
          Card">Payment By Card</label><br/>
          <label><input type="radio" name="iCheck"   value="Payment By
          Cash" checked>Payment By Cash</label><br/>
</form><br/>
      <input type="button" id="btnSubmit" value="Submit" />
  </body>
</html>
```

The minimal.css file in the minimal folder is accessed to apply different CSS styles to the checkboxes and radio buttons. Also, the plugin's icheck.js file is included after the jQuery file.

A <p> element displays the "Select your fast-food item:" text. Below the paragraph element three pairs of <label> and <input> elements show three checkboxes. The three checkboxes are each named *food* and are assigned Pizza, Hot Dog, or Burger values, respectively. The checked property is applied to the Burger checkbox to make it appear as checked by default.

Radio buttons appear after the checkboxes. Another <p> element is defined, with the text, "Select the payment method:". Because only one radio button can be selected, both must be nested inside a <form> element. To access in jQuery code, the <form> element is assigned the id, pay. With the <form> element two pairs of <label> and <input> elements are defined to show radio buttons and their respective labels. Because the radio buttons are meant to display different payment methods, the value and label of the two radio buttons are set to Payment By Card and Payment By Cash, respectively. To access them in jQuery code, both radio buttons are assigned the name iCheck. Also, the checked property is applied on the second radio button as you want it selected by default. Finally, a Submit button is assigned to it.

The following is the jQuery code to apply different styles and other dimensions to the checkboxes and radio buttons.

Usingicheckjq.js

```
$(document).ready(function() {
    $('input').iCheck({
            checkboxClass: 'icheckbox_minimal',
            radioClass: 'iradio_minimal',
            increaseArea: '20%' // optional
    });
    $("#btnSubmit").click(function() {
       var selected = [];
                    $.each($("input[name='food']:checked"), function(){
                            selected.push($(this).val());
            });
            paymethod = $('input[name="iCheck"]:checked', '#pay').val();
            selected.push(paymethod)
            alert("Selected food items and pay method is: " +
            selected.join(", "));
    });
});
```

You can see that on all the input elements, the plugin's iCheck method is executed to apply the desired CSS styles to the radio buttons and checkboxes. When the button with id, btnSubmit is clicked. In other words, when the Submit button is clicked, the click event occurs. Its callback function is executed where the "selected" is defined. The values of all the checkboxes that are checked are pushed (i.e., added to the "selected" array). Whether Pizza, Hot Dog, or Burger is selected, its value is added to the "selected" array.

After observing all the checkboxes, the radio buttons are observed (i.e., all the input elements named iCheck are observed). If any of them is checked, its value is accessed and assigned to the paymethod variable. Recall, all the radio buttons are assigned the name iCheck. Whether the user checked the Payment By Card button or the Payment By Cash radio button, the respective payment method is assigned to the paymethod variable. The value in paymethod is pushed to the "selected" array, which means it has the food items selected by the user and the payment method chosen by the user.

When running the application, a screen asks you to select as many food items you want and choose either of the payment method, as shown in Figure 11-9(a). Whatever food items and payment method the user selects are stored in the "selected" array. Finally, all the information in the that array is displayed on the screen using the alert dialog box, as shown in Figure 11-9(b).

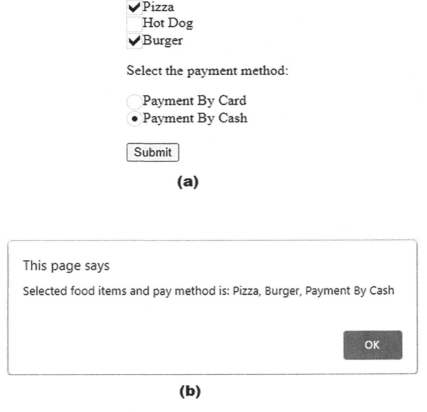

Figure 11-9. *(a) Screen to select the food items and either of the payment method appears. (b) Food items and payment method chosen is displayed via the alert dialog box*

In this HTML program, you used the minimal.css style sheet from the minimal folder. This iCheck plugin provides you many different CSS style sheets to make the checkboxes and radio buttons appear attractive and dynamic. You can use the futurico.css style sheet in the futurico folder in the HTML program. To do this, modify the statement in the HTML file to include the plugin's CSS style sheet.

```
<link href="futurico/futurico.css" rel="stylesheet">
```

To apply styles mentioned in the futurico.css file to the checkboxes and radio, you need to make changes in the jQuery file. Recall, in the jQuery code, the following two lines make use of minimal style classes.

```
checkboxClass: 'icheckbox_minimal',
radioClass: 'iradio_minimal',
```

To apply the futurico style classes instead of minimal style classes, modify the preceding two lines in the jQuery code as follows.

```
checkboxClass: 'icheckbox_futurico',
radioClass: 'iradio_futurico',
```

That's it. No other changes are required. On running the HTML program, you can see that the empty checkboxes are no longer white but black. Also, a checked checkbox is green. Similarly, the radio buttons are black. When selected, a radio button has a small green circle (see Figure 11-10).

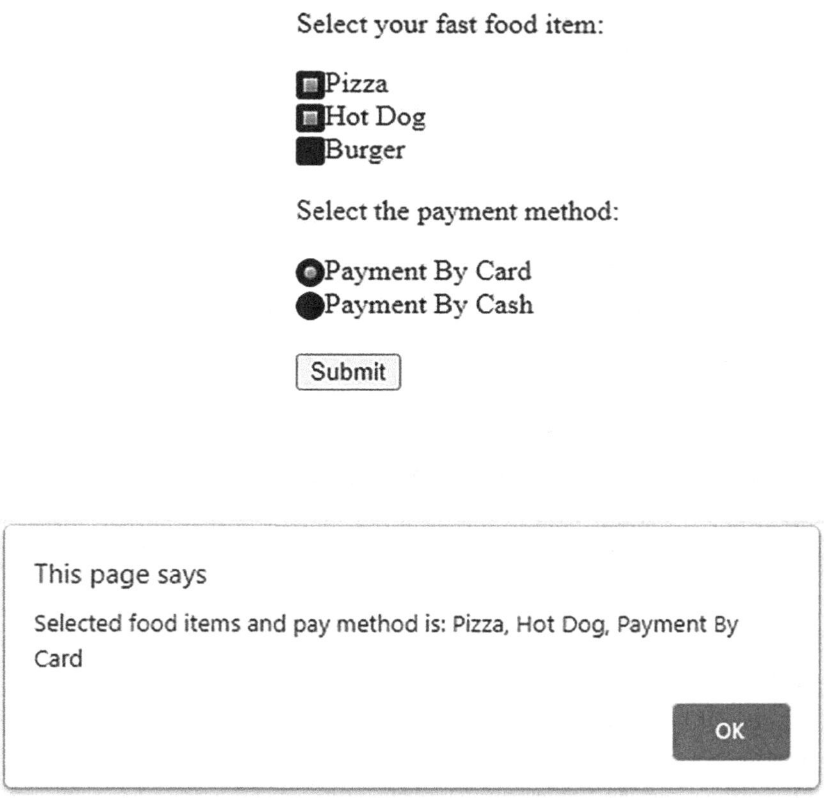

Select your fast food item:

☐Pizza
☐Hot Dog
■Burger

Select the payment method:

◉Payment By Card
●Payment By Cash

[Submit]

This page says

Selected food items and pay method is: Pizza, Hot Dog, Payment By
Card

OK

Figure 11-10. *The empty checkboxes are black color, and when checked, they are green. The radio buttons are black, and when selected, they include a small green circle*

The iCheck plugin also provides a CSS style sheet called line.css in the line folder, which usually takes the complete row to display a checkbox or a radio button. The checkbox and radio button labels share the same background (i.e., background color of the checkbox), and its label is the same. Similarly, the background color of the radio button and its label is the same. To apply the style classes properly, the <label> elements must be below the checkbox or radio button element (not the way you did earlier when the checkbox and radio buttons were nested inside the <label> elements). The following is the modified HTML code.

Usingicheck2.html

```
<!DOCTYPE html PUBLIC "-//W3C//DTD XHTML 1.0 Transitional//EN"
        "http://www.w3.org/TR/xhtml1/DTD/xhtml1-transitional.dtd">
```

```html
<html xmlns="http://www.w3.org/1999/xhtml" xml:lang="en" lang="en">
  <head>
    <meta http-equiv="Content-Type" content="text/html; charset=utf-8"/>
    <title></title>
    <link href="line/line.css" rel="stylesheet">
    <script src="jquery-3.5.1.js" type="text/javascript"></script>
    <script src="icheck.js" type="text/javascript"></script>
    <script src="usingicheck2jq.js" type="text/javascript"></script>
  </head>
  <body>
      <p> Select your fast food item: </p>
      <input type="checkbox"  name="food" value="Pizza">
      <label>Pizza</label><br/>
       <input type="checkbox" name="food" value="Hot Dog">
      <label>Hot Dog</label><br/>
       <input type="checkbox"  name="food" value="Burger" checked>
      <label>Burger</label><br/>
       <p> Select the payment method: </p>
       <form id="pay">
           <input type="radio" name="iCheck"  value="Payment By Card">
           <label>Payment By Card</label><br/>
           <input type="radio" name="iCheck"   value="Payment By Cash"
           checked>
           <label>Payment By Cash</label><br/>
       </form><br/>
       <input type="button" id="btnSubmit" value="Submit" />
  </body>
</html>
```

You can see in the HTML code that the <p> element displays the text asking the user to choose the desired food item. Also, notice that the <label> element follows the checkbox and radio button elements. The rest of the code is the same as the previous HTML code.

To apply the style classes mentioned in line.css style sheet file, the jQuery code has to be modified as follows.

Usingicheckjq.js

```
$(document).ready(function() {
    $('input').each(function(){
            var self = $(this),
              label = self.next(),
              label_text = label.text();

            label.remove();
            self.iCheck({
                    checkboxClass: 'icheckbox_line',
                    radioClass: 'iradio_line',
                    insert: '<div class="icheck_line-icon"></div>' + label_text
            });
    });
    $("#btnSubmit").click(function() {
        var selected = [];
                    $.each($("input[name='food']:checked"), function(){
                            selected.push($(this).val());
                });
                paymethod = $('input[name="iCheck"]:checked', '#pay').val();
                selected.push(paymethod)
                alert("Selected food items and pay method is: " +
                selected.join(", "));
    });
});
```

You can see in the code that all the input elements are selected, and to each input element, a callback function is executed. In the callback function, the text of the <label> element is accessed and assigned to the label_text variable. After that, the plugin's iCheck method is applied to the <input> element, where the respective style classes are applied to the checkbox and radio button elements. Besides this, a <div> element is defined with the text in the label_text variable. To apply specific styles to it automatically, the icheck_line-icon class is assigned to the <div> element. In other words, each checkbox and radio button is replaced by a <div> element with a specific class. The rest of the code is the same, which senses the checkboxes that are checked and radio button and displays the food items selected via checkboxes and the payment method chosen via radio button. The selected choices are displayed through an alert dialog, as shown in Figure 11-11.

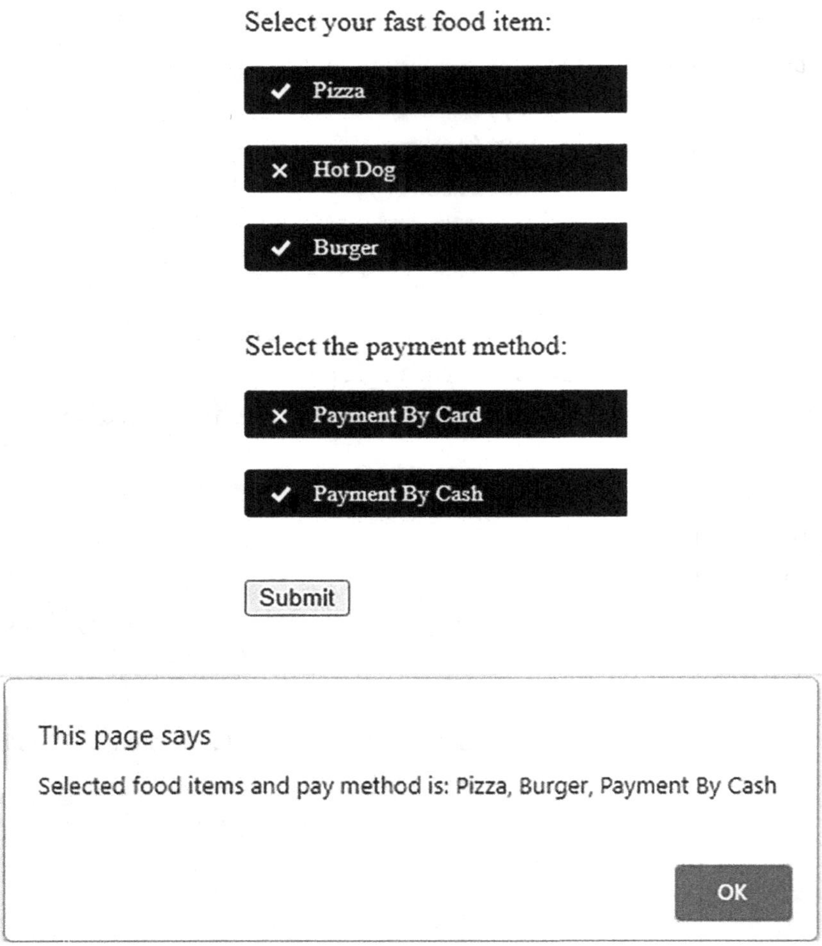

Select your fast food item:

✔	Pizza

✗	Hot Dog

✔	Burger

Select the payment method:

✗	Payment By Card

✔	Payment By Cash

Submit

This page says

Selected food items and pay method is: Pizza, Burger, Payment By Cash

OK

Figure 11-11. *Each checkbox and radio button is replaced by a <div> element with a specific class. Style classes are applied to the checkbox and radio button elements. Selected choices are displayed through an alert dialog*

11-6. Creating an Image Gallery and Carousel Using a blueimp Gallery Plugin

The blueimp Gallery plugin is created by Sebastian Tschan. It is a touch-enabled, responsive, and customizable image and video gallery, carousel, and lightbox optimized for both mobile and desktop applications. It supports features such as swipe, mouse and keyboard navigation, and transition effects. It is easy to use.

You can find complete information on the blueimp Gallery plugin at `https://plugins.jquery.com/blueimp-gallery/`. The page shows the links for a demo, download, documentation, the home page, and so on. Click the "Download now" link to download the code. A code bundle in zip format is downloaded to your computer. Unzip the file. From the js subfolder, copy the blueimp-gallery.js file into your site's folder. From the css subfolder, copy the blueimp-gallery.css file into your site's folder. Now, you are ready to use the blueimp Gallery plugin on your web page.

Note   I used images for making recipes with this plugin, so you need to copy the images folder provided in the code bundle of this book and copy that images folder in your site's folder.

Problem

You are learning to make an image carousel using the blueimp Gallery plugin, but that is a step-by-step approach. First, you learn to make an image gallery. Imagine you have three images, and you want to create an image gallery using the blueimp Gallery plugin. Initially, a thumbnail of the images is displayed. Clicking any of the thumbnails displays its larger version in the form of an image gallery with the Next and Previous buttons, which enable navigating to any image. Also, the title of the image being displayed appears at the top left corner of the image gallery.

Solution

Assuming the images folder containing the thumbnail and the zoomed images is copied into your site's folder, create an HTML file showing the three hyperlinks as follows.

Usingblueimp.html

```
<!DOCTYPE html PUBLIC "-//W3C//DTD XHTML 1.0 Transitional//EN"
        "http://www.w3.org/TR/xhtml1/DTD/xhtml1-transitional.dtd">

<html xmlns="http://www.w3.org/1999/xhtml" xml:lang="en" lang="en">
  <head>
    <meta http-equiv="Content-Type" content="text/html; charset=utf-8"/>
```

```
    <title></title>
    <link href="blueimp-gallery.css" rel="stylesheet">
    <script src="jquery-3.5.1.js" type="text/javascript"></script>
    <script src="blueimp-gallery.js" type="text/javascript"></script>
    <script src="usingblueimpjq.js" type="text/javascript"></script>
  </head>
  <body>
      <div
            id="blueimp-gallery"
            class="blueimp-gallery blueimp-gallery-controls"
            aria-label="image gallery"
            aria-modal="true"
            role="dialog"
>
            <div class="slides" aria-live="polite"></div>
            <h3 class="title"></h3>
            <a
                  class="prev"
                  aria-controls="blueimp-gallery"
                  aria-label="previous slide"
                  aria-keyshortcuts="ArrowLeft"
            ></a>
            <a
                  class="next"
                  aria-controls="blueimp-gallery"
                  aria-label="next slide"
                  aria-keyshortcuts="ArrowRight"
            ></a>
            <a
                  class="close"
                  aria-controls="blueimp-gallery"
                  aria-label="close"
                  aria-keyshortcuts="Escape"
            ></a>
            <a
                  class="play-pause"
```

```
                aria-controls="blueimp-gallery"
                aria-label="play slideshow"
                aria-keyshortcuts="Space"
                aria-pressed="false"
                role="button"
        ></a>
        <ol class="indicator"></ol>
    </div>
    <div id="links">
            <a href="images/chip.jpg" title="Preprocessor">
                    <img src="images/chipthumnail.jpg" alt="Preprocessor" />
            </a>
            <a href="images/chip2.jpg" title="RISC chip">
                    <img src="images/chip2thumnail.jpg" alt="RISC chip" />
            </a>
            <a href="images/chip3.jpg" title="CISC chip">
                    <img src="images/chip3thumnail.jpg" alt="CISC chip" />
            </a>
    </div>
  </body>
</html>
```

The CSS style sheet file, blueimp-gallery.css, is included in the HTML code. The blueimp-gallery.js file is included in the HTML file. Besides this, you can see that a <div> element is defined and is assigned the links". The id is assigned to auto apply styles mentioned in the CSS style sheets and to make it accessible in jQuery code. Within the <div> element are three hyperlinks. These three hyperlinks show the three thumbnail images and link to their large versions. The title attribute of all the <a> elements (i.e., hyperlinks are set to show the title of the three images being displayed).

The following is the jQuery code required to display the three thumbnails and show the image slider when any of the thumbnails is clicked.

Usingblueimpjq.js

```
$(document).ready(function() {
      document.getElementById('links').onclick = function (event) {
            event = event || window.event
```

```
            var target = event.target || event.srcElement
            var link = target.src ? target.parentNode : target
            var options = { index: link, event: event }
            var links = this.getElementsByTagName('a')
            blueimp.Gallery(links, options)
        }
});
```

When the running the program, you see three thumbnail images in the top-left corner of the browser window, as shown in Figure 11-12(a). Clicking any image displays its zoomed version with the title in the top-left corner as shown in Figure 11-12(b). Also there are left and right buttons on the image. You can navigate to any image. For example, clicking the Next button at the last image displays the first image again. Similarly, clicking the Previous button on the first image shows the last image.

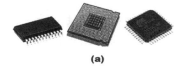

(a)

(b)

Figure 11-12. *(a) Three thumbnail images appear on the top left corner. (b) Clicking any of the images makes its zoomed version appear with its title*

Stretching Images

Sometimes, you feel like stretching the smaller images in your image gallery to the dimensions of the gallery container while keeping the image aspect ratio. To do so, add the blueimp-gallery-contain CSS class to the Gallery widget. That is, modify the class of the outermost <div> element in the HTML file. In the HTML program, you see that the outermost <div> class is blueimp-gallery blueimp-gallery-controls. Those lines are repeated as follows for your reference.

```
<div
   id="blueimp-gallery"
   class="blueimp-gallery blueimp-gallery-controls"
```

Change the class of the <div> element to blueimp-gallery blueimp-gallery-contain by modifying the preceding statements as follows.

```
<div
   id="blueimp-gallery"
   class="blueimp-gallery blueimp-gallery-contain"
```

No other changes are required. When running the program, you see three thumbnail images on the top left corner of the browser window. Clicking any of the thumbnail images enlarges the image, keeping its aspect ratio intact. The height of the image becomes equal to the height of the gallery. The left and right buttons on the image enable you to navigate to any image (see Figure 11-13).

Figure 11-13. *The clicked thumbnail image appears fully stretched*

Making an Image Carousel

The blueimp Gallery plugin enables you to make an image carousel with minimum effort. The image carousel is the one that shows an image at the center of the browser window. After a few seconds, that image automatically slides toward the left border of the browser window and vanishes. Next, another image appears from the right border of the browser window, slides toward the left, and stops at the center of the browser window. Again, after a few seconds, this image automatically slides toward the left border, and the procedure continues. To make an image carousel, where each image keeps sliding continuously, you need to modify the HTML code as follows.

Usingblueimp.html

Modify the html file as follows.

```
<!DOCTYPE html PUBLIC "-//W3C//DTD XHTML 1.0 Transitional//EN"
        "http://www.w3.org/TR/xhtml1/DTD/xhtml1-transitional.dtd">

<html xmlns="http://www.w3.org/1999/xhtml" xml:lang="en" lang="en">
  <head>
    <meta http-equiv="Content-Type" content="text/html; charset=utf-8"/>
    <title></title>
    <link href="blueimp-gallery.css" rel="stylesheet">
    <script src="jquery-3.5.1.js" type="text/javascript"></script>
    <script src="blueimp-gallery.js" type="text/javascript"></script>
    <script src="usingblueimpjq.js" type="text/javascript"></script>
  </head>
  <body>
      <div
            id="blueimp-gallery-carousel"
            class="blueimp-gallery blueimp-gallery-carousel"
            aria-label="image carousel"
      >
            <div class="slides" aria-live="off"></div>
            <h3 class="title"></h3>
            <a
                  class="prev"
                  aria-controls="blueimp-gallery-carousel"
```

```
                aria-label="previous slide"
        ></a>
        <a
                class="next"
                aria-controls="blueimp-gallery-carousel"
                aria-label="next slide"
        ></a>
        <a
                class="play-pause"
                aria-controls="blueimp-gallery-carousel"
                aria-label="play slideshow"
                aria-pressed="true"
                role="button"
        ></a>
        <ol class="indicator"></ol>
    </div>
    <div id="links">
        <a href="images/chip.jpg" title="Preprocessor">
                <img src="images/chipthumbnail.jpg" alt="Preprocessor" />
        </a>
        <a href="images/chip2.jpg" title="RISC chip">
                <img src="images/chip2thumbnail.jpg" alt="RISC chip" />
        </a>
        <a href="images/chip3.jpg" title="CISC chip">
                <img src="images/chip3thumbnail.jpg" alt="CISC chip" />
        </a>
    </div>
</body>
</html>
```

You can see in the HTML code, that wherever the blueimp-gallery class was used, it is replaced by the blueimp-gallery-carousel class so that the style classes mentioned in the plugin's CSS style sheets are automatically applied to the image hyperlinks and the respective jQuery code can be applied to them.

To convert the images hyperlinks into the image carousel, the jQuery code needs to be modified as follows.

Usingblueimpjq.js

```
$(document).ready(function() {
        document.getElementById('links').onclick = function (event) {
                event = event || window.event
                var target = event.target || event.srcElement
                var link = target.src ? target.parentNode : target
                var options = { index: link, event: event }
                var links = this.getElementsByTagName('a')
                blueimp.Gallery(links, options)
        }
        blueimp.Gallery(document.getElementById('links').
        getElementsByTagName('a'), {
                container: '#blueimp-gallery-carousel',
                carousel: true
        })
});
```

When you run the program, you find the first image at the center of the browser screen. After few seconds, that image slide toward the left edge of the browser and vanishes. The second image appears from the right edge of the browser, slides toward the left, and stops in the center of the browser window. After a few seconds, this second image slides toward the left edge of the browser window and vanishes. The third image appears from the right edge, slides to the left, and stops in the center of the browser window. The procedure continues endlessly.

If you click any image, the Next and Previous buttons appear. You can use them to navigate to any image (see Figure 11-14). And the moment you stop your navigation, the image auto-sliding begins.

Figure 11-14. Images appear at the center of the browser screen one after the other. The Next and Previous buttons appear after clicking any image

11-7. Validating a Form Using a jQuery Validation Plugin

The jQuery validation plugin v1.19.3 is written and maintained by Jörn Zaefferer, a member of the jQuery team.

This jQuery plugin provides an easy technique for client-side form validation and provides several customization options to suit your needs. The plugin has several validation methods to validate email address, URL, username, and so on, and all methods have their default error messages in English and translations into 37 other languages. The plugin also provides an API to write your own methods. All bundled

You can find more information on the jQuery validation plugin at `https://jqueryvalidation.org`. The page shows the links for Demos, Download, Documentation, GitHub Repository, and more. Click the "Download now" link and then the "Source code" link to download the code. A code bundle in zip format is downloaded to your computer. Unzip the file. From the dist subfolder, copy the jquery.validate.js file into your site's folder. Now, you are ready to use the blueimp Gallery plugin on your web page.

Problem

You have a form through which you ask the user to enter the user's name, email address, URL, and comments. You want to validate this form using the jQuery validation plugin.

Solution

You need an HTML form prompting the user to enter their name, email address, URL, and comments. The following is the HTML code to display a form asking the user to enter this information.

Usingformvalidate.html

```
<!DOCTYPE html PUBLIC "-//W3C//DTD XHTML 1.0 Transitional//EN"
        "http://www.w3.org/TR/xhtml1/DTD/xhtml1-transitional.dtd">

<html xmlns="http://www.w3.org/1999/xhtml" xml:lang="en" lang="en">
  <head>
    <meta http-equiv="Content-Type" content="text/html; charset=utf-8"/>
    <title></title>
    <script src="jquery-3.5.1.js" type="text/javascript"></script>
    <script src="jquery.form.js" type="text/javascript"></script>
    <script src="usingformvalidatejq.js" type="text/javascript"></script>
  </head>
  <body>
    <form class="cmxform" id="myform" method="get" action="">
        <fieldset>
            <legend>Please provide your name, email address and a
            comment</legend>
            <p>
                <label for="cname">Name (required, at least 2
                characters)</label>
                <input id="cname" name="name" minlength="2"
                type="text" required>
            </p>
            <p>
                <label for="cemail">E-Mail (required)</label>
                <input id="cemail" type="email" name="email" required>
            </p>
            <p>
                <label for="curl">URL (optional)</label>
                <input id="curl" type="url" name="url">
```

```
            </p>
            <p>
                    <label for="ccomment">Your comment (required)</label>
                    <textarea id="ccomment" name="comment" required></textarea>
            </p>
            <p>
                    <input class="submit" type="submit" value="Submit">
            </p>
        </fieldset>
    </form>
  </body>
</html>
```

You can see that a form is defined with id, commentForm, and the cmsform class. The id and class are assigned to automatically apply CSS styles and make it accessible in jQuery code. Within the <form> element is the <fieldset> element that groups the elements of the form. Also, a box is drawn around the nested elements. "Please provide your name, email address, and a comment" is displayed in the outline of the box using the <legend> element. Afterward, whatever information is required by the user is asked via <label> and <input> element pair, and each pair is wrapped inside <p> element. The <label> and <input> elements ask the user to enter a name, email address, URL of user's web site, and comments. The <input> element is used with the "required" attribute where data is essential.

The minlength attribute is used with the <input> element asks for the user name to inform the user that a minimum of two characters is required for a name. The <input> elements for seeking name, email address, URL, and comments are assigned the unique ids, cname, cemail, curl, and ccomment, respectively. It is through these ids that the plugin methods validate these elements of the form. No validation is applied on URL as that input element is set to optional (i.e., the user can leave that input box empty as well).

The jQuery code to apply form validation is as follows.

Usingformvalidatejq.js

```
$(document).ready(function() {
    $("#myform").validate({
        submitHandler: function(form) {
```

```
                form.submit();
        }
    });
});
```

You can see that the form with id, myform is accessed, and the plugin's validate method is invoked. When the user clicks the Submit button, submitHandler invokes the callback back function to submit the form. But the form is not be submitted if all the <input> elements are validated. A popup dialog appears, showing you the error if the <input> element does not match the criteria. The popup dialog automatically vanishes when the user starts typing in the <input> element. The popup appears again if the user clicks the Submit button and any of the <input> elements do not validate.

On running the HTML program, there are four input boxes and a Submit button at the bottom. The input boxes ask the user to enter the user's name, email address, URL, and comments (see Figure 11-15(a)).

Minimum two characters are a must while entering a name, so an error popup appears, asking to enter at least two characters if the user enters nothing or just one character in the name box (see Figure 11-15(b)).

If the user does not enter an email address or enters an invalid email address without the @ symbol, an error pops up, asking for a valid email address (see Figure 11-15(c)). No error appears if the URL box is empty or any invalid URL is entered because no validation is performed on the URL box. Because the comments box cannot be left empty and something must be entered in the comments box, an error popup asks the user to fill the comments box if it is left empty (see Figure 11-15(d)).

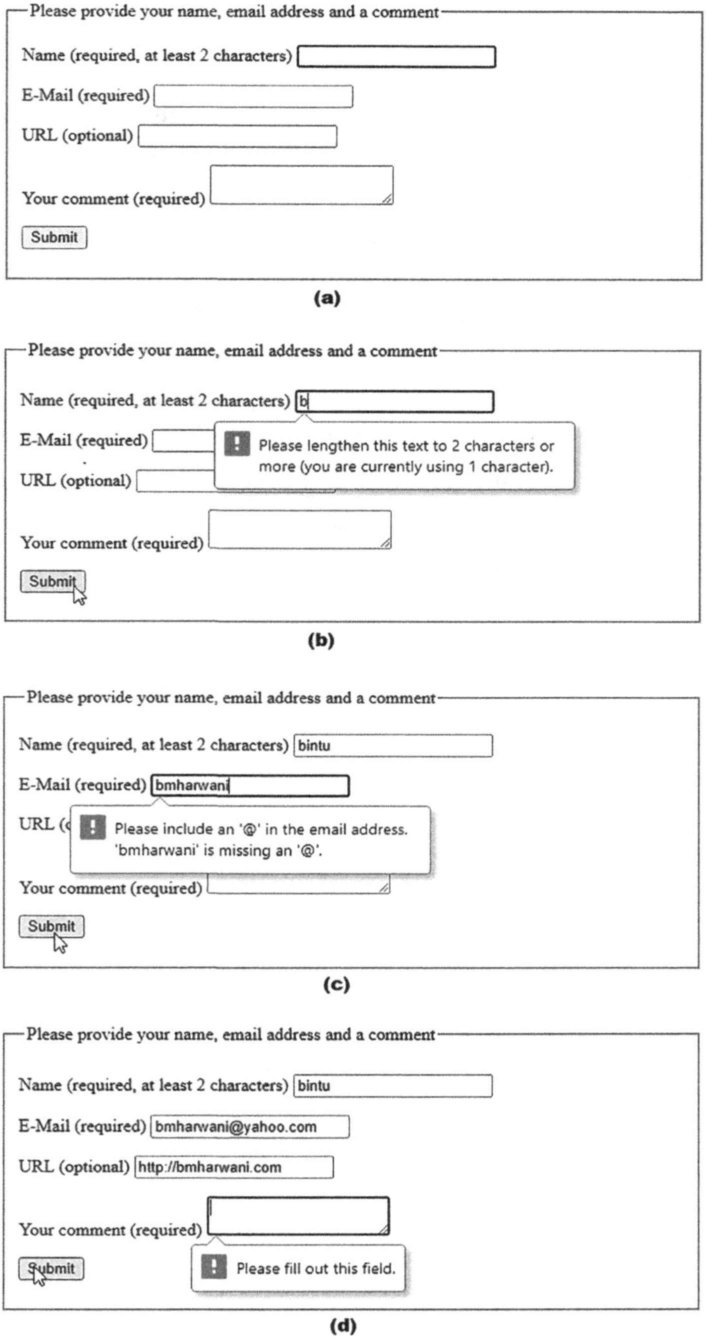

Figure 11-15. *(a) Four input boxes and a Submit button appear. (b) Error popup appears asking to enter at least two characters for the name. (c) Error popup on entering an invalid email address. (d) Error popup appears asking to fill the comments box if it is left empty*

11-8. Summary

In this chapter, you learned how to create a plugin that changes the font size, font style, and foreground and background color of an element. You also learned to make a plugin chainable. You also learned to customize the plugin as needed. You learned to use plugins, including the Magnific Popup plugin to display an images slider, the iCheck plugin to display dynamic checkboxes and radio buttons, the blueimp Gallery plugin to create an image gallery and carousel, and the jQuery validation plugin to validate a form.

The next chapter focused on using CSS. You learn to use CSS to distinguish HTML elements, apply styles to nested elements, indenting paragraphs, and apply an initial cap to a paragraph. You also learned to apply CSS in removing the gap between heading and paragraph, applying styles to heading text, indenting the first line of multiple paragraphs, creating paragraphs with hanging indents, and creating a bordered pull quote. The concept of using CSS becomes clearer after going through more recipes.

CHAPTER 12

Using CSS

This final chapter provides a set of recipes that rely heavily on CSS. These recipes complement the others in this book, as CSS is never far away from a JavaScript developer's work. I've included some of the CSS techniques that I use most often for quick reference as you develop your own web applications.

This chapter covers the following recipes.

- Distinguishing HTML elements

- Applying styles to an element nested inside another element

- Indenting paragraphs

- Applying an initial cap to a paragraph

- Removing the gap between heading and paragraph

- Applying styles to heading text

- Indenting the first line of multiple paragraphs

- Creating paragraphs with hanging indents

- Creating a bordered pull quote

- Creating a pull quote with images

- Applying list properties to list items

- Applying styles to only selected list items

- Placing dividers between list items

- Applying image markers to the list

- Creating inline lists

- Applying styles to hyperlinks and mailto

- Assigning different dimensions to HTML elements

© Bintu Harwani 2022
B. Harwani, *jQuery Recipes*, https://doi.org/10.1007/978-1-4842-7304-3_12

- Placing HTML elements

- Creating a multicolumn layout

- Wrapping text around images

- Placing a drop shadow behind an image

- Changing the cursor when the mouse moves over a link

- Displaying a long piece of text within a specific area

- Making a rounded corner column

- Applying text decorations

- Scaling images

- Setting a background image

- Centering a background image in the browser

- Making the background image stationary

12-1. Distinguishing HTML Elements
Problem

When you want to apply different styles to two different paragraphs or two different h1 elements of an HTML file, you must differentiate them by assigning different classes to them. Also, you need to write style rules that can be individually applied to these classes.

Solution

You first write an HTML file consisting of two paragraphs and two h1 elements. To differentiate them, you assign them different classes. The paragraph elements are assigned the feature1 and feature2 classes, respectively. The h1 elements are assigned the feature2 and feature3 classes, respectively.

Distinguishhtml.html

```
<!DOCTYPE html PUBLIC "-//W3C//DTD XHTML 1.0 Transitional//EN"
        "http://www.w3.org/TR/xhtml1/DTD/xhtml1-transitional.dtd">
```

```
<html xmlns="http://www.w3.org/1999/xhtml" xml:lang="en" lang="en">
  <head>
    <meta http-equiv="Content-Type" content="text/html; charset=utf-8"/>
    <title></title>
    <link rel="stylesheet" href="style.css" type="text/css" media="screen" />
    <script src="jquery-3.5.1.js" type="text/javascript"></script>
    <script src="distinguishhtmljq.js" type="text/javascript"></script>
  </head>
  <body>
    <p class="feature1">Styles make the formatting job much easier and
    efficient.</p>
    <p class="feature2">To give an attractive look to web sites, styles
    are heavily used.</p>
    <h1 class="feature2">Using jQuery</h1>
    <h1 class="feature3">Power of selectors</h1>
  </body>
</html>
```

To apply styles to these HTML elements of different classes, you write following style rules in the stylesheet.

Style.css

```
.greencolor{color:green;font-style:italic}
.highlight{background-color:aqua;color:blue;font-family:arial;}
.redandbold{color:red;font-family:arial;font-weight:bold}
```

The following is the jQuery code to apply the style rules to the paragraphs and H1 elements.

Distinguishhtmljq.js

```
$(document).ready(function() {
  $('p.feature1').addClass('greencolor');
  $('.feature2').addClass('highlight');
  $('h1.feature3').addClass('redandbold');
});
```

How It Works

The first statement applies the properties defined in the greencolor to only the paragraph elements and that also the ones that belong to feature1 class (i.e., those that begin with <p class="feature1"> tag). The second statement applies the properties defined in the highlight style rule to any HTML element in the feature2 class. In the HTML file, one paragraph element and one h1 element belong to the feature2 class (represented by <p class="feature2"> and <h1 class="feature2"> tags), so the properties defined in this rule is applied to both. The third statement applies the properties defined in the feature3 style rule to only the h1 element(s) that belongs to the feature3 class. The output can be seen as shown in Figure 12-1.

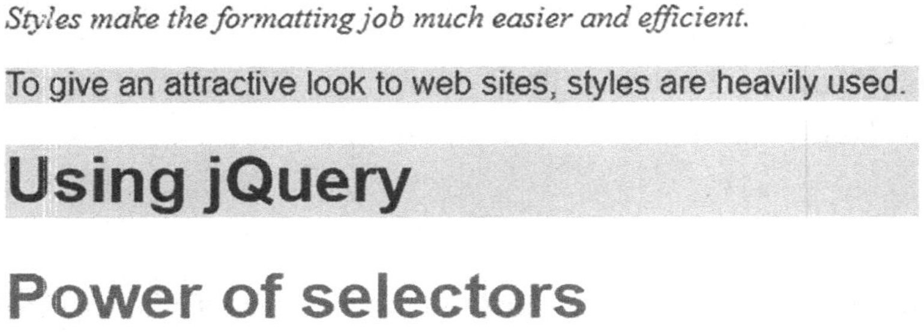

Styles make the formatting job much easier and efficient.

To give an attractive look to web sites, styles are heavily used.

Using jQuery

Power of selectors

Figure 12-1. *Different classes applied to <p> and <h1> tags*

12-2. Applying Styles to an Element Nested Inside Another Element

Problem

Sometimes, the span element is nested inside another HTML element of a specific id or a class and you need to apply styles to that nested span element.

Solution

In the following HTML file, you define a paragraph element of the feature class. In this paragraph element, you define a span element.

Stylenested.tml

```
<!DOCTYPE html PUBLIC "-//W3C//DTD XHTML 1.0 Transitional//EN"
        "http://www.w3.org/TR/xhtml1/DTD/xhtml1-transitional.dtd">

<html xmlns="http://www.w3.org/1999/xhtml" xml:lang="en" lang="en">
  <head>
    <meta http-equiv="Content-Type" content="text/html; charset=utf-8"/>
    <title></title>
    <link rel="stylesheet" href="style.css" type="text/css" media="screen" />
    <script src="jquery-3.5.1.js" type="text/javascript"></script>
    <script src="stylenestedjq.js" type="text/javascript"></script>
  </head>
  <body>
    <p class="feature">Styles make the formatting job much easier and
    efficient. <span>To give an attractive look to web sites,</span>
    styles are heavily used.</p>.
  </body>
</html>
```

The style rules applied to the paragraph element of a feature class and the span element nested inside it are written in the stylesheet and may appear as follows.

Style.css

```
.greencolor{color:green;font-style:italic}
.highlight{background-color:aqua;color:blue;font-family:arial;}
```

To apply styles to the paragraph element of the feature1 class and to the span element nested inside the paragraph element of a feature class. The following is the jQuery code.

Stylenestedjq.js

```
$(document).ready(function() {
  $('p.feature').addClass('greencolor');
  $('p.feature span').addClass('highlight');
});
```

How It Works

First, let's look how you define CSS styles.

`.feature{property:value; property:value;...}`

It defines a style that can be applied to any HTML elements with class="feature".

`.feature span {property:value; property:value;...}`

It defines a style that can be applied to the span element nested inside any HTML elements with class="feature".

`p.feature span {property:value; property:value;...}`

It defines a style that can be applied to the span element nested inside the paragraph element with class="feature".

`feature1 span.feature2 {property:value; property:value;...}`

It defines a style that can be applied to the span element with class="feature2" nested inside the any HTML elements with class="feature1".

`p.feature1 span.feature2 {property:value; property:value;...}`

It defines a style that can be applied to the span element with class="feature2" nested inside the paragraph element with class="feature1".

The first jQuery statement applies the style properties defined in the greencolor to the paragraph element with class="feature". The second statement applies the properties defined in the highlight style rule to the span element defined within the paragraph element with class="feature". In other words, the styles are applied to the region of text enclosed between <span> and </span> tags that are defined within the paragraph element with class="feature". The output on the application of styles can be seen as shown in Figure 12-2.

Styles make the formatting job much easier and efficient. To give an attractive look to web sites, *styles are heavily used.*

Figure 12-2. *Applying style to span element nested in another HTML element*

12-3. Indenting Paragraphs

Problem

You have three paragraphs in a HTML file and you want to indent them at three different levels.

Solution

The following is the HTML containing the three paragraphs.

Indentingparagraph.thml

```
<!DOCTYPE html PUBLIC "-//W3C//DTD XHTML 1.0 Transitional//EN"
        "http://www.w3.org/TR/xhtml1/DTD/xhtml1-transitional.dtd">

<html xmlns="http://www.w3.org/1999/xhtml" xml:lang="en" lang="en">
  <head>
    <meta http-equiv="Content-Type" content="text/html; charset=utf-8"/>
    <title></title>
    <link rel="stylesheet" href="styleindenting.css" type="text/css"
    media="screen" />
    <script src="jquery-3.5.1.js" type="text/javascript"></script>
    <script src="indentingparagraphjq.js" type="text/javascript"></script>
  </head>
  <body>
    <p class="feature1">Styles make the formatting job much easier and
    efficient. To give an attractive look to web sites, styles are heavily
    used. Styles can be written within HTML document or can be attached
    externally. External styles are considered better</p>
    <p class="feature2">JQuery is a powerful JavaScript library that
    allows us to add dynamic elements to our web sites. Not only it is
    easy to learn but easy to implement too.</p>
```

```
<p class="feature3"> jQuery Selectors are used for selecting the area
of the document where we want to apply styles. JQuery has the power
of handling events also meaning we can apply styles when a particular
action takes place</p>
  </body>
</html>
```

You can see that the three paragraphs are assigned three different class names: feature1, feature2, and feature3 respectively. You are using the margin property to indent these paragraphs. The following are the style rules written in the external style sheet.

Styleindenting.css

```
.indent1{
    margin-left:10%;
}
.indent2{
    margin-left:20%;
}
.indent3{
    margin-left:30%;
}
```

To apply the style rules to the three paragraphs, you write the following jQuery code.

Indentingparagraphjq.js

```
$(document).ready(function() {
  $('p.feature1').addClass('indent1');
  $('p.feature2').addClass('indent2');
  $('p.feature3').addClass('indent3');
});
```

How It Works

The first statement selects the paragraph element of the feature1 class from the HTML file and applies the properties defined in the indent1 style rule to it. Similarly, the second and third statements select the paragraph elements of feature2 class and feature3 class and apply the properties defined in the indent2 and indent3 style rules, respectively. The output is shown in Figure 12-3.

> Styles make the formatting job much easier and efficient. To give an attractive look to web sites, styles are heavily used. Styles can be written within HTML document or can be attached externally. External styles are considered better
>
> > JQuery is a powerful JavaScript library that allows us to add dynamic elements to our web sites. Not only it is easy to learn but easy to implement too.
> >
> > > jQuery Selectors are used for selecting the area of the document where we want to apply styles. JQuery has the power of handling events also meaning we can apply styles when a particular action takes place

Figure 12-3. *Three paragraphs indented at three different levels*

12-4. Applying an Initial Cap to a Paragraph

Problem

You want to make the first character of a paragraph an initial cap. Initial caps could be in a different font, different color, or you can even use images for the initial caps.

Solution

Let's consider the following HTML file with a single paragraph element.

Initialcap.html

```
<!DOCTYPE html PUBLIC "-//W3C//DTD XHTML 1.0 Transitional//EN"
        "http://www.w3.org/TR/xhtml1/DTD/xhtml1-transitional.dtd">

<html xmlns="http://www.w3.org/1999/xhtml" xml:lang="en" lang="en">
  <head>
    <meta http-equiv="Content-Type" content="text/html; charset=utf-8"/>
    <title></title>
    <link rel="stylesheet" href="styleinitialcap.css" type="text/css"
    media="screen" />
    <script src="jquery-3.5.1.js" type="text/javascript"></script>
```

```
    <script src="initialcapjq.js" type="text/javascript"></script>
  </head>
  <body>
    <p><span class="cap">S</span>tyles make the formatting job much easier
    and efficient. To give an attractive look to web sites, styles are
    heavily used. Styles can be written within HTML document or can be
    attached externally. External styles are considered better
  </body>
</html>
```

The following is the style rule that you apply is written in the stylesheet.

Styleinitialcap.css

```
.initialcap{
    font-size: 2em;
}
```

The following is the jQuery code to apply the style rule to the span element with the name cap class.

Initialcapjq.js

```
$(document).ready(function() {
  $('span.cap').addClass('initialcap');
});
```

How It Works

You can see in the HTML that to distinguish the first character of the paragraph from the rest of the body, it is enclosed in a span tag and is assigned a cap class. To this cap class, you apply the style rule via jQuery code. You can see that the font size of the first character is made double the size of the default font (of the rest of the paragraph), as shown in Figure 12-4.

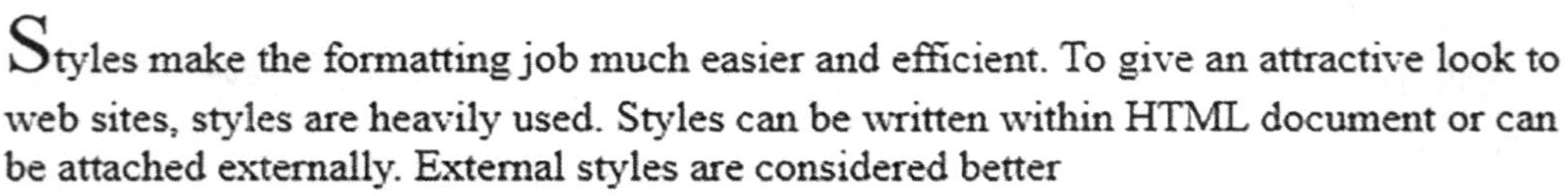

Styles make the formatting job much easier and efficient. To give an attractive look to web sites, styles are heavily used. Styles can be written within HTML document or can be attached externally. External styles are considered better

Figure 12-4. *The first character of the paragraph is set to initial cap*

You can also change the foreground and background color of the first character, as shown in the following style rule.

Styleinitialcap.css

```
.initialcap{
    font-size:2em;
    background-color:black;
    color:white;
}
```

12-5. Removing the Gap Between Heading and Paragraph

Problem

Whenever you apply a heading to any paragraph, there is a gap between the heading and the paragraph. You want to remove this gap.

Solution

The following is the HTML of the heading and the paragraph.

Removinggap.html

```
<!DOCTYPE html PUBLIC "-//W3C//DTD XHTML 1.0 Transitional//EN"
        "http://www.w3.org/TR/xhtml1/DTD/xhtml1-transitional.dtd">

<html xmlns="http://www.w3.org/1999/xhtml" xml:lang="en" lang="en">
  <head>
    <meta http-equiv="Content-Type" content="text/html; charset=utf-8"/>
    <title></title>
    <link rel="stylesheet" href="styleremovinggap.css" type="text/css"
    media="screen" />
    <script src="jquery-3.5.1.js" type="text/javascript"></script>
    <script src="removinggapjq.js" type="text/javascript"></script>
  </head>
```

```
<body>
    <h3>Formatting Makes Attractive</h3>
    <p>Styles make the formatting job much easier and efficient. To give
    an attractive look to web sites, styles are heavily used. Styles
    can be written within HTML document or can be attached externally.
    External styles are considered better</p>
</body>
</html>
```

The following is the style rule to remove the gap between the paragraph and the heading.

Styleremovinggap.css

```
.heading{
    margin:0;
    padding:0;
}

p{
    margin:0;
    padding:0;
}
```

The following is the jQuery code to apply the style to the h3 element.

Removinggapjq.js

```
$(document).ready(function() {
  $('h3').addClass('heading');
});
```

How It Works

The original output of the HTML without applying any jQuery code is shown in Figure 12-5. You can see that there is a large gap between the heading and the paragraph.

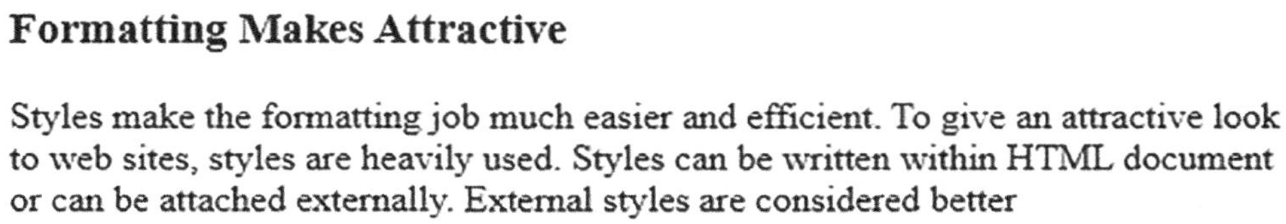

Formatting Makes Attractive

Styles make the formatting job much easier and efficient. To give an attractive look to web sites, styles are heavily used. Styles can be written within HTML document or can be attached externally. External styles are considered better

Figure 12-5. *The paragraph and heading along with a usual gap in between*

In this style sheet, a heading class selector is applied to the h3 element and a p{} type selector is applied to the paragraph element directly.

On applying styles to the paragraph and heading, you find that the gap between them is removed, as shown in Figure 12-6.

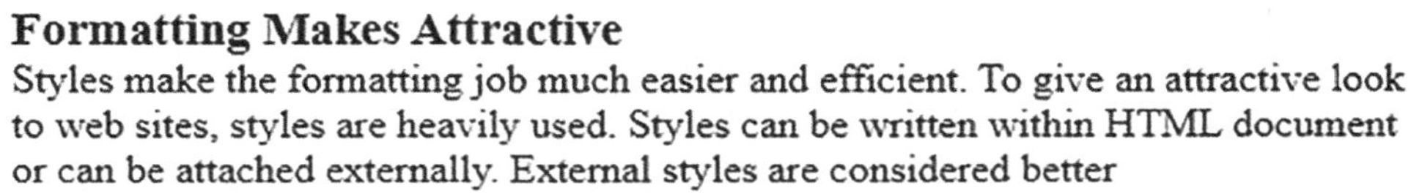

Formatting Makes Attractive
Styles make the formatting job much easier and efficient. To give an attractive look to web sites, styles are heavily used. Styles can be written within HTML document or can be attached externally. External styles are considered better

Figure 12-6. *The usual gap between the paragraph and heading removed*

12-6. Applying Styles to Heading Text
Problem

You want to apply styles to the heading of a text.

Solution

You use the same HTML in Recipe 12-4, which contains a paragraph and a heading. To highlight the heading, you first need to remove the usual gap between the heading and the paragraph. Then, you make it italic and apply borders to it. You write the following style rules in the style sheet.

Stylestoheading.css

```
.heading{
    margin:0;
    padding:0;
    font-style: italic;
    border-top:5px solid black;
```

```
    border-bottom:5px solid black;
}

p{
    margin:0;
    padding:0;
}
```

Let's apply the style to the h3 element with the following jQuery code.

Stylestoheadingjq.js

```
$(document).ready(function() {
  $('h3').addClass('heading');
});
```

How It Works

The margin and padding properties in the style rules remove the usual gap between the heading and paragraph, and the font style makes the heading appear in italic. The border property attaches a top and a bottom border to the heading.

The heading of the paragraph after applying the styles is shown in Figure 12-7.

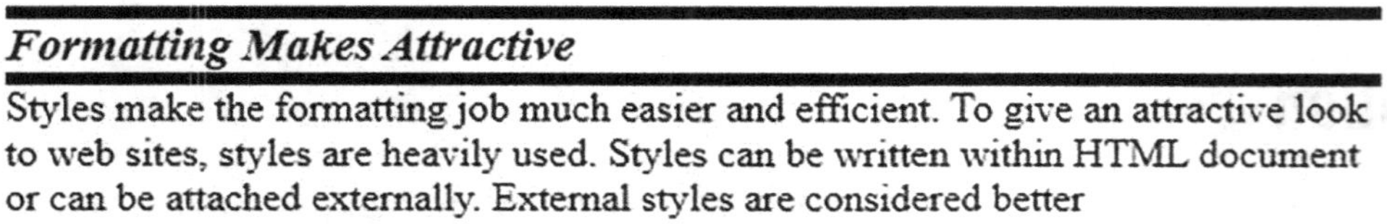

Formatting Makes Attractive

Styles make the formatting job much easier and efficient. To give an attractive look to web sites, styles are heavily used. Styles can be written within HTML document or can be attached externally. External styles are considered better

Figure 12-7.   *The paragraph with a styled heading*

12-7. Indenting the First Line Of Multiple Paragraphs

Problem

You want to indent the first line of the paragraphs in your document.

Solution

Let's write some HTML with a few paragraphs in it as follows.

Indentingfirstline.html

```
<!DOCTYPE html PUBLIC "-//W3C//DTD XHTML 1.0 Transitional//EN"
        "http://www.w3.org/TR/xhtml1/DTD/xhtml1-transitional.dtd">

<html xmlns="http://www.w3.org/1999/xhtml" xml:lang="en" lang="en">
  <head>
    <meta http-equiv="Content-Type" content="text/html; charset=utf-8"/>
    <title></title>
    <link rel="stylesheet" href="styleindentfirstline.css" type="text/css"
    media="screen" />
    <script src="jquery-3.5.1.js" type="text/javascript"></script>
    <script src="indentingfirstlinejq.js" type="text/javascript"></script>
  </head>
  <body>
      <p>Styles make the formatting job much easier and efficient. To give
      an attractive look to web sites, styles are heavily used. Styles
      can be written within HTML document or can be attached externally.
      External styles are considered better</p>
      <p>jQuery is a powerful JavaScript library that allows us to add
      dynamic elements to our web sites. Not only it is easy to learn but
      easy to implement too.</p>
      <p> jQuery Selectors are used for selecting the area of the document
      where we want to apply styles. JQuery has the power of handling
      events also meaning we can apply styles when a particular action
      takes place</p>
  </body>
</html>
```

The HTML display three paragraphs without any indentation. To apply the indentation in the first line of the paragraphs, you need to use the text-indent property. The following is the style rule in the style sheet.

Styleindentfirstline.css

```
.firstindent{
    text-indent:10%;
}
```

The following is the jQuery code to apply the firstindent to all the paragraph elements of the HTML file.

Indentingfirstlinejq.js

```
$(document).ready(function() {
  $('p').addClass('firstindent');
});
```

How It Works

On application of the style, the paragraphs of the HTML file have the first line indented, as shown in Figure 12-8.

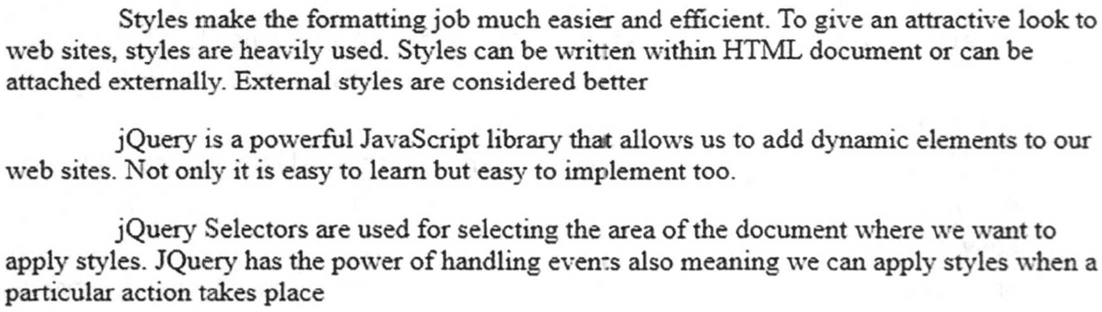

Styles make the formatting job much easier and efficient. To give an attractive look to web sites, styles are heavily used. Styles can be written within HTML document or can be attached externally. External styles are considered better

jQuery is a powerful JavaScript library that allows us to add dynamic elements to our web sites. Not only it is easy to learn but easy to implement too.

jQuery Selectors are used for selecting the area of the document where we want to apply styles. JQuery has the power of handling events also meaning we can apply styles when a particular action takes place

Figure 12-8.   *The paragraphs with the first line indented*

12-8. Creating Paragraphs with Hanging Indents
Problem

You want to have hanging indents in the first line of the paragraphs in your document.

Solution

In this recipe, you use the same HTML that you used in Recipe 12-6. The HTML has three paragraph elements.

You make use of the text-indent and margin-left properties for creating hanging indents. The following is the style rule.

Stylehangingindent.css

```
.hangingindent{
    text-indent:-10%;
    margin-left:10%;
}
```

The following is the jQuery code to apply the hanging indent style rule to the paragraphs.

Hangingindentjq.js

```
$(document).ready(function() {
  $('p').addClass('hangingindent');
});
```

How It Works

By setting the margin-left property to 10%, you set the paragraph to 10% of the browser window width from the left side of the browser window (i.e., the whole paragraph is shifted right by 10% of the browser window's width). By making the value of text-indent –10%, you make the first line of the paragraph shift toward the left equal to 10% of the browser window's width, hence giving it a hanging indentation look.

On application of style, the first line of each paragraph has a hanging indentation, as shown in Figure 12-9.

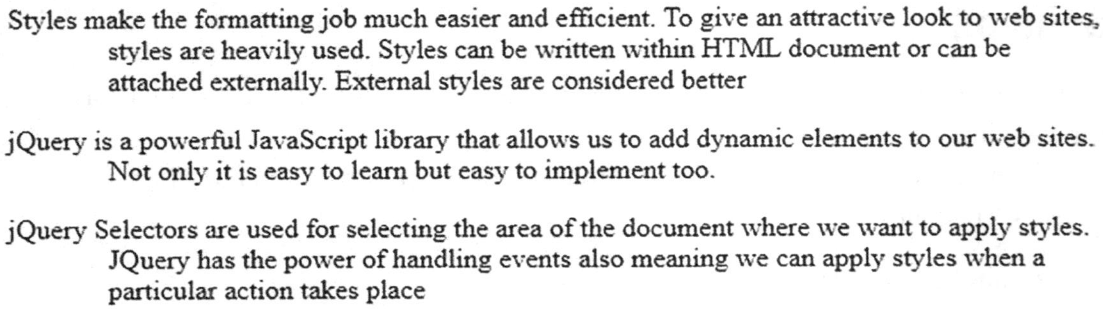

Styles make the formatting job much easier and efficient. To give an attractive look to web sites, styles are heavily used. Styles can be written within HTML document or can be attached externally. External styles are considered better

jQuery is a powerful JavaScript library that allows us to add dynamic elements to our web sites. Not only it is easy to learn but easy to implement too.

jQuery Selectors are used for selecting the area of the document where we want to apply styles. JQuery has the power of handling events also meaning we can apply styles when a particular action takes place

Figure 12-9. *The paragraphs with the hanging indented first line*

12-9. Creating a Bordered Pull Quote

Problem

In the middle of a large piece of text, you want to highlight certain text to catch the visitor's eye. That is, you need to make a bordered pull quote.

Solution

Let's write some HTML with three paragraphs and the paragraph you want to highlight is differentiated from the rest by assigning it a feature class name. The following is the HTML.

Pullquote.html

```
<!DOCTYPE html PUBLIC "-//W3C//DTD XHTML 1.0 Transitional//EN"
        "http://www.w3.org/TR/xhtml1/DTD/xhtml1-transitional.dtd">

<html xmlns="http://www.w3.org/1999/xhtml" xml:lang="en" lang="en">
  <head>
    <meta http-equiv="Content-Type" content="text/html; charset=utf-8"/>
    <title></title>
    <link rel="stylesheet" href="stylepullquote.css" type="text/css"
    media="screen" />
    <script src="jquery-3.5.1.js" type="text/javascript"></script>
    <script src="pullquotejq.js" type="text/javascript"></script>
  </head>
```

```
<body>
    <p>Styles make the formatting job much easier and efficient. To give
    an attractive look to web sites, styles are heavily used. Styles
    can be written within HTML document or can be attached externally.
    External styles are considered better</a>
    <p class="feature">jQuery is a powerful JavaScript library that allows
    us to add dynamic elements to our web sites. Not only it is easy to
    learn but easy to implement too.</a>
    <p> jQuery Selectors are used for selecting the area of the document
    where we want to apply styles. JQuery has the power of handling events
    also meaning we can apply styles when a particular action takes
    place</a>
  </body>
</html>
```

You make use of the margin, color, and font-style properties to highlight the text. The following are the style rules that you write in the external style sheet.

Stylepullquote.css

```
.quote{
    margin:5%;
    color:#00a;
    font-style: italic;
    border:5px solid black;
    padding: .5em;
}
```

The following is the jQuery code to apply the style rule quote to the paragraph with the feature class name.

Pullquotejq.js

```
$(document).ready(function() {
  $('p.feature').addClass('quote');
});
```

How It Works

The margin property indents the paragraph to 5% from all four boundaries. The color property makes the color of the paragraph blue. The font-style property makes it italic. To make a border around the pull quote, add two more properties to the quote style rule: border creates a border of a specified width around the paragraph, and the padding property creates a gap between the border and the paragraph text.

On applying the style rule, the paragraph appears as a bordered pull quote, as shown in Figure 12-10.

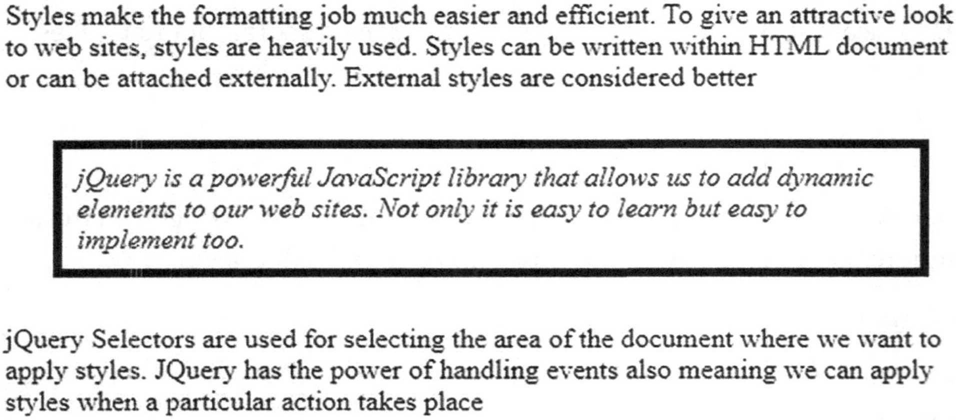

Styles make the formatting job much easier and efficient. To give an attractive look to web sites, styles are heavily used. Styles can be written within HTML document or can be attached externally. External styles are considered better

> *jQuery is a powerful JavaScript library that allows us to add dynamic elements to our web sites. Not only it is easy to learn but easy to implement too.*

jQuery Selectors are used for selecting the area of the document where we want to apply styles. JQuery has the power of handling events also meaning we can apply styles when a particular action takes place

Figure 12-10. *The paragraph distinguished as a bordered pull quote*

12-10. Creating a Pull Quote with Images

Problem

To make text appear attractive and dynamic among a larger piece of text, you want to make a pull quote with images to make it stand out. Pull quotes can act like images to give text-heavy documents something to focus on without needing an image.

Solution

For this recipe, you use the same HTML that you used in Recipe 12-7. You know that in that HTML, the paragraph that you want to distinguish from the rest of the text is assigned a feature class name.

To apply images in the two opposite corners of the pull quote, you make two figures: leftfig.jpg and rightfig.jpg. The leftfig.jpg is shown in Figure 12-11.

Figure 12-11. *Figure in leftfig.jpg file*

The image to be placed in the bottom-right corner of the paragraph is shown in Figure 12-12.

Figure 12-12. *Figure in rightfig.jpg file*

You need to apply two images to the paragraph to be highlighted: one in the top-left corner and the other in the bottom-right corner. Since you can apply only one style to an element, so to apply two images to the paragraph element, you enclose it in a div element. Now, you can apply one style to the paragraph element (to add one image) and another style to the div element to add another image. The following is the HTML file after enclosing the paragraph of the feature class name in the div element.

Pullquoteimages.html

```
<!DOCTYPE html PUBLIC "-//W3C//DTD XHTML 1.0 Transitional//EN"
        "http://www.w3.org/TR/xhtml1/DTD/xhtml1-transitional.dtd">

<html xmlns="http://www.w3.org/1999/xhtml" xml:lang="en" lang="en">
  <head>
    <meta http-equiv="Content-Type" content="text/html; charset=utf-8"/>
    <title></title>
    <link rel="stylesheet" href="stylepullquoteimages.css" type="text/css"
    media="screen" />
    <script src="jquery-3.5.1.js" type="text/javascript"></script>
    <script src="pullquoteimagesjq.js" type="text/javascript"></script>
```

```
  </head>
   <body>
      <p>Styles make the formatting job much easier and efficient. To give
      an attractive look to web sites, styles are heavily used. Styles
      can be written within HTML document or can be attached externally.
      External styles are considered better</p>
      <div>
         <p class="feature">jQuery is a powerful JavaScript library that
         allows us to add dynamic elements to our web sites. Not only it is
         easy to learn but easy to implement too.</p>
      </div>
      <p> jQuery Selectors are used for selecting the area of the document
      where we want to apply styles. jQuery has the power of handling events
      also meaning we can apply styles when a particular action takes
      place</p>
   </body>
</html>
```

The following are the style rules to apply two images to the pull quote.

Stylepullquoteimages.css

```
.quote{
     background-image:url(leftfig.jpg);
     background-repeat: no-repeat;
     margin:5%;
     color:#00a;
     font-style: italic;
     padding:30px 5px 5px 30px;
}

.closing{
     background-image:url(rightfig.jpg);
     background-repeat: no-repeat;
     background-position: bottom right;
}
```

The following is the jQuery code to add the style rules quote and closing to the feature class name paragraph and the div element.

Pullquoteimagesjq.js

```
$(document).ready(function() {
  $('p.feature').addClass('quote');
  $('div').addClass('closing');
});
```

How It Works

The quote style rule applies leftfig.jpg in the top-left corner of the paragraph. The value of background-repeat is set to no-repeat to display the image only once. The margin property makes the paragraph indented to 5% of the browser window's width from all four sides. The font-style property makes the paragraph appear in italic, and the padding property sets the distance between the paragraph text and the images. The closing style rule applies rightfig.jpg in the bottom-right corner of the paragraph.

On application of styles, you see that the pull quote is displayed along with two images in the two opposite corners, as shown in Figure 12-13.

Styles make the formatting job much easier and efficient. To give an attractive look to web sites, styles are heavily used. Styles can be written within HTML document or can be attached externally. External styles are considered better

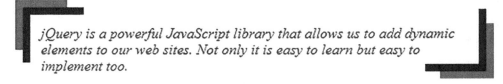

jQuery is a powerful JavaScript library that allows us to add dynamic elements to our web sites. Not only it is easy to learn but easy to implement too.

jQuery Selectors are used for selecting the area of the document where we want to apply styles. jQuery has the power of handling events also meaning we can apply styles when a particular action takes place

Figure 12-13. *The paragraph distinguished as a Pull Quote with images*

12-11. Applying List Properties to List Items

Problem

List items are used heavily in drop-down menus, displaying the hierarchy of items, and so forth. You want to apply list properties to list items.

Solution

Let's make HTML that contains certain list items. The following is the HTML file.

Listproperties.html

```
<!DOCTYPE html PUBLIC "-//W3C//DTD XHTML 1.0 Transitional//EN"
        "http://www.w3.org/TR/xhtml1/DTD/xhtml1-transitional.dtd">

<html xmlns="http://www.w3.org/1999/xhtml" xml:lang="en" lang="en">
  <head>
    <meta http-equiv="Content-Type" content="text/html; charset=utf-8"/>
    <title></title>
    <link rel="stylesheet" href="stylelistproperties.css" type="text/css"
    media="screen" />
    <script src="jquery-3.5.1.js" type="text/javascript"></script>
    <script src="listpropertiesjq.js" type="text/javascript"></script>
  </head>
  <body>
<ul>
  <li>Tea
    <ul>
      <li>Darjeeling</li>
      <li>Assam
        <ul>
          <li>Green Leaves</li>
          <li>Herbal</li>
        </ul>
      </li>
```

```
        <li>Kerala</li>
      </ul>
    </li>
    <li>Coffee
      <ul>
        <li>Cochin</li>
        <li>Kerala</li>
      </ul>
    </li>
  </ul>
  </body>
</html>
```

The list items appear before applying list properties to them, as shown in Figure 12-14.

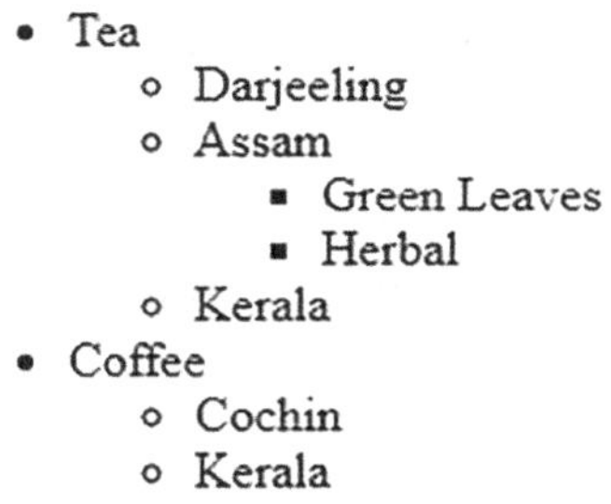

- Tea
  - Darjeeling
  - Assam
    - Green Leaves
    - Herbal
  - Kerala
- Coffee
  - Cochin
  - Kerala

Figure 12-14. *Unordered List Items without applying any style*

Let's define the style rule as follows.

Stylelistproperties.css

```
.dispdisc{list-style-type:disc}
```

The dispdisc style rule makes a disc appear before list items. The following is the jQuery code to apply the dispdisc style rule to the list items.

Listpropertiesjq.js

```
$(document).ready(function() {
  $('li').addClass('dispdisc');
});
```

How It Works

The list style type is set to disc. Figure 12-15 shows all list items are preceded with a disc shape.

- Tea
    - Darjeeling
    - Assam
        - Green Leaves
        - Herbal
    - Kerala
- Coffee
    - Cochin
    - Kerala

Figure 12-15. *Unordered and list items after applying list style*

12-12. Applying Styles to Only Selected List Items

Problem

To highlight them, you want to apply styles to only a part of the list items.

Solution

To apply a style to only the selected list items, you need to distinguish them from others. For selecting a part of a list, you assign it a class name or an id. In this solution, you assign the id as intro to the list item you want to highlight.

Selectedlist.html

```
<!DOCTYPE html PUBLIC "-//W3C//DTD XHTML 1.0 Transitional//EN"
        "http://www.w3.org/TR/xhtml1/DTD/xhtml1-transitional.dtd">

<html xmlns="http://www.w3.org/1999/xhtml" xml:lang="en" lang="en">
  <head>
    <meta http-equiv="Content-Type" content="text/html; charset=utf-8"/>
    <title></title>
    <link rel="stylesheet" href="styleselectedlist.css" type="text/css"
    media="screen" />
```

```
  <script src="jquery-3.5.1.js" type="text/javascript"></script>
  <script src="selectedlistjq.js" type="text/javascript"></script>
</head>
<body>
<ul>
  <li>Tea
    <ul id="intro">
      <li>Darjeeling</li>
      <li>Assam
        <ul>
          <li>Green Leaves</li>
          <li>Herbal</li>
        </ul>
      </li>
      <li>Kerala</li>
    </ul>
  </li>
  <li>Coffee
    <ul>
      <li>Cochin</li>
      <li>Kerala</li>
    </ul>
  </li>
</ul>
</body>
</html>
```

Let's define a style rule applied to the list items with the intro in the style sheet file.

Styleselectedlist.css

```
.dispdisc{color:green;font-style:italic}
```

To apply the properties defined in the style rule to the list items of the intro id, you write the jQuery code as follows.

Selectedlistjq.js

```
$(document).ready(function() {
  $('#intro').addClass('dispdisc');
});
```

The style rule applies the color and font-style properties to the list items with the intro id. You can see that only a part of the list is highlighted, as shown in Figure 12-16.

- Tea
  - *Darjeeling*
  - *Assam*
    - *Green Leaves*
    - *Herbal*
  - *Kerala*
- Coffee
  - Cochin
  - Kerala

Figure 12-16. *Applying style properties to the list items with id intro*

Applying Styles to the List Items Selected with Child Selector

The symbol > is a child combinatory that finds each list item that is a child of the element with the specified id (or class) and applies the given style rule. To understand how the child selector works, let's assign an id named drink to an unordered list as shown in the following HTML.

Listselectedchildselector.html

```
<!DOCTYPE html PUBLIC "-//W3C//DTD XHTML 1.0 Transitional//EN"
        "http://www.w3.org/TR/xhtml1/DTD/xhtml1-transitional.dtd">

<html xmlns="http://www.w3.org/1999/xhtml" xml:lang="en" lang="en">
  <head>
    <meta http-equiv="Content-Type" content="text/html; charset=utf-8"/>
    <title></title>
    <link rel="stylesheet" href="stylechildselector.css" type="text/css"
    media="screen" />
    <script src="jquery-3.5.1.js" type="text/javascript"></script>
    <script src="childselectorjq.js" type="text/javascript"></script>
```

```
  </head>
  <body>
<ul>
  <li>Tea
    <ul id="drink">
      <li>Darjeeling</li>
      <li>Assam
        <ul>
          <li>Green Leaves</li>
          <li>Herbal</li>
        </ul>
      </li>
      <li>Kerala</li>
    </ul>
  </li>
  <li>Coffee
    <ul>
      <li>Cochin</li>
      <li>Kerala</li>
    </ul>
  </li>
</ul>
</body>
</html>
```

Let's assume that the style sheet contains a highlight style rule that applies a green color and makes the text appear in italics.

Stylechildselector.css

```
.highlight {
    font-style: italic;
    background-color: #0f0;
}
```

The following is the jQuery code to apply the highlight style rule to the child of the unordered list with the drink id.

Childselectorjq.js

```
$(document).ready(function() {
  $('#drink >li').addClass('highlight');
});
```

When working with the child selector, it simply finds each list item that is a child of the element with the drink id and applies the highlight class to it.

Applying Styles to List Items to Which a CSS Class Is Not Applied

You can also apply styles to the elements to which a particular CSS class is not applied. Let's write the following jQuery code in the JavaScript file.

Stylestocssnotjq.js

```
$(document).ready(function() {
  $('#drink >li').addClass('highlight');
  $('#drink li:not(.highlight)').addClass('redandbold');
});
```

The style sheet file is assumed to contain two style rules: highlight and redandbold, as follows.

Stylechildselector.css

```
.highlight {
    font-style: italic;
    background-color: #0f0;
}
.redandbold{
    color:red;
    font-family:arial;
    font-weight:bold
}
```

How It Works

This example finds all list items onto which highlight is not applied and applies the properties defined in the redandbold class. The output may be as shown in Figure 12-17.

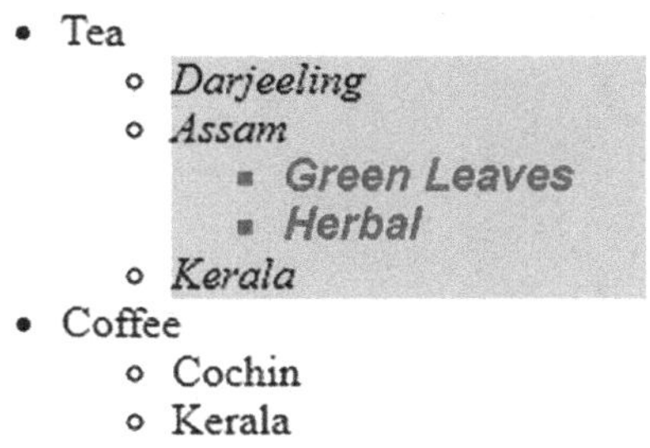

- Tea
  - ○ *Darjeeling*
  - ○ *Assam*
    - ▪ *Green Leaves*
    - ▪ *Herbal*
  - ○ *Kerala*
- Coffee
  - ○ Cochin
  - ○ Kerala

Figure 12-17. *Applying two different styles*

12-13. Placing Dividers Between List Items

Problem

You want list items displayed in a straight line (without indentation) that separates every list item.

Solution

For this recipe, you use the same HTML that you used in Recipe 12-10. The HTML displays certain list items as shown in Figure 12-14.

The following is the style rules.

Styledividerbetlist.css

```
.applytopborders
{
    border-top: 1px solid black;
}

.applybottomborder
{
    border-bottom: 1px solid black;
}

.liststyle {
    list-style-type:none;
    padding-left:0;
}
```

You apply one style rule to the unordered list, one to all list items except the last, and a third to the last list item.

Dividerbetweenlistjq.js

```
$(document).ready(function() {
  $('ul').addClass('liststyle');
  $('li').addClass('applytopborders');
  $('li:last').addClass('applybottomborder');
});
```

How It Works

You use three style rules for this recipe.

- liststyle on the unordered list to remove the traditional bullets from the list items and the hierarchical indentation.

- applytopborder on all the list items except the last one to apply the top border to each of them.

- applybottomborder on the last list item to apply the bottom border to it.

The output that you get by applying these styles is shown in Figure 12-18.

| Tea |
| Darjeeling |
| Assam |
| Green Leaves |
| Herbal |
| Kerala |
| Coffee |
| Cochin |
| Kerala |

Figure 12-18. *List items in a straight line with dividers in between*

12-14. Applying Image Markers to the List Problem

You want to replace the traditional bullets from list items with an image.

Solution

For this recipe, you create HTML that displays certain list items, as follows.

Imagemarkerlist.html

```
<!DOCTYPE html PUBLIC "-//W3C//DTD XHTML 1.0 Transitional//EN"
        "http://www.w3.org/TR/xhtml1/DTD/xhtml1-transitional.dtd">

<html xmlns="http://www.w3.org/1999/xhtml" xml:lang="en" lang="en">
  <head>
    <meta http-equiv="Content-Type" content="text/html; charset=utf-8"/>
    <title></title>
    <link rel="stylesheet" href="styleimagemarker.css" type="text/css"
    media="screen" />
    <script src="jquery-3.5.1.js" type="text/javascript"></script>
    <script src="imagemarkerjq.js" type="text/javascript"></script>
  </head>
<body>
<ul>
  <li>Tea
    <ul>
      <li>Darjeeling</li>
      <li>Assam
        <ul>
          <li>Green Leaves</li>
          <li>Herbal</li>
        </ul>
      </li>
      <li>Kerala</li>
    </ul>
  </li>
  <li>Coffee
    <ul>
      <li>Cochin</li>
      <li>Kerala</li>
    </ul>
```

```
    </li>
</ul>
</body>
</html>
```

In this recipe, the style rule makes use of two properties list-style-type and list-style-image. The former is removes the traditional bullets from the list items, and the latter applies the specified image instead of the bullets.

The image that you want to apply instead of bullets is flower.jpg. The following is the style rule in the stylesheet.

Styleimagemarker.css

```
.liststyle {
    list-style-type: none;
    list-style-image:url(flower.jpg);
}
```

The following is the jQuery code to apply the liststyle style rule to the unordered list.

Imagemarkerjq.js

```
$(document).ready(function() {
  $('ul').addClass('liststyle');
});
```

How It Works

By assigning none to the list-style-type property, the bullets disappear from the list items, and by assigning flower.jpg to the list-style-image property, the image stored in this file is applied to the list items.

When applying the style rule, the traditional bullets from the list items are replaced by the image stored in flower.jpg. The output is shown in Figure 12-19.

Figure 12-19. *List items in a straight line with dividers in between*

12-15. Creating Inline Lists

Problem

You want list items to appear in a horizontal row without any hierarchical levels.

Solution

For this recipe, you create HTML that displays certain list items, as follows.

Inlinelist.html

```
<!DOCTYPE html PUBLIC "-//W3C//DTD XHTML 1.0 Transitional//EN"
        "http://www.w3.org/TR/xhtml1/DTD/xhtml1-transitional.dtd">
<html xmlns="http://www.w3.org/1999/xhtml" xml:lang="en" lang="en">
  <head>
    <meta http-equiv="Content-Type" content="text/html; charset=utf-8"/>
    <title></title>
    <link rel="stylesheet" href="styleinlinelist.css" type="text/css"
    media="screen" />
    <script src="jquery-3.5.1.js" type="text/javascript"></script>
    <script src="inlinejq.js" type="text/javascript"></script>
  </head>
<body>
<ul>
  <li>Tea
```

```
<ul>
  <li>Darjeeling</li>
  <li>Assam
    <ul>
      <li>Green Leaves</li>
      <li>Herbal</li>
    </ul>
  </li>
  <li>Kerala</li>
  </ul>
</li>
<li>Coffee
  <ul>
    <li>Cochin</li>
    <li>Kerala</li>
  </ul>
</li>
</ul>
</body>
</html>
```

In this recipe, the style rule uses properties like display, list-style, margin, and padding, as shown in the following stylesheet.

Styleinlinelist.css

```
.liststyle {
    display: inline;
    list-style:none;
    margin:0;
    padding:0;
}
```

The following is the jQuery code to apply the liststyle style rule to the unordered list and its list items.

Inlinejq.js

```
$(document).ready(function() {
  $('ul').addClass('liststyle');
  $('li').addClass('liststyle');
});
```

How It Works

The inline value of the display property makes the list items display in a row (i.e., on the same line). Setting the value of list-style to none removes the traditional bullets from the list items. Finally, the value 0 assigned to margin and padding removes the hierarchical indentation in the list items.

On application of the style properties, the list items are displayed in a row without any traditional bullets, as shown in Figure 12-20.

Tea Darjeeling Assam Green Leaves Herbal Kerala Coffee Cochin Kerala

Figure 12-20. *List items displayed in a row as inline*

12-16. Applying Styles to Hyperlinks and mailto
Problem

Hyperlinks carry a traditional underline to distinguish them from static text. You want to remove these underlines and apply other styles to these links.

Solution

To apply styles to the hyperlinks, let's make an HTML file that has a hyperlink.

Hyperlinks.html

```
<!DOCTYPE html PUBLIC "-//W3C//DTD XHTML 1.0 Transitional//EN"
        "http://www.w3.org/TR/xhtml1/DTD/xhtml1-transitional.dtd">
<html xmlns="http://www.w3.org/1999/xhtml" xml:lang="en" lang="en">
  <head>
```

```
    <meta http-equiv="Content-Type" content="text/html; charset=utf-8"/>
    <title></title>
    <link rel="stylesheet" href="stylehyperlinksmailto.css" type="text/css"
    media="screen" />
    <script src="jquery-3.5.1.js" type="text/javascript"></script>
    <script src="hyperlinksjq.js" type="text/javascript"></script>
  </head>
  <body>
    <div>Styles make the formatting job much easier and efficient. To give
    an attractive look to web sites, styles are heavily used. A person
    must have a good knowledge of HTML and CSS and a bit of Javascript.
     jQuery is a powerful JavaScript library that allows us to add dynamic
    elements to our web sites. Not only it is easy to learn but easy to
    implement too.
jQuery is an open source project. <a href="abc.com">Click Here</a> for more
information </div>
  </body>
</html>
```

You can see that "Click Here" is a hyperlink and is underlined on the web page. When a visitor clicks this link, he is navigated to the abc.com site.

To remove the underline from the hyperlink and apply other style properties to it, you write the following style rule in the external style sheet file.

Stylehyperlinksmailto.css

```
.linkstyle{
    font-weight:bold;
    background-color: #00f;
    color:#fff;
     text-decoration:none;
}
```

To apply the linkstyle style rule to the hyperlink, the jQuery code may be written as follows.

hyperlinksjq.js

```
$(document).ready(function() {
    $('a[href]').addClass('linkstyle');
});
```

Now let's see how to apply styles to a mailto hyperlink. Here is an HTML file that has a mailto hyperlink, which when selected opens a mail client program to email the concerned person.

mailto.html

```
<!DOCTYPE html PUBLIC "-//W3C//DTD XHTML 1.0 Transitional//EN"
        "http://www.w3.org/TR/xhtml1/DTD/xhtml1-transitional.dtd">
<html xmlns="http://www.w3.org/1999/xhtml" xml:lang="en" lang="en">
  <head>
    <meta http-equiv="Content-Type" content="text/html; charset=utf-8"/>
    <title></title>
    <link rel="stylesheet" href="stylehyperlinksmailto.css" type="text/css"
    media="screen" />
    <script src="jquery-3.5.1.js" type="text/javascript"></script>
    <script src="mailtojq.js" type="text/javascript"></script>
  </head>
  <body>
      <div>Styles make the formatting job much easier and efficient. To
      give an attractive look to web sites, styles are heavily used.
      A person must have a good knowledge of HTML and CSS and a bit of
      Javascript.
      jQuery is a powerful JavaScript library that allows us to add dynamic
      elements to our web sites. Not only it is easy to learn but easy to
      implement too.
      jQuery is an open source project. <a href="mailto:bmharwani@yahoo.com">
      Contact Us</a> for more information </div>
  </body>
</html>
```

The following is the content of the JavaScript file containing jQuery code.

mailtojq.js

```
$(document).ready(function() {
  $('a[href^="mailto:"]').addClass('linkstyle');
});
```

How It Works

Our CSS style rule uses the font-weight property to make the hyperlink appear in bold. The background-color property sets the hyperlink background color to blue, the color property is set to white, and the value of the text-decoration property is set to none to remove the traditional underline from the hyperlink.

The following is the jQuery statement.

```
$('a[href]').addClass('linkstyle');
```

Select all the anchor elements (a) that have an href attribute in the document and apply the linkstyle class to them. The output is shown in Figure 12-21.

Styles make the formatting job much easier and efficient. To give an attractive look to web sites, styles are heavily used. A person must have a good knowledge of HTML and CSS and a bit of Javascript. jQuery is a powerful JavaScript library that allows us to add dynamic elements to our web sites. Not only it is easy to learn but easy to implement too. jQuery is an open source project. **Click Here** for more information

Figure 12-21. *Removing traditional underline from the hyperlink*

The following statement selects all the anchor elements ('a') in the document that have the href attribute and begin with mailto and applies the linkstyle class to them.

```
$('a[href^="mailto:"]').addClass('linkstyle');
```

The output may be as shown in Figure 12-22.

Styles make the formatting job much easier and efficient. To give an attractive look to web sites, styles are heavily used. A person must have a good knowledge of HTML and CSS and a bit of Javascript. jQuery is a powerful JavaScript library that allows us to add dynamic elements to our web sites. Not only it is easy to learn but easy to implement too. jQuery is an open source project. **Contact Us** for more information

Figure 12-22. *Applying linkstyle to mailto option*

12-17. Assigning Different Dimensions to HTML Elements

Problem

You want to constrain the size of certain paragraph elements.

Solution

For this solution, you create an HTML file that contains two paragraph elements that are assigned feature1 and feature2 class names.

Differentdimension.html

```
<!DOCTYPE html PUBLIC "-//W3C//DTD XHTML 1.0 Transitional//EN"
       "http://www.w3.org/TR/xhtml1/DTD/xhtml1-transitional.dtd">
<html xmlns="http://www.w3.org/1999/xhtml" xml:lang="en" lang="en">
  <head>
    <meta http-equiv="Content-Type" content="text/html; charset=utf-8"/>
    <title></title>
    <script src="jquery-3.5.1.js" type="text/javascript"></script>
    <script src="differentdimensionjq.js" type="text/javascript"></script>
  </head>
   <body>
       <p class="feature1">Styles make the formatting job much easier and
       efficient. To give an attractive look to web sites, styles are
       heavily used. A person must have a good knowledge of HTML and CSS and
       a bit of Javascript.  </p>
       <p class="feature2">jQuery is a powerful JavaScript library that
       allows us to add dynamic elements to our web sites. Not only it is
       easy to learn but easy to implement too.  jQuery is an open source
       project that provides a wide range of features with cross platform
       compatibility. JQuery has hundreds of plug-ins to extend its features.
       jQuery helps in increasing interactions with a web site </p>
   </body>
</html>
```

To apply the width property to the paragraph elements with feature1 and feature2 class names, you write the following jQuery code.

Differentdimensionjq.js

```
$(document).ready(function() {
  $('.feature1').css({'width':'50%', 'padding':'10px', 'border':'1px dashed'});
  $('.feature2').css({'padding':'30px', 'border':'2px solid'});
});
```

How It Works

The solution uses the css() method (described in Recipe 3-7). In the jQuery code, the first statement confines the first paragraph to 50% of the width of the browser window. The border property creates a border of dashes of 1 px thickness, and the padding property creates a spacing of 10px between the paragraph text and the border. The second statement makes the paragraph text use up the whole width of the browser window. The border property creates a solid border of 2px thickness, and the padding property creates a spacing of 30px between the paragraph text and the border. The output is shown in Figure 12-23.

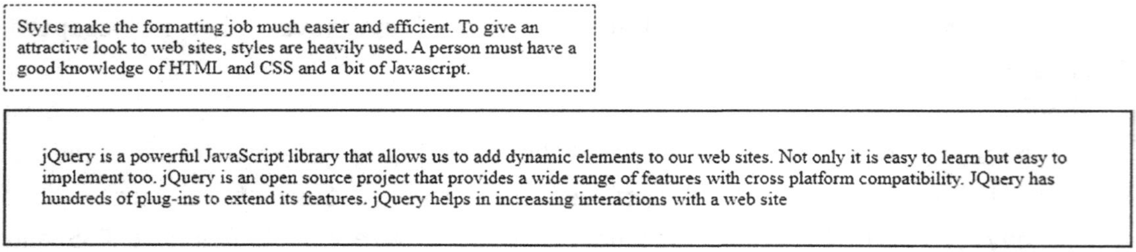

Styles make the formatting job much easier and efficient. To give an attractive look to web sites, styles are heavily used. A person must have a good knowledge of HTML and CSS and a bit of Javascript.

jQuery is a powerful JavaScript library that allows us to add dynamic elements to our web sites. Not only it is easy to learn but easy to implement too. jQuery is an open source project that provides a wide range of features with cross platform compatibility. JQuery has hundreds of plug-ins to extend its features. jQuery helps in increasing interactions with a web site

Figure 12-23. *Specifying width attribute in percentage*

You can also specify the width in terms of pixels as shown in the following jQuery code.

```
$('.feature1').css({'width':'300px', 'padding':'10px', 'border':'1px dashed'});
$('.feature2').css({'padding':'30px', 'border':'2px solid'});
```

The width of the first paragraph is limited to the size of 300 pixels as shown in Figure 12-24.

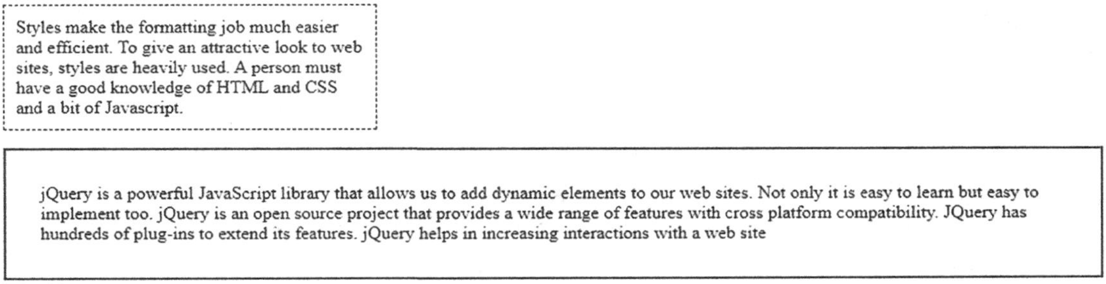

> Styles make the formatting job much easier and efficient. To give an attractive look to web sites, styles are heavily used. A person must have a good knowledge of HTML and CSS and a bit of Javascript.

> jQuery is a powerful JavaScript library that allows us to add dynamic elements to our web sites. Not only it is easy to learn but easy to implement too. jQuery is an open source project that provides a wide range of features with cross platform compatibility. JQuery has hundreds of plug-ins to extend its features. jQuery helps in increasing interactions with a web site

Figure 12-24. *Specifying width attribute in pixels*

12-18. Placing HTML Elements
Problem

You want to make a paragraph element appear to the right or left of another paragraph element.

Solution

Let's create an HTML file that contains two paragraph elements that are assigned the feature1 and feature2 class names.

Placinghtml.html

```
<!DOCTYPE html PUBLIC "-//W3C//DTD XHTML 1.0 Transitional//EN"
        "http://www.w3.org/TR/xhtml1/DTD/xhtml1-transitional.dtd">
<html xmlns="http://www.w3.org/1999/xhtml" xml:lang="en" lang="en">
  <head>
    <meta http-equiv="Content-Type" content="text/html; charset=utf-8"/>
    <title></title>
    <script src="jquery-3.5.1.js" type="text/javascript"></script>
    <script src="placinghtmljq.js" type="text/javascript"></script>
  </head>
  <body>
```

```
<p class="feature1">Styles make the formatting job much easier and
efficient. To give an attractive look to web sites, styles are
heavily used. A person must have a good knowledge of HTML and CSS and
a bit of Javascript.  </p>
<p class="feature2">jQuery is a powerful JavaScript library that
allows us to add dynamic elements to our web sites. Not only it is
easy to learn but easy to implement too.  jQuery is an open source
project that provides a wide range of features with cross platform
compatibility. jQuery has hundreds of plug-ins to extend its features.
jJQuery helps in increasing interactions with a web site </p>
  </body>
</html>
```

To apply the float property to the paragraph elements with feature1 and feature2 class names, you write the following jQuery code.

Placinghtmljq.js

```
$(document).ready(function() {
  $('.feature1').css({'width':'50%', 'border':'1px dashed', 'float':'left'});
  $('.feature2').css({'border':'2px solid'});
});
```

Making a Two-Column Layout

You can also make the first paragraph float left and the second paragraph float right. Let's modify the following jQuery code.

Twocolumnsjq.js

```
$(document).ready(function() {
  $('.feature1').css({'width':'50%', 'border':'1px dashed',
  'float':'left'});
  $('.feature2').css({'width':'48%','border':'2px solid',
  'float':'right'});
});
```

Reversing the Columns

You can also interchange the positions of the columns. That is, the first paragraph can be set to float right and the second paragraph to float left. The jQuery code for the purpose may be written as follows.

Reversingcolumnsjq.js

```
$(document).ready(function() {
  $('.feature1').css({'width':'50%', 'border':'1px dashed', 'float':'right'});
  $('.feature2').css({'width':'48%', 'border':'2px solid', 'float':'left'});
});
```

How It Works

In the jQuery code, the first statement specifies the property float:left that makes the first paragraph appear on the left side of the browser window, making a space of 50% on the right side, which is then occupied by the second paragraph (see Figure 12-25). The border property creates a border of dashes of 1 px thickness around the first paragraph. The second statement creates a solid border of 2px thickness around the second paragraph.

Styles make the formatting job much easier and efficient. To give an attractive look to web sites, styles are heavily used. A person must have a good knowledge of HTML and CSS and a bit of Javascript.	jQuery is a powerful JavaScript library that allows us to add dynamic elements to our web sites. Not only it is easy to learn but easy to implement too. jQuery is an open source project that provides a wide range of features with cross platform compatibility. jQuery has hundreds of plug-ins to extend its features. jQuery helps in increasing interactions with a web site

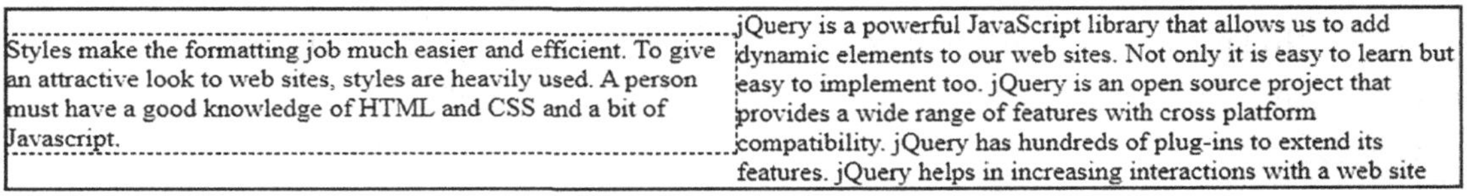

Figure 12-25. *Applying float property*

When the first paragraph is set to float left in the two-column layout, it creates a space on its right (which is used by the second paragraph). Similarly, when the property float:right is applied to the second paragraph, it creates a space on its left of the browser window that can be used by the first paragraph. The output of the application of styles is shown in Figure 12-26.

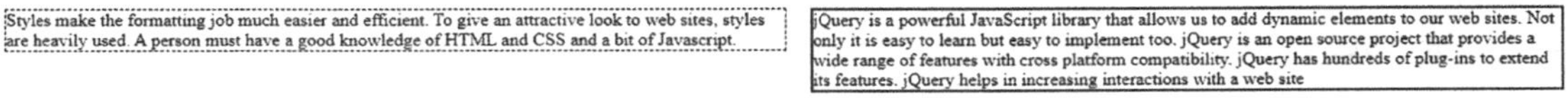

Styles make the formatting job much easier and efficient. To give an attractive look to web sites, styles are heavily used. A person must have a good knowledge of HTML and CSS and a bit of Javascript.	jQuery is a powerful JavaScript library that allows us to add dynamic elements to our web sites. Not only it is easy to learn but easy to implement too. jQuery is an open source project that provides a wide range of features with cross platform compatibility. jQuery has hundreds of plug-ins to extend its features. jQuery helps in increasing interactions with a web site

Figure 12-26. *Applying float property*

The reversed layout is shown in Figure 12-27.

jQuery is a powerful JavaScript library that allows us to add dynamic elements to our web sites. Not only it is easy to learn but easy to implement too. jQuery is an open source project that provides a wide range of features with cross platform compatibility. jQuery has hundreds of plug-ins to extend its features. jQuery helps in increasing interactions with a web site	Styles make the formatting job much easier and efficient. To give an attractive look to web sites, styles are heavily used. A person must have a good knowledge of HTML and CSS and a bit of Javascript.

Figure 12-27. *Interchanging the two columns*

12-19. Creating a Multicolumn Layout
Problem

You want to create a three-column layout (i.e., three paragraphs positioned at particular locations on the page).

Solution

You create a three-column layout by positioning the columns at three different positions of the web page. Let's make an HTML file with three paragraph elements with class names assigned as leftalign, centeralign, and rightalign. The following is the HTML file.

Multicolumn.html

```
<!DOCTYPE html PUBLIC "-//W3C//DTD XHTML 1.0 Transitional//EN"
        "http://www.w3.org/TR/xhtml1/DTD/xhtml1-transitional.dtd">
<html xmlns="http://www.w3.org/1999/xhtml" xml:lang="en" lang="en">
  <head>
    <meta http-equiv="Content-Type" content="text/html; charset=utf-8"/>
    <title></title>
    <script src="jquery-3.5.1.js" type="text/javascript"></script>
    <script src="multicolumnjq.js" type="text/javascript"></script>
  </head>
  <body>
    <p class="leftalign">Styles make the formatting job much easier and
    efficient. To give an attractive look to web sites, styles are heavily
    used. A person must have a good knowledge of HTML and CSS and a bit of
    Javascript.   </p>
```

```
<p class="centeralign">jQuery is a powerful JavaScript library that
allows us to add dynamic elements to our web sites. Not only it is
easy to learn but easy to implement too. </p>
<p class="rightalign">jQuery is an open source project that provides
a wide range of features with cross platform compatibility. jQuery
has hundreds of plug-ins to extend its features. JQuery helps in
increasing interactions with a web site. </p>
</body>
</html>
```

The following is the jQuery code to place the three paragraph elements in the respective positions.

Multicolumnjq.js

```
$(document).ready(function() {
  $('.leftalign').css({'position':'absolute', 'left':'50px',
  'width':'300px'});
  $('.centeralign').css({'position':'absolute', 'left':'400px',
  'width':'300px'});
  $('.rightalign').css({'position':'absolute', 'left':'750px',
  'width':'300px'});
});
```

Applying Floats

You can have the same output (three-column layout) by applying the float property demonstrated in the following solution. In the following HTML file, you define three paragraph elements (without assigning any class names).

Applyfloats.html

```
<!DOCTYPE html PUBLIC "-//W3C//DTD XHTML 1.0 Transitional//EN"
       "http://www.w3.org/TR/xhtml1/DTD/xhtml1-transitional.dtd">
<html xmlns="http://www.w3.org/1999/xhtml" xml:lang="en" lang="en">
  <head>
    <meta http-equiv="Content-Type" content="text/html; charset=utf-8"/>
    <title></title>
```

```
    <script src="jquery-3.5.1.js" type="text/javascript"></script>
    <script src="applyfloatsjq.js" type="text/javascript"></script>
  </head>
  <body>
      <p>Styles make the formatting job much easier and efficient. To give
      an attractive look to web sites, styles are heavily used. A person must
      have a good knowledge of HTML and CSS and a bit of Javascript. </p>
      <p>JQuery is a powerful JavaScript library that allows us to add
      dynamic elements to our web sites. Not only it is easy to learn but
      easy to implement too. </p>
<p>JQuery is an open source project that provides a wide range of features
with cross platform compatiblity. JQuery has hundreds of plug-ins to extend
its features. JQuery helps in increasing interactions with a web site. </p>
  </body>
</html>
```

You then write the following jQuery code.

Applyfloatsjq.js

```
$(document).ready(function() {
  $('p').css({'float':'left',  'width':'300px','margin':'5px'});
});
```

Increasing Gutters Size Between Columns

Gutter means the spacing between the columns. You can also increase the gutter size between the columns by settings the values of the width and margin properties. By reducing the width of columns and increasing the size of the margin, you can increase the spacing (gutter size) between columns.

Let's reduce the width property and increase the margin value by a small amount as shown in the following jQuery code.

Applyfloatsjq.js

```
$('p').css({'float':'left',  'width':'375px','margin':'15px'});
```

How It Works

In the first set of jQuery code, you see that the first statement sets the CSS properties of the HTML element of class="leftalign". It displays the paragraph element with a width of 300 pixels and positions it at 50 pixels from the left in its containing element (the browser window in this case). Similarly, the second statement positions the HTML element of class="centeralign" at 400 pixels from the left of the browser window. The third statement positions the HTML element of class="rightalign" at 750 pixels from the left of the browser window. The output is shown in Figure 12-28.

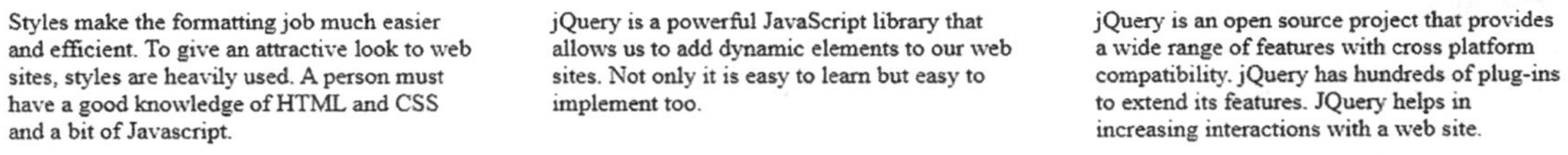

Styles make the formatting job much easier and efficient. To give an attractive look to web sites, styles are heavily used. A person must have a good knowledge of HTML and CSS and a bit of Javascript.

jQuery is a powerful JavaScript library that allows us to add dynamic elements to our web sites. Not only it is easy to learn but easy to implement too.

jQuery is an open source project that provides a wide range of features with cross platform compatibility. jQuery has hundreds of plug-ins to extend its features. JQuery helps in increasing interactions with a web site.

Figure 12-28. *Three-column layout using the position property*

In the float example, you give each paragraph element a width of 300 pixels and make them float to the left of the browser window one after the other. The first paragraph appears first and takes a width of 300 pixels. After a margin of 5 pixels, the second paragraph appears (i.e., after 305 pixels from the left of the browser window). The second paragraph also takes the width of 300 pixels. Finally, the third paragraph appears after keeping the margin of 5 pixels for the second paragraph (i.e., to the rightmost of the browser window), as shown in Figure 12-29.

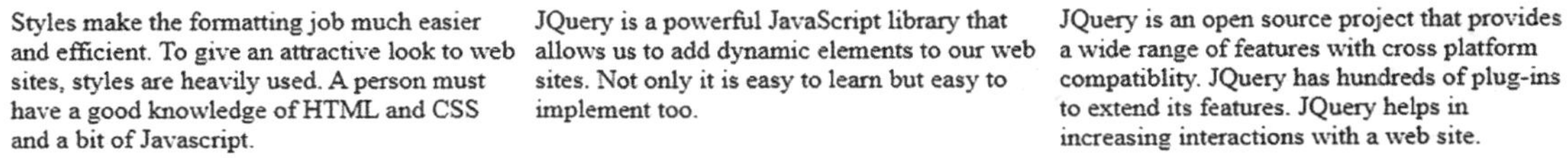

Styles make the formatting job much easier and efficient. To give an attractive look to web sites, styles are heavily used. A person must have a good knowledge of HTML and CSS and a bit of Javascript.

JQuery is a powerful JavaScript library that allows us to add dynamic elements to our web sites. Not only it is easy to learn but easy to implement too.

JQuery is an open source project that provides a wide range of features with cross platform compatiblity. JQuery has hundreds of plug-ins to extend its features. JQuery helps in increasing interactions with a web site.

Figure 12-29. *Three column layout using float property*

Finally, Figure 12-30 shows the example after increasing the gutter size. The gutter size refers to the spacing between columns.

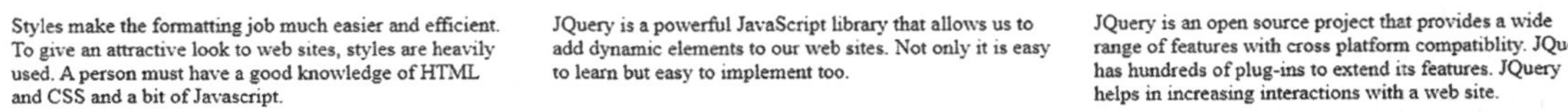

Styles make the formatting job much easier and efficient. To give an attractive look to web sites, styles are heavily used. A person must have a good knowledge of HTML and CSS and a bit of Javascript.

JQuery is a powerful JavaScript library that allows us to add dynamic elements to our web sites. Not only it is easy to learn but easy to implement too.

JQuery is an open source project that provides a wide range of features with cross platform compatiblity. JQuery has hundreds of plug-ins to extend its features. JQuery helps in increasing interactions with a web site.

Figure 12-30. *Three columns with increased gutters size*

12-20. Wrapping Text Around Images

Problem

Usually, when you display an image and text on a web page, both appear one after the other. Either the image follows text or text follows the image (depends on the placement in HTML file); both don't appear adjacent to each other by default. Sometimes, you want the image to appear wrapped by the text around it.

Solution

Let's place an image in an HTML file as follows.

Wraptext.html

```
<!DOCTYPE html PUBLIC "-//W3C//DTD XHTML 1.0 Transitional//EN"
        "http://www.w3.org/TR/xhtml1/DTD/xhtml1-transitional.dtd">
<html xmlns="http://www.w3.org/1999/xhtml" xml:lang="en" lang="en">
  <head>
    <meta http-equiv="Content-Type" content="text/html; charset=utf-8"/>
    <title></title>
    <script src="jquery-3.5.1.js" type="text/javascript"></script>
    <script src="wrapjq.js" type="text/javascript"></script>
  </head>
  <body>
      <img src="cell.jpg"/>
  </body>
</html>
```

You now write jQuery code to wrap the img element within a div element and then append a paragraph element with some text to the div element. The following is the jQuery code.

Wrapjq.js

```
$(document).ready(function() {
  $('img').wrap('<div></div>');
```

```
$('<p>Styles make the formatting job much easier and efficient. To give
an attractive look to web sites, styles are heavily used. A person must
have a good knowledge of HTML and CSS and a bit of Javascript. jQuery
is a powerful JavaScript library that allows us to add dynamic elements
to our web sites. Not only it is easy to learn but easy to implement
too.  jQuery is an open source project that provides a wide range of
features with cross platform compatiblity. jQuery has hundreds of plug-
ins to extend its features. JQuery helps in increasing interactions with
a web site. </p>').appendTo('div');
$('img').css({'float':'left',  'width':'200px','height':'200px'});
$('p').css({'clear':'right'});
});
```

How It Works

The CSS properties applied to the image use the float property to make it float to the left in the browser window (allowing the text to appear on its right). The width property confines the image to 200px (any size less than the browser window's total width), so there's space for the text to wrap around the image. The height property limits the height of an image to a particular size.

When "right" is assigned to the clear property, it makes the extra paragraph text move to the left. It tries to make the space on the right side clear (i.e., it tries to fill the space on the left if available). Hence, the extra text of the paragraph extending beyond the image height moves to the left side, wrapping the image by the text around it.

Applying the preceding CSS properties to the image and paragraph elements, you get the output as shown in Figure 12-31.

Styles make the formatting job much easier and efficient. To give an attractive look to web sites, styles are heavily used. A person must have a good knowledge of HTML and CSS and a bit of Javascript. jQuery is a powerful JavaScript library that allows us to add dynamic elements to our web sites. Not only it is easy to learn but easy to implement too. jQuery is an open source project that provides a wide range of features with cross platform compatiblity. jQuery has hundreds of plug-ins to extend its features. JQuery helps in increasing interactions with a web site.

Figure 12-31. *Wrapping the text around the image*

12-21. Placing a Drop Shadow Behind an Image

Problem

You want to place a drop shadow behind an image.

Solution

To create a drop shadow, you need to make two images, one to create a drop shadow on the right side of the image and the other to create a shadow effect at the bottom. These images can be made using a paint brush or any technique. Let's name the image shadowright.jpg for the drop shadow on the right of the image, as shown in Figure 12-32.

Figure 12-32. *The background shadow image for right side*

Similarly, the image to drop shadow at the bottom of the image is named shadowbottom.jpg. It is shown in Figure 12-33.

Figure 12-33. *The background shadow image for the bottom*

Let's assume that an image file is named image4.jpg. The following is the HTML code to display it.

Dropshadow.html

```
<!DOCTYPE html PUBLIC "-//W3C//DTD XHTML 1.0 Transitional//EN"
        "http://www.w3.org/TR/xhtml1/DTD/xhtml1-transitional.dtd">
```

```
<html xmlns="http://www.w3.org/1999/xhtml" xml:lang="en" lang="en">
  <head>
    <meta http-equiv="Content-Type" content="text/html; charset=utf-8"/>
    <title></title>
    <script src="jquery-3.5.1.js" type="text/javascript"></script>
    <script src="dropshadowjq.js" type="text/javascript"></script>
  </head>
  <body>
      <span class="shadow"><img src="scene.jpg" /></span>
  </body>
</html>
```

The style rules to be applied to the img element and span element are applied via the css() method as shown in the following jQuery code.

Dropshadowjq.js

```
$(document).ready(function() {
  $('span').css({'background':'url(shadowright.jpg)', 'background-
  position':'right',   'background-repeat':'no-repeat', 'padding':'195px
  15px 0px 0px'});
  $('img').css({'width':'200px','height':'200px','background':
  'url(shadowbottom.jpg)',  'background-repeat':'no-repeat','background-
  position':'bottom', 'padding':'0 0 10px 0' });
});
```

How It Works

Observe that the img element is enclosed within a span element. The reason for doing so is that you need to apply two style rules to the img element, one to drop shadow on the right side of the image and the other to drop shadow at the bottom of the image being displayed. But you cannot apply more than one style rule to an element. So, to apply two style rules to the img element, enclose it with a span element so that one style rule can be applied to the span element (which eventually be applied to the img element), and other style rules can be applied to the img element itself.

The first css() call contains four properties.

- The background:url property is set to display the image stored in the file shadowright.jpg in the background of the image.

- The background-repeat property is set to no-repeat to display the shadow image only once.

- The background-position is set to "right" to display the shadow image on the right side of the image aligned to the bottom.

- The padding property sets the distance of the shadow image from the actual image. This helps in deciding the width of the shadow.

- Similarly, the second css() call contains six properties.

- The width and height properties are set to 200px to constraint the width and height of the actual image being displayed to 200 pixels.

- The background:url property is set to display the image stored in the file shadowbottom.jpg in the background of the image.

- The background-repeat is set to no-repeat to display the shadow image only once.

- The background-position is set to bottom to display the shadow image at the bottom of the actual image.

- The padding property sets the distance of the shadow image from the actual image.

Applying these properties to the image gives it drop shadows on the right and bottom as shown in Figure 12-34.

Figure 12-34. *An image with a shadow at the back*

12-22. Changing the Cursor When the Mouse Moves Over a Link

Problem

You want to change the style of the cursor when it moves over a link.

Solution

For this problem, you make a HTML file that contains some information in a div element along with a Click Here link, which when selected, navigates to the abc.com site. The following is the HTML.

Changecursor.html

```
<!DOCTYPE html PUBLIC "-//W3C//DTD XHTML 1.0 Transitional//EN"
        "http://www.w3.org/TR/xhtml1/DTD/xhtml1-transitional.dtd">
<html xmlns="http://www.w3.org/1999/xhtml" xml:lang="en" lang="en">
  <head>
    <meta http-equiv="Content-Type" content="text/html; charset=utf-8"/>
    <title></title>
    <script src="jquery-3.5.1.js" type="text/javascript"></script>
    <script src="changecursorjq.js" type="text/javascript"></script>
  </head>
  <body>
```

```
<div>Styles make the formatting job much easier and efficient. To give
an attractive look to web sites, styles are heavily used. A person
must have a good knowledge of HTML and CSS and a bit of Javascript.
jQuery is a powerful JavaScript library that allows us to add dynamic
elements to our web sites. Not only it is easy to learn but easy to
implement too.
jQuery is an open source project. <a href="abc.com">Click Here</a> for
more information </div>
  </body>
</html>
```

To apply different cursor property to the hyper link, you write following jQuery code.

Changecursorjq.js

```
$(document).ready(function() {
  $(a).hover(
    function(){
      $(this).css({'cursor': 'wait', 'color': 'blue' , 'background-
      color':'cyan'});
    },
    function(){
      $(this).css({'cursor': 'default', 'color': '#000000' , 'background-
      color':'#ffffff'});
    });
});
```

How It Works

The hover() method contains two functions: one is executed when the mouse pointer hovers over the selected element, and the other function is executed when the mouse pointer is moved away from the selected element. Initially, the output is shown in Figure 12-35. You can see that the hyperlink is underlined, and the mouse pointer is the default pointer.

Styles make the formatting job much easier and efficient. To give an attractive look to web sites, styles are heavily used. A person must have a good knowledge of HTML and CSS and a bit of Javascript. jQuery is a powerful JavaScript library that allows us to add dynamic elements to our web sites. Not only it is easy to learn but easy to implement too. jQuery is an open source project. Click Here for more information

Figure 12-35. *Default cursor when link is not visited*

On moving the mouse over the link, the CSS properties defined in hover() are applied on it, changing the shape of the mouse pointer to appear as if it is waiting for something to happen and the background color of the link changes to cyan and its foreground color changes to blue as shown in Figure 12-36.

Styles make the formatting job much easier and efficient. To give an attractive look to web sites, styles are heavily used. A person must have a good knowledge of HTML and CSS and a bit of Javascript. jQuery is a powerful JavaScript library that allows us to add dynamic elements to our web sites. Not only it is easy to learn but easy to implement too. jQuery is an open source project. Click Here for more information

Figure 12-36. *Cursor changes when mouse moves over the link*

12-23. Displaying a Long Piece of Text Within a Specific Area

Problem

You want to display a long piece of text within a specific area.

Solution

The following HTML file defines a paragraph element that you want to confine to a smaller area of the page.

Longtextinarea.html

```
<!DOCTYPE html PUBLIC "-//W3C//DTD XHTML 1.0 Transitional//EN"
        "http://www.w3.org/TR/xhtml1/DTD/xhtml1-transitional.dtd">
<html xmlns="http://www.w3.org/1999/xhtml" xml:lang="en" lang="en">
  <head>
    <meta http-equiv="Content-Type" content="text/html; charset=utf-8"/>
    <title></title>
```

```
    <script src="jquery-3.5.1.js" type="text/javascript"></script>
    <script src="longtextinareajq.js" type="text/javascript"></script>
</head>
<body>

    <p>Styles make the formatting job much easier and efficient. To
    give an attractive look to web sites, styles are heavily used. A
    person must have a good knowledge of HTML and CSS and a bit of
    Javascript.   <br/>
    jQuery is a powerful JavaScript library that allows us to add dynamic
    elements to our web sites. Not only it is easy to learn but easy
    to implement too.   jQuery is an open source project that provides
    a wide range of features with cross platform compatibility. jQuery
    has hundreds of plug-ins to extend its features. jQuery helps in
    increasing interactions with a web site </p>
</body>
</html>
```

To confine the text and apply the overflow property to the paragraph element, you use the following jQuery.

Longtextinareajq.js

```
$(document).ready(function() {
    $('p').css({ 'width':'50%', 'height':'100px','overflow':'scroll' });
});
```

How It Works

You assign 50% of the browser window and a height of 100 pixels to the paragraph. By setting the value of overflow to scroll, you make scrollbars appear if the text of the paragraph element is not completely visible in the specified height and width. The output is shown in Figure 12-37.

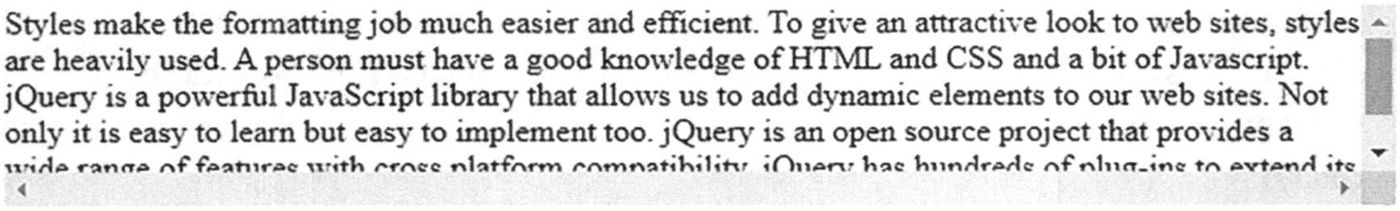

Styles make the formatting job much easier and efficient. To give an attractive look to web sites, styles
are heavily used. A person must have a good knowledge of HTML and CSS and a bit of Javascript.
jQuery is a powerful JavaScript library that allows us to add dynamic elements to our web sites. Not
only it is easy to learn but easy to implement too. jQuery is an open source project that provides a
wide range of features with cross platform compatibility. jQuery has hundreds of plug-ins to extend its

Figure 12-37. *Applying overflow element with scroll option*

Let's see what happens when you set the value of the overflow property to hidden.
The text of the paragraph which is not able to appear within the assigned area becomes
invisible as shown in Figure 12-38.

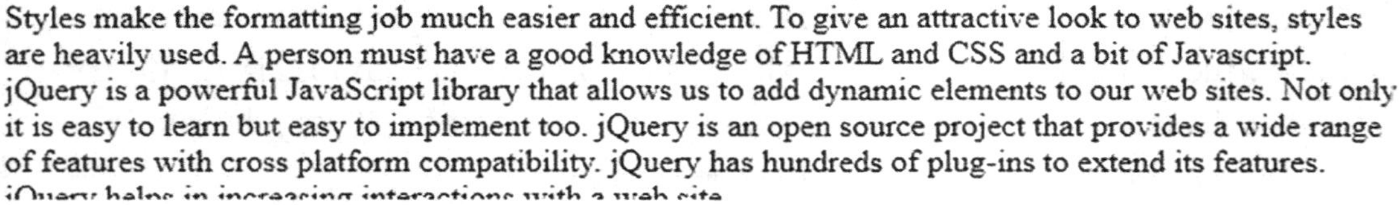

Styles make the formatting job much easier and efficient. To give an attractive look to web sites, styles
are heavily used. A person must have a good knowledge of HTML and CSS and a bit of Javascript.
jQuery is a powerful JavaScript library that allows us to add dynamic elements to our web sites. Not only
it is easy to learn but easy to implement too. jQuery is an open source project that provides a wide range
of features with cross platform compatibility. jQuery has hundreds of plug-ins to extend its features.
jQuery helps in increasing interactions with a web site

Figure 12-38. *Applying overflow element with hidden option*

Let's set the value of the overflow property to auto. The scroll bar is only for the
height and not the width (unlike the value scroll) (i.e., the scrollbar appears only where it
is needed). The output of this style is shown in Figure 12-39.

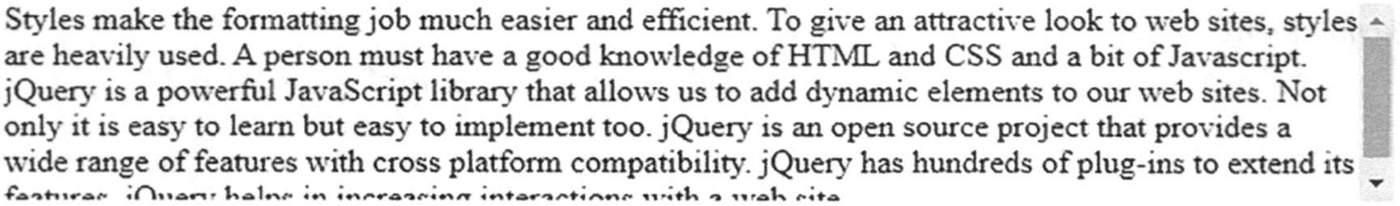

Styles make the formatting job much easier and efficient. To give an attractive look to web sites, styles
are heavily used. A person must have a good knowledge of HTML and CSS and a bit of Javascript.
jQuery is a powerful JavaScript library that allows us to add dynamic elements to our web sites. Not
only it is easy to learn but easy to implement too. jQuery is an open source project that provides a
wide range of features with cross platform compatibility. jQuery has hundreds of plug-ins to extend its
features. jQuery helps in increasing interactions with a web site

Figure 12-39. *Applying overflow element with auto option*

Let's set the value of the overflow property to visible. The text of the paragraph is
entirely visible (i.e., it is not confined to the region assigned to it), as shown in Figure 12-40.

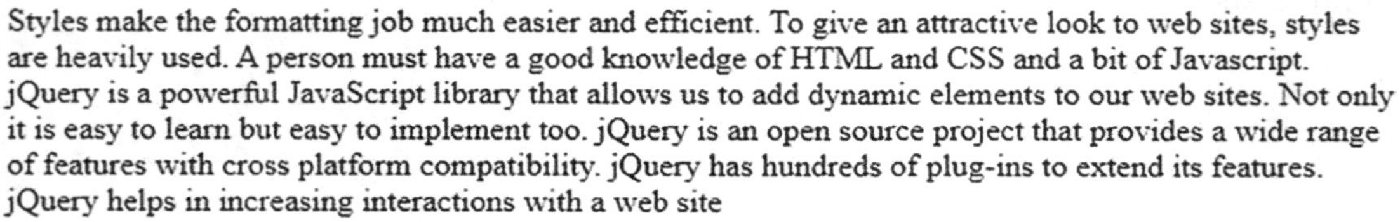

Styles make the formatting job much easier and efficient. To give an attractive look to web sites, styles
are heavily used. A person must have a good knowledge of HTML and CSS and a bit of Javascript.
jQuery is a powerful JavaScript library that allows us to add dynamic elements to our web sites. Not only
it is easy to learn but easy to implement too. jQuery is an open source project that provides a wide range
of features with cross platform compatibility. jQuery has hundreds of plug-ins to extend its features.
jQuery helps in increasing interactions with a web site

Figure 12-40. *Applying overflow element with visible option*

12-24. Making a Rounded Corner Column

Problem

You want to make a single column with rounded corners.

Solution

To make the column appear rounded, you need to make a rectangle with rounded corners and paste it in the background of the text. Let's make a rounded cornered rectangle, as shown in Figure 12-41, and name it columnfig.jpg.

Figure 12-41. *Rounded cornered rectangle*

This image is set as the background of the text. Let's make an HTML file with a paragraph element with some text, as follows.

Roundedcolumn.html

```
<!DOCTYPE html PUBLIC "-//W3C//DTD XHTML 1.0 Transitional//EN"
        "http://www.w3.org/TR/xhtml1/DTD/xhtml1-transitional.dtd">
<html xmlns="http://www.w3.org/1999/xhtml" xml:lang="en" lang="en">
  <head>
    <meta http-equiv="Content-Type" content="text/html; charset=utf-8"/>
    <title></title>
```

```
<link rel="stylesheet" href="styleroundedcolumn.css" type="text/css"
media="screen" />
<script src="jquery-3.5.1.js" type="text/javascript"></script>
<script src="roundedcolumnjq.js" type="text/javascript"></script>
</head>
<body>
    <p>Styles make the formatting job much easier and efficient. To give
    an attractive look to web sites, styles are heavily used. A person
    must have a good knowledge of HTML and CSS and a bit of Javascript.
    jQuery is powerful JavaScript library used to make dynamic sites.</p>
</body>
</html>
```

In the style sheet, let's write a style rule to paste the rounded rectangle as the background of the paragraph element. The style rule includes properties like width, padding, background, and background-repeat, as follows.

Styleroundedcolumn.css

```
.backfig{
    width:150px;
    padding:10px;
    background:url(columnfig.jpg);
    background-repeat:no-repeat;
}
```

Let's write jQuery code to apply the backfig style rule to the paragraph element. The following is the jQuery code.

Roundedcolumnjq.js

```
$(document).ready(function() {
  $('p').addClass('backfig');
});
```

How It Works

The backfig style rule assigns a width to the paragraph text that is equal to the width of the rounded rectangle, so that the text of the paragraph remains confined within the boundaries of the rounded rectangle. The padding property keeps a gap between the rectangle boundary and the paragraph text. The background property is for setting the rounded rectangle image stored in columnfig.jpg as the background of the paragraph text and the value of background-repeat is set to no-repeat to make the rounded rectangle to appear just once.

After applying the rounded rectangle image as the background, the paragraph text looks as shown in Figure 12-42.

Styles make the formatting job much easier and efficient. To give an attractive look to web sites, styles are heavily used. A person must have a good knowledge of HTML and CSS and a bit of Javascript. jQuery is powerful JavaScript library used to make dynamic sites.

Figure 12-42. *A single column with rounded corners*

12-25. Applying Text Decorations
Problem

You want to apply text decorations, such as overline and underline styles, to certain text to draw attention to it. You also need to apply effects, such as strike-through, for comparison purposes. For example, to demonstrate the earlier discount and the current discount on a certain item.

Solution

The following is HTML that contains three paragraph elements that are assigned the class names feature1, feature2, and feature3.

Textdecor.html

```
<!DOCTYPE html PUBLIC "-//W3C//DTD XHTML 1.0 Transitional//EN"
        "http://www.w3.org/TR/xhtml1/DTD/xhtml1-transitional.dtd">
<html xmlns="http://www.w3.org/1999/xhtml" xml:lang="en" lang="en">
  <head>
    <meta http-equiv="Content-Type" content="text/html; charset=utf-8"/>
    <title></title>
    <script src="jquery-3.5.1.js" type="text/javascript"></script>
    <script src="textdecorjq.js" type="text/javascript"></script>
  </head>
  <body>
        <p class="feature1">jQuery is powerful</p>
        <p class="feature2">Styles make the formatting job much easier and
        efficient. To give an attractive look to web sites, styles are
        heavily used. A person must have a good knowledge of HTML and CSS
        and a bit of Javascript. jQuery is powerful JavaScript library used
        to make dynamic sites.</p>
        <p class="feature3">10% Discount on all products</p>
        <p>20% Discount  on all products</p>
  </body>
</html>
```

The following is the jQuery to apply text decoration to the paragraph elements.

Textdecorjq.js

```
$(document).ready(function() {
  $('p.feature1').css({'text-decoration':'underline'});
  $('p.feature2').css({'text-decoration':'overline'});
  $('p.feature3').css({'text-decoration':'line-through'});
});
```

You can also apply both overline and underline values to the heading (i.e., to the feature1 class paragraph) to highlight it.

```
<div>
    <p class="feature1">jQuery is powerful</p>
</div>
```

The style rules now change.

Textdecor2jq.js

```
$(document).ready(function() {
  $('p.feature1').css({'text-decoration':'underline'});
  $('div').css({'text-decoration':'overline'});
  $('p.feature3').css({'text-decoration':'line-through'});
});
```

How It Works

The first call to css() displays the text of the paragraph of class="feature1" as underlined text. Similarly, the second call displays the text of the paragraph of class="feature2" with a line over it. The third call displays the text of paragraph of class="feature3" with a line through it as if the text is stroked. The output is shown in Figure 12-43.

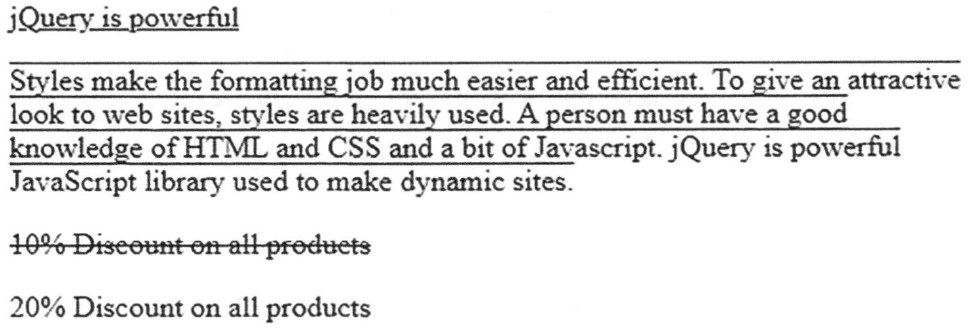

jQuery is powerful

Styles make the formatting job much easier and efficient. To give an attractive look to web sites, styles are heavily used. A person must have a good knowledge of HTML and CSS and a bit of Javascript. jQuery is powerful JavaScript library used to make dynamic sites.

10% Discount on all products

20% Discount on all products

Figure 12-43. *Applying different options of text-decoration with class*

The advantage of using line-through is that the visitor can know what the earlier contents were and can compare with the current contents. As the preceding solution shows, the earlier discount rate was 10% which is increased now to 20%.

To highlight the heading, since you cannot apply two style rules to the same element, you enclose the feature1 class paragraph inside a div element so that you can apply one style rule to the div and another style rule to the paragraph element. You can see that the first style rule makes the feature1 class paragraph appear underlined. The second style rule makes an overline appear on the contents of the div element (i.e., on the feature2 class paragraph). The third style rule makes the feature2 class paragraph appear struck out. The output is shown in Figure 12-44.

jQuery is powerful

Styles make the formatting job much easier and efficient. To give an attractive look to web sites, styles are heavily used. A person must have a good knowledge of HTML and CSS and a bit of Javascript. jQuery is powerful JavaScript library used to make dynamic sites.

~~10% Discount on all products~~

20% Discount on all products

Figure 12-44. *Applying overline and underline to the heading of the text*

12-26. Scaling Images
Problem

You an image to be scalable (i.e., if the size of the block in which the image is placed is reduced), the size of the image should also be reduced automatically. Similarly, if the size of the enclosing block is increased, you want the size of the image also to be increased.

Solution

Let's make use of the same HTML that you used in Recipe 12-19 (refer to Figure 12-30 for the results of that recipe). This time, you define the width of the image in terms of % (percentage) of the containing block element. Since the containing block of the image is the browser window, the width of the image increases or decreases in response to the changes made in the size of the browser window. The following are the modified style rules.

Stylescaling.css

```css
.moveleft
{
    width:40%;
    float:left;
}

.imagewrap {
    clear:right;
}
```

The following is the jQuery code to apply the style rules to the image and the paragraph element.

Scalingimagesjq.js

```js
$(document).ready(function() {
    $('img').wrap('<div></div>');
    $('<p>Styles make the formatting job much easier and efficient.
    To give an attractive look to web sites, styles are heavily used.
    A person must have a good knowledge of HTML and CSS and a bit of
    Javascript. jQuery is a powerful JavaScript library that allows us to
    add dynamic elements to our web sites. Not only it is easy to learn
    but easy to implement too.  jQuery is an open source project that
    provides a wide range of features with cross platform compatiblity.
    jQuery has hundreds of plug-ins to extend its features. JQuery helps
    in increasing interactions with a web site. </p>').appendTo('div');
     $('img').addClass('moveleft');
     $('p').addClass('imagewrap');
});
```

How It Works

If you increase the width of the browser window from Recipe 12-19, you find that the size of the image remains the same and is not scaled according to the change in the width of the browser window, as shown in Figure 12-45.

Styles make the formatting job much easier and efficient. To give an attractive look to web sites, styles are heavily used. A person must have a good knowledge of HTML and CSS and a bit of Javascript. jQuery is a powerful JavaScript library that allows us to add dynamic elements to our web sites. Not only it is easy to learn but easy to implement too. jQuery is an open source project that provides a wide range of features with cross platform compatiblity. jQuery has hundreds of plug-ins to extend its features. JQuery helps in increasing interactions with a web site.

Figure 12-45. *The image is not scaled on increasing the width of browser window*

The reason the image is not scaled lies in the original styles applied to it. The styles have been added to a style rule for reference.

Stylescaling.css

```
.moveleft
{
    width:200px;
    height:200px;
    float:left;
}
```

You can see that the width of the image is set fixed to 200px, as a result, the width of the image remains fixed despite any change in the browser window size.

The new moveleft style rule contains two properties.

- The width property is set equal to 40% of the browser window's width (i.e., whenever the width of the browser window is changed), the width of the image changes to maintain the 40% ratio).

- The float property is set to left to keep the image on the left of the browser, making space for the paragraph text to appear on its right side.

The imagewrap style rule is applied to the paragraph text and contains a single property clear to make the extra paragraph text (the text which extends the size of the image) appear below the image so that the image appears wrapped inside the text. The impact of this property is visible only when the size of the browser window is so adjusted that the paragraph text extends the height of the image.

When applying the styles, you find that the image becomes scalable with the browser window's size, as shown in Figure 12-46.

Styles make the formatting job much easier and efficient. To give an attractive look to web sites, styles are heavily used. A person must have a good knowledge of HTML and CSS and a bit of Javascript. jQuery is a powerful JavaScript library that allows us to add dynamic elements to our web sites. Not only it is easy to learn but easy to implement too. jQuery is an open source project that provides a wide range of features with cross platform compatiblity. jQuery has hundreds of plug-ins to extend its features. JQuery helps in increasing interactions with a web site.

Figure 12-46.   *The image is scaled (increased in size) on increasing the width of browser window*

12-27. Setting a Background Image
Problem

You want an image to appear as the background of your text.

Solution

Let's assume that the following HTML contains a paragraph element to display simple text.

Backgroundimage.html

```
<!DOCTYPE html PUBLIC "-//W3C//DTD XHTML 1.0 Transitional//EN"
        "http://www.w3.org/TR/xhtml1/DTD/xhtml1-transitional.dtd">
<html xmlns="http://www.w3.org/1999/xhtml" xml:lang="en" lang="en">
  <head>
    <meta http-equiv="Content-Type" content="text/html; charset=utf-8"/>
    <title></title>
    <link rel="stylesheet" href="stylebackgroundimage.css" type="text/css"
    media="screen" />
    <script src="jquery-3.5.1.js" type="text/javascript"></script>
```

```
    <script src="backgroundimagejq.js" type="text/javascript"></script>
  </head>
  <body>
      <p>Styles make the formatting job much easier and efficient. To give
      an attractive look to web sites, styles are heavily used. A person
      must have a good knowledge of HTML and CSS and a bit of Javascript.
      jQuery is a powerful JavaScript library that allows us to add dynamic
      elements to our web sites. Not only it is easy to learn but easy to
      implement too.
      jQuery is an open source project that provides a wide range of
      features with cross platform compatiblity. jQuery has hundreds
      of plug-ins to extend its features. jQuery helps in increasing
      interactions with a web site. </p>
  </body>
</html>
```

In order to apply an image as the background of the text, you need to write a style rule, as follows.

Stylebackgroundimage.css

```
.placeimage
{
    background-image:url(cell.jpg);
    background-repeat:no-repeat;
}
```

You now need to write the jQuery code to apply the placeimage to the body tag. The following is the jQuery code.

Backgroundimagejq.js

```
$(document).ready(function() {
  $('body').addClass('placeimage');
});
```

How It Works

Let's assume there is an image file named cell.jpg. In the placeimage style rule, you have used two properties: background-image and background-repeat. With the help of background-image, you make the image stored in cell.jpg appear as the background of the text. By default, the image is repeated several times to fill up the containing block. So, you set the value of the background-repeat property to no-repeat so that the image appears only once in the background.

After applying the placeimage style rule to the body of the HTML file, the image stored in the cell.jpg file appears as the background of the text, as shown in Figure 12-47.

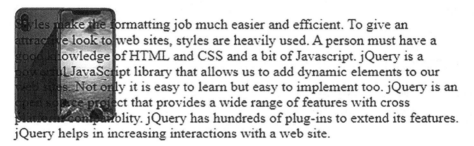

Figure 12-47. *The image is set as the background of the text*

12-28. Centering a Background Image in the Browser

Problem

Usually, when you set an image as the background, it is aligned to the left of the browser window. You want the background image to appear in the center of the browser screen.

Solution

In this recipe, you use the same HTML file you used in Recipe 12-26, which displays an image as the background (that is left-aligned). To make the left-aligned background image appear in the center of the screen, you use the background-position property. By setting the value of the background-position property to the center, the background image appears in the center of the browser screen.

Let's add background-position to the placeimage style rule (see Recipe 12-26) as follows.

Stylecenteringimage.css

```
.placeimage
{
    background-image:url(cell.jpg);
    background-repeat:no-repeat;
    background-position:center;
}
```

The following is the jQuery code to apply the placeimage style rule to the HTML body.

Centeringimagejq.js

```
$(document).ready(function() {
  $('body').addClass('placeimage');
});
```

How It Works

The background-image property makes the image in cell.jpg appear as the background. To make the background image appear only once (i.e., to stop it from repeating itself and filling up the block), you set the value of the background-repeat property to no-repeat. Finally, by assigning the value center to the background-position property, you make sure that the background image appears in the center of the browser window.

After applying the placeimage style rule to the body of the HTML file, the image stored in cell.jpg is the background and in the center of the browser window, as shown in Figure 12-48.

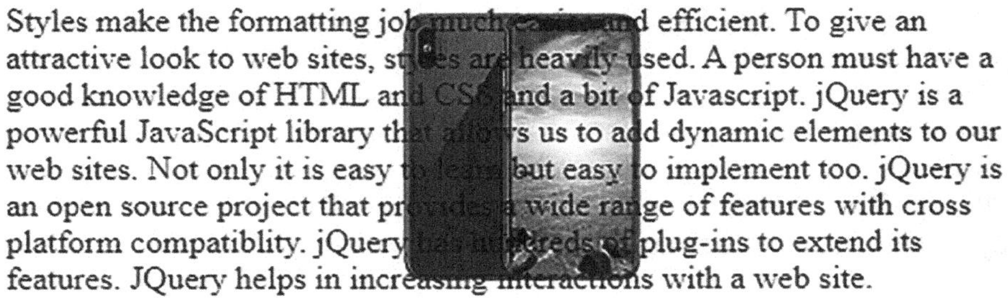

Styles make the formatting job much easier and efficient. To give an attractive look to web sites, styles are heavily used. A person must have a good knowledge of HTML and CSS and a bit of Javascript. jQuery is a powerful JavaScript library that allows us to add dynamic elements to our web sites. Not only it is easy to learn but easy to implement too. jQuery is an open source project that provides a wide range of features with cross platform compatiblity. jQuery has numereds of plug-ins to extend its features. JQuery helps in increasing interactions with a web site.

Figure 12-48. *The background image is placed in the center of the browser screen*

12-29. Making the Background Image Stationary

Problem

When you browse any web page, the image and text scroll up or up the page. You want the background image to remain stationary even when you scroll up or down the page.

Solution

In this recipe, you use the same HTML file that you used in Recipe 12-26. Here you add more text to the paragraph to make it large enough to apply scrolling to it. To keep the background image stationary while scrolling the web page, you use the background-attachment property. By setting the value fixed to the background-attachment property, you set the background image to stay stationary while scrolling the web page. So, let's add the background-attachment property to the style sheet you used in the previous recipe.

Styleimagestationary.css

```
.placeimage
{
    background-image:url(cell.jpg);
    background-repeat:no-repeat;
    background-position:center;
    background-attachment: fixed;
}
```

The following is the jQuery code to apply the placeimage style rule to the body of the HTML file.

Imagestationaryjq.js

```
$(document).ready(function() {
  $('body').addClass('placeimage');
});
```

How It Works

The following is the function of each of the properties used in the placeimage style rule.

- The background-image property makes the cell.jpg image appear as the background.

- The background image is set to appear only once by assigning the value no-repeat to the background-repeat property.

- The background-position property is set to the center to make the background image appear in the center of the browser screen.

- The background-attachment property is set to fixed to make the background image remain stationary when scrolling the web page.

After applying the placeimage style rule to the body of the HTML file, the background image appears as the background, as shown in Figure 12-49.

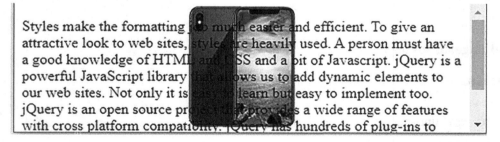

Figure 12-49. *The scroll bar appears when the text is larger than the size of the browser window*

Now, when you scroll the web page down (see the scroll bar on the right), the background image remains in the center of the browser screen, whereas the text scrolls as shown in Figure 12-50.

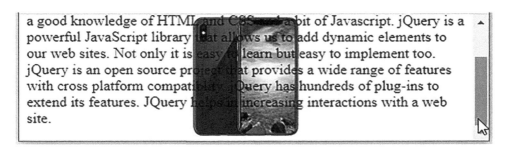

Figure 12-50. *The background image remains stationary even when the text is scrolled*

12-30. Summary

In this chapter, you saw recipes that explain CSS techniques that are frequently applied to web pages. This includes distinguishing HTML elements, applying styles to an element nested inside another element, indenting paragraphs, applying an initial cap to a paragraph, removing the gap between heading and paragraph, applying styles to heading text and indenting the first line of multiple paragraphs.

You saw the process for creating paragraphs with hanging indents, a bordered pull quote, a pull quote with images. You learned how to apply list properties to list items and styles to selected list items, place dividers between list items, apply image markers to a list, and create inline lists.

Finally, you saw how to apply styles to hyperlinks and mailto, assign different dimensions to HTML elements, place HTML elements, create a multicolumn layout, wrap text around images, place a drop shadow behind an image, change the cursor when the mouse moves over a link, display a long piece of text within a specific area, make a rounded corner column, apply text decorations, scale images, set a background image, center a background image, and make the background image stationary.

APPENDIX A

Installing WampServer

The full name of AJAX is **Asynchronous JavaScript And XML** and it enables web pages to be updated asynchronously by exchanging data with a web server in the background. The AJAX technique makes web pages quite responsive because most of the job is done in the background. It is also possible to update parts of a web page instead of reloading the whole web page.

To test AJAX code, you need a server and that is why I installed WampServer on my Windows computer.

The Wamp in WampServer stands for **Windows (operating system), Apache (web server), MySQL (database), and PHP programming language**. There is another server called XAMPP which can be used for Linux and Mac OS as well.

A-1. Downloading WampServer

The first step is to download WampServer. Visit the official website at `www.wampserver.com/en/` and download the WampServer setup. You will find two versions of WampServer, 64-bits (x64) and 32-bits (x86), so choose the version that matches your computer's configuration. The latest version of WampServer at the time of this writing is 3.2.3.

After you click the Download button, the executable (.exe) setup file of WampServer will be downloaded onto your machine. If upon clicking the Download button you are shown certain dialogues, look for the "download directly" link and click it. On my computer, the file is named `wampserver3.2.3_x64.exe`.

© Bintu Harwani 2022
B. Harwani, *jQuery Recipes*, https://doi.org/10.1007/978-1-4842-7304-3

A-2. Installing WampServer

Once the executable file is downloaded, simply double-click it to begin the installation process. The first dialog asks you to choose your preferred language (see Figure A-1). I picked the English language. Choose your desired language and click the OK button.

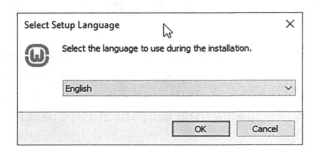

Figure A-1. *Choosing your language*

Figure A-2 shows the license agreement. Read the terms and conditions mentioned in the agreement and if you agree, click the "I accept the agreement" radio button and then the Next button to continue with the installation procedure

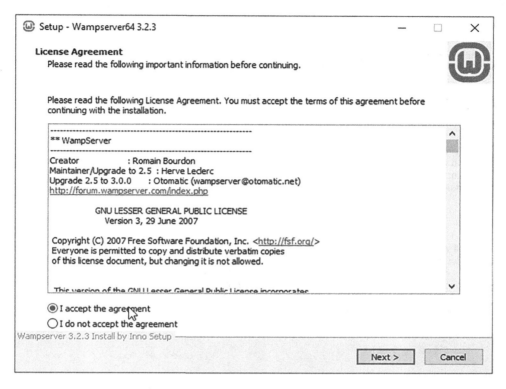

Figure A-2. *Agreeing to the License Agreement*

The next dialog confirms whether the elements that are essential for the proper functioning of WampServer are installed on your system or not. The dialog asks you to make sure that the redistributable package, VC9, VC10, etc. are up to date. It also warns you to not install WampServer over an existing version and that WampServer needs to be installed in a folder at the root of the disk (as shown in Figure A-3). If you are sure about the things mentioned in the dialog, click the Next button to continue.

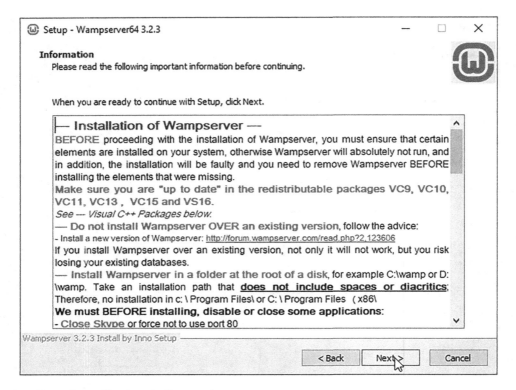

Figure A-3. *Installation information*

The next dialog prompts for the location to install WampServer on your computer (see Figure A-4). The dialog will show you the default folder where WampServer can be installed. You can always select the Browse button to specify your desired folder. Click the Next button to continue with the installation.

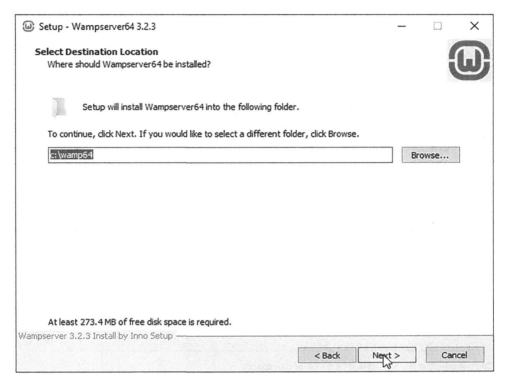

Figure A-4. *WampServer location*

The next dialog asks you to select the components that you want to be installed (see Figure A-5). If you want to choose any specific PHP version or any specific MariaDB version, you can select the respective component. The dialog also shows the disk space required to install the selected components. Click the Next button to continue.

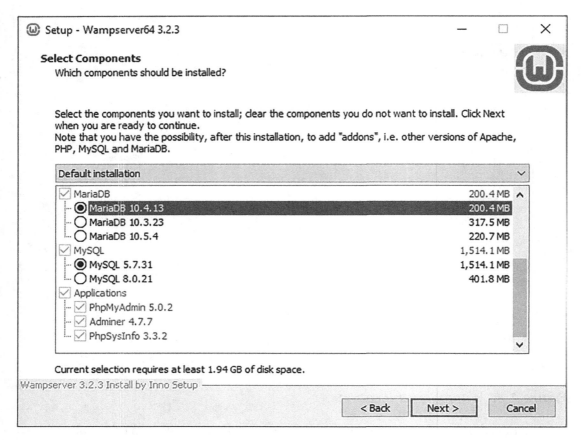

Figure A-5. *Selecting components*

The next dialog asks you to select the Start Menu folder where you want to create the program's shortcut (see Figure A-6). You can select any folder of your choice or you can continue with the default folder. Click the Next button to continue.

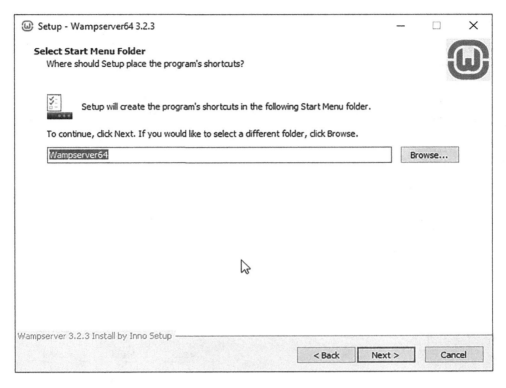

Figure A-6. *Shortcut location*

The next dialog informs you that the setup is now ready to begin installing WampServer on your machine. Click the Install button shown in Figure A-7 to begin with the installation procedure.

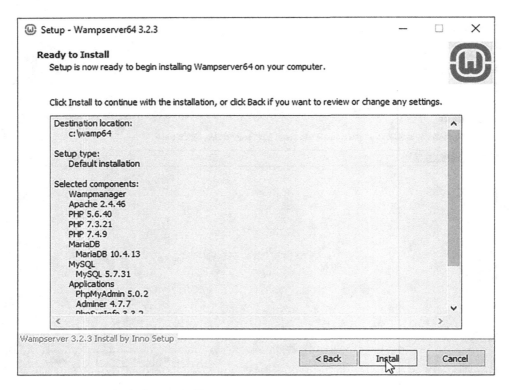

Figure A-7. *Beginning the installation*

The WampServer files will be extracted into the selected folder location. You will be asked to select the browser that you want to be used by WampServer, as shown in Figure A-8. Internet Explorer is the default browser. If you want to use a different browser, click the Yes button.

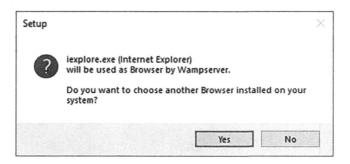

Figure A-8. *Picking a browser*

The next dialog asks you to choose the text editor that you want to be used by WampServer. Notepad is the default editor. You can choose another text editor by clicking the Yes button. See Figure A-9.

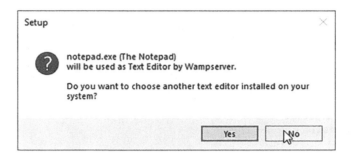

Figure A-9. *Picking a text editor*

The next dialog shows you the location of different help files that help you understand how WampServer works and how SQL statements work in MariaDB (see Figure A-10). Click the Next button to continue.

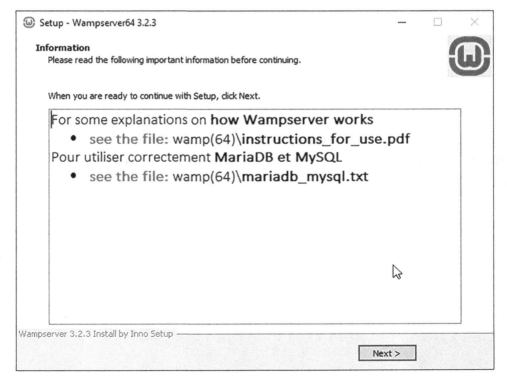

Figure A-10. *Help files*

The next dialog, shown in Figure A-11, confirms that installation is done. Simply click Finish to exit the setup.

Figure A-11. *Success!*

To launch WampServer, type **wamp** in the search box of your computer and WampServer64 will appear with several options like Open, Run as administrator, and more (see Figure A-12). Seelct the Run as administrator option.

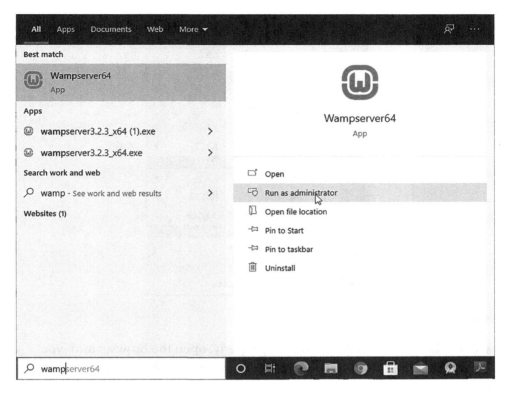

Figure A-12. *Running as an administrator*

WampServer will be launched if the W, the icon of WampServer in the status bar, is turned fully green. This means it is ready to be used. If the color of WampServer is red or orange, that means it is not yet started. In that case, select the W icon in the status bar to open its menu. Select the Start All Services option to start WampServer services (see Figure A-13).

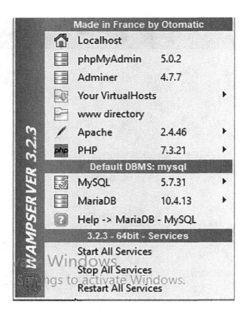

Figure A-13. *Starting WampServer*

To ensure that WampServer is working properly, open the browser and type
`http://localhost/` in the address bar. If you get output similar to Figure A-14, it means
that WampServer is installed and is working properly.

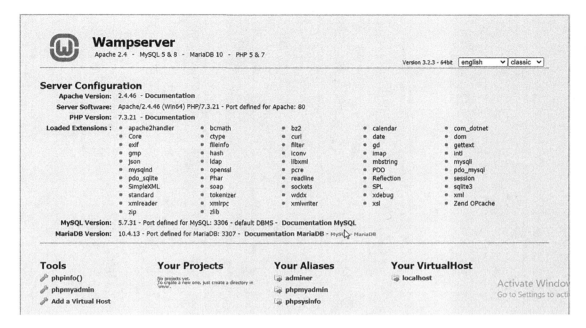

Figure A-14. *WampServer is working properly!*

Note   Copy the code provided in Chapter 10 (with the source code bundle of the book) into the www folder of your computer, the C:\wamp64\www folder.

Index

A

addClass() method, 11, 12
after() method, 354
AJAX
    create database, 495
    create table statement, 496, 497
    INSERT INTO statement, 498–501
    JSON object, images, 482–486
    multiple line of text, 476, 478
    name/value pair, 479
    price of product, 492–495
    SELECT statement, 497, 498
    show databases, 496
    show table statement, 497
    single line of text, 474, 475
    uppercase, 489–491
    user name, 495
    use statement, 496
    validation, 506, 508
ajax() method, 475, 509, 514, 525
alert() method, 15, 43, 90, 427
animate() method, 132, 133
Animation
    expanding/collapsing list
        electronics class, 335
        HTML code, 333, 334
        jQuery code, 335
        list items, 335, 336
        slideToggle() method, 335, 336
        unordered list, 335, 336

image
    animate method, 307, 308
    chip, 309, 310
    HTML program, 305, 306
    jQuery code, 306, 308
    laptop, 309, 310
    left property, 307
    position property, 307
jQuery queue
    alert dialog box, 313, 314
    HTML program, 311
    pop() function, 314, 315
    slideToggle() method, 313
    tasks, 311
Next/Previous buttons
    alert dialog box, 321, 322
    CSS style sheet, 317, 318
    display property, 319
    first image, 321, 322
    float property, 319, 320
    hidden images, 323, 324
    HTML program, 316
    image sliding, 325, 326
    margin-left property, 321
    overflow property, 318
    padding property, 318
read more link
    HTML program, 330
    hyperlink, 332
    jQuery code, 331

© Bintu Harwani 2022
B. Harwani, *jQuery Recipes*, https://doi.org/10.1007/978-1-4842-7304-3

Animation (*cont.*)
    <p> elements, 330
    read less, 332
  zooming in
    css() method, 328
    CSS style sheet, 327
    HTML code, 326, 327
    jQuery code, 328
    mouse pointer, 328, 329
append() method, 22, 53
Apply styles, 213
  Form Button, 216
  HTML file, 213, 214
  select element, 215
  Submit Button, 217–219
Arrays
  concatenating
    complete list, 65, 66
    <div> and <p> elements, 64
    grep() method, 65
    HTML file, 63
    jQuery code, 64
    merge() method, 66
    nums array, 65
  creation
    displaying content, 78, 79
    <div> element, 80
    jQuery code, 79, 80
    sort() method, 81
  elements
    HTML file, 71
    jQuery code, 71–73
    list, 75
    map() method, 74, 75
    ordered-list, 72, 73
    toUpperCase() method, 72, 74, 75
  objects, 83–85

sorting, 52–54
splitting
    <div> and <p> elements, 57
    electronics, 58, 59
    garments, 59
    HTML file, 56, 57
    jQuery code, 57
    splice() method, 58
arrItems, 487
arr.push() method, 481
Associative arrays
  contents, 83
  <div> element, 82
  HTML file, 81
  jQuery code, 82
  <p> element, 82
attr() method, 39, 40, 221
Attributes
  alert dialog box, 40, 41
  attr() method, 39, 40
  HTML file, 38, 39
  hyperlink, 40, 41
autocomplete.php script file, 512
Autofill, 513

B

background-color property, 146, 294, 389
background-image property, 258, 301, 648
background-position
    property, 258, 301
background-repeat property, 152, 258, 294
Blueimp Gallery plugin, 531, 533, 562, 563
blur() method, 91
border-bottom property, 266, 273, 277,
    282, 294
border property, 347, 374, 379, 618

C

callback function, 463, 475, 561

Cascade style sheet (CSS)

    applying initial cap, paragraph, 585–587

    applying styles, 580–582

    apply text decorations, 639, 641, 642

    background image, centering, 647, 648

    background images, 645, 647

    background image stationary, 649–651

    bordered pull quote, 594–596

    changing cursor, 632, 633

    definition, 577

    displaying long piece text, 634–636

    hanging indents, 592–594

    HTML elements, 578–580, 617–619

    hyperlinks/malito, 613, 615, 616

    image markers, 608–611

    indenting first line paragraph, 590–592

    indenting paragraphs, 583–585

    inline lists, 611, 612

    list applying styles, 602–607

    list items, 600–602

    multicolumn layout

        applying floats, 623, 624

        gutter size, 624, 625

        HTML, 622

    placing dividers, 607, 608

    placing drop shadow, 628–630, 632

    placing HTML elements, 619, 621

    pull quote, 596, 597, 599

    remove gap, between heading/ paragraph, 587–590

    rounded corner columns, 637–639

    scaling images, 642–645

    wrapping text, images, 626–628

Chaining

    Cell Phones, 25

    end() method, 25

    jQuery code, 24

    style rules, 24

    styles, 24, 25

    unordered list, 23

Checkboxes

    class selectors, 198, 201

    error message, 202

    HTML file, 197

    length method, 200

children() method, 27

class selector, 155, 158, 175, 176, 178

concat() method, 65

Content delivery networks (CDNs), 3

Create table statement, 496, 497

css() method, 146, 244, 278, 320, 618, 630

D

Data variable, 183, 186, 189, 192, 509

Date

    class selectors, 191

    error message, 192, 193

    HTML file, 190

dateFormat property, 444

datepicker() method, 440

die() method, 504

disabled property, 453, 459, 471

Disable the fields

    error message, 236, 237

    style sheet file, 233

Document Object Model (DOM), 3

    cloning

        applying style, 34

Document Object Model (DOM) (*cont.*)
    classes, 35
    clone() method, 33
    cloningdomstyle.css, 34, 35
    HTML program, 32, 33
    jQuery code, 33
    paragraph elements, 33–35
  nodes, counting, 42–44
  removing, 20, 22
  replacing, 29, 30

E

.each() function, 44, 73, 201, 244, 481
Email address
  class selectors, 194
  error message, 197
  HTML file, 194
Error message, 182, 510
Event handling function, 183, 261
Event model
  add/remove text, 155–157
  applying animation, 131, 132, 134–136
  avoid event bubbling, 119–122
  CSS style
    HTML file, 96, 97
    mouse pointer, 96
    working, 101
  disabling button, 139–141
  displaying text, animation effect,
    163–168
  displaying word balloons, 157, 159–161
  display message
    HTML file, 88
    solution, 88, 89, 91
    working, 91, 92
  fading effect, image, 128–130
  highlight text, 144–146

image-based rollover, 150–154
image bright/blurred, 147–149
key pressed
  HTML file, 124, 125
  input box, 124
  keydown() event, 125
  keypress(), 126
  keyup, 126
  working, 127
mouse button
  HTML file, 93
  problem, 93
  working, 95, 96
mouse hover event
  button, 102
  HTML file, 102, 104
  working, 104
mouse up/down event
  button, 105
  HTML file, 106
  working, 109, 110
replacing text, sliding effect, 168–171
return to top, 161, 162
screen coordinates, 142, 143
triggering events, 136–138
two buttons
  HTML file, 110
  individual tasks, 110
  working, 114, 115
zoom in and out image
  CSS style, 117
  HTML file, 116
  toggleclass(), 117, 118
  working, 118, 119
event.preventDefault() method, 331
event property, 459, 471
event.which property, 94, 95
External style sheet, 106, 137, 208

F

fadeIn() method, 108, 109, 111, 114
fadeOut() method, 108, 109, 114
fadeTo() method, 129, 130
find() method, 19, 24, 25
font-weight property, 294, 301
for loop
    alert dialog box, 27, 28
    ElectronicsProducts, 27
    jQuery code, 27
    range, 28
    string variable, 28
    unordered list, 26
Form
    common elements, 254
    data, 247
    error message, 245, 246
    HTML file, 238
    input fields, 247
    jQuery code, 243
    style sheet, 250
    validation, 238

G

getJSON() method, 480
grep() method, 61, 62, 65, 70

H

hide() method, 113–115
hover() method, 104, 633
HTML file
    desired elements, 519
    hyperlink, 519
    import, 518
    web page, 521

I

iCheck, 531, 554
Image carousel, 563, 568, 570
index() method, 69, 393, 400, 402
indexOf() method, 68, 69
INSERT INTO statement, 498
.is() method, 221, 222

J, K

JavaScript Object Notation, 478
join() method, 58, 481
jQuery
    applying styles, paragraphs
        CSS styles, 11
        HTML file, 10
        <p> elements, 12, 13
    counting paragraphs,specific class
        alert() method, 15
        alert dialog box, 15, 16
        CSS file, 14
        .filter() method, 15
        HTML file, 13, 14
    definition, 2
    features, 2
    installation, 3
    library, web page, 5, 6
    ready() method, 7
    replacing text, 31, 32
    same class name, HTML
        elements, 48, 49
    selectors, 4
    tasks, 7
jQuery ajax() method, 479
jQuery plugins
    chaining, 537, 538
    creating, 533, 534

jQuery plugins (*cont.*)

    customization options, 539–543

    definition, 533

    dynamic checkboxes/iCheck, 554–556, 558–562

    font size/fonts style/foreground/ background, 535–537

    image carousel, 568, 569, 571

    image gallery, 562–566

    Magnific Popup, 544–553

    stretching images, 567

    validation plugin, 571, 573–575

jQuery UI

    accordion, 453–459

    autocomplete widget, 448–453

    datepicker widget

        applying styles, 446, 447

        change date format, 444–446

        configuring properties, 441, 442, 444

        definition, 439

        HTML file, 440

    dialogs, 460–466

    table widget, 466–471

L

leftanimator function, 375

left_rightanimator() function, 380

List items

    collapsed mode, 412

    event handler, 411

    first list item, 412

    HTML file, 408, 409

    jQuery code, 410, 411

    minus (-) icon, 408

    nested, 412, 413

    plus (+) icon, 408

    removing, 412

    second list item, 413

    sorting

        each() function, 424

        HTML file, 422

        jQuery code, 423, 424

        sort algorithm, 424

        unsorted items, 422, 423

    style.css, 410, 411

    unordered, 409, 410

list-style property, 287

list-style-type property, 266, 272, 277

load() method, 520

M

Magnific Popup, 531, 533, 544, 546

margin property, 160, 266, 287, 379

merge() method, 65

mousedown() method, 94, 108

mouseenter() method, 98

mouseleave() method, 99

mouseout() method, 100

mouseover() method, 99

mouseup() method, 107

mysqli_num_rows() function, 503, 505

mysqli_query() method, 505

N

nextAll() method, 232

Numerical array

    arrstring class, 76, 77

    div> and <p> elements, 60

    grep() method, 62

    HTML file, 59, 76

    integer, 62

    into string, 77, 78

    jQuery code, 60, 77

origarr class, 76
partstring class, 76, 77
Numerical value, 177, 178
error message, 182–184
HTML code, 177
label message, 178
negative value, 179
range, 180

O

off() method, 90, 112, 115
one() method, 113
on() method, 89, 112
opacity property, 148
overflow property, 374

P

padding property, 266, 273, 278, 282, 287, 293, 294
Page navigating
access keys
HTML file, 268, 270–272
web development, 272, 273
accordion menu, 290–294, 296
breadcrumb menu, 255–258, 304
context menu, right click, 275
attribute, 278
HTML file, 274, 276
style rules, 275
style sheet file, 277
contextual menu
HTML file, 263–266
jQuery code, 267, 268
creating two menu items, 279–283
dynamic visual menu
HTML file, 296, 297

jQuery code, 299, 300
style.css file, 298
working, 301–303
hover effect, menu items, 258–262
submenu items
first instance, 288–290
HTML file, 284, 286
style sheet file, 287
type selector, 288
Paginating tables, 527, 529–531
Paragraph element
html() method, 47
HTML file, 46, 47
jQuery code, 47
parent element, 48
span element, 48
parent() method, 46
Password\Confirm Password
error message, 233
HTML file, 229
style sheet, 230, 231
Phone number field, 184
class selectors, 185, 186
error message, 187
HTML file, 184
pop() function, 314, 315
position property, 342, 364, 374, 379
prepend() method, 21
preventDefault() method, 176, 182, 183, 232, 245, 376
Prior selection, returning
CSS file, 17
end() method, 18
highlight1 style, 17–19
HTML file, 16
hyperlink, 19
info class, 18
jQuery code, 18

Q

queue() method, 312, 313

R

Radio buttons, 203
    dropdown list, 207
    error message, 206, 210, 213
    HTML file, 204
    multiple select, 210, 212, 213
    style sheet file, 205, 209
remove() method, 21
replaceWith(new_content) method, 30
reverse() method
    ascending order, 56
    items count, 55
    jQuery code, 55
    syntax, 54
rightanimator function, 375

S

scrollTop property, 354
SELECT statement, 497, 498
show()/hide() methods, 303
Siblings
    <div> element, 36, 37
    highlight style, 37, 38
    HTML program, 35
    jQuery code, 37
    style rules, 36
slideDown() method, 111, 112, 170
slideToggle() method, 312
Sliding/visual effects
    after(), 355
    ball bounce, 346–348
    display image vertically, HTML file,
        352–354

displaying image
    appendTo(), 344
    <div> element, 341
    end(), 344
    HTML code, 340
    next(), 343
    position property, 342
    setInterval(), 344
    slice(), 343
images pagewise, 367–371
pendulum scroller, 377–380
scroller
    HTML code, 357, 358
    jQuery code, 359
    stop(), 359–361
scroll images, 348, 349, 351, 352
scrolling images, arrays
    fading out/replacing image,
        384–386
    hover, 383, 384
    HTML file, 381
    jQuery code, 382, 383
scrollTop property, 355
showing images,
    hover, 362, 364, 365
shuffling images, 371–376
sort() method, 53
splice() method, 57, 58
SQL statements, 496, 516
stopPropagation() method, 122, 123
String array
    complete list, 69, 70
    <div> elements, 68, 70
    HTML program, 67
    jQuery code, 68
    <p> elements, 68–70
strtoupper() function, 491
style_products() method, 538, 540, 541

T

Table
  alternate columns, highlighting
    column heading, 394, 395
    hovered over, 392
    .index() method, 393, 394
    individual cells, 395, 396
    jQuery code, 390
    nth-child() method, 391
    style.css, 390
  alternate rows, highlighting, 392
  ascending order
    event handler, 429
    jQuery code, 427, 428
    names, 430
    roll numbers, 429
    > selector, 428
    sort() function, 429
    unsorted table, 429
  column headings
    column name, 427
    jQuery code, 426, 427
    style sheet file, 426, 427
  descending/ascending order
    column headings, 433
    jQuery code, 430, 432
    names, 433, 434
    sort function, 433
    style rules, 430, 432
    unsorted table, 433
    values, 433
  filtering out columns
    colindex variable, 400, 402
    column heading, 402, 403
    event handler, 402

    jQuery code, 401, 402
    not() selector, 402
    selected column, 403
  filtering rows
    hiding, 398
    highlighted row, 397
    HTML file, 396, 434, 435
    input text field, 437, 438
    jQuery code, 396, 397, 436, 437
    label class, 436, 437
    .preventDefault() method, 437
    selected row, 398
    style sheet, 396, 436
  hovering over
    highlighted row, 390
    HTML file, 388, 389
    initial stage, 390
    jQuery code, 389
    style.css, 388, 389
  list items (see List items)
  paginating
    blank table, 406
    event handler, 405
    HTML file, 403, 406
    jQuery code, 404, 405, 407, 408
    page number, 406
    span elements, 405
    style rules, 403, 405
  rows, 413
    designating groups, 417
    event handler, 416, 417
    hovering over, 417, 418
    HTML file, 414, 415
    jQuery code, 415, 416
    plus/minus icons, 418–421

Table (*cont.*)
    spanning elements, 415
    style.css, 415, 416
    table headings, 415
  selected column, hiding
    colindex variable, 400
    column heading, 400, 401
    event handler, 400
    HTML file, 399
    jQuery code, 399, 400
    style.css, 399, 400
  sorting, 424, 425
text-align property, 301
text-decoration property, 266, 273, 277,
    282, 294, 301
text() method, 44, 45
trigger() method, 91, 138
trim() function, 503
two fields
  error message, 225, 228
  HTML file, 223, 225
  Submit Button, 226, 227

U

unbind() method, 140
Unchecking, 219
  checkboxes, 222
  HTML file, 221
  style sheet, 220
User id
  class selectors, 188
  error message, 190
  HTML file, 187

V

validate_date() function, 192
validate_email() function, 195, 196, 244
validate_phoneno() method, 186
validate_userid() function, 189

W

WampServer
  administrator, 663
  choose language, 654
  download, 653
  help files, 661
  installation, 654, 656, 660
  License Agreement, 655
  location, 657
  select components, 658
  shortcut location, 659
  start, 664
  text editor, 661
width property, 266, 273, 277
Wrapper set
  addClass method, 9
  applying styles, 10
  highlight class, 10
  <p> elements, 8, 9
  wrapperstyle.css file, 9

X, Y, Z

XML file, 521–523
  tags, 524–526
  web page, 526

Printed in the United States
by Baker & Taylor Publisher Services